Weapons of Mass Destruction

Weapons of Mass Destruction

THE ESSENTIAL REFERENCE GUIDE

Eric A. Croddy, Jeffrey A. Larsen, and James J. Wirtz, Editors

ABC-CLIO™

An Imprint of ABC-CLIO, LLC

Santa Barbara, California • Denver, Colorado

Library of Congress Cataloging-in-Publication Data

Names: Croddy, Eric, 1966- editor | Larsen, Jeffrey Arthur, 1954- editor | Wirtz, James J.,
   1958- editor
Title: Weapons of mass destruction : the essential reference guide / Eric A.
   Croddy, Jeffrey A. Larsen, and James J. Wirtz, editors.
Description: Santa Barbara, California : ABC-CLIO, [2018] | Includes
   bibliographical references and index.
Identifiers: LCCN 2018015125 (print) | LCCN 2018015927 (ebook) | ISBN
   9781440855757 (eBook) | ISBN 9781440855740 (hardcopy : alk. paper)
Subjects: LCSH: Weapons of mass destruction—Encyclopedias. | Weapons of mass
   destruction—Handbooks, manuals, etc.
Classification: LCC U793 (ebook) | LCC U793 .W427 2018 (print) | DDC
   358/.303—dc23
LC record available at https://lccn.loc.gov/2018015125

ISBN: 978-1-4408-5574-0 (print)
     978-1-4408-5575-7 (ebook)

22 21 20 19 18   1 2 3 4 5

This book is also available as an eBook.

ABC-CLIO
An Imprint of ABC-CLIO, LLC

ABC-CLIO, LLC
130 Cremona Drive, P.O. Box 1911
Santa Barbara, California 93116-1911
www.abc-clio.com

This book is printed on acid-free paper ∞

Manufactured in the United States of America

Contents

PRIMARY DOCUMENTS

Preface

This is a book about a challenging subject. Most of the entries you find herein reflect the dark side of international relations, and some readers will find certain elements difficult to stomach because of that. It is a book about some of the nastiest weapons ever invented, those meant to kill large numbers of people in wartime—or to threaten to do so, and by so doing to deter an adversary from starting a war in the first place. Finding themselves at the center of security policy for many nations, weapons of mass destruction (WMD) remain important subjects that did not disappear with the end of the Cold War nearly 30 years ago. Indeed, these weapons are back, as shown by interest among many states who once again find themselves in a world of great power rivalry.

The term *weapon of mass destruction* is a relatively modern expression. It was first used by the press following international uproar over Germany's aerial bombardment of the Spanish city of Guernica in April 1937. During the anxious years leading up to World War II, WMD referred to the indiscriminate killing of civilians by modern weaponry, especially aircraft. It also echoed the fear of chemical weapons that was unleashed by World War I, memories of which were still fresh in popular consciousness.

Much has been written about WMD during the nearly three decades since the end of the Cold War. The meaning of the term itself is somewhat controversial, although there is a formal definition. According to U.S. Code Title 50, "War and National Defense," a weapon of mass destruction is "any weapon or device that is intended, or has the capability, to cause death or serious bodily injury to a significant number of people through the release, dissemination, or impact of toxic or poisonous chemicals or their precursors; a disease organism; radiation or radioactivity."

So, what makes a weapon massively destructive? Is it the type of injurious agents involved (radioactive, chemical, or biological)? Is it that the attack itself produces significant casualties or destruction? What does "significant" mean in this context? What if very few people are actually killed or hurt by an attack that was thwarted, an attack in space, or a cyberattack? Analysts and policy makers are still sorting out these challenges.

The U.S. military never liked chemical or biological weapons and treated them as a deterrent, to be used only in retaliation for the use of chemical or biological weapons by an opponent. By the early 1990s, the United States had abandoned offensive use of these weapons, although it maintained a research and development program designed to produce effective equipment, procedures, medications, and inoculations to defend against chemical and biological attack.

Nuclear weapons, however, are a different story. The nuclear age began on the morning of July 16, 1945, with the detonation of the world's first atomic bomb—the Trinity test in the high desert of central New Mexico. This explosion marked the culmination of three years of frantic scientific and engineering research and development under the auspices of the U.S. Manhattan Project, which the United States had instituted in 1942 to ensure that the Allies developed atomic weapons before Germany. There had been scientific discoveries and research in the field of radiology prior to World War II, but the threat of an adversary achieving the "ultimate weapon" before the Allies was a strong motivating factor in the efforts of the Manhattan scientists.

Following the war, the world entered a long twilight period known as the Cold War. The United States and its allies faced off against a seemingly implacable foe, the Soviet Union. Both sides rapidly built up their nuclear arsenals until there were more than 70,000 atomic warheads pointed at one another. After years of "standing toe to toe," threatening nuclear war, and "looking into the abyss," reason slowly began to enter into the equation. Concepts such as arms control and nuclear disarmament began to play a role in international relations. Stockpile levels were already coming down dramatically by the time the Soviet Union dissolved in 1991, following which the world shifted from a bilateral standoff to a less well-defined multilateral era.

Nearly 30 years later, however, the world once again seems to have resumed its fascination with WMD, making international relations more dangerous. North Korean nuclear tests; Chinese military adventurism in the South China Sea; the rise of ISIS in the Middle East; increased terrorist attacks in Europe and North America; Iraq's use of chemical weapons on the battlefield against Iran, and later against its own people; Syria's use of chemical weapons in its civil war; and, perhaps most ominously, the return of Russia as a potential adversary trying to revise the post–Cold War international order are all examples of this new security environment.

Russian behavior under President Putin has become particularly worrisome, including the annexation of Crimea, the instigation of civil war in Ukraine, a significant military modernization program, and a new military doctrine. All of this emphasizes the role of nuclear weapons, which have played a role in Russia's overt nuclear threats against its European neighbors. Some analysts say this heralds the beginning of a new Cold War. Yet, today's arsenals are smaller than they have been since the early 1950s, the nuclear taboo still holds, and the United Nations passed a nuclear weapons ban treaty in 2017. Hope remains for a future in which nuclear weapons are never again used in anger.

About the Encyclopedia

The very presence of chemical, biological, and nuclear weapons in international arsenals and the potential that they might fall into the hands of terrorist organizations guarantees that weapons of mass destruction will be of great policy, public, and scholarly interest for years to come. We cannot resolve the debates prompted by WMD, but we believe that our contributors have provided the level of detail to help the reader sort through the controversies that are likely to emerge in the years ahead.

Much that is contained in this volume is disturbing and even frightening; it is impossible to write a cheery encyclopedia about weapons whose primary purpose is to conduct postindustrial-scale mass murder.

The sad truth of the matter is that chemical, biological, radiological, and nuclear weapons reflect the willingness of humans to go to great lengths to find increasingly lethal and destructive instruments of war and violence. We are pleased to note, however, that much of what is reported in this book is historical in nature and that civilized people everywhere now reject the use of chemical and biological weapons. International law is replete with treaties, agreements, and regimes whose purpose is to proscribe the use of these weapons or to mitigate the consequences of any such use. In addition, the world has successfully avoided using nuclear weapons for almost 75 years, reserving them as deterrent weapons of last resort.

Our encyclopedia covers a wide range of topics, some historical and some drawn from today's headlines. We describe many of the pathogens, diseases, substances, and machines that can serve as weapons of mass destruction. (For reasons of space, however, we do not emphasize the vehicles that are used to deliver WMD payloads.) We encouraged our contributors to highlight ongoing controversies and contemporary concerns about WMD and current international arms control and nonproliferation efforts intended to reduce the threat they pose to world peace and security. Even a work of this length, however, cannot completely cover the history, science, and personal stories associated with a topic of this magnitude, so we have included references to help readers take those initial steps for further study of the topics we survey.

Acknowledgments

The editors' primary debt is to the contributors who made this volume a reality. It is nearly impossible for three people to be experts on all the subjects covered in this volume, and without the contributions of our authors, this encyclopedia would never have been completed.

We also want to express our appreciation to our acquisition editors at ABC-CLIO, initially Steve Catalano and then Pat Carlin, as well as the copyeditors who worked diligently to help get this manuscript into print. The commitment of our publisher to this topic and the dedication of the production staff at ABC-CLIO greatly facilitated the completion of this volume.

We hope that this encyclopedia will help inform the public debate about weapons of mass destruction and international security policy, with the goal of never again seeing such weapons used in anger.

Jeffrey A. Larsen
Rome, March 2018

Chemical and Biological Warfare as Weapons of Mass Destruction: A U.S. Perspective

Despite the trauma of World War I and "gas warfare," in the early and even late 20th century, there remained dedicated apologists for the use of chemical weapons (CW). Objectively speaking, those who advocated for CW had supportable arguments on their side. The rationalization was that conventional artillery, bullets, and bombs caused the vast majority of dead (at least 10 million) in the Great War—not gas. And in addition to millions more who were injured, at least 140,000 soldiers from all sides also suffered the loss of at least one limb.[1] In contrast, chemical casualties usually recovered with no significant permanent injury. To this point, Brigadier General Harold Hartley, a chemist turned soldier, reported to the British Association ("On Chemical Warfare") in 1919, "There is no comparison between the permanent damage caused by gas, and the suffering caused to those who were maimed and blinded by shell and rifle fire. It is now generally admitted that in the later stages of the war many military objects could be attained with less suffering by using gas than by any other means."[2]

Still, the real or perceived horror of gas in World War I led the international community to reinvigorate treaties to outlaw such methods of warfare. Previous attempts, such as The Hague Convention (1899),

seemed to have it covered, prohibiting "asphyxiating or deleterious gases." But two of the major belligerents in the Great War never signed on to the convention (the United States and Great Britain), and even ones that did (Germany) exploited its wide loopholes to justify their use of chemicals in World War I. The same could be said for the 1925 Geneva Protocol for the Prohibition of the Use in War of Asphyxiating, Poisonous or Other Gases, and of Bacteriological Methods of Warfare. Although the 1925 protocol may have outlawed such use, it had no provisions against the research, development, production, and possession of such weaponry.

During the 1930s, the Geneva Protocol notwithstanding, chemical weapons were seen as a future threat to urban populations, as they could lead to "mass destruction." In her 1934 argument for both chemical and biological toxin disarmament, Elvira Fradkin predicted that citizens of all nations were at risk from the combination of aerial warfare and chemical weapons. Wholesale urban populations faced being

massacred by gas bombs from thousands of airplanes (the number of planes necessarily decreasing as the deadliness of lethal burning phosphorus and smoke released increases) and peace will be concluded only over the dead bodies of the enemy nation. Poison gas . . . is ideal for *mass destruction. Mass destruction* means you and me (emphasis added).[3]

Similar warnings also included those of Major Leon A. Fox, U.S. Army Medical Corps, who envisioned the potential combination of air power with biological weapons (BW): "An airplane could carry enough of the botulinus toxin to destroy every living thing in the world if administration of the toxin were as simple a process as production and transportation."[4]

As for the first coinage of the term "weapons of mass destruction" (WMD), some point to a December 28, 1937, statement by the archbishop of Canterbury, Cosmo Gordon Lang. In the wake of the German Luftwaffe attack on Guernica (also eponymously depicted in Picasso's famous painting), he bemoaned the use of such "weapons of mass destruction."[5] But we would note here that this was in reference to the terror bombing using conventional weaponry and not to the use of chemical or biological agents.[6]

As it happens, at least in the parlance of U.S. military and government agencies, it is relatively new that conventional explosives have been added to the category of WMD, that is, chemical, biological, radiological, nuclear, and explosive (CBRNE). Thus, the U.S. Department of Defense's recent (and long-winded) definition of WMD includes "chemical, biological, radiological, or nuclear weapons or devices capable of a high order of destruction and/or causing mass casualties. This does not include the means of transporting or propelling the weapon where such a means is separable and divisible part of the weapon."[7]

World War II—Prepared for CBW

Hitler will send no warning—so always carry your gas mask.
—British Ministry of Home Security Poster

During World War II, despite offensive and defensive preparations to do so by the Allied and German militaries, neither side used chemical or biological weapons in the European theater. Although Japan employed chemical (and biological) weapons against Chinese troops and civilians in the Sino-Japanese War, it was careful to avoid such use against U.S. or British troops.

Although having the most advanced CW capability among the World War II belligerents, Germany never employed chemical weapons. This was mostly because Hitler's advisers were certain the United States and Great Britain were similarly armed and that a return to gas warfare would not be in Germany's best strategic interests. As for BW, according to high-ranking German military staff, Hitler had received (false) reports that the Allies were looking to use ticks and beetles to attack Germany's agriculture. Even in response to this purported threat, as well as what had been learned from initial French investigations in 1940, Hitler authorized appropriate ("extreme efforts") in developing BW defenses in April 1942, but "the Führer . . . has ordered that no preparations for bacterial warfare are to be made by [Germany]."[8]

For its part, the United States was well prepared to use chemical weapons for the Pacific theater. Millions of chemical munitions, including land mines filled with mustard, had been produced by 1945, and many had been forward deployed to regions closer to Japan, including Australia, Hawaii, Luzon, and

Okinawa. As desperate fighting continued in the Philippines and Iwo Jima, there were public calls in the United States for using chemical weapons. "You Can Cook Them with Gas," recommended the March 11, 1945, headline of the *Chicago Tribune*. It further argued that "the use of gas might save the lives of many hundreds of Americans and of some of the Japanese as well."[9]

In June 1945, as the United States drew closer to an invasion of the main Japanese island of Honshū, serious thought was again given to using chemical weapons against Japan. Based on a study by the U.S. Chemical Warfare Service, initial plans called for thousands of bombs filled with phosgene gas to be dropped on Tokyo in the morning hours. Additional CW agents under consideration to bring Japan to her knees included "blood agents"—hydrogen cyanide (HCN) and cyanogen chloride (CK)—as well as mustard (a blister agent). As for the main thrust against the other main island of Kyūshū, U.S. Army chemical planners recommended a concentrated gas bombardment against Japanese troops on the beaches in advance of U.S. amphibious operations. And although it was known that many noncombatants would likely be killed, the study also drew up detailed plans for the use of CK against military targets around the city of Kagoshima. These preparations were never employed, of course, as the Pacific War ended with the Hiroshima and Nagasaki atomic bombings in August 1945.

WMD in the Cold War

Sixteen months before the Soviet Union detonated its first nuclear device (August 29, 1949), the well-known military historian Hanson Baldwin noted in the *Saturday Evening Post*,

There are . . . many mass killers besides the atomic bomb, and for some of them no practical form of even partial physical control can possibly be devised. For some of the new weapons, notably biological agents, no scheme of control, no matter how extensive and inclusive, can possibly be established that would mean safety. For biological agents are of tremendous importance to peacetime medicine as well as to wartime destruction. Small, not large, installations produce them. Tiny laboratories, easily concealed, could quickly amass "weapons" adequate to kill 1,000,000 people.[10]

In the face of a standoff between Western countries and a real or perceived growing Soviet military threat, the need to prepare for chemical, biological, and radiological (CBR) warfare was highlighted by the statements of Soviet marshal Georgy Konstantinovich Zhukov. At the 20th meeting of the Communist Party of the Soviet Union (February 1956), Zhukov declared that "future war, if it is unleashed, will be characterized by the mass use of air power, various types of rocket weapons, and various means of *mass destruction* such as atomic, thermonuclear, chemical and bacteriological weapons (emphasis added)."[11]

Biological Weapons Development in the Cold War

During the Cold War, many of the biological weapons tests conducted by the United States included live agent experiments, such as those performed at Fort Detrick, Maryland, and Dugway Proving Ground, Utah. Below are some examples of such research studies performed by U.S. biological weapons scientists with their approximate dates:

- "Epidemiological Investigation of Occupational Illness of Joel E. Willard," 1958
- "The Pathogenesis of Brucellosis Employing *Brucella* [Brucellosis] Variants," 1950
- "Studies of LE [Plague Bacteria] Aerosols at Two Humidities," 1958
- "Evaluation of Dry Minigenerator Disseminating Dry N [Anthrax Bacteria]," 1960
- "Aerogenic Challenge of Volunteers with *Coxiella burnetii* [Q Fever]," 1965
- "Microbiological Laboratory Hazard of Bearded Men," 1967

Of these selected studies, one in particular (the first bulleted item) speaks to the human cost and the utilitarian nature of bioweaponeering during the Cold War. Joel Eugene Willard, then a 53-year-old electrician, worked at Fort Detrick, Maryland, in the late 1950s. At the Fort Detrick biological weapons research and development facility, the testing of BW agents was often performed using live animals. In late June 1950, Joel Willard accidentally inhaled anthrax spores while working in the "hot zone." He was admitted in the hospital on June 30, 1958, and died from inhalational anthrax on July 5.[12] His wasn't the only fatality from a laboratory-acquired infection at this facility. Seven years earlier, a microbiologist, William A. Boyles (46), also died from inhalational anthrax. Then, in the early 1960s, another worker, Bernard Victor Kreh, developed a cutaneous anthrax infection in his finger (he survived). In each of these cases, scientists at Fort Detrick isolated the bacteria from these patients, taking these now more virulent anthrax strains for weaponization. One such strain that was produced for the U.S. BW program was isolated from Bernard V. Kreh's finger and coded "BVK-1."[13]

In 1965, the United States conducted a field test called Operation Shady Grove in the Pacific Ocean, near Johnston Atoll. U.S. bioweaponeers brought in hundreds of rhesus monkeys on open barges, and a jet aircraft sprayed 36 gallons of a liquid suspension containing *Francisella tularensis* bacteria over a large ocean area. Half the monkeys became ill from inhaling this aerosolized preparation. It was further determined that using 10 times the experimental amount of BW agent could result in about 50 percent casualties in an area roughly the size of Atlanta, Georgia.

But having demonstrated to the scientists its potential value, the U.S. Department of Defense was much less sanguine. It concluded in 1967 that "biological weapons were relatively poor weapons at their current state of development, that they could be developed into reliable, useful weapons, and that their development would be expensive, time consuming, and of marginal impact on the overall strategic balance between the U.S. and the U.S.S.R."[14]

Due in part to this pessimistic assessment, President Richard Nixon cancelled U.S. offensive BW agent research in 1969. His decision was typically Nixonian realpolitik. First, the focus at the time was on nuclear weapons disarmament in terms of dealing with the Soviet Union; biological weapons only complicated things. Next, Nixon's advisers were not impressed by BW in an offensive capacity, finding it lacking in both operational benefits and strategic deterrence value. Finally, it was fully realized that other state actors could develop biological weapons that could threaten the U.S. homeland. A treaty to rid the world of this weaponry, it was reasoned, would provide the United States (and NATO allies) real security benefits.[15]

As the United States was demilitarizing its biological weapons program and facilities, the former Soviet Union was just getting started. Ken Alibek reports a case in which a scientist by the name of Ustinov was accidentally infected with Marburg hemorrhagic fever virus. When Ustinov died, the Soviets wasted no time in harvesting the virus—now likely to be even more lethal after having passed through an organism's immune system—and in 1990s, they prepared a "Variant U" of Marburg virus for weaponization in his "honor."[16]

Chemical Disarmament

In 1990, the former Soviet Union and the United States agreed to stop producing chemical weapons and to make significant reductions in their respective chemical weapons stockpiles. On June 26, 1990, an operation named both Operation Steel Box and Operation Golden Python began the withdrawal of 100,000 U.S. chemical munitions from Germany. By September 22, the mission for their removal had been completed, and the chemical weapons were shipped to Johnston Atoll in the Pacific for their destruction.[17]

Following the agreement between the United States and the former Soviet Union, and the signing of the Chemical Weapons Convention (CWC) in 1993, both countries have continued to destroy their CW agent and munition stocks. Already proving to be a Herculean and messy task, delays due to political, environmental, and technical issues (usually in various combinations of these) have pushed out the final destruction dates for Russia (2017) and the United States (2023). Given the large quantity of chemicals slated for demilitarization—40,000 tons for Russia and 30,000 tons for the United States—this still represents a remarkable milestone for chemical

weapons elimination. In contrast, negotiations for establishing a similar regime to enforce the Biological and Toxin Weapons Convention (1972) have stalled, and it is unlikely any meaningful action will take place by 2020.

Syria and Chemical Weapons in the 21st Century

Despite having signed and acceded to the CWC in 2013, the Assad regime in Syria has continued to use chemical weapons against its own people. Observers have since noted that the U.S. government and the international community failed to account for Syria's obviously hidden cache of chemical weapons. In response to Syria's April 4, 2017, attack on Idlib with sarin nerve agent, days later the United States carried out missile strikes at the Syrian airfield from which the chemical attacks had been staged. Even as late as February 2018, the Syrian regime has continued to indiscriminately use chemicals—probably chlorine gas—against the rebel-held town of Saraqeb in Idlib province. Despite efforts by the international community and the Organization for the Prohibition of Chemical Weapons (OPCW), Syria represents a signal failure in the chemical arms control regime.

Conclusion: CBW—Low Risk, High Consequence

All told, the risks for both military and civilian populations from chemical and biological weapons remain low, but they still represent very high consequences in the unlikely event of such an attack. The question, then, is what to do about it.

Today, the Centers for Disease Control and Prevention (CDC) maintains the Strategic National Stockpile with the charge to deal with an expanding number of potential public health crises:

- bacterial and viral diseases
- pandemic influenza
- radiation/nuclear emergencies
- chemical attacks

According to the official website, the "CDC's Strategic National Stockpile is the nation's largest supply of potentially life-saving pharmaceuticals and medical supplies for use in a public health emergency severe enough to cause local supplies to run out. The stockpile ensures the right medicines and supplies are available when and where needed to save lives."[18]

All told, the annual cost of $7 billion to maintain this overarching WMD defensive program, which represents less than 1 percent of the U.S. total defense budget, appears to be a reasonable insurance measure against an unlikely but possible WMD attack.

Eric A. Croddy

Notes

1. Combined numbers from Germany, France, Britain and the United States. Beth Linker, *War's Waste: Rehabilitation in World War I America* (Chicago: University of Chicago Press, 2011), 98.

2. Victor Lefebure, *The Riddle of the Rhine: Chemical Strategy in Peace and War* (New York: Chemical Foundation, 1923), 240–241.

3. Elvira K. Fradkin, *The Air Menace and the Answer* (New York: Macmillan Company, 1934), 40.

4. Fradkin, *Air Menace*, 57.

5. Diana Preston, *A Higher Form of Killing: Six Weeks in World War I That Forever Changed the Nature of Warfare* (New York: Bloomsbury Press, 2015), 268.

6. Dan Radu, "Weapons of Mass Destruction and Terrorism," in *Enhancing Cooperation in Defence against Terrorism*, ed. Kenan Tokgöz (Washington, D.C.: IOS Press, 2012), 57, fn 2.

7. James B. Burton, F. John Burpo, and Kevin Garcia, "20th CBRNE Command," *Military Review* 96, no. 4 (July/August 2016): 64–65.

8. Erhard Geissler and Jeanne Guillemin, "German Flooding of the Pontine Marshes in World War II: Biological Warfare or Total War Tactic?" *Politics and the Life Sciences* 29, no. 1 (March 2010): 6.

9. Norman Polmar and Thomas B. Allen, "Another Alternative—poison gas!" *Naval History* 29, no. 4 (August 2015): 42–43.

10. Hanson Baldwin, "We Need Not Fight Russia," *Saturday Evening Post* 220, no. 40 (April 3, 1948): 27.

11. U.S. Foreign Broadcast Information Service, "Radio Propaganda Report" (originally marked confidential), Current Developments Series, CD.62, April 5, 1957, 3.

12. United States Army Medical Unit, United States Army Medical Research and Development Command, Document AD492734, Autopsy Report: Joel E. Willard, April 1960.

13. Scott Shane, "Army Harvested Victims' Blood to Boost Anthrax," *Baltimore Sun* (December 23, 2001) (online). http://articles.baltimoresun.com/2001-12-23/news/0112230059_1_anthrax-bacteria-spores

14. Daniel M. Gerstein, *National Security and Arms Control in the Age of Biotechnology: The Biological and Toxin Weapons Convention* (Lanham, MD: Rowman & Littlefield, 2013), 19.

15. Jonathan B. Tucker and Erin R. Mahan, *President Nixon's Decision to Renounce the U.S. Offensive Biological Weapons Program*, Center for the Study of Weapons of Mass Destruction Case Study 1 (Washington, D.C.: National Defense University Press, October 2009), 9.

16. Ken Alibek with Stephen Handelman, *Biohazard: The Chilling True Story of the Largest Covert Biological Weapons Program*

in the World—Told from the Inside by the Man Who Ran It (New York: Random House, 1999), 133.

17. Robert L. Gunnarsson Sr., *American Military Police in Europe, 1945–1991: Unit*

Histories (Jefferson, NC: McFarland & Company, 2011), 308.

18. Centers for Disease Control and Prevention, "Strategic National Stockpile," accessed April 30, 2018, https://www.cdc.gov/phpr/stockpile/index.htm.

Nuclear Weapons

On July 16, 1945, the world changed forever when British and American scientists and engineers tested an implosion-type atomic device in the desert near Alamogordo, New Mexico, producing the first nuclear explosion. Developed under the code name "Manhattan Project," this first-generation fission device was quickly weaponized, and when the U.S. Army Air Corps dropped atomic bombs on the Japanese cities of Hiroshima and Nagasaki in August 1945, World War II in the Pacific quickly ended.

The United States did not retain a nuclear monopoly for long. The Soviet Union detonated a nuclear device in 1949. By the early 1950s, a second generation of fusion weapons, with explosive power measuring in millions of tons of trinitrotoluene (TNT), was entering Soviet and U.S. nuclear arsenals. As the Cold War unfolded, the Soviet and U.S. militaries deployed tens of thousands of tactical, theater, and strategic nuclear weapons to deter both conventional and nuclear attacks. Soviet-American strategic relations reflected a situation of mutual assured destruction (MAD), which moderated superpower behavior but risked catastrophic destruction if some military or diplomatic insult upset the delicate "balance of terror." People everywhere breathed a collective sigh of relief as the risk of nuclear Armageddon became increasingly remote at the end of the Cold War. Since the early 1990s, Russia and the United States have cut the number of their deployed nuclear forces, ended nuclear testing, and have carried out limited modernization and replacement of their nuclear delivery systems.

By the turn of the century, it indeed appeared that the threat posed by nuclear weapons was diminishing. For a time, South Africa possessed a few nuclear weapons, but it renounced its nuclear ambitions and joined the Nuclear Nonproliferation Treaty (NPT) as a nonnuclear weapons state in 1991. Ukraine, Belarus, and Kazakhstan inherited large nuclear arsenals for a short period following the collapse of the Soviet Union in the early 1990s, but all three states were persuaded to give up those weapons and join the NPT by the mid-1990s. The United States, Russia, France, and Great Britain adopted modest life-extension and modernization programs for their nuclear arsenals, while reducing the overall size of their arsenals. China's nuclear arsenal grew in both size and sophistication, but here too change was modest and measured. India and Pakistan's nuclear weapon tests in the late 1990s and even North Korea's 2006 underground nuclear test—possibly a "fizzle" with a yield of less than 1 kiloton—did not produce systemic changes in international affairs.

The September 11, 2001, terrorist attacks on the World Trade Center and the Pentagon highlighted the fact that terrorists and non-state actors were interested in creating mass-casualty attacks, leaving policy makers and scholars to debate whether nuclear or radiological devices would one day be used as weapons of terror. Officials also worried about the emergence of an international black market in nuclear weapons technology, radiological materials, and even complete weapons. Nevertheless, as world history entered a second nuclear age, nuclear weapons remained a force to be reckoned with, but not all trends were bad.

From the vantage point of 2018, however, proliferation issues have taken center stage. North Korea's nuclear weapons programs and associated missile-delivery systems are advancing at an unprecedented pace. In the span of a decade, North Korea has advanced from a barely functional gun-type fission device to underground testing of what could be a boosted fission weapon. Pyongyang has also tested a missile with an intercontinental range. Matched with the bizarre rhetoric and threats emanating from the "hermit kingdom," these developments constitute a dangerous new twist in the history of nuclear weapons. The 2018 thaw in diplomatic relations between the two Koreas, and between the United States and the regime in Pyongyang, was greeted with a collective sigh of relief around the world. Nevertheless, it remains to be seen if Pyongyang's apparent willingness to terminate its nuclear program will pan out over the coming years.

Was There a Nuclear Revolution?

Nuclear weapons, the advent of long-range delivery systems, and the establishment of a new organization, the U.S. Air Force, produced a revolution in military affairs (RMA) that fundamentally transformed warfare. Bernard Brodie, writing in 1946, was quick to recognize the nature of this RMA when he observed that national objectives for military efforts had changed: whereas militaries traditionally strove to win wars, with the advent of nuclear weapons, their purpose became deterring wars. Nuclear weapons would make major war a calamity, demanding that all military and diplomatic efforts be directed at deterring, by threat of retaliation in kind, nuclear war.

Decades later, Robert Jervis (1989) noted that this RMA had produced a nuclear revolution: stability (the absence of great-power war) now characterized relations between great powers because none dare risk direct military confrontation, given the dark shadow of nuclear escalation. There were warnings that this nuclear stability might actually increase the likelihood of smaller wars, however, especially along the "periphery." Glenn Snyder (1961), for instance, identified a "stability-instability" paradox: stability at the nuclear level of conflict actually made great powers more tolerant of instability (war) in peripheral areas or among clients. But at the end of the Cold War, it did appear that peace, or at least the absence of great-power conflict, was the by-product of the threat of massive nuclear destruction.

Nuclear weapons introduced stability in great-power relations because they produced a modicum of restraint in both diplomatic and military adventures undertaken by Soviets and Americans during the Cold War. Nuclear weapons' effects are also predictable, and nuclear powers tend to share a similar knowledge base about the destructiveness of nuclear weapons. Both U.S. and Soviet officials recognized the destructiveness of a full-scale nuclear exchange. Moreover, as Thomas Schelling (1966) noted, the absence of an effective defense against massive nuclear attack allowed nuclear-armed states to engage in the "diplomacy of violence." States armed with large nuclear arsenals could destroy each other's societies while virtually bypassing direct engagement of the opponent's military forces. To a lesser extent than conventional warfare, which is influenced by strategy, tactics, leadership, equipment, training, and morale, the outcome of nuclear combat is driven by the enormous explosive yield of the nuclear weapons themselves, not by superior strategy.

In other words, once nuclear arsenals became very large and deployed in relatively survivable ways, there was little either the United States or the Soviet Union could do to prevent their opponent from undertaking a nuclear retaliatory strike. The world had indeed gone MAD (believing in the stabilizing effect of Mutually Assured Destruction).

MAD was defense dominant because both sides had the ability to deny victory in a nuclear war to the opponent. No nation with a leader in his right mind would start a nuclear war that it would be sure to lose—at least that was the argument advanced by those who championed the nuclear revolution.

Critics of the nuclear revolution have generally come in two varieties: those who believe that it is a mistake to treat deterrence as the dominant nuclear doctrine and those who believe that nuclear revolutionaries underestimate the risks involved in nuclear deterrence. Those who champion nuclear war-fighting strategies believe that others might think nuclear war is winnable or that deterrence itself is unreliable and can fail because of misunderstandings, irrationality, or simple human frailty. Under these circumstances, they believe that, for deterrence to be effective, it is imperative to develop credible nuclear war-fighting options. Missile defenses that deny opponents the ability to hold U.S. or allied targets at risk thus become an important way to strengthen U.S. deterrent threats. They also believe that nuclear weapons should be integrated into forces and war plans to give national authorities limited nuclear options that could influence battlefield events in positive ways. The 2002 U.S. Nuclear Posture Review, for example, called for the development of highly selective and limited nuclear options to increase the credibility of U.S. deterrent threats and to hold opponents' small nuclear, chemical, and biological weapons arsenals at risk while reducing the prospect of collateral damage.

Other critics worry, however, that the circumstances that make nuclear deterrence "stable" are rare and unlikely to be found in emerging weapons states and regional rivalries. New nuclear weapons states might adopt nuclear doctrines or forces that are shaped by domestic political turmoil, by political dreams of regional domination, or by a specific leader's megalomania. Maintaining negative control over nuclear arsenals (preventing weapons from being used without proper authorization) is daunting in states that face ethnic, fundamentalist, or political unrest. Countries in immediate proximity to each other—here India and Pakistan come to mind—can expect virtually no tactical warning of nuclear attack, increasing the likelihood that they might adopt preventive or preemptive nuclear war-fighting strategies. These critics also suggest that building "safe" nuclear weapons is technically challenging and financially demanding and might be beyond the resources of new nuclear powers. No matter what rich or poor states do, "normal accidents," the tendency of complex systems to interact with humans in unanticipated ways, are likely to defeat safety systems.

Those who champion disarmament as the best way to deal with nuclear weapons believe that nuclear deterrence is fundamentally immoral and misguided. Disarmament advocates suggest that those who believe in deterrence or war-fighting strategies simply perpetuate a war system that is destined to fail catastrophically. They dismiss ideas about a so-called nuclear revolution as window dressing to justify using a nuclear arms race and threats of nuclear warfare as a means of achieving political objectives. In their view, nuclear weapons are so destructive that they are irrational instruments of war that place at risk far more people and infrastructure than their users can hope to protect. They point out that a full-scale nuclear exchange during the Cold War could have eliminated human beings from planet Earth. Disarmament advocates believe that efforts to develop forces for deterrence create arms races, fear, and hostility and that the only way to break this negative trend is to eliminate nuclear weapons as quickly as possible.

Other disarmament advocates believe that nuclear deterrence was epiphenomenal when it came to maintaining stability during the Cold War. They believe that fear of conventional hostilities generally deters war, that most leaders are risk adverse, and often that the spread of democracy throughout the world will soon render nuclear weapons and deterrent strategies obsolete. Others believe that a nuclear taboo—a tradition of nonuse of nuclear weapons—governs the behavior of nuclear weapons states and that nothing should be done to increase the likelihood that nuclear weapons could or would be used in battle.

Disarmament advocates also have done much to shape international priorities. In 2009, for instance, President Barack Obama advanced the Prague Agenda, which reemphasized that nuclear disarmament should be universally embraced as an objective. The International Campaign to Abolish Nuclear Weapons (ICAN) also shepherded the 2017 Nuclear Weapons Ban Treaty to passage by the United Nations. Although existing nuclear states have ignored the treaty, disarmament advocates believe it has opened a new pathway to nuclear disarmament for those states willing to embark on the journey.

Nuclear Weapons Effects: A Primer

Unlike the debate about the political and strategic impact of nuclear weapons, the topic of basic nuclear physics holds few unknowns. The effects that nuclear weapons produce once they are detonated are well documented. *Nuclear weapon* is the general name given to any device that creates an explosion from energy involving atomic nuclei, either through a fission or a fusion reaction. More specifically, an atomic bomb is one that relies on fission, and a nuclear bomb has a fusion core—the design of choice in most modern arsenals. A gun-type fission weapon is relatively simple to construct; the greatest barrier to obtaining this type of nuclear weapon is the difficulty in manufacturing or obtaining weapons-grade fissile material. By contrast, high-yield, low-weight implosion fusion weapons are some of the most complex machines ever developed by human beings. They combine exquisite mechanical and electrical engineering design and manufacturing with innovative applications of nuclear physics and engineering. The details of specific weapons designs and operating principles are considered top secret by governments around the world.

When a nuclear weapon is detonated, it produces a series of weapons effects that occur in a predictable sequence: electromagnetic pulse (EMP), direct nuclear radiation, thermal radiation (which mostly takes the form of light), blast, and fallout. Bomb designers can vary the way the energy of a nuclear explosion is distributed across these effects. The neutron bomb, for instance, shifts more energy toward EMP and direct radiation in an effort to reduce collateral damage when used against targets on the ground (such as enemy armored formations) or to maximize damage to the electronic systems of targets in space (such as an opponent's incoming nuclear warheads). Weapons effects vary depending on a variety of influences, including the height of burst (for example, air burst, ground burst, underwater detonation, or underground detonation); weather; and local geography.

EMP and direct radiation are produced immediately upon detonation of a nuclear weapon. EMP is produced by the interaction of gamma radiation and matter that destroys all electronic systems that are not deliberately hardened against its effects. Although EMP effects fall off relatively quickly and are not harmful to humans, high-altitude air bursts can produce a very strong EMP wave that can affect systems thousands of miles away.

About 35 percent of the energy generated by a nuclear explosion takes the form of thermal radiation (in the form of a light pulse). The thermal radiation produced by a relatively large 1-megaton air burst (a weapon that would have to be detonated at an altitude of about 8,000 feet to prevent the nuclear fireball from touching the ground) can produce first-degree burns on exposed skin at a distance of about 7 miles from the point of detonation, second-degree burns at a distance of about 6 miles, and third-degree burns within a radius of about 5 miles. This weapon would also produce temporary flash blindness in anyone caught out in the open within about 13 miles on a clear day and within 53 miles on a clear night. The thermal light pulse can also produce retinal burn, causing permanent blindness, but this injury would presumably be relatively rare, since those who might suffer it probably would be killed by other weapons effects.

Blast, which arrives a few seconds after the light pulse, takes the form of overpressure (a quick rise in atmospheric pressure) and dynamic overpressure (wind). At about 1 mile away from a 1-megaton air burst, overpressure increases to about 20 pounds per square inch (psi), and wind velocities reach a peak of about 470 miles per hour. This is enough to level steel-reinforced concrete structures. At about 5 miles away from the blast, overpressure reaches about 5 psi, and wind velocities reach about 160 miles an hour, which is sufficient to destroy lightly constructed commercial buildings and most residences.

This "5-psi ring" is an important dividing line in terms of nuclear weapons effects. Planners assume that 50 percent of the people within this ring would be killed promptly by the blast effects of a nuclear weapon. At about 12 miles away from a 1-megaton air burst, overpressure drops to less than 1 psi and wind velocities drop to less than 35 miles per hour, making flying glass and debris the greatest hazard. When planners calculate damage expectancies from nuclear weapons, they generally rely on blast effects, not thermal effects, to predict the damage and casualties that will occur.

Irradiated earth and debris that is carried aloft in a nuclear detonation and then returns to the ground is known as *fallout*. A nuclear ground burst intended to destroy hardened targets, such as missile silos or underground command facilities, would produce the greatest amount of fallout; air bursts intended to destroy area targets such as cities or to barrage attack the operating areas of land-based mobile missiles would produce the least.

How fallout is deposited is highly variable and depends on wind speed and direction; the height to which the fallout is initially lofted by the fireball; weather (rain can wash fallout out of the sky, creating local "hot spots"); and geography (weapons effects can be shaped by local geographic features, such as hills). The amount of radiation produced by fallout will diminish over time as the irradiated materials "decay." Most radioactive materials have short half-lives; in other words, they decay relatively quickly. Some radioactive materials, however, have extremely long half-lives: strontium 90 and cesium 137 remain radioactive for years and can contaminate the food chain.

Exposure to radiation kills at the cellular level. An exposure of 600 rem (Roentgen equivalent man) over about a week has a 90 percent chance of killing an individual.

Living with the Bomb

Three methods of dealing with the presence of nuclear weapons have emerged in international relations: deterrence, arms control, and disarmament. Deterrence remains the dominant strategy of nations to prevent the use of nuclear weapons by other states. It creates a state of mind in an adversary that makes an act of aggression on the part of the opponent less likely. States using this strategy must have the capability to retaliate in kind if the opponent uses nuclear weapons and must make credible threats that nuclear retaliation will occur. There is much debate about the effectiveness of deterrence, when it has failed in the past, and under what circumstances it is likely to fail again in the future. During the Cold War, both the Soviet and U.S. militaries went to great lengths to construct secure second-strike forces and command and control facilities that could survive a nuclear attack and strike a retaliatory blow. But as political motivations for war have diminished among nuclear powers over the past couple of decades, many observers believe that a little nuclear deterrence goes a long way toward reducing the likelihood of war.

Negotiations among enemies to take actions of mutual interest—a process that came to be known as *arms control*—was a revolutionary idea when it emerged in the 1950s as a way to moderate the nuclear arms race. With the goals of making war less likely, reducing death and destruction if war should break out, and reducing the resources devoted to armament, arms control negotiations achieved some successes during the Cold War. Arms control probably made its greatest contribution by allowing the superpowers to clarify their strategic intentions and expectations and by demonstrating to all concerned that negotiation offered an alternative to violent confrontation as a means of managing the nuclear standoff.

Following the end of the Cold War and into the 2000s, traditional approaches to arms control began facing the perception of diminishing returns in Russian-American relations. But arms control, especially new types of confidence-building measures, might help to moderate other regional rivalries that have been exacerbated by nuclear proliferation and an accelerating race in recent years to develop more advanced nuclear delivery systems.

Disarmament efforts have made modest progress over the past half-century. The Nuclear Nonproliferation Treaty (NPT) serves as the basis of the international nonproliferation regime. The NPT is a means by which states not interested in developing nuclear weapons can formally register their nonnuclear status. It also pressures nuclear powers to take action to reduce not only the size of their nuclear arsenals but also their reliance on nuclear weapons in their military and foreign policies. The nonproliferation regime provides a method for regulating legitimate commerce in nuclear materials, and it provides an inspection and monitoring mechanism run by the International Atomic Energy Agency (IAEA) to guarantee that nuclear materials are not diverted into nuclear weapons production.

Since about the turn of the century, however, nonproliferation efforts have suffered a series of setbacks. Nuclear tests by Pakistan and India have led to a gradual buildup of their nuclear capabilities, and Iran's and Syria's clandestine efforts to acquire nuclear capabilities have raised doubts and anxieties about existing surveillance and safeguard procedures associated with the NPT. Most importantly, North Korean nuclear and missile tests have not only raised concerns about nuclear proliferation but have also made the danger of nuclear war an everyday reality. Critics note that well-intentioned efforts such as the newly signed Nuclear Weapons Ban Treaty do little to address states that seem determined to alter the status quo by developing a significant nuclear arsenal.

James J. Wirtz

A

Abrin

Abrin is a highly toxic protein (lectin) that presents a potential bioterrorism threat. But like ricin (a toxin found in the castor bean plant, *Ricinus communis*), abrin is more likely to be used as a poison for murder (e.g., assassinating individual targets) than as a component in a weapon of mass destruction.

Abrin can be extracted from the seeds of the *Abrus precatorius* plant, the beans of which are variously known as rosary peas, precatory beans, crab's eye, the jequirity bean, Indian licorice, and Jumbie bead. Provided the bean is chewed or otherwise processed, one such seed from this plant can be enough to kill a human adult. Both abrin and ricin share similar structures and toxicological properties. Based on testing using laboratory animals, abrin is approximately two to four times more toxic than ricin when administered to mice. Due to the much larger market for castor beans (as a source for ricin but also for vegetable oil and for use in lubricants), the worldwide availability of jequirity seeds is relatively small. As a consequence, and despite the disparity in their toxicities, ricin probably remains a greater overall threat.

If abrin particles are inhaled, abrin can cause the death of tissues in the lungs and airways, leading to severe inflammation and edema. Cell death causes nausea, vomiting, and shock. Death from abrin poisoning would likely occur many hours after exposure.

In a military manual published by members of the Al Qaeda terrorist organization (ca. 2000), the reader is instructed that precatory beans ("red or black and used in prayer beads") could be used to extract abrin for assassination purposes. The recipe described in the manual was probably derived from *The Poisoner's Handbook*, an underground pamphlet published in the 1980s.

Because of its purported role as a biological warfare (BW) agent, under international as well as U.S. federal statutes (under the Biological Weapons Anti-Terrorism Act, 1989), it is a serious crime to acquire, possess, or distribute abrin. Recent cases include a Floridian, Jesse William Korff (January 2014), who was caught in a federal sting operation attempting to sell abrin over the Internet. In April 2015, in Greater Manchester, England, an unnamed juvenile was sentenced to a year in prison for acquiring abrin using the dark web in an undercover sting operation. More recently, in March 2016, a federal court in California sentenced James Christopher Malcolm five years for transporting abrin to customers in New York and San Francisco.

Eric A. Croddy

Further Reading

Griffiths, Gareth D., Christopher D. Lindsay, Paul Rice, and David G. Upshall, "The Toxicology of Ricin and Abrin Toxins: Studies on Immunisation against Abrin Toxicity," in *Proceedings of the Medical Defense Bioscience Review (1993) Held in Baltimore, Maryland, on 10–13 May 1993,*

(Salisbury, UK: Chemical and Biological Defence Establishment, Porton Down, 1993) vol. 3, 1407–1416.

Roxas-Duncan, Virgina I., and Leonard A. Smith, "Of Beans and Beads: Ricin and Abrin in Bioterrorism and Biocrime," *Journal of Bioterrorism & Biodefense* (January 23, 2012), S2:002. doi:10.4172/2157-2526.S2-002.

Accidental Nuclear War

An accidental nuclear war would be the result of nuclear weapons having been used without legitimate political or military authorities having made the decision to launch a nuclear attack. Several potential causes of accidental nuclear war have emerged in the literature.

An accidental war could be caused by the malfunction of some weapon system or from human error involved in the operation of a weapon. In terms of operator error or equipment malfunction, weapons would literally launch or detonate "accidentally," a scenario that could lead to a nuclear exchange, especially in a time of crisis. On March 11, 1958, for example, a B-47 bomber accidentally dropped a Mark 6 atomic bomb on Mars Bluff, South Carolina. Although the weapon lacked its nuclear core, its high-explosive primary detonation charge exploded, injuring bystanders on the ground.

Although many procedures are followed to maintain negative control of nuclear weapons (that is, to guarantee that they will not be used without orders), highly complex systems can interact in unexpected ways, defying the best efforts of operators to maintain or regain control. During the Cold War, for example, observers worried that the Soviet and U.S. early warning networks and command and control systems formed a single and tightly linked mechanism that might produce a ratchet effect, generating a feedback loop that would force both sides to take steps that greatly increased the prospect of war. Another concern was that early warning data could be mislabeled or misinterpreted, leading to a mistaken decision to retaliate. In November 1983, for instance, a North Atlantic Treaty Organization (NATO) nuclear command and control exercise code-named "Able Archer" momentarily alarmed Soviet observers who thought that the exercise was a ruse to conceal preparations for a real nuclear attack.

Inadvertent war is sometimes used interchangeably with the term *accidental war*, but it identifies a different phenomenon. Inadvertent war is caused by the close interaction of opposing military forces in peacetime or during a crisis. Fighting erupts because of locally rational decisions or mistakes made by local commanders, decisions that effectively disconnect the use of force from political control. Inadvertent war is not accidental in the sense that it is caused by mechanical failure or operator error; rather, it is caused by the tendency of military interactions to unfold according to their own logic.

Since the dawn of the nuclear era, substantial thought and effort have gone into preventing accidental and inadvertent nuclear war. Nuclear powers have attempted to construct the most reliable technology and procedures for command and control of nuclear weapons, including robust fail-safe early warning systems for verifying attacks. The United States and the Soviet Union have also maintained secure second-strike capabilities to reduce their incentives to launch a preemptive strike against each other during crisis situations or out of fear of a surprise attack. The two nuclear superpowers worked bilaterally to foster strategic stability by means of arms control and confidence-building measures and agreements, and several agreements were negotiated to reduce the risk of an accidental nuclear war: the 1971 Agreement on Measures to Reduce the Risk of Outbreak of Nuclear War, the 1972 Agreement on the Prevention of Incidents on and over the High Seas, and the 1973 Agreement on the Prevention of Nuclear War.

Following the end of the Cold War, the United States and the Russian Federation have continued to offer unilateral initiatives and to negotiate bilateral agreements on de-alerting and detargeting some of their nuclear forces to further reduce the likelihood of a catastrophic nuclear accident. They have concluded agreements on providing each other with notifications in the event of ballistic missile launches or other types of military activities that could possibly be misunderstood or misconstrued by the other party.

The likelihood of accidental nuclear war has always been viewed as low, but the consequences of such a war or incident were, and remain, viewed as so potentially catastrophic as to require serious diplomatic and scholarly attention and analysis. As additional nuclear powers have emerged, so have concerns about the technology and procedures for command and control of nuclear weapons. The proliferation of nuclear weapons has been thought to increase the probability of accidental or inadvertent nuclear war, especially as stability criteria are less obvious in a multi-player game. In addition, the risks of dramatic political changes in states possessing nuclear weapons, highlighted by the breakup of the Soviet Union, the political fragility of a nuclear-armed Pakistan, and a bizarre North Korean regime, leave many observers uneasy about the safety and security of nuclear arsenals amid politically or militarily chaotic situations.

Steven Rosenkrantz

Further Reading

Jones, Nate, *Able Archer 83: The Secret History of the NATO Exercise That Almost Triggered a Nuclear War* (New York: New Press, 2016).

Larsen, Jeffrey A., and Kerry M. Kartchner, *On Limited Nuclear War in the 21st Century* (Palo Alto, CA: Stanford University Press, 2014).

Sagan, Scott, *The Limits of Safety* (Princeton, NJ: Princeton University Press, 1993).

Schlosser, Eric, *Command and Control: Nuclear Weapons, the Damascus Accident, and the Illusion of Safety* (New York: Penguin Books, 2013).

Agroterrorism (Agricultural Biological Warfare)

Agroterrorism, or agricultural biological warfare (BW), is the deliberate use of pathogens against plant crops or livestock. Because industrialized countries are increasingly dependent on large-scale, dense, and efficient mechanized farms, this industrialized model may be more vulnerable to deliberate attack using plant or animal pathogens. Such attacks—which could include the use of viruses, fungi, bacteria, insects, or poisons—could cause huge economic losses and socioeconomic disruption.

Vulnerability of Livestock

In 1997, in one of the most serious animal disease outbreaks to occur in the previous century, foot-and-mouth disease (FMD) devastated Taiwan's swine industry, leading to some $25 billion in direct and indirect losses to the country's economy. Although FMD is not nearly as deadly to animals as other diseases, it is still among the most feared diseases in agriculture, especially in the cattle and swine industries. The disease generally results in many sick and, therefore, unproductive animals. In addition to fever, anorexia, and general malaise, infected animals manifest blistery sores on and inside the oral cavity and on the teats as well as ulcerating patches on the hooves (thus the name *foot-and-mouth*).

The 1997 outbreak probably began with the smuggling of an infected animal across the Taiwan Strait from mainland China. (Although some suggested this was a deliberate attack perpetrated by the Chinese, most Taiwanese veterinarians believe it was unintentional.) Another outbreak of FMD a few years later, this time in the United Kingdom, also led to billions of dollars in economic losses, primarily in the sheep-rearing industry.

In another example, the virus that causes Newcastle disease in birds results in illness with a very high mortality rate (95–100 percent). Humans can also be infected with the Newcastle disease virus, causing conjunctivitis ("pinkeye"), which is relatively benign; it is possible for people to spread the virus to animals. In 1971, Southern California experienced an outbreak of Newcastle disease that led to the slaughter of 12 million chickens in an effort to control its spread.

Another serious epizootic, avian influenza virus (fowl plague), has been known to jump from one species, such as fowl or pig, to humans (and vice versa). In 1983–1984, an outbreak of avian influenza (H5N5 strain) in Pennsylvania led to a campaign to destroy all infected birds in the vicinity. As a result, prices for poultry rose some $350 million that year. Another strain of avian influenza, H5N1, killed six people in Hong Kong in 1997, also demonstrating the virus's ability (albeit rare) to jump from one species to another.

Food Security: "Farm to Fork"
There is another dimension to the threat from agroterrorism, namely, food safety. In both developed and developing economies, there has recently been an increased focus on security surrounding the "farm to fork" cycle of the food industry—that is, the vulnerability of the food supply to deliberate contamination with toxins or pathogens. Such an attack could occur at the locations where crops or animals are first raised, at the midpoint processing facility, or even on the grocery shelves and at other points of sale. That said, the deliberate poisoning of food or beverages in modern societies has largely been a phenomenon reserved for criminal or malicious activity and not organized warfare or terrorism. During the late 1990s, in China, a substantial number of cases occurred in which jealousy or hatred led individuals to contaminate food or beverages with rat poison, including the acutely toxic rodenticide tetramine (tetramethylenedisulfotetramine). Mass poisonings have sometimes resulted. In a 2002 incident, 40 people died and 300 others became seriously ill from tetramine poisoning.

Attacks on agriculture, however, could stem from purely financial motives. For example, after deliberately spreading a disease among cattle or corn, and thus causing a dramatic rise or fall in their prices on the world market, a malevolent actor might be able to take advantage by speculating on commodity futures.

Like the categories of pathogenic organisms that affect human beings, BW agents that could be used against agriculture include bacteria, viruses, fungi, and insects. Today, a number of possible BW agents have been recognized that could be used against crops or livestock.

Targeting Crops and Animals: World War I and World War II

The devastating consequences of crop diseases were keenly felt by Germany during World War I when large stores of potatoes were destroyed by potato blight (*Phytophthora infestans*), the same disease that had accelerated the famines in Ireland during the mid-1800s. Some have suggested that this potato famine contributed to Germany's capitulation and the end of the war. Also during World War I, Germany was probably the first to employ infectious agents (such as glanders, caused by *Burkholderia mallei* bacteria) against the Allies' horses and mules. It is unclear, however, whether this sabotage operation made any significant impact.

Research programs among the Allies to defend against—as well as to offensively employ—crop and animal diseases began in earnest during World War II. In 1938, the British scientist J. B. S. Haldane proposed the notion that both Germany and England could be vulnerable to an attack on their respective agricultural industries by the highly destructive Colorado potato beetle. In 1939, French veterinary and BW experts even proposed dropping potato beetles on Germany's crops. None of these plans (as far as it is known) were ever carried out. In the early 1940s, the potential BW threat to Allied agricultural targets, as well as possible weaknesses in Axis food supplies, led to further research into a number of pathogens that could cause disease in crops and domesticated animals. Beginning with a recommendation by U.S. governmental experts in March 1942, a number of plant and animal pathogens were considered as possible biological weapons for use by the United States.

Antilivestock Agents: World War II

Animal diseases were very much a security concern for the Allies as well as potential weapons to be used against the Axis powers. During World War II, as far as U.S. intelligence was concerned, rinderpest (cattle plague) was one of the most threatening of the animal pathogens. Falling into the same group of viruses (*Morbillivirus*) as human measles and the distemper virus in dogs, rinderpest only infects animals (primarily cattle). Rinderpest is so deadly and spreads so fast that—as in the case of FMD—the usual method of control is simply to destroy (cull) infected animals. In a joint American and Canadian project conducted at Grosse Ile, on the St. Lawrence River, studies were led to develop large amounts of rinderpest vaccine against a possible BW attack by Germany against Allied agriculture. Allied military scientists also studied the foot-and-mouth virus during World War II.

"Operation Vegetarian"

The most concerted Allied military program to attack Germany's agriculture was codenamed "Operation Vegetarian," in which Great Britain undertook to kill Germany's domestic livestock. In 1943, an English soap factory molded some 5 million cakes impregnated with a slurry of anthrax (*Bacillus anthracis*) spores, which were designed to attract grazing cattle, horses, and sheep. The anthrax bacteria would then cause a gastrointestinal form of the disease. (Although the primary goal was to destroy an important food source, this project also had the potential to cause human anthrax cases as well via secondary infection.) The original plans required at least 1,250 planes to fly across Germany, each aircraft dropping about 10 boxes of the anthrax cakes per sortie. Ultimately, however, the plan to attack Germany's livestock with anthrax-laden cakes never materialized. Thirty years after this operation was conceived, the last of the remaining cakes were destroyed.

Anticrop Agents

In 1943, Dr. E. C. Tullis, at the United States Department of Agriculture (USDA) research facility in Beaumont, Texas, noted that Japanese rice varieties grown in Arkansas were often subject to a fungal disease called rice blast (also known as rotten neck or Pyricularia blight) caused by *Pyricularia oryzae*. This fungal organism—along with another, brown spot of rice caused by *Helminthosporium oryzae* (*Cochliobolus miyabeanus,* code letter E)—was researched for its possible use on Japanese rice fields. Rice blast is a severe threat to rice crops; an outbreak of it was partly responsible for the 1942–1943 Bengal famine that led to the deaths of more than 2 million people. During World War II, the United States investigated this disease as a potential weapon (coded "IR") but found that the conidia spores—the means by which the fungal agent reproduces and spreads from plant to plant—did not survive well in warm weather conditions, diminishing its potential. The development of effective growth regulators for herbicidal applications, primarily the chemical herbicide 2,4-D (now marketed as Roundup), replaced schemes that would have used biological agents to destroy crops during the war. But in the case of Japan, the mitigating factor against targeting rice crops was concern about the imminent military occupation of Japan and the future source of food for the Japanese population.

The Allies also observed that Germany was economically dependent on potatoes. The United States conducted research into southern blight (*Sclerotium rolfsii,* code C), a fungus that appeared to have potential as a BW weapon. By war's end, however, it was found to have little efficacy against resistant Japanese crops and was not pursued further. The fungus that causes potato blight, *Phytophthora infestans*, was known to be a potentially powerful BW agent. But it was difficult to store, and a method of devising its large-scale production remained elusive. One method of delivery devised for potato blight involved the use of navy beans and specially made pellets. Again, these means of BW were never used.

Cold War Activity

During the first half of the Cold War (1950–1969), the U.S. biological weapons program continued research with anticrop agents. Having revived earlier work with such agents as *Sclerotium rolfsii* (the cause of southern blight or Sclerotium rot), the U.S. military later stockpiled some 30 tons of *Puccina graminis tritici* fungal spores (black stem rust). At that time, the United States considered the Chinese rice plantations and the extensive wheat fields in the Soviet Union (Ukraine) as potential targets. Early prototypes of delivery systems used feathers that were to be dropped in 500-pound propaganda leaflet bombs. These were judged by American bioweaponeers to be capable of spreading a widespread epidemic to the enemy's major cereal crops. U.S. biological weapons scientists also experimented with, among others, the following agents in both defensive and offensive capacities: brown spot of rice, rinderpest, blight of potatoes, Newcastle disease, and rice blast. All U.S. work regarding the use of BW agents against crops and animals was halted in 1969 with President Richard Nixon's announcement that further offensive biological weapons research was forbidden.

The former Soviet Union also led a significant research and development program into agricultural BW agents, many of these being similar to those studied in the West. Under one program, *Ekology*, for example, the Soviet Union studied a large number of both antiplant and antianimal agricultural BW agents. From 1973 to the early 1990s, Soviet research included the causative bacterial agent in psittacosis (*Chlamydia psittaci*), African swine fever, as well as rinderpest and foot-and-mouth disease viruses. For crops (grains and cereals), Soviet bioweaponeers focused on, among others, fungal rust (*Puccinia* spp.) and rice blast (e.g., *Magnaporthe oryzae*). However, the full extent of Soviet and Russian work in offensive agricultural BW is still unknown.

Allegations—all unfounded—that the United States practiced offensive agricultural warfare continued throughout the Cold War. These included claims by Fidel Castro's government in Cuba that the United States was deliberately disseminating an aggressive, fruit-burrowing insect (*Thrips palmi*) against Cuba's citrus crops. The former East Germany often accused the West of using Colorado potato beetles (the so-called *Ami-Käfer*) against Soviet bloc countries. Even in the late 1990s, the Russian BW expert General Valentin Yevstigneyev suggested that the United States was responsible for past beetle infestations in the former Soviet Union. These and similar charges were never substantiated.

During the 1980s, the Iraqi bioweapons program also conducted investigations into the use of anticrop agents, including *Tilletia* fungus. Recognized as a serious disease in

wheat since the 1700s (then described by the English agronomist Jethro Tull), *Tilletia* grows in the kernel of grains and develops into a "dirty" black center that completely devours the food portion of the plant. This cover smut (or bunt) of wheat continues to devastate field grains throughout the world. In their work with fungi, Iraqi BW scientists tested wheat cover smut (*Tilletia* spp.) fungal spores in field trials, in combination with aflatoxin derived from *Aspergillus flavus*. During their experiments, Iraqi BW scientists used fine-powdered silica as a carrier for dry dissemination of a mixture of aflatoxin and wheat smut fungi. This could have served as a means to attack the food supply of Iraq's neighbor Iran or perhaps Iraq's Kurdish populations to the north. In other areas, Iraq apparently worked with camel pox, a close relative to human smallpox (*Variola major*). The ultimate goals of this research are still unclear.

Defense against Livestock Diseases

Although vaccines are available for a number of animal diseases—to include those for FMD, rinderpest, and *peste des petits ruminants* ("goat plague")—for various reasons, these are not normally used in the developed world due to unit costs of the vaccine and the demands of regulated livestock markets. Furthermore, as with human viral diseases, effective chemotherapeutic treatments are lacking. Viruses also happen to be the cause of the most worrying of animal diseases—FMD, Newcastle, highly pathogenic avian influenza, and the like. As a consequence, the primary defenses against agroterrorism are early detection of disease outbreaks, the separation of diseased animals (usually by culling) from healthy ones, and the vaccination of a ring of livestock around the affected populations to stop the outbreak.

In the United States, the primary defense against exotic and otherwise devastating diseases in plants and animals is the U.S. Department of Agriculture's (USDA) Animal and Plant Health Inspection Service (APHIS). The research and development of diagnostic, surveillance, and detection techniques are conducted at the Foreign Animal Disease Diagnostic Laboratory at the Plum Island Animal Disease Center in New York. To develop an advanced warning capability, the USDA has also established its own intelligence units to analyze and predict future animal disease outbreaks.

Eric A. Croddy

Further Reading

Foxell, Joseph W., Jr., "Current Trends in Agroterrorism (Antilivestock, Anticrop, and Antisoil Bioagricultural Terrorism) and Their Potential Impact on Food Security," *Studies in Conflict & Terrorism* 24, no. 2 (April 2001): 107–129.

Frazier, Thomas W., and Drew C. Richardson, eds., *Food and Agricultural Security: Guarding against Natural Threats and Terrorist Attacks Affecting Health, National Food Supplies, and Agricultural Economics* (New York: The New York Academy of Sciences, 894, 1999).

Yeh, J. Y., J. H. Lee, J. Y. Park, Y. S. Cho, and I. S. Cho, "Countering the Livestock-Targeted Bioterrorism Threat and Responding with an Animal Health Safeguarding System," *Transboundary & Emerging Diseases* 60, no. 4 (August 2013): 289–297.

Zilinskas, Raymond A., "The Anti-Plague System and the Soviet Biological Warfare Program," *Critical Reviews in Microbiology* 32 (2006): 47–64.

Airborne Alert

The U.S. bomber alert operation, code-named "Chrome Dome," was a realistic training mission designed by the Strategic Air Command (SAC) to deter enemy forces from a surprise attack on the United States. Chrome Dome was established in 1960 following a series of planning and training flights in the late 1950s; a portion of the U.S. strategic nuclear bombing fleet remained on continuous airborne alert until 1968. In later years, these missions operated under the code names "Head Start," "Round Robin," and "Hard Head." The alert ensured that up to a dozen nuclear-armed bombers were airborne 24 hours a day. It greatly improved SAC's retaliatory capability in case of a Soviet surprise attack, thus strengthening America's nuclear deterrent.

The southern airborne alert route crossed the Atlantic Ocean and Mediterranean Sea before returning to the United States; the northern route went up the eastern coast of Canada, west across Canada toward Alaska, and then down the western coast of North America. Other mission routes were substituted as required. The Hard Head missions were intended to ensure continuous visual surveillance of Thule Air Base, Greenland, and its vital Ballistic Missile Early Warning System (BMEWS) radar, critical elements of the U.S. early warning and surveillance network guarding North America. If voice or data links were lost to these critical installations due to enemy action, the B-52 crews were supposed to provide visual confirmation and then follow subsequent orders to proceed to their designated targets.

Airborne alert flights ended following two serious accidents involving nuclear bombs and B-52s. On January 17, 1966, a B-52 collided with its KC-135 tanker during aerial refueling and crashed off the coast of Palomares, Spain. On January 22, 1968, a B-52 crashed near Thule, Greenland. SAC thereafter placed 30 percent of its bomber force on ground alert, with crews ready to take off within minutes of a warning being received from a BMEWS site or other radar.

Gilles Van Nederveen

Further Reading

Polmar, Norman, ed., *Strategic Air Command: People, Aircraft, and Missiles* (Annapolis, MD: Nautical and Aviation Publishing Company of America, 1979).

Schlosser, Eric, *Command and Control: Nuclear Weapons, the Damascus Accident, and the Illusion of Safety* (New York: Penguin Books, 2013).

Al Qaeda

Al Qaeda (Arabic for *base* or *foundation*) is the Islamic terrorist organization responsible for the September 11, 2001, attacks on the United States. The history of Al Qaeda is closely tied to the life of its leader, Osama bin Laden (d. 2011), and is mostly shaped by his experiences as part of the Arab mujahideen (holy warriors) in Afghanistan in the 1980s and his role as a Saudi political dissident.

In the early 1980s, the Saudi government supported the mujahideen resistance against the Soviet Union's invasion of Afghanistan, recruiting and sending Arab men from Saudi Arabia and other countries to fight in the name of Islam. At that time, bin Laden, with the help of the Saudi government, established the Islamic Salvation Foundation with the same purpose. After the withdrawal of the Soviet Union from Afghanistan—which was seen by the mujahideen as a victory for Islam produced by their efforts—many of these volunteer soldiers returned to their native Saudi Arabia, only to be disaffected and alienated from a government that they felt no longer appreciated them or upheld the values of Islam. Sharing this sentiment, bin Laden became a key player in the founding of a dissident organization known as the Advice and Reform Council.

Meanwhile, bin Laden was also active in South Asia. The World Muslim League and the Muslim Brotherhood organizations in Peshawar, Pakistan, led by Abdullah Azzam, served as the center for the Arab mujahideen that had remained in the vicinity. After Azzam's assassination in 1989, bin Laden took over these organizations and formed them into Al Qaeda, with the goal of developing a broad-based alliance among former Arab mujahideen.

Al Qaeda's ideology is based on the Wahhabi branch of Sunni Islam, which demands the strict application of Islam to every aspect of political and social life. Additionally, Al Qaeda has elevated the concept of jihad (holy war) to a position of central importance in its interpretation of Islam. Al Qaeda defines *jihad* as a duty for all Muslims to fight against kafirs (infidels or unbelievers). For Al Qaeda, unbelievers include all non-Muslims as well as those Muslims it believes do not adequately uphold the teachings of Islam. The Saudi royal family is among the Muslims targeted for destruction.

Throughout its growth as a terrorist organization, Al Qaeda has maintained four main ideological grievances. First, it claims that the Saudi royal family is corrupt and does not uphold its professed Wahhabi beliefs. Second, it opposes Saudi cooperation with and reliance on the United States. Third, it sees the U.S. military presence in Saudi Arabia since the end of the First Gulf War as an "occupation" of Islamic holy sites. Fourth, it opposes U.S. support for Israel. But Al Qaeda is not only geographically disparate; it is also ideologically diffuse. In different geographical locations, certain issues are given emphasis by local cells. In all cases, however, local conflicts between cells are seen in the broader context of jihad against unbelievers.

The combination of jihadi ideology with Al Qaeda's grievances against what it saw as insufferable American cultural influences led bin Laden to declare jihad against the United States in 1998. The original fatwa specifically mentions the United States, but it also includes U.S. allies.

However, even before declaring jihad against the West, Al Qaeda was on the path to war. Al Qaeda is believed to have been responsible for previous attacks against Americans: 18 U.S. soldiers killed in Mogadishu, Somalia, in 1993; 5 U.S. soldiers killed in a Riyadh, Saudi Arabia, bomb attack in 1995; and 19 U.S. military personnel killed in Dhahran, Saudi Arabia, in the Khobar Towers bombing, in 1996. Iran also may have played a role in the Khobar Towers bombing. Al Qaeda is also suspected of being involved in the 1992 bombings in Aden, Yemen; the 1993 World Trade Center bombing; a 1994 plot to assassinate President Bill Clinton; and a 1995 plan to blow up a dozen U.S. jetliners over the Atlantic Ocean. Al Qaeda has also been charged with perpetrating the U.S. embassy bombings in Kenya and Tanzania in 1998 as well as the attack on the USS *Cole* in 2000.

Since its formation, Al Qaeda has reportedly attempted to acquire or develop weapons of mass destruction, including chemical, biological, radiological, and nuclear (CBRN) weapons. In November 2001, U.S. forces in Afghanistan discovered the blueprints for a crude nuclear bomb in a house in Kabul. It has been reported that Al Qaeda has tried on numerous occasions to obtain uranium or other radioactive materials. Reports by both U.S. and British intelligence sources indicate that Al Qaeda was successful on at least one occasion.

Al Qaeda has also made attempts to develop chemical and biological weapons (CBW). Bin Laden expressed his desire for the group to develop a CBW capability. Files recovered from Al Qaeda computers and equipment found in Al Qaeda laboratories in Afghanistan support bin Laden's statements and indicate that the group at one time had the capability to produce limited quantities of some CBW agents. For example, one lab near Kandahar was equipped to produce anthrax. Finally, in August 2002, the Cable News Network (CNN) broadcast Al Qaeda–produced videotapes that it had obtained in Afghanistan that showed dogs being killed by clouds of unknown toxic chemicals. These were probably trials or demonstrations of hydrogen cyanide gas.

Although still an active terrorist organization, Al Qaeda has in many ways allowed itself to be eclipsed by the Islamic State of Iraq and Syria (ISIS), especially since the death of Osama bin Laden at the hands of U.S. Navy SEALs in May 2011. In 2013, U.S. government officials estimated Al Qaeda's ranks of operatives numbered no more than 100 in Pakistan and Afghanistan. However, by 2016, Al Qaeda had staged a comeback of sorts, with affiliated fighters numbering some 5,000 in Syria and a dozen or more affiliated branches in the Middle East, Africa, and South and Central Asia. After nearly a decade of an uneasy relationship, Al Qaeda formally renounced any links with ISIS in February 2014.

Led by Osama bin Laden's second-in-command, Ayman al-Zawahiri, Al Qaeda has attempted to distinguish and separate itself from the more bloodthirsty and indiscriminate killing for which ISIS is now infamous, preferring instead to refocus on targeting its main enemies, namely, the United States and its allies. This moderation (if it can be called that) has not endeared itself with jihadist fighters, however, who seem to gravitate toward ISIS and its more sanguineous acts of terrorism.

In 2015, Michael Morell, a former Central Intelligence Agency (CIA) deputy director, cautioned that Al Qaeda and its associated organizations have attempted to acquire CBRN technologies and use them in some weaponized form, and that "they will try again." But for all real or imagined intent by Al Qaeda to obtain and potentially employ WMD, thus far (2018) there have been no confirmed instances of its group members having employed chemical, biological, or radiological weapons. There are likely a number of reasons for Al Qaeda not resorting to using such weapons for mass-casualty attacks, but two very important factors include (1) the technological hurdles involved in developing WMD and (2) the likely withering military response by the United States and other nations that could spell the end of Al Qaeda as an organization.

Sean Lawson and Eric A. Croddy

Further Reading

Gunaratna, Rohan, *Inside Al Qaeda: Global Network of Terror* (New York: Columbia University Press, 2002).

Holbrook, Donald, "Al-Qaeda and the Rise of ISIS," *Survival* 57, no. 2 (April–May 2015): 93–104.

Morell, Michael, with Bill Harlow, *The Great War of Our Time* (New York: Twelve, 2015).

Stone, John, "Al Qaeda, Deterrence, and Weapons of Mass Destruction," *Studies in Conflict & Terrorism* 32 (2009): 763–765.

Ammonium Nitrate Fuel Oil

Ammonium nitrate fuel oil (ANFO) is a low-velocity (meaning the speed of expansion following a blast is less than higher-yield explosives such as TNT), pushing-type secondary explosive primarily used to move earth and rock. Because the materials involved in its production are readily available, it is relatively easy for individuals to produce large volumes of ANFO without attracting unwanted attention. This ease of acquisition and manufacture makes ANFO ideal for use in terrorism. ANFO explosives have also been used to simulate the effects of nuclear detonations.

Background

In the 1650s, a chemist by the name of J. R. Glauber prepared what he called "nitrum flammans," now known as ammonium nitrate, but at the time he did not recognize its utility as a component in explosives. In the early 19th century, researchers Grindel and Robin used ammonium nitrate instead of potassium nitrate for the manufacture of black powder, the classic explosive of the time until smokeless powder was introduced.

In 1955, a large coal mining concern achieved an effective result by using a combination of ammonium nitrate and coal (as the fuel). Later, other mining companies discovered the use of fuel oil further enhanced its properties, and, thus, the ammonium nitrate fuel oil (ANFO) combination for modern explosives was born.

In 1966, based on the mining industry's decade-long experience with the use of ANFO as an explosive, scientists from the U.S. Naval Surface Weapons Center suggested replacing TNT with ANFO to simulate nuclear weapon blasts. On October 6, 1976, Operation DICE THROW detonated a 628-ton ANFO device on the White Sands Missile Range, New Mexico, to simulate the damage from a nuclear device on military equipment and other targets.

Oklahoma City Bombing, 1995

The most horrific domestic use of ANFO as a weapon was the bombing of the Alfred P. Murrah Federal Building in Oklahoma City in 1995. In seeking out an explosive for his purposes, Timothy McVeigh selected ANFO for several reasons. The primary components were easily acquired in bulk in the agricultural communities of the Midwest without drawing any attention from law enforcement, and the materials for bomb construction were inexpensive. McVeigh created a very large device because he believed that, due to the lower yield of ANFO in relation to other high explosives, a large container would be needed to construct a very powerful weapon. McVeigh probably did not realize that the compressed air shock wave produced by slower detonating materials (e.g., ANFO) is highly effective against rigid building components.

McVeigh rented a delivery truck, filled it with ANFO in 55-gallon drums, added booster charges, and parked it at the curb next to the Alfred P. Murrah Federal Building. The tricky part of the operation involved setting all the detonators to go off simultaneously. Due to the comparatively low sensitivity of ANFO, a single detonation might have pushed most of the ANFO harmlessly away from the primary blast. Ultimately, McVeigh succeeded in creating a simultaneous detonation of the ANFO, which produced extensive damage to the federal building and hundreds of casualties. The federal courthouse across the street was severely damaged, and glass was broken in the windows of many downtown buildings. Injuries in other buildings from the shock wave and flying glass added to the number of victims.

The Oklahoma City bombing, coming just weeks after the Aum Shinrikyo sarin attack on the Tokyo subway system, led the U.S. Congress to take more specific actions to help the nation's largest cities to prepare to respond to terrorist attacks.

Dual Use for Industry and Terrorism

The simplicity of ANFO and the availability of materials have made it popular among various terrorist groups for decades. In Europe, ANFO explosives have been used so widely that government regulations require ammonium nitrate to be produced in prills too large for use in explosives. Vehicle-borne improvised explosive devices (VBIEDs) employing ANFO have become more common in the last few decades, such as in the case of the Provisional Irish Republican Army (1990s), and were extensively employed by insurgent terrorists in Iraq, beginning in 2003, and by the Islamic State of Iraq and Syria (ISIS) from 2011 to the present. Over time, the size of these vehicle bombs has grown to include massive truck-sized VBIEDs.

ANFO-based explosives and its key component, ammonium nitrate, are still used every day by law-abiding individuals in their legal pursuits (e.g., coal mining, demolitions). Following the Oklahoma City bombing, increased law enforcement awareness and legislation have been pursued surrounding fertilizers with heavy ammonium nitrate concentrations. Due to the huge volume of this material used in agricultural and commercial operations, it is highly unlikely that complete control over its sale and movement will ever be established.

Dan Goodrich and Eric A. Croddy

Further Reading

Explosives and Demolitions, U.S. Army Field Manual 5-250 (Washington, D.C.: Department of the Army, 1992).

Military Explosives, Technical Manual No. 9-1910 (Washington, D.C.: Departments of the Army and the Air Force, April 14, 1955).

Petes, Joseph, Robert Miller, and Frank McMullan, *User's Guide and History of ANFO as a Nuclear Weapons Effect Simulation Explosive*, Report No. DNA-TR-82-156 (Washington, D.C.: Defense Nuclear Agency, March 31, 1983). http://www.dtic.mil/dtic/tr/fulltext/u2/a151623.pdf.

Anthrax

Anthrax is an acute infectious disease caused by *Bacillus anthracis*. Because of its high fatality rate, it is one of the most feared biological warfare (BW) agents. Anthrax is classified by the Centers for Disease Control and Prevention (CDC) as a Category A bioterror threat because it can be easily disseminated and could result in a high number of deaths. According to the CDC, a large, dedicated attack using aerosolized anthrax bacteria against a populated city could result in hundreds of thousands of casualties. In September 2001, Bruce Ivins, a U.S. biological weapons defense scientist, is believed to have deliberately spread anthrax spores through the U.S. postal system. This attack caused 22 cases of infection and 5 deaths.

Background

Anthrax was the first disease for which a microbial origin was definitively established (by Robert Koch in 1876). *Bacillus anthracis*, the causative agent of anthrax, is a disease of grazing mammals (sheep, cattle, etc.) that can be transmitted to humans. When conditions become unfavorable for this microbe's survival (e.g., lack of nutrients), it forms a rigid outer shell through a process called *sporulation*. These spores are oval, colorless, odorless, tasteless, microscopic, and hardy, capable of surviving in the soil for years.

B. anthracis can cause three distinct diseases in humans, depending on the route of exposure. The first and deadliest form, inhalation anthrax, is contracted by inhaling the spores and is the only form that poses a serious BW threat. Inhalation anthrax is characterized by flulike symptoms, including a sore throat, fever, muscle aches, and malaise. After this acute phase, there is sometimes a brief improvement that is followed by respiratory failure and shock. Chest X-rays usually show a characteristic widening of the mediastinum—tissues surrounding the lymph in the chest—due to hemorrhaging of the local lymph nodes. Case-fatality estimates are extremely high, even with treatment.

The second and most common form of anthrax, making up some 95 percent of all cases, is cutaneous anthrax. This type usually occurs after contact with infected animals or animal products and is usually related to occupational exposure (anthrax was once called "woolsorter's disease"). The bacterium gains entry through a break in the skin, and infection begins as a papule, progressing into an ulcer with a central black necrotic area. (The term *anthrax* is derived from the Greek word for coal, *anthrakis*, because of the characteristic black skin lesions). Fatality of this type is less than 1 percent with treatment and 5–20 percent without.

The third form, gastrointestinal anthrax, is rare and usually follows consumption of contaminated meat. The fatality rate is 25–60 percent, even with treatment.

History

Anthrax has played a long and devastating role in human history. An epidemic in 17th-century Europe caused 60,000 deaths.

Today, only approximately 2,000 human cases are reported worldwide annually; these are usually the cutaneous type and occur mostly in developing countries (rarely do any cases occur in the United States). The largest international outbreak in modern times was in Zimbabwe (1979–1980), with more than 10,000 people infected and over 180 deaths. Nearly all of these were because of the cutaneous form of anthrax, although some cases of inhalation and gastrointestinal anthrax cannot be ruled out.

Before the advent of safer handling processes, vaccines, and improved veterinary management of domesticated animals, "woolsorter's disease" was a relatively common occupational hazard in wool-related textile mills, especially during the 18th-century industrial revolution. This deadly job-related illness was caused by inhaled anthrax spores liberated from newly spun wool, causing not only cutaneous but also the more deadly inhalation anthrax.

One landmark case occurred in 1957 in Manchester, New Hampshire, when nine workers at a goat hair processing plant became infected after handling a contaminated shipment of skins from Pakistan. Four of the five workers who contracted inhalation anthrax died. Although the number of actual cases was too small for a proper scientific conclusion, one of the lessons learned from this incident was that inoculating workers with anthrax vaccine probably protected them from the inhalational form of the disease.

Bioterrorism

During its occupation of Manchuria (1932–1945), Japan conducted BW research that included weaponizing anthrax and other disease agents. The Japanese research program, designated Unit 731, tested anthrax bombs on humans. Anthrax-contaminated food was dropped on Chinese cities, and anthrax-filled chocolates were given to children in Nanking (Nanjing), China. By the end of World War II, the Japanese BW program had stockpiled nearly 900 pounds of anthrax, to be used in specially designed fragmentation bombs.

The United States and Great Britain weaponized anthrax during World War II as a potential retaliatory weapon against a German BW attack. About 5,000 anthrax-filled bombs were produced at Camp Detrick, Maryland. The British tested anthrax bombs on Gruinard Island, off the northwest coast of Scotland (1942–1943). The Allies also stockpiled anthrax-laced cattle feed cakes in a program called "Operation Vegetarian" that were intended to be dropped on German livestock farms. This plan, however, was never carried out.

On April 2, 1979, Military Compound 19 (the Microbiology and Virology Institute) in Sverdlovsk (now Yekaterinburg) accidentally released anthrax spores into the atmosphere, causing the largest known inhalation anthrax epidemic in the 20th century. The official Soviet statistics reported years later that 96 people were infected, resulting in at least 68 deaths. Others have estimated that between 68 and 600 deaths were caused by this accidental release of anthrax. At the time of the incident—and up until the dissolution of the USSR—Soviet officials attributed the outbreak to contaminated meat. Finally, in 1992, Russian president Boris Yeltsin acknowledged that a "military-related anthrax study" had been conducted at the research institute.

Iraq began an offensive BW program in 1985, and a decade later, Iraq admitted to the UN Special Commission (UNSCOM) that it had amassed 6,000 liters of anthrax, deployed 5 Scud missiles and several 122-mm rockets filled with anthrax, and produced 50 bombs filled with anthrax spores. They also had spray tanks fitted to aircraft that could distribute biological agents over a specific target. These "death-drones" were targeted during Desert Fox, the joint U.S. and U.K. air attack on Iraqi BW installations in December 1998.

In 1993, Aum Shinrikyo, the doomsday cult behind the deadly sarin gas attack in Tokyo's subway in 1995, tried twice to disperse aerosol anthrax from the roof of Aum Shinrikyo's office building in Tokyo. The attacks failed, at least in part, because they used the nonvirulent vaccine strain (Sterne).

As many countries are capable of producing and delivering this weapon, the threat from state-sponsored programs using anthrax as a biological weapon is difficult to assess. But even smaller groups or individuals are capable of causing great harm and anxiety from using anthrax as a weapon of terror.

U.S. Anthrax Attack, 2001

Shortly after the terrorist attacks on the World Trade Center and Pentagon on September 11, 2001, four anthrax-laced letters were mailed from Trenton, New Jersey, to the *New York Post*, the NBC television studios in New York, and Senators Tom Daschle and Patrick Leahy. A fifth letter (sent to American Media, Inc.) was apparently discarded after being opened. An estimated total of 10 grams of spores were contained in the letters, leading to 22 anthrax cases in 4 states (New York, New Jersey, Florida, and Connecticut) and the District of Columbia. The CDC confirmed that 11 victims were infected from inhalation anthrax (5 of these victims died), and 11 others suffered from cutaneous anthrax. Although the death toll was relatively low, the dissemination of anthrax spore–laden envelopes crippled business, government, and postal services, straining the public health system.

Subsequent genetic analyses of the anthrax in the letters matched perfectly with Fort Detrick's 1980 Ames strain. This source was ultimately traced to an employee and scientist, Bruce Ivins, but before he could be charged, he committed suicide in 2008. Ivins was known to have psychiatric problems, and his exact motivations for having carried out these anthrax letter attacks are still unclear.

Current Anthrax Defensive Research

The defensive effort against anthrax primarily involves improving rapid diagnostic methods and prophylactic and advanced therapeutic regimens. In late 2012, the U.S. Food and Drug Administration (FDA) finally approved the use of a monoclonal antibody, raxibacumab, delivered in an injection has been shown to be effective against inhalation anthrax. It is now being stockpiled (over 57,000 doses) under the U.S. Biomedical Advanced Research and Development Authority program (Department of Health and Human Services) in the event of a bioterrorist attack. This is in addition to the stockpiling of over 28 million doses of an FDA-approved vaccine for anthrax (BioThrax).

Beverley Rider and Eric A. Croddy

Further Reading

Alibek, Ken, and Stephen Handelman, *Biohazard: The Chilling True Story of the Largest Covert Biological Weapons Program in the World* (New York: Random House, 1999).

Bower, William A., Katherine Hendricks, Satish Pillai, Julie Guarnizo, and Dana Meaney-Delman, "Clinical Framework and Medical Countermeasure Use during an Anthrax Mass-Casualty Incident CDC Recommendations," *MMWR Recommendations & Reports* 64, no. 4 (December 4, 2015): 1–21.

Anti-Ballistic Missile Treaty

Signed in 1972 between the United States and the Soviet Union, the Anti-Ballistic Missile (ABM) Treaty severely restricted the development and deployment of ballistic missile defenses and was considered a significant milestone in the history of arms control. It was the first formal treaty between the two nations that limited systems related to their central strategic deterrent capabilities. The U.S. government portrayed it as a significant first step in a new era of mutual restraint and arms limitation between the Cold War superpowers that would provide for a more stable strategic balance and lead to a broader, more comprehensive series of arms control agreements.

The treaty also set important precedents that were followed by later arms control treaties, including the legitimization of "national technical means" of verification and the establishment of a commission to oversee implementation and compliance. Over the course of its existence—from May 26, 1972, until June 13, 2002—the ABM Treaty was viewed by many as the basis of Soviet-American and then Russian-American strategic relations. Promoted on the one hand as the cornerstone of strategic stability and vilified on the other as a constraint on U.S. self-defense that shackled Washington to a strategic doctrine of perpetual vulnerability, the ABM Treaty represented both the best and the worst aspects of modern arms control.

Negotiation of the Treaty

Soviet leaders were at first opposed in principle to the very idea of limiting missile defenses—which they believed were entirely defensive weapons. However, within days of the U.S. Senate's June 24, 1968, approval of the U.S. Sentinel ABM system, which had been designed to match the Soviet Union's own ABM system then being deployed around Moscow, they did a complete about-face on the subject and agreed to accept the U.S. proposal to begin immediate discussions on limiting ballistic missile defenses. Although the United States was most interested in achieving a treaty on offensive force limitations, following two years of negotiations, it accepted a treaty limiting ABM systems along with an interim agreement on offensive arms limitations, with the prospect of pursuing a more comprehensive formal treaty on offensive arms in the future.

Terms of the Treaty

The ABM Treaty originally limited the United States and the Soviet Union to two sites of 100 antiballistic missile launchers each, separated by at least 1,300 kilometers. A protocol to the treaty, signed in 1974, reduced this limit to just one site for each side. The treaty banned the deployment of ABM systems for a defense of national territory and obligated the parties to not provide a base for such a defense or for the defense of an individual region, except as provided for in the treaty. ABM systems were defined, for the purposes of the treaty, as ABM interceptor missiles, ABM launchers, and ABM radars. The application of the treaty terms to ABM systems that used mechanisms other than missiles to intercept strategic missiles, such as lasers or directed-energy weapons, became the subject of an intense controversy in the years following the signing of the treaty.

The ABM Treaty further provided for a complete prohibition on developing, testing, or deploying ABM systems or components that were not fixed and land based, that is, sea-, air-, space-, or mobile land-based systems or components. To reduce the potential for circumventing the terms of the treaty, the treaty also prohibited upgrading theater-range antiballistic missiles (which were not otherwise limited by the treaty), testing them concurrently with strategic ABM systems or components, or transferring ABM systems or components to other nations. ABM radars were limited to those at ABM launcher bases or located on the periphery of the national territory and oriented outward (restrictions violated by the Soviet ABM radar at Krasnoyarsk).

Relationship of the Treaty to Other Treaties

Many ABM Treaty supporters considered it the basis of international arms control regimes, which were all predicated to one degree or another on the assumption that the ABM Treaty had forestalled a U.S.-Soviet arms race between offensive and defensive weapons.

The Soviets took steps to codify a linkage between their interest in further strategic offensive arms reductions and preservation of the ABM Treaty. For example, they insisted, prior to the conclusion of the Strategic Arms Reduction Treaty (START), that START would be "effective and viable only under conditions of compliance with" the ABM Treaty as signed on May 26, 1972. Soviet negotiators also made clear in a unilateral statement associated with START that "events related to withdrawal by one of the Parties" from the ABM Treaty could be grounds for exercising the right to withdraw from START. A similar condition was associated with the Russian Duma's consent to ratify START II.

Problems Interpreting the ABM Treaty

Almost from the beginning, the necessarily vague diplomatic language of the ABM Treaty posed serious problems of interpretation. One controversy in particular arose in the mid-1980s, soon after President Ronald Reagan announced the intention of the United States to pursue robust missile defenses through a Strategic Defense Initiative (SDI). Some argued that although the treaty banned the deployment of sea-, air-, space-, and mobile land-based ABM systems, it did not prohibit research and development into ABM systems related to those areas. Advocates of this position, which came to be known as the "broad interpretation," further argued that the language of Agreed Statement D, referring to the potential creation in the future of ABM systems "based on other physical principles," allowed their development and testing but not their deployment. Others believed that the ABM Treaty prohibited the development and testing as well as the deployment of such exotic ABM systems. This position came to be known as the "narrow interpretation."

The Reagan administration officially adopted the broad interpretation in 1985, and this eventually led to a confrontation with the U.S. Congress over which interpretation had been associated with the treaty during its ratification process and whether the executive branch had a right to reinterpret treaties once ratified. In 1992, President Bill Clinton's administration officially renounced the "broad interpretation" and reinstated the "narrow interpretation" as the official policy of the United States. Thereafter, it substantially reduced funding for research into missile defenses and dismantled existing missile defense research and development programs.

The U.S. Decision to Withdraw from the ABM Treaty

Upon assuming office in 2001, President George W. Bush announced that it was the policy of his administration to deploy effective missile defenses against the threat of limited attacks by a handful of missiles launched by rogue states, and to do so as soon as technically feasible. This set the United States on an inevitable collision course with the ABM Treaty.

On December 13, 2001, President Bush gave formal notice to Russia that the United States was withdrawing from the ABM Treaty in accordance with the requirement contained in Article XV of the treaty to give six months' advance notice. In making his announcement, the president noted that the world was vastly different from that which existed in 1972, when the treaty was signed, and that one of the signatories, the Soviet Union, no longer existed—and neither did the hostilities that once characterized relations between the two countries. He cited the imperative of having the freedom and flexibility to develop effective defenses against ballistic missile attack by terrorists or hostile rogue states and the need to move beyond mutual assured destruction (MAD) as the basis of deterrence. This withdrawal became effective on June 13, 2002.

Although the George W. Bush administration had held a series of intense discussions with Russia over the fate of the ABM Treaty, in which ideas for revising or modifying it were discussed as alternatives to withdrawing from the treaty, the administration was increasingly convinced that a clean break with the past was in order. There were three principal reasons for this decision. First, the ABM Treaty was no longer an appropriate basis for what at the time was a relatively cooperative U.S.-Russian relationship. Second, deterrence based solely on mutual assured destruction, as institutionalized by the ABM Treaty, no longer appeared to be a critical necessity vis-à-vis Russia nor desirable against

potential adversaries. Third, the ABM Treaty presented an obstacle to the testing and development activities needed to find the most effective and affordable means of defending against ballistic missiles of all ranges. Moreover, the ABM Treaty prohibited cooperation between the United States and its allies in developing missile defenses, an avenue the United States was determined to pursue through NATO as well as bilaterally with key friends and allies.

Russia reacted with moderation, given the dire warnings its leaders and diplomats had issued up to that time regarding the potentially negative effects that would surely accompany any U.S. effort to withdraw from or substantially modify the ABM Treaty. In a response given the same day as the U.S. withdrawal announcement, President Vladimir Putin said Russia believed the U.S. decision to be mistaken but asserted it would not pose a threat to the national security of Russia.

Fifteen years later, as North Korea ballistic missile tests place renewed emphasis on theater and national missile defenses, few observers bemoan the loss of the ABM Treaty.

Kerry Kartchner

Further Reading

Smith, Gerard C., *Doubletalk: The Story of SALT I* (Garden City, NY: Doubleday, 1980).

U.S. Arms Control and Disarmament Agency, "ABM Treaty," in *Arms Control and Disarmament Agreements: Texts and Histories of the Negotiations* (Washington, D.C.: U.S. Arms Control and Disarmament Agency, 1990), 155–166.

Wirtz, James J., and Jeffrey A. Larsen, eds., *Rockets' Red Glare: Missile Defenses and the Future of World Politics* (Boulder, CO: Westview, 2001).

Antinuclear Movement

The antinuclear movement has raised concerns about the use of nuclear technology for peaceful or military purposes. The movement's main policy goals, its size, and its perceived influence have varied over time, and its history can be divided into four main periods of activity. From 1944 to 1948, the movement consisted of elites who advocated civilian control of nuclear technology and international control of nuclear knowledge under the United Nations. From 1957 to 1963, the movement included the broader public and advocated limits on nuclear testing. From the late 1960s through 1980, the antinuclear movement worked with the emerging environmental movement to oppose the construction and operation of nuclear power plants. From 1979 through 1984, the movement was at its largest and most influential and was focused on the proposal for a U.S. and Soviet "nuclear freeze."

Currently, the movement has adopted a "humanitarian" approach to nuclear disarmament. But in 2017, it achieved a real success when the UN General Assembly passed a nuclear weapons ban treaty (albeit without any of the nuclear weapons states or NATO members as signatories, limiting the immediate effectiveness of the ban).

Early Efforts

Even as research and development of nuclear weapons occurred, some of the scientists involved began to question the long-term implications of their work. Within elite academic, political, and scientific circles, many expressed a mix of fear of the new weapons' power and hope that peaceful uses of nuclear energy might emerge. They came to believe that decisive action to establish control of the new technology was necessary, but there was less agreement on what action should occur. Several leading researchers formed the Federation of Atomic Scientists with the hope of influencing debate. Because of the technical nature of the issues involved, the scientists' views were accorded great weight, but some politicians and military officials believed that the scientists were politically naive. The Federation obtained its initial objective with the passage of the 1946 Atomic Energy Act, which gave the civilian-led Atomic Energy Commission control of commercial and military U.S. nuclear programs.

Debate then shifted to the idea of international control of nuclear arsenals, which brought existing peace groups and world federalist organizations into the antinuclear movement. Their hopes for real action on the Baruch Plan, the U.S.-backed initiative to give control of all nuclear weapons to the United Nations, were dashed by mounting Cold War tensions. As fear of an emerging Soviet threat spread, international control of nuclear arsenals appeared increasingly far-fetched.

The Test Ban Movement

By the mid-1950s, nuclear weapons technology had advanced with the development of the hydrogen bomb and ballistic missiles. Several new groups, notably Pugwash and the Committee for a Sane Nuclear Policy (SANE), were established to inform policy makers and the public about the dangers of nuclear escalation and possible flaws in deterrence strategies.

These new groups generated significant media and policy-maker attention, especially when the issue of nuclear testing became a source of public alarm. In 1954, radioactive fallout from a U.S. test on Bikini Island covered a Japanese fishing boat. There also were mounting reports that radioactive fallout from atmospheric nuclear testing would cause genetic defects and cancer. Polls showed widespread public support for a test ban, and existing antinuclear organizations began to push it as an important first step in arms control. Support for the test ban also came from religious figures, including Pope Pius XII; leaders in the nonaligned movement, such as Jawaharlal Nehru; and political parties from Japan to England. A small number of activists also used direct action, such as sailing boats close to test sites.

It is difficult to say precisely how much influence these polls and various groups had, but it became clear to both U.S. and Soviet leaders that they shared a mutual interest in adopting moratoriums on atmospheric testing. In 1963, the Limited Test Ban Treaty, which banned testing in the atmosphere, underwater, or in outer space, was signed. The treaty was a victory for the antinuclear movement. Lacking a pivotal issue around which to rally support, the movement again receded.

Movement against Commercial Use

During the 1960s and 1970s, smaller groups of people continued to criticize the overall development of nuclear strategy, specific weapons systems, and missile defense systems. Many peace groups and other foreign policy–oriented groups shifted their focus to the Vietnam War. Another branch of the antinuclear movement began to work with environmental and local citizens' groups to protest nuclear power plants. At first, these protests were small, but in time, four factors emerged that strengthened the movement. First, rising oil prices made nuclear energy a more attractive alternative. Second, the U.S. government radically reorganized its energy bureaucracy. Plans for the reorganization gave the movement an issue while

also providing new entry points for lobbying. Third, both government and private research showed that the dangers of nuclear power had been understated. And, fourth, several small accidents and near accidents highlighted potential problems.

In their attempts to limit the spread of nuclear power, movement strategists first used legal action and demands for full environmental impact reports. By 1976, they had moved to an electoral strategy, placing several antinuclear referenda on ballots and supporting the Democratic Party's platform, which called for developing nonnuclear sources of energy. They then added tactics of direct action. For example, members of the Clamshell Alliance occupied the construction site of the Seabrook Nuclear Power Plant in New Hampshire. These actions revitalized the old debate over whether the benefits of nuclear energy would outweigh the dangers. The movement was gradually gaining public support, although it lost a key referendum battle in California in 1976. Then, the debate turned in favor of opponents of nuclear power because of accidents at Three Mile Island, Pennsylvania, and Chernobyl, Ukraine.

Nuclear Freeze

By the late-1970s, many people in both the public and policy-making circles saw Cold War tensions, the dangers of nuclear war, and arms races that were only partially limited by arms control agreements as unpleasant but unavoidable facts of modern life. Randall Forsberg, a researcher trained at the Massachusetts Institute of Technology, disagreed. Forsberg argued that, as the first step toward international security, the United States and the Soviet Union needed to end the arms race by freezing the testing, production, and deployment of nuclear weapons. Forsberg took the idea to existing peace, religious, and antinuclear groups. By early 1980, an Ad Hoc Task Force for a Nuclear Freeze had been created. The idea captured the attention of peace activist Randy Kehler, who then led efforts to put a freeze referendum on the ballot in three western Massachusetts districts. The freeze referendum passed in all three districts and even did well in areas that supported Ronald Reagan for president.

The freeze's expansion into a national movement was due to the actions of one of its greatest opponents. Reagan and many of his top advisers, fearing a rising Soviet threat, spoke repeatedly of increasing U.S. defense spending, purging arms control supporters from the bureaucracy, negotiating only from a position of strength, and fighting and winning a nuclear war. These statements led many to conclude that Reagan was determined to confront the Soviet Union at all costs and that he was not serious about arms control. These people supported the freeze both as a bold policy alternative and as a symbolic sign of disapproval of Reagan's ideas.

As the movement gained strength, Reagan and his supporters argued that a freeze would lock any Soviet superiority in place, potentially worsen the U.S. position if the Soviets cheated on the agreement, and weaken the position of U.S. arms control negotiators. Ironically, these administration arguments only served to further convince many that Reagan was exaggerating the Soviet threat and was unwilling to seriously negotiate.

The spread of the freeze movement was dramatic and reflected a combination of opposition to Reagan's policies, a general antinuclear mood in the country following the accident at Three Mile Island, and a widespread desire to achieve arms control objectives without increasing the Soviet threat. Freeze proposals were passed by dozens of town and city governments, by legislatures from Massachusetts to Oregon, and in eight statewide referenda votes in 1982. Polls consistently showed that over 70 percent of the public supported a freeze, although the numbers significantly declined if the question was worded to suggest that the freeze could lead to Soviet military superiority. In November 1982, a march in New York drew 750,000 people, and an initiative signed by more than 2 million people was delivered to the United Nations.

Proponents of the freeze remained active through the 1984 election, but the movement had begun to wane. Disputes over whether to use legislative or grassroots tactics, what final language would be acceptable, and whether the freeze would really lead to peace or only distract attention from other initiatives began to split the movement.

Humanitarian Initiative

Following the 2010 NPT Review Conference, a series of international meetings was held that highlighted the humanitarian consequences of nuclear weapons. The underlying premise of the movement is that the use of even a single nuclear weapon would produce a catastrophe beyond the scope of existing relief capabilities. Because states have an obligation to comply with existing humanitarian law, the humanitarian movement holds that they share an obligation to work to prevent the actual use of nuclear weapons under all circumstances. This philosophy is captured by the pledge issued by the Austrian government at the close of the Vienna Conference on the Humanitarian Impact of Nuclear Weapons (December 8–9, 2014). Austria "pledges to cooperate with all relevant stakeholders, States, international organizations, the International

Red Cross and Red Crescent Movements, parliamentarians and civil society, in efforts to stigmatize, prohibit and eliminate nuclear weapons in light of their unacceptable humanitarian consequences and associated risks."

The movement achieved a significant milestone on July 7, 2017, when 122 nations adopted the Treaty on the Prohibition of Nuclear Weapons in the General Assembly of the United Nations. The treaty was opened for signature on September 20, 2017. This effort of the nuclear abolition movement was led by the International Campaign to Abolish Nuclear Weapons (ICAN), a loose collection of international organizations that seek the elimination of nuclear weapons. ICAN was awarded the 2017 Nobel Peace Prize for its leadership of the campaign.

John W. Dietrich and Jeffrey A. Larsen

Further Reading

Austrian Ministry of Foreign Affairs, "Austrian Pledge," December 9, 2014. https://www.opendemocracy.net/5050/rebecca-johnson/austrian-pledge-to-ban-nuclear-weapons.Accessed February 20, 2018.

Kojm, Christopher A., ed., *The Nuclear Freeze Debate* (New York: H. W. Wilson, 1983).

Meyer, David S., "Protest Cycles and Political Process: American Peace Movements in the Nuclear Age," *Political Research Quarterly* 46 (1993): 451–479.

Muravchik, Joshua, "The Perils of a Nuclear Freeze," *World Affairs* 145 (1982): 203–207.

Price, Jerome, *The Antinuclear Movement* (Boston: Twayne, 1982).

Waller, Douglas C., *Congress and the Nuclear Freeze: An Inside Look at the Politics of a Mass Movement* (Amherst: University of Massachusetts Press, 1987).

Anti-Satellite Weapons

Anti-satellite (ASAT) weapons are designed to attack satellites in orbit. Potential destruction and disruption mechanisms for ASAT weapons include nuclear warheads, high explosives, directed energy, kinetic energy, and electronic warfare.

The United States became concerned about countering the potential for nuclear weapons delivery systems in orbit soon after the beginning of the space age. It first tested an air-launched ASAT weapon from a B-47 bomber under the U.S. Air Force's Bold Orion program in 1959. In the early 1960s, the U.S. Navy tested systems launched by F-4 fighters. These early ASAT systems would have used nuclear warheads as the kill mechanism, but none of them became operational.

In the early 1960s, Secretary of Defense Robert S. McNamara authorized development and deployment of limited numbers of two ground-based, nuclear-tipped ASAT systems. The army's Program 505 system used a Nike-Zeus launcher to conduct 7 tests from Kwajalein Island, in the Pacific, between 1964 and 1966. Program 437, the U.S. Air Force system, used a Thor booster from Johnson Island and was tested 16 times from 1964 to 1970. The indiscriminate nuclear kill mechanism on these systems could have destroyed or disabled all satellites in low Earth orbit by pumping up radiation belts.

Both the Soviet Union and the United States began work on more discriminating ASAT systems during the 1960s. The Soviets developed a radar and optical guided co-orbital system with a high-explosive warhead that was launched from a Tsyklon-2 (SL-11) booster and tested it at least 20 times between 1968 and 1982. U.S.

efforts during this period culminated in the successful September 13, 1985, test of the Miniature Homing Vehicle (MHV), a direct-ascent kinetic kill ASAT launched from an F-15 fighter.

Congressional restrictions on testing led the administration of President Ronald Reagan to cancel the MHV system in 1988. The superpowers also attempted to address ASAT issues through formal arms control efforts, holding three rounds of dedicated ASAT negotiations in 1978–1979 and discussing the issue in the Defense and Space Talks from 1985 to 1991. None of these negotiations produced an agreement.

Advances in ASAT capabilities accelerated after the turn of the century. The People's Republic of China (PRC) maintains a significant ASAT capability that includes anti-satellite missiles, co-orbital microsatellites, ground-based jammers, and directed energy weapons. In 2007, the PRC destroyed its FY-1C polar orbital satellite using a kinetic kill vehicle, which created much space debris. In 2008, the United States used an SM-3 missile fired from the cruiser USS *Lake Erie* to destroy a radar imaging satellite (NROL-21) that had malfunctioned, creating minimal space debris. Russia also apparently tested ASAT missiles in 2015 and 2016.

Analysts remain concerned that these ASAT capabilities might be used in a conflict to cripple an opponent's command and control, communication, and early warning capabilities, reducing the victim's ability to utilize modern information-enabled weapons and operations. Because both societies and militaries heavily rely on space-based communications for all sorts of activities, a major attack on an opponent's satellites, and the resulting environmental damage produced by space debris, could produce immediate strategic effects in war and lingering damage to the global economy.

Peter Hays and James J. Wirtz

Further Reading

Moltz, James Clay, *Crowded Orbits: Conflict and Cooperation in Space* (New York: Columbia University Press, 2014).

Stares, Paul B., *The Weaponization of Space: U.S. Policy, 1945–1984* (Ithaca, NY: Cornell University Press, 1985).

Wilson, Tom, "Threats to United States Space Capabilities," Space Commission Staff Background Paper, January 11, 2001. http://armedservices.house.gov/Publications/107thCongress/article05.pdf. Accessed January 1, 2018.

Arms Control

Arms control is any tacit or explicit agreement among states aimed at reducing the likelihood of war, the costs of preparing for war, or the damage should war occur. Arms control agreements seek to achieve these goals by restricting or reducing the size of arsenals or by placing limits on their operation. They may include a variety of verification and transparency measures, such as on-site inspections, reciprocal exhibitions of military hardware, notifications, joint exercises, and data exchanges. Arms control encompasses both formal and informal agreements.

As the focus of arms control efforts increasingly shifts to combating the proliferation of weapons of mass destruction and other types of weapons, recent arms control arrangements have come to include agreements among supplier states to limit the export of certain categories of weapons or materials that have military application, such as missiles, conventional arms, land mines, and chemical weapon precursor ingredients. Unilateral measures, undertaken with a view to influencing the military force policies of another state, also may be considered a form of arms control.

Arms control is a relatively modern concept and must be distinguished from *disarmament*, which refers to the elimination of weapons. Arms control may include a mutual freeze in levels of armaments, an agreed-upon reduction, or even a controlled increase in certain areas of weapons (such as those considered more "stabilizing" or "verifiable" than others). It may also include provisions for controlling how subject weapon systems are operated, or even where they are based.

The modern concept of arms control arose in the late 1950s and early 1960s as a response to the nuclear competition between the United States and the Soviet Union. Its tenets were originally formulated by mathematicians and game theorists seeking to resolve the instabilities inherent in the interplay between the fear of nuclear surprise attack and the buildup of nuclear weapons stockpiles. The arms race then emerging between the two superpowers, which many feared would spiral out of control without some concerted effort to check it, provided the incentive and urgency for exploring diplomatic and political means of slowing, stopping, or eventually reversing the U.S.-Soviet competition in nuclear weapons.

Arms control theory arose out of these concerns. It postulated that given the means to independently verify military capabilities through newly developed satellite technology, distrust could be surmounted through the implementation and mutual verification of incremental arms control arrangements. In theory, these incremental arrangements, initially very modest, would in turn engender sufficient trust to proceed toward more complete arms control agreements and eventually toward a process of actual disarmament.

Arms Control Objectives

Early arms control theorists developed a series of principles to guide negotiators and policy makers:

Arms control was not an end in itself but a means to an end, specifically the enhancement of security, especially prevention of nuclear war.

The superpowers shared a common interest in avoiding nuclear war, and that common interest could be the basis for effective arms control agreements.

Arms control and a nation's national security strategy should work together to promote national objectives.

Arms control encompassed more than the conclusion of formally negotiated agreements. It could include informal arrangements and unilateral confidence-building measures.

Determining Success or Failure

Debate about the prospects and necessary conditions for the success or failure of arms control measures accompanied the creation of modern arms control theory. On the one hand, the pro–arms control community has largely focused on the intangible benefits allegedly accruing from the process of negotiation, which include greater mutual understanding, a deliberate shift to more stable avenues of competition, a lessening of political tension, and improvements in the learning curve each nation experiences with security policies and structures. This school of thought has generally assumed that arms control could transcend political tensions among prospective arms control partners and could be used as an instrument to ameliorate those tensions. The successful negotiation of increasingly ambitious arms control arrangements by more and more states on both a bilateral and multilateral basis is taken as evidence of the benefits of this approach.

On the other hand, those skeptical of arms control have focused on the allegedly poor track record of tangible arms control results, the modest negotiated outcomes of arms control processes, and their impact on other national security objectives. They have also taken issue with the very assumptions of arms control theory, arguing that arms control has emphasized the inherently futile task of finding technical solutions to essentially political problems.

For example, many skeptics have held that arms control theory and practice pay too little attention to problems of verification and compliance. The essential verification problem is the limited ability of surveillance technology to monitor the activities of a treaty party determined to find ways to cheat. The compliance problem consists of the reluctance of some states to act on unavoidably ambiguous evidence of cheating, where standards of evidence are set unrealistically high, out of concern that raising such issues would itself complicate the prospects for further progress in the arms control process. These two problems are, according to the critics of arms control, compounded by the asymmetries between an open and basically law-abiding Western culture and those closed, controlled, and distrusting governments bent on exploiting advantages to be gained by cheating on assumed international obligations. Critics also alleged that arms control often became an end in itself, out of sync with larger national security objectives.

Nevertheless, arms control evolved into an important instrument of national security and a forum for international conflict management. Early bilateral U.S.-Soviet efforts were soon complemented by a series of multilateral arms control efforts, many under the auspices of the United Nations, others as ad hoc arrangements among various nations. Beginning with the 1968 multilateral Nuclear Nonproliferation Treaty, several international arms control agreements emerged in the 1970s, 1980s, and early 1990s. These arms control efforts involved, for example, arrangements for nuclear-weapons-free zones, constraints on specific weapon systems, agreements on measures designed to promote transparency and confidence-building among states, and nuclear testing constraints. Another series of multilateral arms control agreements have been directed at limiting and reducing the proliferation of conventional weapons and ballistic missile technology. See table 1 for a representative list of international arms control treaties and regimes.

The Process of Arms Control Negotiations

When negotiating an arms control agreement, delegations from the prospective parties often meet on neutral ground. Geneva, Switzerland, has been a favored location. Once draft treaty text has been agreed to, a summit meeting is held between the heads of state of the various parties (so called because this is the highest possible level of meeting between representatives of states) and copies of the actual text in all relevant languages are signed. It also is common for modern arms control agreements to incorporate annual reviews of compliance as one of their obligations. Most review conferences take place in Geneva, but Vienna, Austria, has also become home to several key arms control implementation bodies, such as the International Atomic Energy

Table 1: Examples of arms control regimes

Nuclear weapons–free zones (NWFZ)	Weapons systems constraints	Confidence-building measures	Nuclear-testing constraints	Suppliers club and export controls
• Outer Space Treaty • Seabed Treaty • Africa NWFZ • Treaty of Tlatelolco (Latin America and Caribbean NWFZ) • South Pacific NWFZ	• Anti-Ballistic Missile (ABM) Treaty • Intermediate-Range Nuclear Forces (INF) Treaty • START I Treaty • START II Treaty • Biological and Chemical Weapons Conventions • Strategic Offensive Reductions Treaty (SORT)	• Hot line agreements • Accidents Measures Agreement • Confidence-and security-building measures (CSBMs) • Open Skies Treaty • ICBM and SLBM launch notifications • Detargeting Agreement	• Limited Test Ban Treaty (LTBT) • Threshold Test Ban Treaty (TTBT) • Peaceful Nuclear Explosions Agreement • Comprehensive Test Ban Treaty (CTBT)	• Non-Proliferation Treaty (NPT) and Zangger Committee • Australia Group • Missile Technology Control Regime (MTCR) • Fissile Material Cut-Off Treaty (FMCT)

Agency, which has responsibility for overseeing compliance with the Nuclear Nonproliferation Treaty.

Arms Control after the Cold War

Arms control, like many other aspects of national security, has been subject to considerable rethinking in the aftermath of the collapse of the Soviet empire. For some, the end of the bilateral U.S.-Soviet competition has meant that arms control has lost its primary relevance, that the new era of American preeminence requires that the United States free itself from as many arms control constraints as possible, and that legally binding treaties incorporating complex verification measures have outlived their usefulness. For others, the end of the Cold War meant a realignment of the arms control agenda but not diminishment of arms control as an instrument of national strategy.

Most agree that the new focus of arms control must be on combating the proliferation of weapons of mass destruction through a new focus on multilateral mechanisms. Other multilateral nonproliferation efforts

also enlarge the definition of arms control because they are not based on legally binding or formal treaties but instead involve nonbinding supplier groups, or groups of nations that have formed voluntary associations to restrict international trade in weapon systems deemed destabilizing. Such is the case, for example, with the Missile Technology Control Regime, which includes more than 30 countries agreeing to restrict the international transfer of missiles and missile technology.

Since the first decade of the 2000s, Russia has consistently objected to the constraints it faces due to arms control regimes, and it has unilaterally withdrawn from several Cold War–era treaties. Among those no longer in force is the CFE Treaty, and the INF Treaty is facing severe challenges, as the United States has accused Russia of testing a new cruise missile whose range violates treaty limits. In response, in the 2018 Nuclear Posture Review, the United States threatened to consider the development of new theater range missiles as well. Selective Russian observance of the Open

Skies Treaty is an ongoing concern, as are the prospects for extension of the New START Treaty when it expires in 2021.

Kerry Kartchner and Jeffrey A. Larsen

Further Reading

Adler, Emanuel, ed., *The International Practice of Arms Control* (Baltimore: Johns Hopkins University Press, 1992).

Bull, Hedley, *The Control of the Arms Race*, 2nd ed. (New York: Praeger, 1965).

Burns, Richard Dean, ed., *Encyclopedia of Arms Control and Disarmament*, 3 vols. (New York: Scribner's Sons, 1993).

Goldblat, Jozef, *Arms Control: A Guide to Negotiations and Agreements* (London: Sage, 1994).

Larsen, Jeffrey A., and James J. Wirtz, *Arms Control and Cooperative Security* (Boulder, CO: Lynne Rienner, 2009).

Aum Shinrikyo

The Japanese apocalyptic group Aum Shinrikyo (Supreme Truth) has been credited with opening the Pandora's box of WMD terrorism with its sarin nerve agent attack on the Tokyo subway system on March 20, 1995. Although it was not the first ever chemical or biological terror attack, it was of such a scale that it is generally regarded as the benchmark for the beginning of modern WMD terrorism.

The subway attack in March 1995 killed 12 people and injured hundreds more, but it was not the first Aum Shinrikyo chemical terror attack. It was preceded by attempts to develop and employ biological weapons, all of which were complete failures. Thus, Aum Shinrikyo stands as a valuable case study regarding the dangers of WMD terrorism and the difficulty in employing WMD, even for a well-financed group with technical expertise.

Aum Shinrikyo represented a "new religion," a fanatical apocalyptic cult willing to use mass casualty terrorism to accelerate and achieve what it saw as its preordained destiny. The group was founded by a charismatic blind charlatan named Shoko Asahara. He promulgated the belief that Armageddon was inevitable and that only the devout believers in Aum Shinrikyo would survive the end of the world.

As a new religion, Aum Shinrikyo was successful in drawing recruits and donations. The group specifically targeted its recruitment at technical universities and enjoyed a relatively well-educated and wealthy membership. From such recruiting and fund-raising, the group was able to employ its wealth and some of its technically expert members to support its WMD program.

As a cult, Aum Shinrikyo was a particularly violent one, committing assault and murder against its real or perceived rivals and opponents. However, although Japanese legal authorities compiled a growing body of evidence on Aum Shinrikyo's terrorist objectives and chemical and biological programs preceding the Tokyo subway attacks, they hesitated to take action because of provisions in Japanese law protecting religious freedom. Largely unmolested by the police, the cult enjoyed the benefits as a self-described religious organization to further its political agenda, which also included acts of terrorism. Aum Shinrikyo developed hierarchical operational organs, a highly sophisticated infrastructure, and extensive support mechanisms. At the same time, Aum Shinrikyo developed business enterprises and internally selected technical experts to support its action program. These included conventional, chemical, and biological weapons labs derived from legitimate cover enterprises.

Aum Shinrikyo tried to develop and employ biological and chemical weapons as early as 1990. Testimony during the legal proceedings following the 1995 Tokyo subway attacks indicated that the targets of the mostly unsuccessful attempts included the general Japanese public, specific rival groups, disaffected cult members, investigative journalists, the Japanese legal system and government, members of the Japanese royal family, and U.S. military installations based in Japan.

Aum Shinrikyo had extensive biological and chemical agent development programs, but its actual employment of WMD had mixed results. In April 1990, the group attempted to employ botulinum toxin for mass casualty effects in Tokyo. (To not fall victim to the attack, the operation coincided with an island retreat for the Aum Shinrikyo leadership and membership.) The group's operatives attempted to disperse the toxin from truck-mounted dispensers: one outside the Diet (national parliament) building downtown, one outside the U.S. naval facilities in the southern port suburbs, and one at Narita International Airport. For various reasons (including having selected the wrong *Clostridium botulinum* strain), these attacks were complete failures.

The group again attempted to disperse botulinum toxin in June 1993, again from a truck-mounted spray dispenser. The target in this attack was the gathering of world dignitaries in conjunction with the wedding of Crown Prince Naruhito, but no casualties resulted from this failed attempt.

Aum Shinrikyo then turned to anthrax as its agent of choice. Just weeks after the 1993 royal wedding attempt, the group dispensed anthrax bacteria from the roof of a cult-owned building in downtown Tokyo. Although a few people reported being affected by noxious fumes, this attack also failed to cause casualties. The anthrax strain Aum Shinrikyo used was an American animal vaccine (Sterne) strain, not a toxic strain.

Aum Shinrikyo's unsuccessful experience with biological weapons caused them to switch to chemical weapons. Beginning in 1993, reports suggested they had successfully experimented with sarin employed against sheep on a cult-owned ranch in Australia. (Later investigations, however, showed that tests on the sheep carcasses may have confused sarin with commercial organophosphate pesticides used in "sheep dip.") In early 1994, Aum Shinrikyo leadership chose the leader of a rival "new religion" and its associated political party for a chemical attack, but their effort to create a gaseous form of sarin resulted in the dispersal van catching fire.

The group's second sarin attack, in June 1994, was not fully successful. The intent was to kill three judges who were presiding at a trial involving Aum Shinrikyo. The plan was to gas the judges, their courthouse, and an adjacent police station. Poor planning caused the attack team to arrive after the judges had left the courthouse. Then, improvising, they released sarin gas in a residential area where the judges lived, but it was dispersed in an uncontrolled fashion, forming large clouds of poisonous vapor over a large area, and then the wind shifted. While some of the magistrates fell ill with poisoning, seven other people unrelated to the case were killed. (It was only after a long and tragically misguided investigation that the authorities were finally able to trace the attack back to Aum Shinrikyo.)

Finally, as the cult was put under intense pressure by Japanese law enforcement, the March 1995 Tokyo subway attacks had the dual purposes of producing mass casualties and intimidating the authorities for Aum's own self-preservation. Having amassed sufficient evidence to raid Aum Shinrikyo, the Japanese National Police Agency planned to raid the cult compound on March 22.

Tipped off to the impending raid, Aum Shinrikyo's first agent attack was focused on the Kasumigaseki subway station using botulinum toxin on March 15. The cult specifically chose Kasumigaseki station because it was near the Ministry of Justice offices. The timing (morning commute) of the attack would have meant that many of the passengers on those trains would have likely been Ministry of Justice employees. In this case, Aum attempted to dispense botulinum toxin hidden in briefcases, but this attack also failed.

Aum Shinrikyo then reverted to sarin, again attacking the subway system on March 20. This subway attack employed an unsophisticated dispersal method—plastic bags of liquid sarin punctured by the pointed ends of umbrellas. The operation involved rush-hour attacks on five separate subway trains in the Tokyo system, trains that were all due to arrive at Kasumigaseki station shortly before eight o'clock on a weekday morning. A dozen people died, and hundreds fell ill. It is likely that the preparation of sarin used in this makeshift attack was impure, which helps to explain why relatively few people were killed.

Finally, as the investigations and arrests following the March 1995 subway attacks began, Aum Shinrikyo members returned to target the Tokyo subway system one more time. On May 5, 1995, the group attempted to employ cyanide in Shinjuku station. In this case, they rigged a crude binary acid-cyanide device, but it was discovered before it could do any harm.

In sum, Aum Shinrikyo had only limited success in some 14 separate biological and chemical attacks. The group employed or attempted to employ sarin and cyanide as well as VX and phosgene gas. In terms of biological weapons, Aum Shinrikyo at various times was developing or seeking to develop anthrax bacterial spores, botulinum, Q-fever, and even Ebola virus for use as weapons. Aum Shinrikyo had up to 20 people dedicated to biological weapon production and testing.

After the Tokyo subway attack, Japanese police found enough sarin precursors (e.g., phosphorus trichloride) in the group's possession to produce tons of sarin nerve agent. At that time, work at the Aum Shinrikyo labs also suggested that the group was continuing to develop or experiment with a variety of nerve agents—including VX, soman, and tabun—and other chemical weapons, such as mustard and hydrogen cyanide. At its peak, as many as 80 Aum Shinrikyo members worked on chemical weapons development.

Aum Shinrikyo was also involved with and had specific interest in both nuclear and conventional weapons. The group widely sought nuclear weapons materials and expertise—from Australian uranium to Russian lasers (an experimental technology for producing fissile materials). They also showed interest in other exotic weapons that had relevance to Japan, including seismological weapons. They also procured and produced conventional weapons, notably AK-74 rifles. The variety of weapons and systems that Aum Shinrikyo procured, as well as insight into their future plans, was demonstrated by their efforts to employ a Russian military helicopter and some unmanned drone aircraft, all to be outfitted with aerial spray dispersal systems for chemical weapons.

Following the Tokyo subway attacks, the main Aum Shinrikyo leadership, operational cadre, and weapons personnel were arrested, tried, and imprisoned. Having lost their final appeal of their death sentences in July 2018 Shoko Asahara, along with six other original Aum cult members, were executed by hanging.

James M. Smith

Further Reading

Brackett, D. W., *Holy Terror: Armageddon in Tokyo* (New York: Weatherhill, 1996).

Croddy, Eric, "Urban Terrorism and Chemical Warfare in Japan," *Jane's Intelligence Review* 7, no. 11, (November 1995): 520–523.

Kaplan, David E., and Andrew Marshall, *The Cult at the End of the World: The Incredible Story of Aum Shinrikyo* (London: Hutchison, 1996).

Lifton, Robert Jay, *Destroying the World to Save It: Aum Shinrikyo, Apocalyptic Violence, and the New Global Terrorism* (New York: Metropolitan, 1999).

Rosenau, William, "Aum Shinrikyo's Biological Weapons Program: Why Did It Fail?," *Studies in Conflict & Terrorism* 24, no. 4 (July 2001): 289–301.

Australia Group

The Australia Group (AG) is an informal network of 42 countries and the European Commission that aims to ensure that their exports do not contribute to the development of chemical or biological weapons (CBW). The Australia Group does this by licensing the exports of certain chemicals, biological agents, and dual-use chemical and biological manufacturing equipment that can be used in CBW programs, based on common control lists.

History

In April 1984, a special investigation mission sent by the UN secretary-general to Iran found that chemical weapons (CW) had been used against Iran in the Iran-Iraq War: a clear and unequivocal violation of the 1925 Geneva Protocol. There was also evidence that Iraq had obtained materials for its CW program from the international chemical industry. In response to these findings, a number of countries placed licensing measures on the export of chemicals used in the manufacture of chemical weapons.

The countries concerned saw an urgent need to address the problem posed by the spread of CW and to ensure that their industries were not, either deliberately or inadvertently, helping other countries to acquire and use such weapons in violation of international law and norms.

The measures originally imposed by these countries, however, were not uniform either in scope or application. It also became apparent that attempts were being made to use this lack of uniformity to circumvent these initial controls. This led Australia to propose, in April 1985, that representatives from the 15 countries that had introduced licensing for exports should meet to examine ways to standardize the measures taken at the national level to prevent illicit trafficking in chemical weapons precursors.

The first meeting of what came to be known as the Australia Group (AG) took place in Brussels, Belgium, in June 1985. Participating countries agreed that there was benefit in continuing the process, and meetings of the group are now held in Paris on an annual basis.

Technical Details

AG participants have developed, through a consensus approach, common export control lists that specify items that each AG participant undertakes to control through its respective national export licensing procedures. Licensing procedures allow each participating country to consider whether a particular export could contribute to CBW and therefore breach the country's obligations under the Biological and Toxin Weapons Convention (BTWC) or the Chemical Weapons Convention (CWC). Every export license application is examined by the national authority on a case-by-case basis, with the decision about whether to supply the requested items resting solely with the country approached. An export request is denied only when there is particular concern about potential diversion for CBW purposes.

Current Status
Participating countries in the Australia Group include Argentina, Australia, Austria, Belgium, Bulgaria, Canada, Croatia, Cyprus, Czech Republic, Denmark, Estonia, Finland, France, Germany, Greece, Hungary, Iceland, Ireland, Japan, Republic of Korea, Lithuania, Luxembourg, Malta, Mexico, the Netherlands, New Zealand, Norway, Poland, Portugal, Romania, Slovakia, Slovenia, Spain, Sweden, Switzerland, Turkey, Ukraine, the United Kingdom, and the United States. The European Union is also a participant. Australia chairs the group and provides a secretariat within its Department of Foreign Affairs and Trade.

Although a small number of countries criticize the Australia Group for what they claim are restrictions on legitimate trade and technology transfers, there appears to be an increasing acceptance by most countries of the idea that adopting national export licensing measures based on the Australia Group's common control lists raises the barriers to both chemical and biological weapons proliferation and chemical or biological terrorism. Many countries also believe that the group provides a tool for implementing nonproliferation obligations under the CWC and BTWC. A number of participants and other countries have also used the various common control lists as a basis for domestic monitoring of listed items as a means to increase the barriers to terrorism. The importance of the Australia Group and the use of lists of chemical and biological materials of concern are likely to increase in the years ahead.

Robert Mathews

Further Reading
Australia Group. http://www.australiagroup .net. Accessed February 1, 2018.

B

Baruch Plan

On June 14, 1946, Bernard M. Baruch, the U.S. representative to the recently created United Nations Atomic Energy Commission, presented a U.S. proposal for controlling nuclear weapons. This was the first nuclear arms control proposal in history and drew on the work of a team led by Dean Acheson, the undersecretary of state, and David Lilienthal, who was soon to become the first chairman of the U.S. Atomic Energy Commission. The major technical contributions to the plan were made by J. Robert Oppenheimer, the physicist who had been the science leader of the World War II project to develop the atomic bomb.

The Baruch Plan was significant in several important respects. It represented a difficult decision by the United States to give up its sole possession of the atomic bomb if an acceptable political regime to control the new weapon could be established. It sought to pursue arms control through the multilateral channels of the newly created United Nations instead of bilaterally negotiating details with the Soviet Union. It recognized the uniquely threatening character of nuclear weapons by proposing to set aside the Security Council veto for nuclear matters. And when the plan was debated, the question of the legitimacy of anticipatory defense was raised at the United Nations for the first time.

Recognizing that the key to nuclear weapons production was obtaining fissile materials, the plan called for the creation of an International Atomic Energy Development Authority, which would control all phases of the development and use of atomic energy, starting with the raw material. When an adequate system for control of atomic energy, including the renunciation of the bomb as a weapon, had been agreed to and put into operation, and when sanctions had been set up for violations of the rules of control (violations that would be stigmatized as international crimes), then national manufacture of atomic bombs would stop, existing bombs would be disposed of pursuant to terms of the treaty, and the authority would possess full information on how to produce atomic energy.

The Soviet Union objected to the phased approach, insisting that stockpiles first be destroyed and possession or use of nuclear weapons be characterized as an international crime prior to establishing a technical control regime. Talks quickly stalemated as the Cold War set in. Although some critics have argued that with a different approach to the negotiations the United States might have secured a compromise, most scholars of the Baruch Plan today recognize that Soviet leader Joseph Stalin was set on acquiring nuclear weapons, negotiations notwithstanding.

Michael Wheeler

Further Reading

Acheson, Dean, *Present at the Creation* (W. W. Norton, 1969).

U.S. Department of State, *The International Control of Atomic Energy: Growth of a Policy* (Washington, D.C.: U.S. Government Printing Office, March 31, 1947).

Bikini Island

Bikini Island is an atoll in the Marshall Islands in the western Pacific Ocean that was used for early atomic testing by the United States. Located north of the equator and 225 miles northwest of Kwajalein, the atoll comprises 2 square miles of dry land forming a ring around a 15- by 25-mile lagoon. It was occupied by Japan until 1944 and administered by the United States from 1947 to 1979 as part of the Trust Territory of the Pacific Islands. In 1979, it became a part of the Republic of the Marshall Islands.

In 1946, Bikini became the site of Operation CROSSROADS, a joint military and scientific project to determine the impact of nuclear bombs on naval vessels. The 166 native Micronesians living on the atoll had to be relocated to Kili Island, about 500 miles southeast. Less than a year after the Hiroshima and Nagasaki bombings, Bikini experienced the first of what became more than 20 atomic tests at seven locations on or near the island over the next 12 years as the initial U.S. atomic testing site. On July 1, 1946, with some 78 surplus naval vessels as targets, the Able test witnessed a 20-kiloton atomic bomb dropped from a B-29 Superfortress. Only five ships were sunk as a result, so on July 25, 1946, the Baker test became the world's first underwater atomic explosion, raising a column of radioactive water and a shock wave that sank an additional nine ships.

From 1946 through 1958, Bikini and Enewetak Atoll, which is located about 150 miles southwest of Bikini, became the Pacific Proving Grounds for the U.S. Atomic Energy Commission. Tests included thermonuclear devices, and on March 1, 1954, the first hydrogen bomb was tested near Bikini. Castle Bravo was the largest nuclear test ever conducted by the United States, with a yield of 15 megatons. This and subsequent tests resulted in severe radioactive contamination of the atoll.

In the 1960s, some of the original islanders tried to return to Bikini, but the radiation levels proved unsafe. In 1969, the United States began work on a long-term project to reclaim the islands. The islanders filed a suit against the government in 1985, and as a result of this action, the U.S. government funded a cleanup that started in 1991. The first radiation cleanup project was completed in 1998. Although radiation levels were too high for residence, the Bikini Lagoon was reopened for scuba diving in 1996, and sport fishing was again permitted in 1998.

Frannie Edwards and Jeffrey A. Larsen

Further Reading

McGee, William L., *Operation Crossroads— Lest We Forget!: An Eyewitness Account, Bikini Atomic Bomb Tests 1946* (Tiburon, CA: BMC Publications, 2016).

Shurcliff, W. A., *Bombs at Bikini: The Official Report of Operation Crossroads* (New York: William H. Wise & Co, 1947).

Binary Chemical Munitions

Binary chemical munitions consist of two separate components that, by themselves, are relatively nontoxic, but when mixed together, they produce a toxic chemical warfare (CW) agent. With advantages that include safer production and handling, binary chemical weapons are more advanced than unitary chemical munitions that simply contain the CW agent in the warhead fill. Some binary chemical weapon designs can also be used in terrorist attacks, with relatively simple designs using common chemical ingredients (e.g., cyanide).

During the late 1980s, the United States produced a number of binary weapons, including artillery projectiles and the Bigeye VX nerve agent glide bomb, a ground attack weapon that sprayed agent as it flew over a defined area.

The idea of binary chemical munitions is not new. Some concepts for binary chemical weapons were devised during World War II. In one design of an aerial bomb, for example, military chemists separated two components, magnesium arsenide and sulfuric acid, into divided chambers. When the bomb struck the ground, the partition would shatter, and the chemical components would mix to produce toxic arsine (AsH_3) gas (blood agent). It does not appear, however, that this chemical ordnance ever found service in any conflict.

Another idea considered during the 1940s included the formation of a vesicant (blister agent). Here, a nontoxic molecule would react with another to form the toxic chemical product, the nitrogen-based blister agent methyl N-(2-chloroethyl)-N-nitrosocarbamate (code-named "KB-16"). As far as it is known, this design was never fully developed into a chemical weapon.

Maritime traditions are replete with exacting standards of safety. It should not be surprising that the hazards involved in transport and handling of chemical weapons were of special concern to the U.S. Navy. During the mid-1960s, the U.S. Navy had patented a design for a binary chemical weapon utilizing two chemicals—one liquid and one solid—that would react to form a toxic CW agent. This was the basic prototype for the VX Bigeye bomb.

By 1972, the U.S. military had been able to build a prototype of a binary chemical weapon for use in land-based artillery. This would later become M-687, the 155-millimeter howitzer projectile. The M-687 projectile produced sarin by mixing difluoromethylphosphonate (difluor) and isopropyl alcohol. After the weapon was fired, the membrane separating the component chemicals was shattered by the initial shock from its launch. Now spinning at thousands of revolutions per minute, the weapon's rotation in flight facilitated the mixing of the binary components to form sarin. When the projectile neared its target, a special fuse mechanism ensured efficient dissemination of the agent through the back of the projectile.

The VX Bigeye glide bomb, developed under the auspices of the U.S. Navy, was intended to spray VX from an aerial munition that would glide over the target. Two relatively nontoxic compounds, sulfur and a chemical code-named "QL," would combine to form VX within the bomb itself. Although a working prototype was built, the project was plagued with technical problems, not the least of which was a tendency for the munition to burst prematurely. The BLU-80/Bigeye was designed to deliver some 180 pounds of VX nerve agent.

Other Designs

Because of its ability to fire a large and redundant number of volleys, the multiple-launch rocket system (MLRS) has long been considered one of the more effective delivery platforms to increase the concentration of chemical warfare agent on a given target. During the Cold War, for example, the U.S. military had outfitted sarin and VX unitary warheads for the M55 rocket.

It is likely that Soviet chemical weapons designers developed designs for sarin binary and perhaps VX nerve agent munitions. Following the breakup of the Soviet Union in the early 1990s, an intriguing story that came to light was the research into novel CW agents conducted by Soviet chemical weapons scientists. These included *novichok* (Russian for *newcomer*) chemical compounds, some being up to 10 times more toxic than VX nerve agent. According to Russian dissident scientists, *novichok* agents were to be used in binary weapons. The usual means of treating nerve agent casualties would not be effective against this highly toxic chemical. Details on this and other novel CW agents reportedly developed in the former Soviet Union are still classified.

Terrorists may also utilize the basic concept of binary chemical systems for sabotage or even large-scale attacks. In 1995, immediately following the sarin nerve agent attack on the Tokyo subway by the Japanese cult Aum Shinrikyo, cyanide binary devices were discovered in subway restrooms. Consisting of two containers, one holding solid cyanide salt and the other a dilute acid solution, a crude timer was to combine the components to form hydrocyanic acid (HCN) gas. Fortunately, these chemical devices were deactivated before they could do any harm. Another design found in the open literature proposes to mix two relatively nontoxic compounds to form phosgene gas, a toxic lung irritant. It is uncertain whether such a system could create sufficient concentrations of phosgene gas to cause death or injury.

Eric A. Croddy

Further Reading

Stockholm International Peace Research Institute (SIPRI), *The Problem of Chemical and Biological Warfare*, vol. 2, *CB Weapons Today* (Stockholm: Almqvist & Wiksell, 1973).

Wise, David, *Cassidy's Run: The Secret Spy War over Nerve Gas* (New York: Random House, 2000).

Biological and Toxin Weapons Convention

The 1972 Biological and Toxin Weapons Convention (BTWC—often referred to as the Biological Weapons Convention (BWC)) prohibits the development, production, and stockpiling of biological weapons. There are currently 175 countries that are signatories to the BTWC (as of 2016). Although not explicitly stated in its preamble, by inference, the BTWC prohibits the use of microbial or other biological agents or toxins as a means of warfare. Unlike the Chemical Weapons Convention (signed in 1993), however, the BTWC has no verification protocol—that is, the BTWC has no set rules or guidelines to verify compliance by its members. Although its current status as a toothless disarmament treaty does not make its obligations any less binding on its parties, the BTWC is little more than a gentleman's agreement.

Background

The first effort to prohibit the use of biological weapons—albeit with important loopholes and exceptions—can be found in the 1925 Geneva Protocol. Its full title was Geneva Protocol for the Prohibition of the Use in War of Asphyxiating, Poisonous, or Other Gases, and of Bacteriological Methods of Warfare. The inclusion of the term *bacteriological methods of warfare* was made nearly at the last minute by the suggestion of the Polish delegate. Problematically, the Geneva Protocol of 1925 only prohibited the first use of such weapons against other parties to the treaty—and not the development, production, or stockpiling of such weapons.

Prior to the 1925 Protocol, there had been reported acts of sabotage during World War I that used bacteria. The German American agent Anton Dilger conducted a number of attacks on Allied horses and pack mules in 1915–1916, using the causative agents of glanders (*Burkholderia mallei*) and anthrax (*Bacillus anthracis*). Working from a makeshift laboratory in Washington, D.C., Dilger hired other agents—including longshoremen—to infect animals in their stockades along ports in the eastern United States. However, these acts of biological warfare (BW) were barely noticed by Allied authorities.

During the 1930s, biological weapons were still very much an unknown quantity. In December 1932, a report from the Special Committee on Chemical, Incendiary, and Bacterial Weapons for the Conference for the Limitation and Reduction of Armaments downplayed the likelihood of bacteriological warfare as not being very practical.

As military aviation made rapid advances during the early 20th century, public and official concern about the threat posed by incendiary bombs or toxic biological and chemical mists increased. Elvira K. Fradkin, in a 1934 treatise titled *The Air Menace and the Answer*, described how biological agents could rain death from the skies and that "an airplane could carry enough of the botulinus toxin to destroy every living thing in the world if administration of the toxin were as simple a process as production and transportation" (Fradkin 1934).

In 1938, the British scientist John Burdon Sanderson (J. B. S.) Haldane—later identified as an agent working for Soviet military intelligence (GRU) in the 1940s—warned that yellow fever could be utilized as a biological weapon. A year later, Imperial Japanese agents visited the Rockefeller Institute in the United States in an attempt to acquire cultures of yellow fever virus. As yellow fever was not a disease endemic to the Far East, these surreptitious inquiries aroused suspicions by Western intelligence. These reports of Japanese efforts to obtain and develop potential BW agents—as well as intelligence (often spurious) indicating that Nazi Germany had an interest in biological weapons—provided impetus for the Allies to undertake their own BW programs.

During World War II, the United States, Canada, and the United Kingdom initiated substantial programs for BW defense and offense, including the production of virulent organisms, such as anthrax spores. Although committed to not using such weapons unless for retaliation in kind, Presidents Roosevelt and Truman continued offensive research and development of biological weapons. North Korea and the People's Republic of China alleged that the United States used biological weapons during the Korean War (1951–1953). However, these allegations were entirely fabricated by China.

Throughout the Cold War and until renouncing biological weapons in 1969, the United States tested and weaponized several offensive BW agents, including *Brucella*, anthrax, tularemia, staphylococcal enterotoxin B, and anticrop agents. Although U.S. military commanders were somewhat skeptical, American BW scientists were confident by the 1960s that their validated biological delivery systems could be effective in shutting down enemy ports or even bringing an entire country to its knees with debilitating viruses, bacteria, or toxins.

Until the late 1960s, for much of the U.S. public, the idea of using chemical and biological agents was not particularly controversial, or at least so it appeared. The use of chemical herbicides (including Agent Orange) and CS tear gas during the Vietnam War, however, led to protests against the perception that chemical warfare (CW) agents were being employed by the United States in that conflict. In March 1968, some 6,000 sheep were killed near Dugway Proving Ground, Utah. Their owner claimed that the U.S. Army was responsible when aircraft dropped VX nerve agent during training runs near Skull Valley, Utah. Although the U.S. Army paid the farmer $1 million in restitution, it did not admit to being culpable.

Still, the impact of this incident—and ongoing operations by the United States in destroying obsolete chemical weapons by dumping them into the ocean—led to public questions concerning U.S. offensive CBW policies. In response, the Nixon administration reviewed the U.S. position with regard to both CW and BW in May 1969. Two months later, a chemical spill on a U.S. military base in Okinawa, Japan, exposed 24 people (including one civilian) to sarin nerve agent. Protests erupted in Japan as a result, and further revelations that U.S. chemical weapons were stored in West Germany added more fuel to the controversy.

Makings of a Convention

As the public outcry in the United States against chemical and biological weapons grew, the United Kingdom brought forth a proposal, on July 10, 1969, to the United Nations' Eighteen-Nation Disarmament Committee that would ban the production, development, and stockpiling of biological weapons. Significantly, in 1969, President Richard M. Nixon made the decision to renounce biological warfare, specifically the use of disease-causing organisms.

Nixon based this decision on practical grounds but also realpolitik: as a technology, biological weapons were not easy to develop and employ. But just as important, enemies of the United States could also threaten large populated cities in the United States. Finally, by supporting biological weapons disarmament, Nixon also hoped that this decision would improve the public image of his administration. After some further internal debate, by 1970, biological toxins (not just disease-causing pathogens) were included in the unilateral renunciation of BW by the United States.

In the years 1970 and 1971, negotiations in Geneva over a biological and toxin weapons treaty had been making little progress for a number of reasons, most having to do with an insistence by the Soviet Union that chemical weapons also be included in the treaty. The Soviets finally relented on this point, however, and the final version of the BTWC was approved on September 28, 1971; opened for signature in April 1972; and entered into force in March 1975.

Five years following the treaty's entry into force, the first Review Conference of the BTWC was held in March 1980. Intense discussions at this conference were spurred in part by the advances already made in genetic engineering as well as by the increased military interest around the world in the biological sciences. Two controversies were brought forward during this time: the Sverdlovsk anthrax outbreak in 1979 and U.S. allegations of yellow rain (T-2 mycotoxin) being used by Soviet client states in the Middle East and Southeast Asia. Reports concerning the Sverdlovsk outbreak appeared at the same time as the first Review Conference took place. Not surprisingly, the (now confirmed) release of a biological warfare agent (anthrax) raised great concerns not only about Soviet BW programs but also about the implications of future verification, inspections, and BTWC compliance.

During the second Review Conference in 1986, four important confidence-building measures (CBMs) were established to increase the level of trust among signatories and improve transparency: (1) annual provision by signatories of data on high-containment facilities designed for work on dangerous biological materials; (2) annual notification to signatories of outbreaks of unusual diseases; (3) encouragement of publication of results of biological research related to the BW convention; and (4) promotion of contact between scientists engaged in research, including exchanges of staff for joint research.

The overall response to the CBMs was tepid, with fewer than 40 countries reporting regularly on an annual basis since the 1986 review. Most developing nations either did not send declarations or their declarations were incomplete. Although China and the Soviet Union did supply information detailing their BW-related programs, by 1991, only 40 signatories out of 117 had established their own domestic legislation for implementing proper declarations, and only 70 (out of 135) had done so by 1996.

Current Status

In late 2001, BTWC protocol negotiations came to an impasse. Since that time, little progress has been made, and, conservatively, a verification protocol for the BTWC is not likely to be agreed upon by 2020.

Although it seems naïve to suggest that criminalizing biological weapons will dissuade individuals or governments determined to acquire them, many believe that making the possession or use of biological weapons a universal crime could further biological weapons disarmament. In the United States, for example, the Biological Weapons Anti-Terrorism Act of 1989 (BWATA)—which has been since updated and expanded—was originally implemented to establish legal penalties in the enforcement of the BTWC. Numerous convictions under the BWATA have taken place since, usually involving the production, possession, or dissemination of biological agents (e.g., ricin and abrin toxins).

Eric A. Croddy

Further Reading

Fradkin, Elvira K., *The Air Menace and the Answer* (New York: Macmillan, 1934).

Morales Pedraza, Jorge, "The Need to Establish the Organisation for the Prohibition of Biological Weapons: A Proposal for the Future," *Public Organization Review* 12, no. 1 (March 2012): 57–70.

Sims, Nicholas A., *The Evolution of Biological Disarmament* (New York: Oxford University Press, 2001).

Tucker, Jonathan B., "A Farewell to Germs: The U.S. Renunciation of Biological and Toxin Warfare, 1969–1970," *International Security* 27, no. 1 (summer 2002): 107–148.

Bioregulators

Bioregulators (or bioregulatory peptides) are genetically coded chains of amino acids that are naturally produced in the human body and are essential for normal physiological functioning. In that they are chemicals of biological origin, these substances resemble toxins in their nature and action, and in technical terms, they can in fact be defined as toxins. Although the role of bioregulators in controlling biological processes has only begun to be understood, their effects are known to range from the mediation of sensations such as fear and

Table 2: Select bioregulators and some of their effects

Type	Prototype bioregulator(s)	Primary effect(s)
Algogen	Substance P	Sensory transmission of pain
Endogenous opioid	Endorphins, enkephalins	Analgesia similar to morphine
Hormone	Vasopressin	Water retention, vasoconstriction
Endothelium-derived factor	Endothelin	Vasoconstriction

pain to the regulation of the body's vital signs: blood pressure, heart rate, and respiration. When present at inappropriately elevated levels (e.g., as a result of intentional introduction into the body), a bioregulator can overwhelm the body's compensatory mechanisms, and its actions can go unchecked. Potential consequences include the sensation of pain, loss of consciousness, altered blood pressure, and psychological changes. Death is possible, but these effects—although profoundly incapacitating—are generally not lethal.

In theory, a bioregulator can be introduced into the body in one of two ways. First, it can be introduced by using well-established genetic engineering techniques; the gene that codes for the bioregulator can be inserted into a microorganism, which is then delivered into the body via injection, ingestion, or inhalation. Upon gaining entry to the body, the microorganism produces the bioregulator, and its effects are felt. Second, the bioregulator itself can be chemically or enzymatically synthesized in a laboratory. Once a quantity of the bioregulator has been produced, it can be delivered on its own, again via injection, ingestion, or inhalation, in the same manner as any other biological weapon (or pharmaceutical agent, for that matter).

Research in the Former Soviet Union

Soviet bioweaponeers engaged in extensive research on bioregulators throughout the 1980s under the code name "Project Bonfire." As reported during a conference of Soviet scientists in 1989, the project had been a success: the gene coding for the bioregulator myelin toxin had been identified. Through the application of advanced recombinant DNA techniques, the myelin toxin gene was then inserted into the bacterium *Yersinia pseudotuberculosis*. In laboratory tests, this single agent caused both the symptoms of the pathogen and the paralytic effects of myelin toxin. Notably, *Yersinia pestis*, the causative agent of plague, is closely related to *Y. pseudotuberculosis*, suggesting the possibility of transfer of similar genetic material into this lethal pathogen to create an enhanced and truly formidable biological weapon. It has been reported that Soviet scientists did in fact successfully perform such a transfer before the collapse of the Soviet Union, but that the agent was not developed any further. It is not known whether other bioregulators were researched within the former biological weapons program. It is known, however, that a number of other bioregulators were studied, ostensibly for peaceful purposes, in the Soviet Union throughout the later years of the Cold War and later during the Russian Federation.

Bioregulators of Importance

Though in fact comprising a very broad category of chemicals, for practical purposes, bioregulators can be narrowed in spectrum, based largely on their action and amenability to synthesis, to those with biological warfare (BW) implications. A selection of bioregulators often referred to in a BW context is represented in table 2.

Rich Pilch

Further Reading

Bokan, Slavko, John G. Breen, and Zvonko Orehovec, "An Evaluation of Bioregulators as Terrorism and Warfare Agents," *ASA Newsletter* 02–3, no. 90 (June 28, 2002): 16–19.

Leitenberg, Milton, James Leonard, and Richard Spertzel, "Biodefense Crossing the Line," *Politics and the Life Sciences* 22, no. 2 (2004): 1–2.

Tucker, Jonathan B., "The Body's Own Bioweapons: The Next Biothreat Could Come from Chemicals Derived from the Human Body That Can Incapacitate and Kill— And Which Skirt Existing Arms Controls," *Bulletin of the Atomic Scientists* 64, no. 1 (March/April 2008): 16–22.

Blood Agents

Poisonous compounds that include hydrogen cyanide, phosphine, and arsine gases have traditionally been referred to as blood agents. Although the term *blood agents* is both anachronistic and a misnomer, because of its widespread use in military parlance, the term is used here simply out of convention.

Cyanide

Cyanide and related compounds have been recognized for centuries as toxic substances. In 1782, the Swedish chemist Karl Wilhelm Scheele first described the chemical formula for hydrogen cyanide (or hydrocyanic acid). Although the exact cause is not known for certain, it is widely believed that his sudden death in the laboratory four years later was a result of his working with this compound. According to one account, in 1813, a pharmacist suggested to the Prussian general Bülow that cyanide could be used on bayonets. (A similar story is told concerning Napoleon III having gotten this idea during the Franco-Prussian War.) In World War I, France was equipped early on with cyanide-filled artillery munitions. Possibly out of concern that using chemicals by means of projectile weaponry was in violation of The Hague Convention (1899), French military forces did not use them right away. After the major gas (chlorine) attack by Germany at Ypres in April 1915, such reservations quickly seemed irrelevant. However, due to its high volatility, cyanide dissipates very quickly in the open air. As a consequence, efforts to utilize cyanide as a weapon were largely failures.

Cyanide was once widely found in pesticide formulations to kill rodents, especially in barns and other large structures, such as naval vessels. Before World War II, Germany employed the so-called cyclone method, using hydrogen cyanide adsorbed onto wood chips or another material. Held in canisters, the contents would be released when ready for use. In the interest of safety, this "Zyklon" rodenticide also employed a very noticeable warning odor. Eventually, Zyklon B—commercially produced in Nazi Germany—was employed to massacre millions of Jews during the Holocaust. Needless to say, this preparation had no telltale odor in it to warn its human victims.

Of all the recognized blood agents, hydrogen cyanide (HCN) is probably the most likely chemical agent for use in warfare or terrorism. Still, HCN suffers from many of the disadvantages of carbon monoxide and other highly volatile compounds. It is liquid at room temperature, but just barely. HCN volatilizes so quickly that it can leave behind a congealed spot due to rapid dissipation of heat.

The process of weaponizing HCN is also problematic. Left to its own devices, HCN will spontaneously polymerize—reacting with itself chemically in a violent explosion. Metals, including cobalt and nickel in oxalate salts, have been used in attempts to stabilize this compound. During World War II, some Japanese soldiers were equipped with glass jars filled with liquid HCN that had been chemically stabilized with copper or arsenic trichloride. Although some were thrown at British tanks during World War II, no Allied soldiers were reported to have been affected by these gas grenades.

Throughout the war, the United States, Germany, and the Soviet Union continued searching for effective methods of HCN delivery. Though most of these attempts ended in failure, some aerial dissemination techniques were developed that could have had potentially devastating impact on the battlefield. German military intelligence reported that ongoing Soviet trials, using HCN delivered at low altitude and from slow-moving aircraft, were apparently successful in creating lethal concentrations over large areas.

Terrorists could devise means of delivering HCN, either in its original form (perhaps having been acquired through the chemical industry) or by producing it in vapors from a reaction between cyanide salts with acid. In 1995, Aum Shinrikyo cult operatives placed binary chemical devices in Tokyo subway restrooms. These contained one container full of cyanide salt and another of dilute sulfuric acid that were rigged to combine their contents by means of a timer. These binary cyanide devices were discovered before they could do any harm, but they clearly demonstrated how terrorists could deliver HCN by using simple equipment.

According to witness accounts and intelligence reports, it is quite likely that Al Qaeda terrorist operatives have experimented with cyanide compounds. Video footage seized in Afghanistan in 2002, for example, shows what appears to be Al Qaeda members using a compound that has similar properties to HCN in tests using dogs.

Humans can survive even multiple lethal doses of HCN poisoning—if medical intervention is timely. Antidotes prescribed for cyanide poisoning vary depending on the country. Generally speaking, the formation of methemoglobin from hemoglobin in the blood—the latter instrumental for carrying oxygen through the body—by sodium nitrite (or amyl nitrite) helps to scavenge cyanide, increasing the victim's chances of survival. Sodium thiosulfate is used to further remove cyanide from the body by means of other enzyme reactions (by combining free cyanide with sulfur to form relatively harmless thiocyanate). Modern protective masks also decrease the risk of cyanide exposure by means of a chemical barrier.

Cyanogen Chloride (CN)

Cyanogen chloride (and related compounds such as the bromide form) held some promise for U.S. military use in World War I, but these compounds were also quite unstable due to spontaneous polymerization (self-reacting). Cyanogen chloride (CNCl) is about half as toxic as HCN. The immediate effects of cyanogen chloride are quite noticeable, especially in the mucosa, with a very strong irritating effect on the eyes and upper respiratory tract. In World War I, the French military utilized a mixture of HCN and cyanogen chloride called *manguinite*.

The goal was to create such an irritant to enemy troops that they would remove their protective masks, allowing HCN to finish them off.

Other Systemic Poisons

Two other compounds, arsine and phosphine gas (in older literature referred to as arseniuretted hydrogen and hydrogen phosphide, respectively), were investigated during World War I as potential CW agents. Neither proved to be very effective as CW agents.

Eric A. Croddy

Further Reading

Baud, F. J., "Cyanide: Critical Issues in Diagnosis and Treatment," *Human & Experimental Toxicology* 26 (2007): 191–201.

Prentiss, Augustin M., *Chemicals in War: A Treatise on Chemical Warfare* (New York: McGraw-Hill, 1937).

Botulism (Botulinum Toxin)

Due to its extreme toxicity, botulinum toxin was among the first agents to be considered as a biological weapon. In a list compiled by the Centers for Disease Control and Prevention (CDC) that includes bacteria, viruses, and toxins thought to pose the greatest risk for use in a bioterrorist attack, *Clostridium botulinum* falls under Category A—the level of highest immediate risk. Clostridial neurotoxins are among the most toxic substances known to science. Their inclusion as a high-risk agent in bioterrorism is due not only to the very high toxicity of botulinum toxin, but also to its past development as a weapon and its relative ease of production. Clinically, botulinum toxin has been estimated to be lethal at very small doses for the average adult when ingested. When aerosolized, the lethal dose when inhaled is approximately five times larger than the lethal dose when ingested.

Background

In 1897, Émile van Ermengem, a Belgian student of the renowned microbiologist Robert Koch, isolated a bacterium (*Clostridium botulinum*) that had caused an outbreak of botulism in 23 people, of whom 3 eventually died. (The source was a ham that had not been adequately preserved with salt.) Since then, botulinum toxin has earned its reputation as one of the deadliest neurotoxins known. Occasional cases of botulism still occur as a cause of food poisoning, especially in societies that practice traditional forms of charcuterie.

Botulism is a disease that paralyzes muscles with a toxin produced by the bacterium *Clostridium botulinum*. The main categories of botulism in the context of infectious disease are those of food-borne illness (particularly among infants) and complications arising from wounds that become contaminated with *Clostridium botulinum* spores.

Food-borne botulism usually occurs when a person ingests the causative bacteria or the botulinum toxin, leading to illness within about 24 hours. Until the ultimate source is found, such individual cases are considered a potential public health emergency, as many other people could be affected as well. Infant botulism occurs in a small number of children, probably because their digestive tracts at their early stage of growth are more susceptible to ingestion of *C. botulinum*. (This is the concern that has prompted warnings against feeding honey to infants, as sometimes *C. botulinum* spores are found in honey.) Wound botulism takes place when wounds are infected with *C. botulinum*, which is naturally found in soils and other materials in the environment.

Symptoms of botulism are anticholinergic, including double vision, blurred vision, drooping eyelids, slurred speech, difficulty swallowing, dry mouth, and muscle weakness (flaccid paralysis) that starts at the shoulders, spreads to the upper arms, and descends through the body. In the instance of paralysis of the breathing muscles, an individual can stop breathing and die unless assistance with breathing (mechanical ventilation) is given. If administered early in the course of the disease, the antitoxin is effective in reducing the severity of symptoms. Most patients eventually recover after weeks to months of supportive care.

History

During World War II, intelligence information indicated that Germany was attempting to develop botulinum toxin as a weapon to be used against Allied invasion forces. At the time the Allied work to defend against this threat began, the composition of the toxic agent produced by *C. botulinum* was not clear, nor was the mechanism of lethality in animals and humans. Therefore, the earliest goals of research on botulinum toxin were to isolate and purify the toxin and to determine its pathogenesis. As it happened, there was apparently no effort on the part of German military scientists to utilize botulinum toxin against potential invasions. But due to this early intelligence—and the strict rules regarding the compartmentalization of this intelligence—the Allies produced some 300,000 doses of botulinum toxoid (vaccine) for D-Day troops in 1944. For reasons that are lost to history, apparently none of these doses were ever administered. In yet another historical question mark, the assassination (1942) of the notorious SS-*Obergruppenführer* Reinhard Heydrich by anti-Nazi Czech partisans is rumored to have involved the use of botulinum toxin.

Botulinum toxin was one of several agents tested at the Soviet site code-named "Aralsk-7" on Vozrozhdeniye Island in the Aral Sea. A former senior scientist of the Russian civilian bioweapons program reported that the Soviets had attempted splicing the botulinum toxin gene from *C. botulinum* into other bacteria. In the 1980s, Iraq chose to weaponize more botulinum toxin than any of its other known biological agents. However, Iraq in general found botulinum difficult to weaponize. Counterintuitively, the more Iraqi scientists exerted themselves in purifying botulinum, the less toxic it became, and ultimately it was not much of an improvement over VX nerve agent.

Seven distinct serotypes (classification within species of pathogens based on immune response) of botulinum toxin have now been isolated, designated A through H. It is interesting that not all serotypes have been associated with poisoning of humans.

Medical Response to Botulism

There are two basic alternatives for prophylaxis from botulinum poisoning: active immunization using a vaccine (toxoid) and passive immunotherapy using immunoglobulin, an antibody that helps to neutralize the toxin. The vaccine currently available is a toxoid that protects against serotypes A through E that was developed by scientists at Fort Detrick, in Frederick, Maryland, during the 1950s. The toxin produced from the culture is made nontoxic with the addition of formaldehyde for use as a toxoid, using strains of *C. botulinum* that produce the respective serotypes. As of 2012, the U.S. Strategic National Stockpile (SNS) had acquired over 100,000 doses of botulinum antitoxin in the event of a bioterrorist event involving cases of botulism.

Botulinum toxin ("Botox") is the first microbial toxin to become licensed for treatment of human disease. In 2010, only seven companies worldwide were licensed to produce pharmaceutical-grade botulinum. In the United States, it is currently licensed for treatment of cervical torticollis (muscular disorder of the neck), strabismus (crossed eyes), and blepharospasm (involuntary blinking) associated with dystonia (the general term for the neurological condition typified by involuntary muscular contraction). More recently, Botox has been used as a means to decrease facial wrinkles by paralyzing certain facial muscles.

Kalpana Chittaranjan

Further Reading

Arnon, Stephen, Robert Schechter, Thomas V. Inglesby, Donald A. Henderson, John G. Bartlett, Michael S. Ascher, Edward Eitzen, Anne D. Fine, Jerome Hauer, Marcelle Layton, Scott Lillibridge, Michael T. Osterholm, Tara O'Toole, Gerald Parker, Trish M. Perl, Philip K. Russell, David L. Swerdlow, and Kevin Tonat, "Botulinum Toxin as a Biological Weapon: Medical and Public Health Management," *Journal of the American Medical Association* 285, no. 8 (February 28, 2001): 1059–1070.

Hedinsdottir Hammer, Tóra, Sanne Jespersen, Jakob Kanstrup, Vibe Cecilie Ballegaard, Anne Kjerulf, and Allan Galvan, "Case Report: Fatal Outbreak of Botulism in Greenland," *Infectious Diseases* 47 (2015): 190–194.

Wein, Lawrence M., and Yifan Liu, "Analyzing a Bioterror Attack on the Food Supply: The Case of Botulinum Toxin in Milk," *Proceedings of the National Academy of Sciences of the United States of America* (PNAS) 102, no. 28 (July 12, 2005): 9984–9989.

Brinkmanship

Brinkmanship is a deliberate effort to create or exacerbate a crisis to coerce an adversary into complying with demands by increasing the likelihood of nuclear or conventional war. At the heart of the strategy is the assumption that an asymmetry of commitment or capability exists in the looming confrontation. Sometimes, the party engaged in brinkmanship believes that the opponent is relatively less committed to achieving its stated objectives in a crisis, which should make the opponent less willing to risk war to achieve these objectives. Other times, the party engaged in brinkmanship believes that once it appears that its superior military capabilities could be brought into play, the weaker opponent will back down from the brewing conflict. Regardless of the underlying assumptions motivating adoption of this strategy, brinkmanship involves manipulation of the risk of war as an instrument of coercion to achieve objectives.

As a policy, brinkmanship is most closely associated with statements made by Secretary of State John Foster Dulles and U.S. actions during the Offshore Islands Crises between the United States and China (1954–1955, 1958). Thomas Schelling, who eventually won a Nobel Prize for his work in game theory, further developed the logic behind "threats that leave something to chance"—how the manipulation of risk can be used to gain leverage over opponents in situations in which neither party prefers to go to war. Oddly enough, Schelling and others drew lessons from showdowns between teenage miscreant drivers—the game of chicken—to draw strategic lessons on how to threaten to use force to gain political leverage in a nuclear standoff.

Schelling also noted that strategic advantage can be gained in a crisis by denying yourself freedom to maneuver to avoid war. In other words, one can gain a superior position in a conflict by shifting the onus of escalation onto others or by taking steps to shift the burden of avoiding war onto others. These observations constitute refinements in the strategy of brinkmanship.

Although the term *brinkmanship* is generally used in a historical context today, *gray zone* and *hybrid* tactics have become increasingly prevalent; these also constitute a form of brinkmanship. In attempting to alter the status quo without prompting the eruption of war, state and nonstate actors engage in the fait accompli, proxy warfare, and the exploitation of ambiguous deterrence situations, which came to be known during the Cold War as "salami tactics."

A recent example of the fait accompli is the Russian annexation of Crimea in 2014, which shifted the onus of escalation onto the United States and its North Atlantic Treaty Organization (NATO) allies to reverse the Russian land grab. Chinese efforts at fortifying islands and recently constructed artificial reefs in the South China Sea constitutes the most vivid example of the practice of salami tactics in international relations. Not only do these initiatives constitute a gradual shift in the status quo, they have antagonized the United States, Japan, and a host of nations with strategic, territorial, and economic interests in the region. China's policy is a form of brinkmanship because it reflects assumptions of asymmetric interests and forces the onus of escalation onto others.

James J. Wirtz

Further Reading

Lebow, Richard Ned, *Between Peace and War: The Nature of International Crisis* (Baltimore: Johns Hopkins University Press, 1981).

Broken Arrow

Broken arrow and *bent spear* are U.S. Department of Defense terms used to report accidents involving nuclear weapons or components. Broken arrow denotes the most serious accidents, including the following: (1) accidental or unauthorized launching, firing, or use of a nuclear-capable weapons system by the United States or a U.S. ally; (2) accidental, unexplained, or unauthorized nuclear detonation; (3) nonnuclear detonation or burning of nuclear weapons or components; (4) radioactive release and contamination; (5) actual or perceived public hazard; or (6) jettisoning of a nuclear weapon or its components.

An example of a broken arrow incident occurred in Goldsboro, North Carolina, in 1961 when two MK39 nuclear bombs were jettisoned from a B-52. The plane had disintegrated due to structural failure. One bomb parachuted to the ground and was found intact. The other struck the soggy ground of a farm at terminal velocity. The mechanisms designed to prevent detonation worked.

A bent spear mishap involves (1) radioactive contamination from the burning, theft, seizure, or destruction of a radioactive limited-life component; (2) evident damage to a nuclear weapon or nuclear component that requires major rework, replacement, examination, or recertification by the U.S. Department of Energy; (3) events requiring immediate action in the interests of nuclear surety or which could result in adverse national and international public reaction or the premature release of information; (4) events indicating that a nuclear weapon or warhead has been armed; or (5) events that could lead to a nuclear weapon system accident.

An example of a bent spear incident occurred in August 2007 when a B-52 bomber accidentally carried six cruise missiles armed with nuclear weapons in a flight across the United States.

Zachariah Becker

Further Reading

Gregory, Shaun, *The Hidden Cost of Deterrence: Nuclear Weapons Accidents* (Dulles, VA: Brassey's, 1990).

Sagan, Scott D., *The Limits of Safety: Organization, Accidents, and Nuclear Weapons* (Princeton, NJ: Princeton University Press, 1993).

Schlosser, Eric, *Command and Control: Nuclear Weapons, the Damascus Accident, and the Illusion of Safety* (New York: Penguin Books, 2013).

Secretary of Defense Task Force on DoD Nuclear Weapons Management, *Report of the Secretary of Defense Task Force on DOD Nuclear Weapons Management: Phase II: Review of the DOD Nuclear Mission*, December 18, 2008. https://www.defense.gov/Portals/1/Documents/pubs/PhaseIIReportFinal.pdf.Accessed January 15, 2018.

Brucellosis (*Brucella* Bacterium)

Brucella bacteria are notable for being among the first to be weaponized in a modern U.S. military program for biological warfare (BW). The *Brucella* bacterium, however, is best described as an incapacitant (versus a deadly pathogen), because (especially in the era of antibiotics) the lethality of brucellosis is quite low (5 percent mortality or less without treatment). Both the United States and the former Soviet Union prepared *Brucella* bacteria for use in biological weapons. Later, both countries replaced this organism with other BW agents that proved more reliable.

Background

Brucella comprises at least four types of bacteria that cause brucellosis in humans, but nowadays it is mostly found in domesticated and wild animals: *Brucella suis* (swine), *Brucella melitensis* (sheep), *Brucella abortus* (cattle), and *Brucella canis* (dogs). Named after David Bruce, who isolated the organism, brucellosis has been called Malta fever (as it was widespread among British soldiers stationed there during the Crimean War); Mediterranean gastric remittent fever; and undulant fever. *Brucella* bacteria can infect humans by means of ingestion of contaminated milk or meat as well as through broken skin. Workers in slaughterhouses have often acquired brucellosis through contact with diseased animals and infectious aerosols. It is not surprising, therefore, that *Brucella* would be researched for its potential use in warfare.

In March 1944, according to the official history of the U.S. biological weapons program, the U.S. Chemical Warfare Service (CWS) undertook investigations into *Brucella* as a potential BW agent. (Other sources suggest that the utilization of *Brucella* bacteria was actually proposed two years earlier.) Although the bacterial species *Brucella melitensis* is most often associated with serious human infection, it also proved more difficult to grow and to keep virulent. Animal experiments conducted at that time using guinea pigs also showed that much fewer *Brucella suis* bacteria were required to cause infection when disseminated as an aerosol. Thus, during World War II, the U.S. Army selected *Brucella suis* for weaponization.

Pilot production of bacteria commenced in summer 1945 at Camp Detrick, Maryland. *Brucella* bacteria were produced in crude fashion by infecting laboratory animals and then harvesting their bacteria-laden spleens. These bacteria were then added in small amounts into glassware containing growth media and gradually transferred into larger vessels. Production of *Brucella* was halted in September 1945.

At the end of World War II, the technology of the day was limited to liquid suspensions of *Brucella*. Refrigeration was required to maintain live bacterial cultures for weapons fill. Thus, when it came to practical designs, this organism was problematic as a weapon. But *Brucella* bacteria performed rather well during aerosol tests.

In 1949, a year before the outbreak of the Korean War, the U.S. Army Chemical Corps selected *B. suis* as the first standardized biological weapon in the American arsenal. In 1950 and 1951, preliminary tests using aerial munitions dropped from B-29s were conducted at Dugway Proving Ground, Utah. Validating field trials in 1952 eventually gave way to the first standardized biological weapon in the U.S. arsenal. This consisted of M114 bombs (108 of them) that were clustered in formation with the M26 adapter. Provided to the U.S. Air Force, the weapon was named the M33 *Brucella* cluster bomb. With each M33 package weighing about a quarter of a ton, up to 16 of these clustered munitions were deemed necessary to cover a square mile of territory. But ultimately, mostly due to the refrigeration requirements, this biological ordnance proved to be a logistical nightmare and was never used.

Technical Aspects

In an aerosol, *Brucella* bacteria are among the more infectious, requiring only 10–100 bacteria to cause disease in humans. Its effects are also widely variable. Some people may be exposed but remain non-symptomatic, but others may develop symptoms over 5–60 days after exposure.

Like other bacterial diseases found in BW contexts, brucellosis infection starts as a flulike illness, with fever, headache, chills, and general malaise. Up to three-fourths of victims may develop gastrointestinal upset, with nausea, vomiting, or diarrhea. In a small number of cases, infection of the heart and nervous system can result in very poor outcomes. Endocarditis, while a rare condition, has been responsible for 80 percent of the deaths that have occurred as a result of *Brucella* infection. Transmission from person to person is not likely during the infectious stage of the disease. Although vaccines are routinely used for animals (e.g., cattle), no prophylactic treatment is currently available for human use.

When compared to other BW threats, such as anthrax, brucellosis is not expected to top the list of bioterrorist or BW threats for the modern battlefield. However, its endemic nature as a zoonotic in some regions of the globe may present a public health threat for overseas operations. Also, one cannot rule out the possibility of the use of *Brucella* as an antianimal disease to cause disruptions in the agricultural sector (agroterrorism).

Eric A. Croddy

Further Reading

Cochrane, Rexmond C., *History of the Chemical Warfare Service in World War II*, vol. 2, *Biological Warfare Research in the United States* (Fort Detrick, MD: Historical Section, Plans, Training and Intelligence Division, Office of Chief, Chemical Corps, November 1947).

Regis, Ed, *The Biology of Doom* (New York: Henry Holt, 1999).

Yagupsky, Pablo, and Ellen Jo Baront, "Laboratory Exposures to Brucellae and Implications for Bioterrorism," *Emerging Infectious Diseases* 11, no. 8 (August 2005): 1180–1185.

C

Chemical Weapons Convention

The 1993 Convention on the Prohibition of the Development, Production, Stockpiling, and Use of Chemical Weapons and on Their Destruction (known more simply as the Chemical Weapons Convention (CWC)) entered into force on April 29, 1997. It was the first verifiable treaty to ban an entire category of weapons of mass destruction. As of 2017, there are 192 nations that are states parties to the CWC.

Definition of a Chemical Weapon

The CWC defines a chemical weapon as essentially consisting of one or more of three elements: (1) toxic chemicals and their precursors in a type and quantity not consistent with the object and purpose of the treaty, (2) munitions and devices that are specifically designed to cause death or harm through the use of such chemicals, and (3) any equipment specifically designed for use directly in connection with the employment of munitions and devices specified in (2). A key element in the CWC's definition of a chemical weapon is that it bans the production, development, stockpiling, and use of *all* toxic chemicals and their precursors, except when used for peaceful purposes. This general-purpose criterion encompasses the overarching definition of a chemical weapon, taking into account any relevant future technological and scientific developments that could be utilized in chemical weaponry.

Background

The main international legal instrument dealing with chemical weapons prior to the CWC's entry into force was the Geneva Protocol for the Prohibition of the Use in War of Asphyxiating, Poisonous, or Other Gases, and of Bacteriological Methods of Warfare (the Geneva Protocol, 1925). However, the Geneva Protocol did not prevent the stockpiling of chemical weapons. Furthermore, many of the major powers attached conditions to their instruments of ratification: for example, provisions that a state would not consider itself bound by treaty obligations if first attacked with chemical weapons or if it were involved in a military conflict with nonsignatory states or with military coalitions that included one or more nonsignatory states.

Other agreements regarding chemical weapons included the International Declaration Concerning the Laws and Customs of War, signed at the Brussels Conference of 1874; the conventions signed at the First International Peace Conference (The Hague, 1899) and the Second International Peace Conference (The Hague, 1907); the Treaty of Peace with Germany (also known as the Treaty of Versailles, signed on June 28, 1919); and the Treaty of Washington of 1922, Relating to the Use of Submarines and Noxious Gases in Warfare (signed in Washington, D.C., on February 6, 1922).

Groundwork in CWC negotiations began in 1968 within the framework of the United Nations' Eighteen-Nation Committee on Disarmament (the present-day Conference on Disarmament). Decades later, the United States and the Soviet Union negotiated a bilateral agreement on chemical weapons in parallel with the multilateral negotiations on chemical disarmament. The bilateral negotiations resulted in the Agreement on Destruction and Nonproduction of Chemical Weapons and on Measures to Facilitate the Multilateral Convention on Banning Chemical Weapons, signed on June 1, 1990. Although the latter agreement was never fully implemented, the CWC's verification of compliance procedures are largely based on that bilateral agreement.

Organization for the Prohibition of Chemical Weapons (OPCW)

The Organization for the Prohibition of Chemical Weapons (OPCW), based in The Hague, Netherlands, is mandated to verify the destruction of chemical weapons—including old and abandoned chemical weapons—as well as to verify the destruction or conversion of former chemical weapon production facilities. It is also tasked to ensure that national defense establishments and national chemical industries are not engaged in prohibited activities. The OPCW also provides parties with technical expertise and advice on chemical weapon–related matters, such as the planning and implementation of weapon destruction programs.

Parties are required to provide annual declarations on defense-related activities and on the production, consumption, and transfer of certain chemicals. Chemical weapon–related facilities (including chemical weapon storage and destruction facilities) and facilities working with small quantities of chemical warfare agents for research, medical, pharmaceutical, or protective purposes are then subject to international inspections. Segments of the chemical industry are also subject to visits by inspectors.

Schedule 1, 2, and 3 Chemicals

Although any use of chemicals as a means of warfare is prohibited under the CWC, certain chemicals known to have been used as CW agents are listed in schedules; others are included due to their potential use as CW agent precursors. In the Schedule 1 category, CW agents that have typically been developed for warfare—and have no other practical purpose—are listed, including the nerve agents (e.g., sarin) and mustard agent. States may produce these in small quantities only for peaceful defensive purposes, and there are strict reporting guidelines in these cases. Schedule 2 chemicals include toxic chemicals that could be utilized as a means of warfare, such as amiton (a nerve agent), and other chemicals that could be used to produce Schedule 1 chemicals. Countries may produce Schedule 2 chemicals, but only for peaceful purposes, and their trade is restricted to CWC parties. Finally, Schedule 3 includes classic World War I–era gases such as chlorine. These chemicals are often used in commercial products, and their strict regulation would be too burdensome for the chemical industry worldwide. These can be produced in large quantities so long as they are for peaceful uses.

Implementation of the CWC

The CWC is implemented by the OPCW. The OPCW consists of the Conference of the States Parties (CSP), the Executive Council (EC), and the Technical Secretariat. The CSP is the highest decision-making body. It meets in a regular session once per year. The EC, which is composed of 41 members representing five geographical groupings, meets in regular sessions three to four times per year. It develops and considers draft recommendations, decisions, and guidelines for the approval of the CSP, including the annual draft program and budget. It also plays a key role in implementing the CWC's provisions on consultations, cooperation, and fact-finding, up to and including challenge inspections—that is, states must comply with on-the-spot, "anytime, anywhere" inspections if and when approved by the OPCW—and investigations of alleged chemical weapon use. The Secretariat is responsible for carrying out the treaty's verification measures and providing administrative and technical support to the CSP, EC, and various subsidiary organs.

The countries that have declared chemical weapon production facilities—defined as any facility that has produced chemical weapons at any time since January 1, 1946—are Bosnia and Herzegovina, China, France, India, Iran, Japan, Libya, Russia, South Korea, Syria, the United Kingdom, the United States, and Yugoslavia. Three parties have declared having abandoned chemical weapons. The largest quantity of abandoned chemical weapons was those left in China by Japan at the end of World War II, totaling at least 1 million munitions. The CWC does not require that chemical weapons dumped (such as in the ocean) before January 1, 1985, be declared. Nor does it require that chemical weapons buried on a party's territory (and that remain buried) before January 1, 1977, be declared.

In October 2013, the OPCW was awarded the Nobel Peace Prize, highlighting its recent efforts in removing and destroying Syria's chemical weapons stocks in the middle of its civil war. This effort was spurred by the outcry following Syria's use of sarin nerve agent in August of that year that killed more than 1,400 civilians in the suburbs of Damascus. Although Syria has since become a state party to the CWC, the Syrian military continued using chemicals (chlorine and sarin nerve agent) throughout 2017 in its war against its opponents, causing death and injury to hundreds of civilians.

John Hart and Eric A. Croddy

Further Reading

Krutzsch, Walter, and Ralf Trapp, *A Commentary on the Chemical Weapons Convention* (Dordrecht, the Netherlands: Martinus Nijhoff, 1994).

Krutzsch, Walter, and Ralf Trapp, eds., *Verification Practice under the Chemical Weapons Convention: A Commentary* (The Hague, the Netherlands: Kluwer Law International, 1999).

Martin, David, "The Chemical Weapons Convention: Hollow Idealism or Capable Mechanism? The Syrian Intervention as a Test Case," *Loyola of Los Angeles International & Comparative Law Review* 37, no. 1 (2015): 31–66.

Chernobyl

Chernobyl is a nuclear power station located in Pryp'yat, Ukraine, 10 miles southwest of the city of Chernobyl and 65 miles north of Kiev. The plant contains four reactors, each capable of producing 1,000 megawatts of electric power. The reactors were activated between 1977 and 1983. In 1986, Chernobyl became the site of the worst nuclear power disaster in history.

On April 26, 1986, a poorly designed experiment led to a chain reaction in the core of Unit 4, causing the reactor to go out of control. Several explosions triggered a huge fireball that blew off the steel and concrete lid of the reactor. The fire in the graphite reactor core led to a partial meltdown of the core and the release of radioactive material into the atmosphere. On April 27, 30,000 residents of Pryp'yat were evacuated. A Swedish monitoring station initially discovered the release. The accident triggered international criticism of Soviet power plant designs and their unsafe operating procedures.

Between 50 million and 185 million curies of radionuclides escaped into the atmosphere, several times more than were generated by the Hiroshima and Nagasaki bombs. Windborne radioactive contamination was carried as far away as the United Kingdom and Italy. The aftereffects of contamination will diminish over the next century; for instance, in 2012, British authorities stopped monitoring livestock for exposure to radioactive residue on contaminated pasture land.

The rapid cleanup resulted in radioactive material being buried at 800 temporary sites. The core was also encapsulated, but the container was later found to be unsound. Thirty-two people died initially, and dozens of others contracted radiation sickness. It is expected that several thousand radiation-induced illnesses and cancers will develop over time as a result of the accident.

Unit 2 remained operating after the accident, but it was shut down following a fire in 1991. Unit 1 was decommissioned in 1996, and unit 3 was deactivated in 2000.

The accident sparked renewed interest in the Soviet Union's use of nuclear power facilities to create weapons-grade nuclear materials. Some commentators blamed the magnitude of the accident on the design's focus on weapon production. The accident led to a reemergence of a strong international antinuclear lobby in a campaign that almost stopped the construction of new nuclear power plants worldwide.

Frannie Edwards

Further Reading

Read, Piers Paul, *Ablaze: The Story of the Heroes and Victims of Chernobyl* (London: Secker and Warburg, 1993).

China, People's Republic of

The People's Republic of China (PRC) once possessed chemical weapons, but by the mid-1990s, it had completely eliminated its offensive chemical warfare (CW) program. China adamantly refutes any suggestion that it ever had an offensive biological warfare (BW) capability.

Today, in terms of weapons of mass destruction (WMD), China relies on a relatively small (200–300 warheads) nuclear arsenal for strategic deterrence. Furthermore, China has also maintained its stated "no first use" policy; that is, the PRC has pledged to never be the first to use a nuclear weapon, while reserving the right to respond in kind if attacked.

Chemical Weapons

China has long advocated the prohibition and elimination of chemical weapons. To underscore this point, the PRC often cites its having been a victim of Japanese CW during the Sino-Chinese conflict (1931–1945). But after decades of denying ever possessing an offensive chemical warfare capability, in the late 1990s, it finally admitted to having had a chemical weapons program. Although the details of its declaration in 1997 to the Chemical Weapons Convention (CWC) are confidential, Chinese sources indicate the PRC had, at the very least, "pilot" production of chemical warfare agents. Because both the Soviet Union and the United States had pursued vesicants (e.g., mustard) and nerve agents (e.g., VX) in their respective chemical arsenals, it is likely China researched, developed, and produced similar agents, including binary nerve munitions. China's legacy chemical weapons and their production facilities no longer exist in any form.

In 1956, a secret report produced by U.S. Army intelligence (G-2) summarized what little was known about "Communist China's" chemical, biological, and radiological (CBR) warfare:

> There is insufficient information on file in this office and a lack of supporting evidence to justify a valid inventory of CBR items in the hands of the Communist Chinese. It is to be remembered that large stocks of Japanese CBR equipment fell into the hands of the Chinese Nationalists and the Soviet[s] in Manchuria at the end of World War II. The Nationalists in turn, lost or surrendered to the Communists large quantities of material and equipment including U.S. items given or lent to [the Nationalists] by various agreements. (U.S. Army 1956)

Abandoned Chemical Weapons in China

Having signed and ratified the CWC, Japan agreed to take responsibility for some 2 million tons of World War II–era chemical weapons it abandoned in China, with the largest stocks being found in the northeastern provinces of Liaoning, Jilin, and Heilongjiang. The lion's share (some 90 percent) of these are found in Jilin province's Haerbaling (Yanbian Korean Autonomous Prefecture), with over 300,000 chemical munitions awaiting destruction.

Biological Weapons

China's experience in World War II also shaped PRC leaders' attitudes toward biological weapons. The horrific BW experiments conducted by the Japanese Unit 731 and other military organizations continue to leave a disdain by the Chinese in regard to this type of warfare. Today, China continues to state categorically that it has never manufactured nor possessed biological weapons.

Having acceded to the Biological and Toxin Weapons Convention (BWC) in 1984, the PRC has since declared several facilities to be associated with biological defense research, which is allowed under the treaty.

Ken Alibek, who for a time was deputy director of the Soviet Biopreparat BW program, claims that China may have unwittingly unleashed Xinjiang hemorrhagic fever (focused near Lop Nor) in the late 1980s as a result of its biological weapons research. His speculation was based at least in part on the belief by the Soviets that this disease had not been previously known in that area. Nevertheless, as early as 1968, the Xinjiang virus—genetically similar to the one causing Crimean-Congo fever—had already been tentatively identified during an outbreak in southern Xinjiang province. Although it is more likely that this was a natural outbreak, no further information has been found to confirm or deny any connection with BW activity.

Sensationalist reporting also appeared following a devastating foot-and-mouth disease (FMD) outbreak in Taiwan. In this case, some in the Taiwanese defense establishment suspected that mainland China had deliberately infected the island's pig population, intentionally ruining its swine industry. Based on interviews with knowledgeable sources in Taiwan, it was more likely an accidental outbreak due to the smuggling of piglets from China.

It is unclear whether we will see a more complete account of past Chinese research in biological warfare, to include offensive agents and weaponization. In 2014, the U.S Department of State reported that there was no evidence that China was in violation of its BWC obligations.

Nuclear Weapons

On January 15, 1955, during a meeting of the Politburo's Central Secretariat, Mao

Zedong announced his decision to proceed with a nuclear weapons program, designated "02." Two days later, the Soviet Union announced it would assist China with peaceful nuclear energy research. The following year, Mao told a meeting of the Chinese Communist Party Central Committee that the time had arrived for China to acquire nuclear weapons. By 1958, day-to-day direction of the nuclear weapons program was under the leadership of Vice Premier Nie Rongzhen, who would oversee China's nuclear weapons program for the next 30 years. Progress slowed when the Soviet Union withdrew its technical support for the program around 1960. Nevertheless, China tested its first nuclear device—and became the world's fifth nuclear power—in October 1964.

China's nuclear declaratory policy emphasizes "no first use," and its officials and scholars highlight China's responsible stewardship of its nuclear arsenal. Since the turn of the century, China has slowly modernized its nuclear force—estimates of its total size range between 200 and 300 nuclear weapons—deployed on an emerging "triad" of intercontinental ballistic missiles (ICBMs) (DF-5A, DF-31A), submarine-launched ballistic missiles (JL-2), and medium-range bombers. The PRC has also demonstrated a capability to place multiple independently targeted reentry vehicles atop its ICBMs.

The increase in the size and sophistication of China's nuclear arsenal since the end of the Cold War improves the survivability of its arsenal; these developments do not necessarily contradict its no-first-use doctrine. If current trends continue, however, the PRC will soon have the capabilities needed to adopt a more ambitious nuclear strategy that seeks to integrate nuclear weapons into a broader set of deterrent objectives.

Eric A. Croddy and James J. Wirtz

Further Reading

Alibek, Ken, and Stephen Handelman, *Biohazard: The Chilling True Story of the Largest Covert Biological Weapons Program in the World* (New York: Random House, 1999).

Croddy, Eric, "Chinese Chemical and Biological Warfare (CBW) Capabilities," National Intelligence Council Conference, *China and Weapons of Mass Destruction: Implications for the United States*, November 5, 1999. https://fas.org/irp/nic/china_wmd .html. Accessed April 30, 2018.

Frieman, Wendy, *China, Arms Control, and Non-Proliferation* (New York: Routledge, 2004).

Gill, Bates, *Chemical and Biological Weapons and Deterrence, Case Study 6: People's Republic of China* (Alexandria, VA: Chemical and Biological Arms Control Institute, 1998).

Haynes, Susan Turner, *Chinese Nuclear Proliferation: How Global Politics Is Transforming China's Weapons Buildup and Modernization* (Lincoln, NE: Potomac Books, 2016).

U.S. Army Forces Far East Chemical Office, *Status of Chemical, Biological and Radiological Warfare, Communist China*, April 5, 1956.

Chlorine Gas

As a lung irritant, chlorine (Cl_2) is the quintessential choking agent used in gas warfare. The spring 1915 chlorine attack by the German military at Ypres, Belgium, was considered a signal event that heralded the era of modern chemical weaponry. Although not the first offensive use of chemical weapons in World War I, the Ypres gas attack was unprecedented both in terms of its scope and impact.

Background

In 1823, the British chemist Michael Faraday (1791–1867) first liquefied chlorine gas.

Since then, chlorine has been one of the most widely used chemicals. Modern industrial production of chlorine is carried out by electrolysis, using electricity to separate the elements of salt (sodium chloride). Chlorine gas is collected as it separates from the brine, and sodium is also produced for use in making another useful chemical, caustic soda (sodium hydroxide). In World War I, the amount of chlorine brought to the front in April 1915 (approximately 170 tons) represented a sizeable portion of Germany's industrial chemical capacity.

Chlorine gas is mainly effective as a weapon through inhalation, producing an immediate, irritating sensation in the nasal passages, with tightening in the upper airways followed by a very severe cough. Depending on the amount of exposure, damage in the lungs leads to swelling of tissues (pulmonary edema), causing blood to leak from the injured alveoli (the fragile sacs of tissue critical for lung respiration). As body fluids enter the lungs' air spaces, no further gas exchange can take place, and the victim chokes to death—thus the World War I–era term: *dry-land drowning*. Apart from assisted breathing and supportive care, there is little else that can be done in the event of significant exposure to chlorine. By 1916, the treatment of casualties was largely limited to delivering oxygen through the nasal passages with small tubes. Those that did survive usually made full recoveries.

Chlorine Gas at Ypres, April 22, 1915

In early 1915, the great armies in World War I were nearly at a standstill in trenches stretching for hundreds of miles. Desperate to make a breakthrough, the German military chemist Fritz Haber organized a massive gas assault by bringing some 5,730 cylinders of chlorine to a 6-kilometer front at Ypres, Belgium. These chlorine gas canisters were then spaced along the front lines (about one cylinder per meter). Upon their release on April 22, clouds of chlorine gas broke the Allied forces defending the salient, but there was insufficient German infantry to exploit the offensive any further. In this fateful gas attack at Ypres, at least 1,400 Algerian, Canadian, and French soldiers died. (The claim that 5,000 soldiers perished and 15,000 injured was clearly exaggerated for Allied propaganda purposes).

In response to the Ypres gas attack, the British duplicated Haber's tactics on September 24, placing 5,500 chlorine gas cylinders along the front at Loos, Belgium. Unfortunately for the British, the winds were not favorable, and many of the gas casualties were their own. The constant problem presented by shifting winds and other environmental factors convinced both sides to develop chemical-filled artillery projectiles.

Chlorine Gas as a Modern Weapon

Just as Germany utilized chlorine from its domestic chemical industry, chlorine poses a modern risk due to its potential diversion from commercial markets. In 2007, for example, the Islamic State of Iraq and Syria (ISIS) used chlorine gas in various bombings. The Islamic State also reportedly used chlorine gas in attacks against Iraqi police and Kurds in 2014.

During spring 2013, Syrian military forces used chlorine gas against a number of civilian targets, including Aleppo and Damascus. According to the Organization for the Prohibition of Chemical Warfare, in 2014, the Syrian government used chlorine gas during aerial assaults on several villages in northern Syria. In August 2016, Syrian helicopters also reportedly dropped chlorine gas cylinders on civilian populations, and there were at least eight more chlorine attacks on Aleppo during winter of that year, causing hundreds of casualties. These and other chemical attacks were carried out despite Syria's October 2013 commitment to abide by the Chemical Weapons Convention (CWC).

Eric A. Croddy

Further Reading

Padely, A. P., "Gas: The Greatest Terror of the Great War," *Anesthesia & Intensive Care* 44 (2016 History Supplement): 24–30.

Prentiss, Augustin M., *Chemicals in War: A Treatise on Chemical Warfare* (New York: McGraw-Hill, 1937).

Tucker, Jonathan B., *War of Nerves: Chemical Warfare from World War I to Al-Qaeda* (New York: Pantheon Books, 2006).

Comprehensive Test Ban Treaty

The Comprehensive Test Ban Treaty (CTBT) is an international agreement to ban nuclear testing in any environment. The treaty is an extension of efforts begun in the mid-20th century to limit nuclear weapons proliferation. It is not yet in force. The CTBT requires that all member states enact a moratorium on detonating nuclear weapons, in effect preventing new states from acquiring them and current nuclear powers from developing newer and more advanced nuclear weapons. Originally proposed in the 1950s, but not opened for signature until 1996, the treaty will enter into force following ratification by the 44 states listed in Annex 2 of the treaty. As of 2018, North Korea remains the only Annex 2 state that has not signed the treaty, and five Annex 2 states (China, Egypt, Iran, Israel, and the United States) have signed but not ratified the treaty. The U.S. Senate failed to ratify the CTBT in a vote taken in October 1999.

The CTBT consists of 17 articles and various annexes and protocols detailing the scope of the agreement. It will enter into force 180 days after the last of the Annex 2 states ratifies it. The formal organization of the regime includes a Conference of States Parties, an executive council consisting of 51 members that serves as the executive organ of the Comprehensive Test Ban Treaty Organization (CTBTO), and a Technical Secretariat that assists member states with implementation measures.

Following implementation of the treaty, states parties will be able to activate various noncompliance measures, and a verification regime will begin monitoring compliance with the test ban. Verification measures in the CTBT include an International Monitoring System (IMS) of more than 300 seismic, radiological, hydroacoustic, and infrasound detectors around the world set up to detect seismic and other activities that could indicate a nuclear detonation; they will transmit data to the CTBTO headquarters in Vienna. The headquarters will analyze suspected events and distribute the information to member states. The treaty text details the locations of IMS facilities, which were designed to ensure global coverage. In addition to detecting possible nuclear explosions, the monitoring stations can supply member states with information on volcanic, seismic, and nonnuclear radiological activities. IMS facilities are owned by the state in which they are located. In some cases, these facilities are preexisting installations; in others, the CTBTO and relevant state parties must yet fund and initiate their construction.

In the event that member states suspect an illegal nuclear explosion, the CTBT allows for a series of options for on-site inspections, including overflight observation and photography, environmental sampling, and drilling to obtain radioactive samples. The CTBT does not explicitly provide for noncompliance measures other than the suspension or restriction of rights outlined in the framework of the treaty. However, the treaty does recommend that a state found to be in violation of its obligations be subject to actions by the United Nations, including sanctions.

During negotiations, the United States ensured that the treaty banned only nuclear explosions and not all activities resulting in nuclear energy release. Given this wording, the CTBT would allow the United States (and other signatories) to conduct a range of tests of components in nuclear weapons, such as subcritical explosions involving fissile material, which could result in a release of nuclear energy, to guarantee the reliability of its nuclear weapons stockpile.

John Spykerman

Further Reading

Hansen, Keith A., *The Comprehensive Nuclear Test Ban Treaty: An Insider's Perspective* (Stanford, CA: Stanford Law & Politics, 2006).

Holdren, John P. and the Committee on Technical Issues Related to Ratification of the Comprehensive Nuclear Test Ban Treaty, *Technical Issues Related to the Comprehensive Nuclear Test Ban Treaty* (Washington, D.C.: National Academies of Sciences, 2002) http://www.ldeo.columbia.edu/~richards/my_papers/CISAC_CTBT_AllText.pdf. Accessed May 11, 2018.

Cooperative Threat Reduction Program (Nunn-Lugar Program)

Between 1991 and 2013, the United States sponsored the Nunn-Lugar Cooperative Threat Reduction Program to assist the states of the former Soviet Union dismantle their weapons of mass destruction; secure their nuclear weapons and associated materials, technology, and expertise; and convert their nuclear facilities to other purposes. Senators Sam Nunn (D-Ga.) and Richard Lugar (R-Ind.) cosponsored the 1991 legislation that created this program. The term "Nunn-Lugar" was thus used to refer to the full range of threat reduction and nonproliferation programs undertaken by the U.S. government in cooperation with the states of the former Soviet Union, including those managed by the U.S. Departments of Commerce, Energy, and State. Cooperative Threat Reduction (CTR), which was housed in the Defense Threat Reduction Agency, is more accurately applied to the U.S. Department of Defense element of Nunn-Lugar.

At the time of its collapse, the Soviet Union possessed approximately 30,000 strategic and tactical nuclear weapons in its arsenal, in addition to some 1,000 tons of highly enriched uranium, 200 tons of plutonium, 40,000 tons of chemical weapons agents, and a massive biological weapons program. Perhaps more significantly, the Soviet collapse created three new nuclear weapons states in Belarus, Kazakhstan, and Ukraine. In the immediate aftermath of the Cold War, the denuclearization of these three new nuclear powers was not a foregone conclusion. Most analysts believe that the denuclearization of all three states by the mid-1990s—leaving Russia as the sole former Soviet nuclear legacy state—would not have occurred, or would have taken a much longer time, without the assistance of the Nunn-Lugar Program.

Although Nunn-Lugar was a unique program that was fraught with growing pains, bureaucratic battles, and international misunderstandings, it eventually matured into a complex and comprehensive foreign policy and national security mechanism. Nunn-Lugar generated considerable domestic momentum throughout the legislative, executive, industrial, and nongovernmental communities, which for years carried it through the ebbs and flows of U.S.-Russian bilateral relations. Nevertheless, Congress began scaling back funding for Nunn-Lugar at the start of the Barack Obama administration.

Organizational Elements of CTR

The various U.S. government agencies that managed elements of the Nunn-Lugar Program provided specific objectives for their individual programs. For the U.S. Department of Defense, CTR program objectives reflected the fact that Ukraine, Kazakhstan, and Belarus are nonnuclear weapons states. Nunn-Lugar was intended to do the following: (1) assist Russia in accelerating strategic arms reductions to the second Strategic Arms Reduction Treaty (START II) levels; (2) enhance safety, security, control, accounting, and centralization of nuclear weapons and fissile material in the former Soviet Union to prevent their proliferation and encourage their reduction; (3) assist Ukraine and Kazakhstan to eliminate START II limited systems and weapons of mass destruction infrastructure; (4) assist the former Soviet Union to eliminate and prevent proliferation of biological and chemical weapons and associated capabilities; and (5) encourage military reductions and reform while reducing proliferation threats in the former Soviet Union.

The primary Department of Energy initiative dedicated to Nunn-Lugar work in Russia was the Material Protection, Control, and Accounting (MPC&A) Program. Its mission was to support U.S. national security objectives by enhancing the protection of international nuclear weapons and weapons-usable nuclear material at high risk of theft or diversion. The MPC&A Program's goals included assisting Russia and other nations in this endeavor, enhancing Russia's capabilities and commitment to operating and maintaining improved nuclear security and establishing and maintaining a collaborative environment with MPC&A program customers and stakeholders.

Whether coordinated by the U.S. Departments of Defense, Energy, or State, or by other U.S. government agencies, aspects of the Nunn-Lugar Program were negotiated, implemented, managed, and monitored through overarching umbrella agreements maintained between the United States and recipient governments that specified the rights and scope of the country-specific program. These agreements were set for a specific duration and included audit procedures. Separate implementation agreements were negotiated and maintained for each specific initiative. Congress authorized each element of the program annually. The president annually certified the eligibility of each recipient state for assistance against specified criteria required by Congress. U.S. agencies needed to notify Congress of their intent to commit funds to a specific country. The United States executed the program by providing goods and services, not aid.

CTR Termination

In 2012, Moscow informed the U.S. government that it would not extend the cooperation agreements under the aegis of the Nunn-Lugar cooperative security model. In June 2013, the United States and the Russian Federation signed a new bilateral agreement on cooperative threat reduction, but this agreement fell victim to worsening relations between Washington and Moscow. In January 2015, the Russian Federation informed Washington that it would no longer accept U.S. assistance to secure weapons-grade nuclear material. Joint U.S.-Russian security work at various sites was effectively cancelled in January 2015.

Charles L. Thornton and James J. Wirtz

Further Reading

Cerami, Joseph R., *Leadership and Policy Innovation—From Clinton to Bush: Countering the Proliferation of Weapons of Mass Destruction* (London: Routledge, 2013).

Shields, John M., and William C. Potter, eds., *Dismantling the Cold War: U.S. and NIS Perspectives on the Nunn-Lugar Cooperative Threat Reduction Program* (Cambridge, MA: MIT Press, 1997).

Crisis Stability

For a strategic relationship to possess crisis stability, it should not promote incentives during a crisis for either side to initiate conflict or challenge the position of the other in a way that would provoke conflict. Although there might not be any incentive for a state to go to war during normal circumstances, rising political tensions might cause a state to conclude that war is likely, that it faces a higher risk of being attacked itself, and that there are advantages to attacking first if war were to occur. In such circumstances, a normally stable relationship would be unstable in a crisis.

The circumstances that would jeopardize crisis stability typically involve some combination of *vulnerability* and *opportunity*—that is, situations where the state sees an opportunity to reduce its own vulnerability by taking advantage of an opponent's weakness. Improving crisis stability encourages policy choices that sometimes involve not only increasing the survivability of one's nuclear forces but also taking steps to increase the survivability of a potential adversary's nuclear forces. If both sides in a dispute possessed a secure second-strike capability, then neither would feel much incentive to use nuclear forces first in a crisis.

For example, the dominant characteristic of the missile age has been the lack of adequate defense against attack. Such vulnerability means that the only way to avoid unacceptable destruction in a war is to destroy the opponent's attack capability. During the late 1950s and early 1960s, both the United States and the Soviet Union possessed ballistic missiles that were themselves vulnerable to attack; thus, each had an opportunity to destroy that threat before being attacked by launching a nuclear attack first in the hope of catching the opponent's nuclear arsenal on the ground. In a crisis, each would have had an incentive to strike first, in the hopes of eliminating a substantial portion of the missiles against which it could not defend, rather than waiting to be attacked. This situation would be crisis unstable because incentives to attack would become salient at a moment when political tensions peaked.

By contrast, if the missiles in question could survive an attack, then the opportunity to defeat the threat posed by those missiles disappears. By the early 1960s, the United States had not only begun to put its intercontinental ballistic missiles in underground silos and deployed them on submarines at sea, it had also encouraged the Soviet Union to do the same. By deploying their weapons in more survivable ways, both sides increased crisis stability. Because crisis stability largely depends on how states perceive threats, risks, opportunities, and incentives, mechanisms to improve communication in a crisis have also been important—beginning with the Hot Line Agreements from the early 1960s and continuing with the more recent exchange of military personnel in strategic command and warning centers. Beyond the bilateral nuclear relationship, provisions to improve communication and avoid miscalculation in a crisis have become standard elements in managing conflict situations around the world.

Crisis stability is ultimately about keeping all parties in an antagonistic relationship believing that they cannot benefit from initiating hostilities. This involves efforts to reduce the incentives of all parties to use nuclear weapons first in a crisis. Paradoxically, this means that a larger military capability may be more stabilizing than a smaller one, if the smaller one is more vulnerable to being destroyed in a surprise attack. Hence, the pursuit of crisis stability in a deterrent relationship may be at odds with the purposes of disarmament.

Schuyler Foerster

Further Reading

Foerster, Schuyler, ed. *Defining Stability: Conventional Arms Control in a Changing Europe* (Boulder: Westview, 1989).

Freedman, Lawrence, *The Evolution of Nuclear Strategy* (London: Palgrave Macmillan, 2003).

Schelling, Thomas C., and Morton H. Halperin, *Strategy and Arms Control* (Washington, D.C.: Pergamon-Brassey's, 1985).

Criticality and Critical Mass

The key requirement for making a nuclear weapon or a practical nuclear reactor is to create a self-sustaining chain reaction. In such a chain reaction, neutrons released by fission in one atom are likely, on average, to induce the fission of one or more subsequent atoms. An assembly of fissile and other materials that can support a self-sustaining chain reaction is said to be a *critical* assembly or to have achieved *criticality*.

Criticality depends on the type and amount of fissile material as well as assembly details such as mass, surface area, geometry, and the composition of nonfissionable materials used in construction. The primary criterion for criticality is that the multiplication factor (k)—the ratio of neutrons in one generation of fissions to the number produced in the final generation—be greater than unity. The $k > 1$ criterion is a primary design consideration for any practical use of nuclear energy and is achieved by creating designs that balance the production and loss rate of neutrons. The criticality condition can be met with a variety of assembly structures, sizes, and time scales; can be exceeded significantly or barely met; and can be met with different fissionable materials that produce combinations of fast and slow neutrons. The most significant differences in the design of nuclear assemblies are between nuclear weapons and nuclear reactors.

Criticality in Nuclear Weapons

A nuclear weapon explodes because the assembly releases energy from a fission chain reaction so quickly that the fissile material vaporizes. If two subcritical assemblies $(k < 1)$ are brought together too slowly, they will release heat and melt rather than produce an explosion. A nuclear weapon requires an explosive assembly that goes quickly from a subcritical state to a supercritical state ($k \sim 2$: on average, neutrons from any single fission event are likely to produce two subsequent fissions).

Once assembled into the supercritical state, the chain reaction can only occur for a brief moment because criticality causes the fissile material to blow itself apart. The time scale between fissions in a critical assembly is about 10 nanoseconds; for $k \sim 2$, all the atoms in a kilogram of uranium would completely fission in less than a microsecond. The nuclear energy released from the complete fission of 1 kilogram of uranium would be equivalent to the energy released from about 17,000 kilograms of chemical explosives.

Shape has a major impact on the size and mass required for a critical assembly. A long, thin rod, with a large surface area, would lose many neutrons through the surface before they could participate in a chain reaction. The optimum shape for achieving a critical assembly with the smallest possible mass is a sphere; the number of fissionable atoms increases with the cube of the radius, but the surface area for escaping neutrons increases only with the square of the radius. Not all nuclear weapons use spherical assemblies, but early nuclear weapons depended on this optimum shape.

For nuclear weapons, the timing of achieving criticality is very important. The weapon works best if the assembly goes from subcritical to supercritical instantaneously. If subcritical assemblies come together very slowly, fission energy dissipates in heating the materials, possibly moving them out of an appropriate shape to sustain criticality. The spontaneous fissions from uranium or plutonium can also initiate a chain reaction before supercriticality is achieved. Such a premature chain reaction would not use up much of the fissile material and would dramatically reduce the nuclear yield. When this occurs, it is referred to as a "fizzle."

The term *critical mass* is something of a misnomer. Achieving criticality depends on the density, configuration, and timing of a nuclear weapon assembly, and only partly on the total mass of fissile material available to participate in the chain reaction; there is no single "critical mass" used to construct a nuclear weapon. The amount of fissile material used in a nuclear weapon depends on the yield sought, the assembly design and configuration, and the predicted fraction of the nuclear material that will generate the explosion before being explosively disassembled.

Nonetheless, it is common to speak of the critical mass for the primary fissile materials in a particular assembly. In many unclassified books and articles, it is common to see a single number quoted as "the critical mass" for uranium 235 (usually quoted as a number between about 9 kg and 25 kg) or plutonium 239 (usually between 4 kg and 20 kg). These different numbers reflect different assumptions about the assembly requirements needed to construct explosive devices. Efficient designs, involving spheres of pure material that surround the nuclear assembly with materials that reflect neutrons and delay the dispersion of explosive products, require less fissile material. Conservative designs use extra material to ensure that supercritical conditions are met and to make up for uncertainty in the fraction of nuclear material that might be involved in the explosive chain reaction.

There are significant differences when it comes to using fissile uranium and plutonium in designing a nuclear weapon. Plutonium is a denser material, and a smaller amount of plutonium will usually be required to produce a given yield from a particular design. Variations in isotopic content and metallurgic mixture, however, can overwhelm this difference in density.

The spontaneous fission rate for plutonium (and especially of the isotope Pu-240) is also much higher than the spontaneous fission rate of uranium. Because of this higher rate of spontaneous neutron generation, plutonium weapons need to be assembled rapidly to avoid premature fizzle yields.

Weapon designs make efficient use of fissile plutonium or uranium because the cost and effort involved in producing these materials is high. Given the resources put into creating a nuclear weapon, it is not cost-effective unless it is more powerful than a conventional high-explosive device. This was a major concern on the part of scientists working on the Manhattan Project during World War II. The mass of the hardware needed to make a nuclear weapon dwarfs that of the fissile material itself; for example, the nuclear weapon dropped on Nagasaki weighed about 10,000 pounds but used only 10–20 pounds of plutonium. New nuclear powers and terrorists may be satisfied with very inefficient nuclear weapons, and they may tolerate great uncertainties in the percentage of fuel contributing to the explosion.

Criticality in Nuclear Power Production

A nuclear reactor also depends on the property of criticality. A reactor used to generate electric power must maintain a chain reaction to produce more energy than is being used to operate the reactor. Nuclear reactors are usually designed to operate with k near unity. Reactor design balances the loss of neutrons through the surface and by absorption in nonfissile materials (including the coolant that captures the energy for electricity generation) with the generation of many neutrons from a chain reaction in a large amount of fissile material. The fuel rods of nuclear reactors tend to have large surface areas, and the total amount of nuclear fuel used in a single critical assembly is typically measured in tons. The reactor consists of an assembly of fissile material, moderators to slow the neutrons and increase the likelihood of fission, control elements that can absorb neutrons and decrease the likelihood of fission, coolant to take away the heat generated by absorption of neutrons, and other elements as required. Varying the position of control elements and the rate of coolant flow allows the reactor to be operated in a self-sustaining chain reaction or maintained at a subcritical level.

The relatively low multiplication factor in a reactor design means that nuclear energy is released at a much lower rate than in a nuclear explosion. The nuclear energy generated by fission is released over a longer period of time than in a nuclear weapon. At $k = 1$, a kilogram of uranium atoms takes decades to completely fission. The same factors that determine criticality in a nuclear weapon—total amount of fissionable material, density, configuration, and timing—are managed in a nuclear reactor design. But the reactor design creates a barely sustained chain reaction, with the percentage of fissile material participating in the chain reaction during each second very low (approximately 10–14 percent). A high total power level is achieved by arranging large amounts of fissionable materials into a nuclear assembly participating in the chain reaction.

The level of criticality and the kind of chain reaction that occurs is determined by the design of a nuclear assembly. A fast assembly cannot be used to produce a sustained power generation over a long period of time, and a distributed nuclear reactor cannot be made to explode. Even an uncontrolled chain reaction allowed to operate well outside design parameters in a nuclear reactor would only lead to the melting of the fissile materials and a drop below criticality.

Roy Pettis

Further Reading

Serber, Robert, and Richard Rhodes, eds., *The Los Alamos Primer: The First Lectures on How to Build an Atomic Bomb* (Berkeley: University of California Press, 1992).

Smyth, Henry De Wolf, and Philip Morrison, *Atomic Energy for Military Purposes: The Official Report on the Development of the Atomic Bomb under the Auspices of the United States Government* (Berkeley: University of California Press, 1992).

Weisman, Joel, ed., *Elements of Nuclear Reactor Design*, 2nd ed. (Melbourne, FL: Krieger, 1983).

D

De-alerting

De-alerting is a reduction in the day-to-day alert status of strategic nuclear forces that diminishes their readiness for launch or introduces deliberate delays into the process of preparing them for launch. Substantial de-alerting of U.S. heavy bombers, tactical and theater nuclear weapons, and North Atlantic Treaty Organization (NATO) dual-capable aircraft took place under a series of 1991 presidential nuclear initiatives.

In the mid to late 1990s, additional proposals were introduced calling for de-alerting U.S. and Russian strategic nuclear forces, ostensibly as a means of making them more secure from theft, loss, unauthorized access, or accidental launch and as a way to accelerate the dismantling and disarmament process already taking place under the Strategic Arms Reduction Treaties (START I and START II). These proposals were, in part, responses to the perceived deterioration in the Russian command and control of its nuclear forces. Measures proposed included removing nuclear warheads from operationally deployed intercontinental ballistic missiles (ICBMs), submarine-launched ballistic missiles (SLBMs), and bombers and storing them at a small number of centralized locations; removing or deactivating navigational equipment needed to guide strategic nuclear delivery vehicles; piling gravel on top of missile silos; reducing at-sea deployment rates of U.S. Trident submarines; and removing the launch keys or launch codes from command and control facilities and placing them in centralized containers monitored by officials from the United States and Russia. These proposals sometimes had much in common with other similar proposals for "detargeting," "decommissioning," "deactivation," "demating," and "deposturing."

In October 2017, the U.S. Air Force announced that it was renovating its flight line facilities at Barksdale Air Force Base to position itself to shorten the alert times for its nuclear-capable B-52 bombers. This marks the first evidence of a shift in the U.S. day-alert nuclear posture since the Cold War.

Kerry Kartchner and James J. Wirtz

Further Reading

Blair, Bruce G., Harold A. Feiveson, and Frank N. von Hippel, "Taking Nuclear Weapons Off Hair-Trigger Alert," *Scientific American* vol 277 issue 5 (November 1, 1997, pp. 74–81).

Karas, Thomas H., *De-alerting and De-activating Strategic Nuclear Weapons*, Sandia National Laboratories, Report SAND2001-0835, April 2001. http://www.prod.sandia.gov/cgi-bin/techlib/access-control.pl/2001/010835.pdf. Accessed September 15, 2003.

Lamotha, Dan, "The Air Force Hasn't Used Nuclear 'Alert Pads' since the Cold War. Now They're Being Upgraded," *Washington Post*, October 23, 2017. https://www.washingtonpost.com/news/checkpoint/wp/2017/10/23/the-air-force-denies-it-is-considering-cold-war-style-alerts-for-b-52-bombers/?utm_term=.127006d6a092. Accessed January 5, 2018.

Declared Facility

The term *declared facility* is a technical term often associated with arms control and disarmament treaties. A declared facility is a storage site, manufacturing plant, or military base that is subject to inspection and compliance review by other parties to a treaty or by an international governing body created to verify compliance with an international agreement.

Signatories of the 1993 Chemical Weapons Convention (CWC), for example, are subject to a stringent inspection regime in which they must provide a list of declared facilities that are, or once were, involved in the manufacture or storage of chemical weapons. A declared facility identified by a state party is subject to systematic verification or on-site inspection based on declared chemical weapons–related activities or functions. Under the CWC, declared and undeclared facilities are subject to challenge inspections. Other states parties may request that a team of international inspectors visit the site in question to verify that the host nation has abandoned its chemical arsenal. The Organization for the Prohibition of Chemical Weapons (OPCW), created by the CWC, provides an international team of professional inspectors to undertake challenge inspections.

The 1968 Nuclear Nonproliferation Treaty (NPT) also includes a method of monitoring "declared facilities" to verify that nuclear materials are not being diverted to produce weapons. The International Atomic Energy Agency (IAEA) implements an NPT Safeguards agreement by using a system of material accountancy and inspections to make sure that nuclear materials are not being removed from declared facilities (in this context, facilities involved in peaceful nuclear activity).

James J. Wirtz

Further Reading

Busch, Nathan E., and Joseph F. Pilat, *The Politics of Weapons Inspections: Assessing WMD Monitoring and Verification Regimes* (Stanford, CA: Stanford University Press, 2017).

Depleted Uranium (U-238)

Depleted Uranium (DU), or U-238, is a very hard, dense substance that is slightly radioactive. It is a by-product of the production of enriched fuel for nuclear reactors and weapons. In this process, many of the U-235 isotopes that are normally present in uranium are removed—thus "depleting" it—leaving behind a preponderance of U-238 isotopes.

In the process of manufacturing fuel for most nuclear reactors or the pits for nuclear weapons, the isotopic content of the uranium must be enriched in U-235 for these systems to function. At the end of the enrichment process, there are two products. One is the uranium enriched in U-235, ready for its intended nuclear applications. The other, referred to as "tails," is also known as *depleted uranium*.

Depleted uranium was originally viewed as simply a waste product from the enrichment process, but in the 1970s, uses for depleted uranium began to emerge, especially in armor and penetrating weapons for U.S. tanks. This application generated considerable controversy owing to popular speculation that depleted uranium is responsible for illnesses in people exposed to the residue. Although depleted uranium is considered chemically toxic, it is not considered a radiation hazard. Depleted uranium is about 40 percent less radioactive than natural uranium.

Depleted uranium's density makes it ideal for use in tank armor and antiarmor projectiles because its mass-to-size ratio means it carries great penetrating power. Depleted uranium is extremely dense: approximately 19.1 g/cm3 (1.7 times the density of lead). On impact, depleted uranium shears normal to the impact surface, creating a self-sharpening effect that greatly aids its penetration. Shearing makes it an ideal material in making antiarmor ammunition that relies on kinetic energy as its primary mechanism of destruction.

After passing through a target, DU rounds tend to burn up, creating tiny airborne particles of U-238. These particles can be inhaled and ingested and are not only chemically toxic but, because they can lodge in the body for many years and emit small quantities of both alpha and gamma radiation, can be radiologically toxic as well. U-238 dust has been suggested as one source of "Gulf War Syndrome," a series of mysterious illnesses that afflicted U.S. veterans of the First Gulf War. There is some debate, however, over the actual danger that DU represents. The U.S. military denies that it is especially hazardous and continues to use DU because it is an inexpensive and highly effective weapon. In fact, the Department of Energy maintains a stockpile of hundreds of thousands of metric tons of depleted uranium. Alternatives, such as tungsten, are expensive and not as effective.

Depleted uranium is also used in numerous commercial applications requiring dense material, such as stabilizers in planes and boats, counterweights, radiation shielding, and breeding blankets in fast breeder reactors for the creation of plutonium.

Additionally, depleted uranium is sometimes used in nuclear weapons. It serves as a tamping device in nuclear weapons because of its high density and neutron-scattering properties. When used in this manner, the depleted uranium's inertia holds the weapon together longer, allowing it to more thoroughly fission its fuel, thus increasing the yield of the weapon. Also, depleted uranium can undergo fission by fast neutrons. As a result, depleted uranium can be added to the exterior of a thermonuclear weapon to enhance its total yield. This process greatly increases both the amount of yield and the fallout from the weapon. The largest nuclear weapons ever built or tested are of this type.

Rod Thornton and C. Ross Schmidtlein

Further Reading

Bailey, M. R., A. W. Phipps, and Katie Davis, *The Hazards of Depleted Uranium Munitions, Parts 1 and 2* (London: Royal Society, May 2001 and March 2002).

Flounders, Sara, *Metal of Dishonor: Depleted Uranium* (New York: International Action Center, 1997).

Harley, N. H., E. C. Foulkes, L. H. Hilborne, A. Hudson, and C. R. Anthony, *Depleted Uranium*, National Defense Research Institute, vol. 7 (Santa Monica, CA: RAND Corporation, 1999).

Deterrence

Deterrence is the act of dissuading another state or party from undertaking a politically or militarily undesirable action, such as an attack or some sort of fait accompli, that it might otherwise carry out and can be achieved in any of three ways: (1) by implicitly or explicitly threatening to retaliate if the undesirable action is undertaken; (2) by providing a defense to deny an attacker's objectives; or (3) by offering a reward for not carrying out the undesired action.

Popular notions of deterrence mainly revolve around deterrence by threat of retaliation because the threat of a retaliatory nuclear strike became the primary way the United States underwrote its policy of deterrence during the Cold War. Deterrence by threat of retaliation seeks to convince a potential adversary that the benefits of his actions will be outweighed by the costs produced by a retaliatory strike. Deterrence by denial seeks to dissuade a potential adversary by convincing her that she will not be able to achieve her objectives and is a function of some combination of passive and active defenses. Deterrence by reward relies on inducing a potential adversary not to undertake an action by offering him a greater benefit for restraining his behavior.

The policy of détente, or seeking to integrate the Soviet Union more fully into world politics through trade and security enticements, used inducements to deter behavior deemed politically unacceptable by the U.S. government. Deterrence is at times confused with the notion of compellence. Compellence differs from deterrence in that it involves the use of threats to compel the target to take action it would not otherwise do, rather than persuading or dissuading it not to do something it would otherwise be inclined to do.

With the dawning of the nuclear age, deterrence assumed the status of a preeminent national security objective and strategy, supplanting traditional military objectives such as seizing and holding territory or militarily defeating the enemy. As military historian and strategic analyst Bernard Brodie noted in a seminal collection of essays published in 1946, "Thus far the chief purpose of our military establishment has been to win wars. From now on its chief military purpose must be to avert them. It can have almost no other useful purpose." With the advent of large nuclear arsenals, deterrence became the centerpiece of U.S. national security strategy and foreign policy. Deterrence is intended to maintain the peace; in the event that deterrent threats are executed, deterrence as a strategy has failed.

How Deterrence Works

Each of the three approaches to deterrence relies heavily on a rational decision-making process of evaluating costs versus benefits. Each assumes that the potential opponent will rationally choose not to undertake the forbidden action in exchange for avoiding the retaliation or the costs of surmounting a defense or accepting the proffered reward. But for this rational choice to be made, several conditions must obtain.

The deterrent threat (or reward) must be understood. Deterrence is fundamentally a process of communication. The nation making the deterrent threat must know what actions it wants to deter, who it wants to deter from undertaking those actions, and how to communicate that threat. The target of the deterrence strategy must recognize the deterrent threat and understand the costs and consequences of failing to be deterred. Obviously, lack of clear communication channels, differences in the interpretation of deterrent threats, misperceptions, miscommunications, and misunderstandings can all undermine deterrence.

The deterrent threat must also be credible. The credibility of a deterrent threat is a function of the deterring state's collective political will to carry out the deterrent threat (or provide the promised reward) and its perceived ability or capability to carry it out (or provide the reward). If a state threatens to retaliate with means that are not at its disposal, or to carry out retaliatory threats that it may itself not believe to be credible, the chance of deterrence failure increases.

Criticism of Deterrence

Deterrence as a theory, a strategy, and a policy has been the subject of considerable criticism. Much of this criticism is focused on retaliatory deterrence, however, rather than on deterrence that takes the form of denial or rewards. Critics focus on several points. Some suggest that deterrence relies too heavily on the assumption that the prospective opponent is a rational, unitary decision maker. Others note that those making deterrent threats need to set their priorities in advance and communicate threats to targets, two requirements that are difficult to achieve in practice. It is also difficult to design deterrence strategies that correspond to all options open to a potential adversary, creating wiggle room that can lead to small encroachments on the status quo or miscalculations that can lead to war. One might also suggest that deterrence works best when it is least needed. It is most necessary in a crisis, a time when rationality breaks down, communication becomes difficult, and perceptions become distorted.

Today "gray-zone" tactics—significant faits accomplis, incremental changes to the status quo, or minor military actions—are becoming commonplace as state and non-state actors attempt to achieve their objectives without triggering deterrent threats. So far, these activities have not triggered a major conflict, but challenging deterrent threats through gray-zone operations risks miscalculation and war.

Kerry Kartchner

Further Reading

Brodie, Bernard, ed., *The Absolute Weapon* (New York: Harcourt Brace, 1946).

George, Alexander L., and Richard Smoke, *Deterrence in American Foreign Policy: Theory and Practice* (New York: Columbia University Press, 1974).

Green, Philip, *Deadly Logic: The Theory of Nuclear Deterrence* (Columbus: Ohio State University Press, 1966).

Morgan, Patrick M., *Deterrence: A Conceptual Analysis*, 2nd ed. (Beverly Hills, CA: Sage, 1983).

Payne, Keith B., *Deterrence in the Second Nuclear Age* (Lexington: University of Kentucky Press, 1997).

Snyder, Glenn H., *Deterrence and Defense: Toward a Theory of National Security* (Princeton, NJ: Princeton University Press, 1961).

Deterrence and Defense Posture Review

In May 2012, the North Atlantic Treaty Organization (NATO) released a report titled "Deterrence and Defence Posture Review" (DDPR). The DDPR reiterated that NATO would remain a nuclear alliance, and that NATO's nuclear policy is based on NATO's 2010 Strategic Concept and this posture review. It further stated that the fundamental purpose of NATO's nuclear forces is deterrence; that deterrence, based on an appropriate mix of nuclear and conventional capabilities, remains a core element of NATO's overall strategy; that nuclear weapons are a core component of the alliance's overall capabilities for deterrence and defense (alongside conventional and missile defense forces); that NATO is committed to arms control, disarmament, and nonproliferation—but with the proviso that, as long as nuclear weapons exist, it will remain a nuclear alliance; and that the Nuclear Planning Group provides the forum for consultation on NATO's nuclear deterrence policies.

The DDPR did not institute major changes to NATO's existing nuclear sharing arrangements or deterrence policy. Instead, it called for a continuation of the status quo by retaining U.S.-based B-61 tactical nuclear weapons in Europe, to be delivered if necessary by an international strike package that would include dual-capable aircraft (DCA) carrying the warhead from at least one of the states in which nuclear weapons are stored.

There was apparently considerable debate within the alliance over the wording in the DDPR, as some member states wanted to take the opportunity to eliminate all remaining U.S. warheads in Europe, perhaps even changing NATO policy regarding nuclear first use. Nevertheless, after the changes in the European security situation that started in 2014, NATO reiterated its commitment to nuclear sharing and the DCA mission in strongly worded statements about nuclear deterrence in its July 2016 Warsaw Summit declaration.

Jeffrey A. Larsen

Further Reading

North Atlantic Treaty Organization, "Deterrence and Defence Posture Review," NATO Press Release 2012(063), May 20, 2012. https://www.nato.int/cps/en/natohq/official_texts_87597.htm. Accessed February 6, 2018.

Thränert, Oliver, "NATO's Deterrence and Defense Posture Review," *SWP Comments* 34 (November 2011). https://www.swp-berlin.org/fileadmin/contents/products/comments/2011C34_trt_ks.pdf. Accessed February 6, 2018.

Deuterium

Deuterium, also known as *heavy hydrogen*, is one of two stable isotopes of the element hydrogen. Deuterium makes up 0.015 percent of all hydrogen. Deuterium's additional mass occurs because its nucleus contains a neutron in addition to the single proton held by normal hydrogen. Deuterium has properties that are useful in both fission and fusion reactions. It is used in nuclear reactors, where it is combined with oxygen to form heavy water (D_2O). In thermonuclear weapons, deuterium is used in both the primary and secondary stages of the weapon.

German scientists first suggested the existence of a heavy isotope of hydrogen in 1919 to explain hydrogen's departure from an atomic weight of 1. In 1920, W. D. Harkins and E. Rutherford began to suspect that a new particle, the neutron, might exist, which could account for hydrogen's anomalous mass. In 1931, H. C. Urey, F. G. Brickwedde, and G. M. Murphy of the U.S. National Bureau of Standards conducted a search for a heavy hydrogen isotope through an evaporation experiment; they evaporated a large amount of liquid hydrogen to create a concentration of the heavy hydrogen in the remaining liquid. Subsequent analysis of the optical spectra showed spectral lines that indicated an isotope with a mass very near 2, indicating the presence of heavy hydrogen. The discoverers named this heavy isotope *deuterium*, from the Greek word *deuteros* (second).

In fission reactions, deuterium, in heavy water, is used to moderate (slow) neutrons for enhanced absorption of the neutrons in the fuel. This occurs because of deuterium's large scattering-to-absorption cross-section ratio. In fusion reactions, deuterium and tritium collisions have the highest probability of undergoing fusion at the temperatures that exist in most fusion systems and are thus the reaction of choice for most fusion applications. This applies to commercial and military applications of fusion reactions. In a nuclear weapon, deuterium is used in two systems within the weapon. In a nuclear weapon's primary stage, a small quantity of deuterium and tritium gas boosts the yield by accelerating fusion reactions. In the second stage of a thermonuclear weapon, deuterium with lithium in the form lithium-deuteride (LiD) produces a compact fusion energy source, adding greatly to the weapon's total yield.

Deuterium remains important for both fission and fusion nuclear systems. In particular, it is used in Canada Deuterium Uranium (CANDU) and Advanced CANDU reactors. Both magnetic and inertial confinement fusion systems will continue to use deuterium as a fuel. Additionally, deuterium will remain a key component in the primary and secondary stages of thermonuclear weapons.

C. Ross Schmidtlein

Further Reading

Lamarsh, J. R., and A. J. Baratta, *Introduction to Nuclear Engineering*, 3rd ed. (Upper Saddle River, NJ: Prentice-Hall, 2001).

Parrington, Josef R., Harold D. Knox, Susan L. Breneman, Edward M. Baum, and Frank Feiner, *Nuclides and Isotopes: Chart of the Nuclides*, 15th ed. (New York: General Electric and KAPL, 1996).

E

Enrichment

Enrichment is a process that turns natural uranium into a fissionable material. Naturally occurring uranium contains only 0.72 percent of U-235, the highly fissionable isotope, and the rest of the material consists of less fissionable isotopes. The fissile material must be separated from the rest of the uranium through a process called enrichment. Uranium enriched to 20 percent or more U-235 is called *highly enriched uranium* (HEU). Uranium enriched to less than 20 percent is called *low enriched uranium* (LEU).

The earliest successful enrichment methods were electromagnetic isotope separation (EMIS), which utilizes large magnets to separate ions of the two isotopes, and gaseous diffusion, where uranium hexafluoride (UF6) gas is passed through a porous barrier to separate the lighter molecules containing U-235. The first large-scale uranium-enrichment facility, the Y-12 plant at Oak Ridge, Tennessee, used EMIS in devices designated *calutrons*. The United States abandoned EMIS because of its high consumption of electricity, but it was adopted by the Iraqis before the First Gulf War.

More efficient enrichment methods were developed after World War II. Gas centrifuges, in which UF6 gas is whirled inside a complex rotor assembly and centrifugal forces push the molecules containing the heavier isotope to the outside, are the most common. Many stages are required to produce the highly enriched uranium needed for a nuclear weapon, but the gas centrifuge enrichment technique requires substantially less electricity than either of the older technologies. Atomic or molecular laser isotope separation is still under development. This process uses lasers to selectively excite atoms or molecules containing one isotope of uranium so that it can be extracted.

The South African nuclear program used an aerodynamic separation technique in an indigenously designed and built device called a *vortex tube*. In the vortex, a mixture of UF6 gas and hydrogen is injected tangentially into a tube that tapers into a small exit aperture at one or both ends, and centrifugal force causes the separation. The Becker Nozzle Process, another aerodynamic separation technique, was developed in West Germany. Aerodynamic enrichment processes require large amounts of electrical power and are not currently considered economically competitive.

Yellowcake

UF6 is used as the feedstock in the gas-centrifuge and gaseous-diffusion processes, and uranium tetrachloride (UCl4) is used as feed in the EMIS process. Uranium ore concentrates, known as *yellowcake*, typically contain 60–80 percent uranium. There are two commercial processes used to produce purified UF6 from yellowcake: the solvent extraction/fluorination (wet) process and the fluorination/fractionation (dry) process. In each case, chemical reactions are used to convert the yellowcake to a metal or powder for use in the gaseous-diffusion and gas-centrifuge processes.

Electromagnetic Isotope Separation

The EMIS process relies on the principle that a charged particle will follow a circular trajectory when passing through a uniform magnetic field. Two ions with the same kinetic energy and electrical charge but different masses (such as U-235 and U-238) will have different trajectories (the heavier U-238 ion has the larger diameter trajectory). Different trajectories allow for the separation of the two isotopes.

The initial U.S. EMIS process produced weapons-grade material from natural uranium in two stages. The first stage used natural or slightly enriched uranium as feed and enriched it to 12–20 percent U-235. The second stage used the product of the first stage as feed and further enriched it to weapons-grade uranium. To allow more efficient use of magnets and floor space, the individual stages were arranged in continuous oval or rectangular arrays (called *racetracks*, or simply *tracks*) with separator tanks alternated with electromagnetic units.

Thermal Diffusion

Thermal diffusion utilizes the transfer of heat across a thin liquid or gas to accomplish isotope separation. By cooling a vertical film on one side and heating it on the other side, the resultant convection currents will produce an upward flow along the hot surface and a downward flow along the cold surface. Under these conditions, the lighter U-235 gas molecules will diffuse toward the hot surface, and the heavier U-238 molecules will diffuse toward the cold surface. These two diffusive motions, combined with the convection currents, will cause the lighter U-235 molecules to concentrate at the top of the film and the heavier U-238 molecules to concentrate at the bottom of the film. The thermal-diffusion process is simple and inexpensive.

Gaseous Diffusion

The gaseous-diffusion process depends on the separation effect arising from the molecular flow of gas through small holes. Gas is forced through a series of porous membranes with microscopic openings. Lighter molecules are more likely to enter the barrier pores than heavier molecules. For UF6, the difference in velocities between molecules containing U-235 and U-238 is small (0.4 percent). Consequently, the amount of separation achieved by a single stage of gaseous diffusion is small.

The solid UF6 is heated to form a gas, and the gaseous-diffusion enrichment process begins. Because the U-235 is lighter, it moves through the barriers more easily.

Gas Centrifuge

In the gas-centrifuge uranium-enrichment process, gaseous UF6 is fed into a cylindrical rotor that spins at high speed inside a casing. When the flowing gas is rotated, enriched gas gathers at one end and depleted gas at the other end, facilitating separation of enriched from depleted atoms.

Aerodynamic Processes

Aerodynamic uranium-enrichment processes include the separation-nozzle process and the vortex tube–separation process. These aerodynamic separation processes depend on separation produced by pressure gradients, as does the gas-centrifuge method. Aerodynamic processes effectively act as nonrotating centrifuges. In this process, a mixture of gaseous UF6 is compressed and then directed along a curved wall at high velocity. The heavier U-238-bearing molecules move preferentially out to the wall relative to those containing U-235. At the end of the deflection, the gas jet is split by a knife edge into a light fraction and a heavy fraction, which are withdrawn separately.

Atomic Vapor Laser Isotope Separation

The atomic vapor laser isotope separation (AVLIS) process exploits the fact that U-235 and U-238 atoms absorb light at different frequencies (or colors). Although the absorption frequencies of these two isotopes differ only by a very small amount, the dye lasers used in AVLIS can be tuned so that only the U-235 atoms absorb the laser light. In the vaporizer, metallic uranium is melted and vaporized to form an atomic vapor stream. The vapor stream flows through the collector, where it is illuminated by the precisely tuned laser light.

Molecular Laser Isotope Separation

Molecular laser isotope separation (MLIS) is a two-step process. In the first step, UF6 is irradiated by an infrared laser system operating near the 16 mm wavelength, which selectively excites the U-235 atom, leaving the U-238 atoms relatively unexcited. In the second step, a laser system (infrared or ultraviolet) is required for conversion and separation.

Chemical and Ion Exchange

A chemical-exchange isotope segregates two forms of an element into separate streams. For heavy elements such as uranium, achieving a suitable separation factor involves contact between two valence (oxidation state) forms. The U-235 isotope exhibits a slight preference for the higher valence in the laboratory. Currently, no full-scale uranium-enrichment plants based on an exchange process are in operation.

Gilles Van Nederveen

Further Reading

Gardner, Gary T., *Nuclear Nonproliferation: A Primer* (Boulder, CO: Lynne Rienner, 1994).

Wilson, P. D., ed., *The Nuclear Fuel Cycle: From Ore to Wastes* (Oxford: Oxford University Press, 1996).

Extended Deterrence

Extended deterrence is the act of providing security for another state through the threat of punishment against a third party. For the North Atlantic Treaty Organization (NATO), the American guarantee of extended deterrence has provided the basis for security against aggressors, particularly the Soviet Union and Russia. During the Cold War, deterrence was often equated with nuclear weapons. Today, NATO and other U.S. allies around the world, such as Japan and South Korea, rely on continuing promises of deterrence based on America's nuclear arsenal as the ultimate guarantor of their security.

Deterrence (the prevention of action through fear of the consequences) involves a state of mind brought about by the existence of a credible threat of unacceptable counteraction. Extended deterrence is exercised by threatening action or reaction against a third party in an attempt to convince that party not to take some action. This reaction includes, in extreme circumstances, the actual use of military power. The aim of deterrence is to pose the prospect of failure or destruction to a potential attacker. Extended deterrence is simply a geographical extension of this concept.

The U.S. nuclear arsenal was designed and deployed in a manner that would provide credible security guarantees to allies. The United States extended deterrence by making it clear that it would, if necessary, use nuclear weapons in response to a Soviet nuclear or conventional attack on allies, especially in Europe and Japan. Although the United States, together with its NATO allies, sought to deploy a conventional force posture that could avoid an early resort to nuclear weapons, the alliance did not forgo the option of first use of nuclear weapons if needed. The extended deterrence concept (sometimes called *active deterrence* because it involves a clear decision and willful act on the part of the nation that owns the weapons and extends its deterrence) underscored the coupling between the United States and its allies. It existed in a strategic setting in which the United States extended an explicit security guarantee to its allies, backed by vast nuclear and conventional military capabilities and the forward deployment of hundreds of thousands of U.S. troops and their families in Europe and Asia. In a crisis, deterrence involved signaling the U.S. commitment to a particular country or an alliance and expressing national interest by enhancing warfighting capabilities in the theater. In short, extended nuclear deterrence gave the United States and its allies the confidence to stand toe to toe with potential adversaries and not blink.

History and Background: Europe

Nuclear weapons became an integral part of NATO strategy in 1954 when the United States, facing superior Soviet conventional forces in Europe, first threatened "massive retaliation" against the Soviet Union in the case of a Soviet attack against Western Europe. By so doing, the United States extended deterrence to its European allies against a Soviet attack and created what also was referred to as a "nuclear umbrella" sheltering Western Europe. America's nuclear guarantee was backed up by the deployment of some 250,000 U.S. troops and their families to Europe. This substantial U.S. presence in Europe served as a "tripwire" ensuring American vulnerability

to an attack against Western Europe, thereby providing the linkage to U.S. strategic nuclear forces.

By the early 1960s, the credibility of the massive retaliation threat was called into question when the Soviet Union achieved the ability to also hit U.S. cities with its nuclear weapons. Therefore, in 1967, the allies agreed to replace *massive retaliation* with *flexible response*, a doctrine designed to give NATO a variety of nuclear and conventional force responses to a Soviet attack. The discussion over whether to adopt flexible response drove France out of NATO's military arrangements in 1966.

According to early alliance documents, it was clear that both the United States and the European allies understood that the U.S. security commitment to Europe included nuclear protection against coercion or aggression. Much of NATO's history has been marked by debates over the meaning of this nuclear guarantee. During the Cold War, Europe's leaders reached consensus that a U.S. nuclear presence on the ground in their countries was a requirement for credible extended deterrence.

Nuclear weapons, particularly tactical or theater weapons, were the next logical step above conventional forces on the escalatory ladder of conflict and thereby provided a link—coupling—to the United States. To this purpose, nuclear weapons had to be flexible, survivable, have sufficient range, and have a doctrine for their use. Also, allied participation in planning and deterrence through threatened use, known as *nuclear sharing*, helped assuage potential desires for independent nuclear capabilities and made Washington's NATO allies feel a part of the shared risk and responsibilities.

The deployment of U.S. short- and medium-range missiles that could hit Soviet territory from locations in Western Europe was meant to convince the Soviet Union that a war in Europe could not be kept at the conventional level. Escalation would put Soviet territory at risk, too, thus raising the stakes for Russia. Unlike strategic forces, intermediate-range missiles would become vulnerable to preemptive attack early in a European war, potentially forcing the destabilizing decision to use these weapons early rather than risk losing them to capture or destruction.

A question arose regarding the ultimate political purpose of nuclear weapons in Europe: were they there to provide deterrence or to reassure America's allies? Obviously, they served both purposes. Coupling the United States to Europe created a condition where the integrity of the chain of escalation was complete, from conventional forces in Europe, to theater nuclear forces in theater, to the U.S. strategic nuclear force. This symbolized the social, political, and historical links between the two sides of the Atlantic. A challenge, however, resulted from the geographical separation of Europe and the United States and the uncertainty that separation engendered in the minds of European allies. This was one aspect of NATO's nuclear dilemma.

Europeans suspected and feared that the United States *could*, in the event of crisis or war, decouple itself from Europe's problems. Every move made by the alliance since the 1960s, as U.S. nuclear superiority ended, that involved nuclear forces or strategy reinvigorated this worry about the specter of decoupling.

This question revolved around the deliberately ambiguous strategy of flexible response. This strategy marginally satisfied both parties, but only because of its doctrinal ambiguity. Europeans focused on the response side of the equation (deterrence by punishment) and the seamless web of deterrence; the United States, in contrast, focused on flexibility and deterrence by denial (a warfighting approach).

If conflict were to break out in Europe, it was reasoned, the United States and Europe would have different responses. The United States would favor a limited war confined to the Continent, would want to prevent its spread to North America, and would want to keep it conventional as long as possible. This approach reflected its warfighting preference. Tactical nuclear weapons stationed (and, if necessary, used) in Europe would serve these warfighting strategies. Europeans, who did not want to see any type of war break out on their soil, preferred a policy of immediate, catastrophic, and automatic escalation to nuclear war at the highest possible level, thereby increasing the level of deterrence effect. They feared that if war broke out, it could be fought over their heads and that the American preference for smaller tactical weapons could be destabilizing.

Both points of view therefore called for European-based nuclear weapons in NATO's arsenal, though for different reasons. These weapons supported both types of deterrence—one directly, one indirectly. Neither perspective justified nuclear weapons in terms of reassurance, but they were reassuring nonetheless, especially in light of the transatlantic linkage argument, which Europeans stressed. Thus, a constituency arose on both sides of the Atlantic that wanted nuclear weapons in Europe. There was little change in the underlying rationale for more than 30 years, but then it disappeared for a generation when peace seemed to break out in Europe and Russia was considered a strategic partner. Since 2014, however, with renewed Russian belligerence, the concept of deterrence, and the need for extended deterrence, has returned to the forefront of NATO concerns. It is a sensitive topic, and the issues relating to it are normally kept out of the public eye.

Deterrence in Other Regions

Nuclear weapons did not ensure the end of war, but they did appear to limit the size of the conflicts that occurred underneath the nuclear umbrella. It is hard to say whether nuclear deterrence succeeded, as deterrence can only be assessed if it fails. But the lessons of Europe appeared compelling and were thought to be transferable elsewhere in the world.

America's extended nuclear deterrence to Japan and South Korea were overt (with nuclear weapons deployed in Korea until 1992). The United States also implied that it would defend Israel with nuclear weapons (until Israel developed its own nuclear forces). These guarantees were backed up by multiple regional alliances, including NATO, the Australia–New Zealand–U.S. alliance (ANZUS), the Southeast Asia Treaty Organization (SEATO), and the Central Asian Treaty Organization (CENTO).

The Future

American extended deterrence rests on a combination of conventional and nuclear retaliatory capabilities, active and passive defenses, and counterforce policies. This has included consistent allied declarations concerning NATO strategy and the continued importance of U.S. substrategic weapons deployed in Europe. The region that may most need America's extended deterrent today is East Asia. American allies in the region feel and fear the ripple effects of multiple simultaneous strategic changes: North Korea's continuing nuclear aspirations; China's growth into a regional hegemon with the potential for strategic military

capabilities that match its economic strength; instability in regional states; and the ongoing competition between India and Pakistan. All of this points to greater uncertainty and raises the specter of new threats to traditional U.S. allies, such as Japan, South Korea, and Taiwan. The strategic defense leg of the new U.S. strategic "Triad," rather than the offensive nuclear approach that NATO took in Europe, may be appropriate for these states.

All of these measures are based on one key assumption: that the United States retains its role as the leading great power in the world, with commensurate global responsibilities.

Jeffrey A. Larsen

Further Reading

Center for Nonproliferation Research National Defense University and Center for Global Security Research, *U.S. Nuclear Policy in the 21st Century: A Fresh Look at National Strategy and Requirements: Final Report* (Washington, D.C., and Lawrence, CA: National Defense University and Lawrence Livermore National Laboratory, July 1998).

Sloan, Stanley R., "NATO Nuclear Strategy beyond the Cold War," in *Controlling Non-Strategic Nuclear Weapons: Obstacles and Opportunities*, edited by Jeffrey A. Larsen and Kurt J. Klingenberger (Colorado Springs: USAF Institute for National Security Studies, July 2001, pp. 39–62).

Wilkening, Dean, and Kenneth Watman, *Nuclear Deterrence in a Regional Context* (Santa Monica, CA: RAND Corporation, 1995). Highlights from the book can be found in "Regional Deterrence: The Nuclear Dimension," available at http://www.rand.org/publications/RB/RB24/rb24.html.

Yost, David S., *The U.S. and Nuclear Deterrence in Europe*, Adelphi Paper 326, International Institute for Strategic Studies (New York: Oxford University Press, March 1999).

F

Fallout

The term *fallout* refers to radioactive particles created from the soil and debris irradiated by a nuclear detonation. This material is scooped up and carried into the mushroom cloud of the explosion, and the particles return to the earth's surface as fallout.

When the fireball from a nuclear detonation touches the earth's surface, it forms a crater. The earth from this crater is pulverized into microscopic radioactive particles by the force of the explosion. These particles are carried up into the distinctive mushroom-shaped cloud created by the detonation and eventually fall out of the cloud and return to the earth's surface. Each contaminated particle continuously emits radiation while in the mushroom cloud, while descending, and on the ground. There are two categories of fallout: early and delayed. Early fallout descends to earth within 24 hours after the explosion. Delayed fallout arrives after this 24-hour period.

The largest, heaviest fallout particles reach the ground first, landing in locations close to the explosion. The smaller particles could be carried by the wind for hundreds of miles before falling to earth. Some particles fall so slowly that they could remain airborne for weeks to years before reaching the ground. By that time, their dispersal and radioactive decay would make them much less dangerous. The radioactive particles that rise only a short distance (those in the "stem" of the mushroom cloud) fall back to earth within a matter of minutes and land close to ground zero (the focal point of the detonation). Such particles are unlikely to cause many deaths because they will fall into areas where most people have already been killed by other nuclear weapons effects. The radioactivity contained in this fallout, however, will complicate rescue and recovery operations. The particles that rise higher in the cloud will be carried some distance by the wind before returning to earth.

The area and intensity of the fallout is strongly influenced by local weather conditions. Much of the material is simply blown downwind, falling in a plume-shaped pattern on the ground. Rainfall can also influence the way fallout is deposited, as rain will carry contaminated particles to the ground. The areas receiving such contaminated rainfall become "hot spots," with greater radiation intensity than their surroundings.

A nuclear explosion creates four kinds of radiation: alpha, beta, gamma, and neutron. Gamma radiation is by far the most dangerous because its rays are more penetrating and harmful. The roentgen (R) is the unit most commonly used to measure gamma radiation. Most American civil defense instruments give readings in roentgens or roentgens per hour (R/hr). Until 1980, the U.S. military used the rad (radiation absorbed dose) as its unit of measurement. It now uses gray (Gy) for interoperability with the North Atlantic Treaty Organization (NATO).

The danger from fallout radiation lessens with time. The radioactive decay, as this lessening is called, is rapid at first and then becomes slower. The dose rate (the amount of radiation received per hour) decreases accordingly.

Jeffrey A. Adams

Further Reading

Adams, Jeffrey A., and Stephen Marquette, *First Responders Guide to Weapons of Mass Destruction (WMD)* (Alexandria, VA: American Society for Industrial Security (ASIS), February 2002).

Hanchett, J. G., F. W. Hasselberg, and M. H. Singh, *Glossary of Terms: Nuclear Power and Radiation* (Washington, D.C.: U.S. Nuclear Regulatory Commission, June 1981).

Headquarters, Department of the Army, *Treatment of Nuclear and Radiological Casualties*, U.S. Army Field Manual (FM) 4-02.283 (Washington, D.C.: Headquarters, Department of the Army, n.d.).

Fentanyl

The properties of opium poppy–derived medicaments had been known for many centuries, and morphine had already found use as an anesthetic agent by the late 1800s. But morphine also had a poor safety record. In a search for better options, the synthesis of meperidine in 1939 renewed interest in the use of opiates. But arguably the most important development was the synthesis of fentanyl (first patented by Paul Janssen in 1963), which remains among the more commonly used compounds for anesthesia.

Especially during the Cold War, a great deal of research was expended by the United States and the former Soviet Union on chemical substances that would temporarily incapacitate but not kill the enemy. For example, fentanyl was considered for U.S. special operations in Vietnam (1965–1975), but it was never adopted for use in warfare.

In October 1997, the Israeli Mossad (intelligence bureau) reportedly used fentanyl in an attempted snatch-and-grab operation. According to one account, Israeli intelligence operatives traveled to Jordan and followed Khalid Mishal, the leader of Hamas. The plan was to deliver fentanyl in a spray that would be absorbed through Mishal's ear, but he was eventually able to escape. He was reportedly affected by the drug, however, and required significant medical attention afterward.

Moscow Theater Attack

On October 23, 2002, during an evening performance at a Moscow music theater, about 50 Chechen terrorists seized the venue and the 800 people inside. Heavily armed with both firearms and explosives, the terrorists threatened to kill everyone inside unless Russia ended the war in Chechnya. Three days later, after negotiations had stalled, Russian special police units piped an unidentified gas inside the building. When Russian police finally stormed the theater, all the Chechen militants were immobilized, and they were ultimately shot to death. Sadly, 129 civilians also died from the effects of the gas. Previous Russian military writings have specifically mentioned carfentanil as a drug that could be aerosolized and quickly knock down the enemy, and it was suspected that Russia had used fentanyl or a closely related analog such as carfentanil to incapacitate the Chechen terrorists.

After the theater assault, chemists at the United Kingdom Defence Science and Technology Laboratory, Porton Down, obtained clothing and body fluid (blood, urine) samples from British nationals who were present during the Moscow theater siege. From their analysis, they found two fentanyl derivatives: carfentanil and remifentanil. Carfentanil is a more potent fentanyl analog and has been used as an animal tranquilizer. Porton Down concluded that a mixture of carfentanil and remifentanil was likely used in the Moscow incident, speculating that the less potent remifentanil was intended to reduce the toxicity of the dosage. But the authors also warned, "It is highly improbable that a chemical agent exists for which a dose can be calibrated in a tactical environment to incapacitate opponents reliably and without substantial mortality" (Riches et al., 2012).

Eric A. Croddy and Anthony Tu

Further Reading

Carpin, J., C. Whalley, and R. Mioduszewski, *The Evaluation of a Synthetic Opiate Aerosol in Inducing Narcotic Hypnosis in the Rat* (Aberdeen Proving Ground, MD: U.S. Army Chemical Research, Development, and Engineering Center, 1989).

Riches, James R., Robert W. Read, Robin M. Black, Nicholas J. Cooper, and Christopher M. Timperley, "Analysis of Clothing and Urine from Moscow Theatre Siege Casualties Reveals Carfentanil and Remifentanil Use," *Journal of Analytical Toxicology* 36, no. 9 (September 20, 2012): 647–656. https://academic.oup.com/jat/article/36/9/647/785132/Analysis-of-Clothing-and-Urine-from-Moscow-Theatre. Accessed June 15, 2017.

Fissile Material Cutoff Treaty

The purpose of a fissile material cutoff treaty (FMCT) is to ban the production of fissile material used in nuclear weapons. Proposals for an FMCT have been part of international arms control talks since the end of World War II. Almost all variations of FMCT proposals target the activities of nuclear weapons states.

An FMCT is generally considered a disarmament initiative because it would ban the production of fissile materials used in nuclear weapons, although there seems to be little interest in using the FMCT to eliminate existing fissile materials. An FMCT would not address previously produced stockpiles of fissile materials, nor would it apply to fissile materials not used for weapons systems, such as naval nuclear-propulsion systems.

Although there exists no internationally agreed-upon definition of *fissile material*, in the context of proposed negotiations on an FMCT, it usually refers to any fissionable material that could be used to create a nuclear explosion, that is, *weapons-grade* or *weapons-usable* material. This would include any isotope of plutonium, uranium 233, or uranium enriched to the point that it contains 20 percent or more of the isotope U-235. FMCT proponents generally agree that the proposed "fissile material" ban would not apply to other radioactive materials, nor would it apply to exotic materials such as tritium or americium. The International Atomic Energy Agency probably would be called upon to conduct verification activities to support an FMCT, although past U.S. administrations have generally objected to proposed intrusive measures to guarantee compliance with an FMCT.

There have been several proposals for an FMCT, but there is currently no negotiating text. Although the United Nations Conference on Disarmament (CD) established a mandate to negotiate an FMCT in March 1995, formal negotiations have made little progress. In 1998, the mandate for negotiations expired. In 2009, the CD agreed to establish a new FMCT negotiating committee, but a standoff quickly developed. Pakistan's representatives characterized a future FMCT as unequal, discriminatory, and directed specifically against Pakistan. The CD has made little progress in exploiting its most recent mandate.

Guy Roberts

Further Reading

Roberts, Guy, *This Arms Control Dog Won't Hunt: The Proposed Fissile Material Cut-Off Treaty at the Conference on Disarmament,* INSS Occasional Paper 36 (Colorado Springs: USAF Institute for National Security Studies, January 2001).

France

France has pursued its own nuclear weapons programs and policies since the early days of the nuclear age. The instability of the Fourth Republic after World War II and a shortage of financial resources slowed French nuclear research, which lagged behind Soviet and American weapons programs. However, France gradually developed its nuclear weapons infrastructure and delivery systems.

History and Background

In October 1945, General Charles de Gaulle, as president of the Provisional Government, set up the *Commissariat à l'Energie Atomique* (French Atomic Energy Commission) to undertake research related to the use of atomic energy in the fields of science, industry, and national defense. In late 1954, the French government launched a secret program to develop a nuclear weapon. In April 1958, a ministerial top-secret order was given to prepare for the first series of atomic tests, which were to take place in early 1960.

The French decision to acquire nuclear weapons was influenced by several factors. A nuclear arsenal was seen as a way to promote France's position as a great power and to reduce its reliance on the U.S. nuclear deterrent, thereby bolstering its diplomatic and military leverage with its allies and adversaries. Dismissing the North Atlantic Treaty Organization (NATO) concept of integrated forces, de Gaulle established an arsenal capable of acting on behalf of French interests. His aims for the *Force de Frappe* (Strike Force) were the restoration of French grandeur, the reunification of Europe under French leadership, and the subordination of West Germany to French leadership in Europe. Ultimately, a credible French nuclear arsenal would make possible an independent role for Europe in world affairs.

General de Gaulle continued to support the construction of an independent French nuclear arsenal throughout the 1960s. The *Force de Frappe* became a military priority for France.

In February 1960, the French program produced its first French nuclear device. When tested at Reggane, in the Algerian Sahara Desert, the plutonium fission device had a yield of about 65 kilotons. De Gaulle had rejected the moratorium on atmospheric testing proposed by the United States and the United Kingdom, and in a stand that outraged environmentalists worldwide, France refused to sign the Limited Test Ban Treaty banning atmospheric tests in 1963. Testing continued as weapons and test devices were mounted on barges or suspended from balloons at France's Pacific Testing Center in Polynesia. In August 1968, following delays in the uranium isotope-separation process under way at a nuclear complex in Pierre-latte, the French detonated their first fusion device.

General de Gaulle closely monitored the construction of France's emerging nuclear arsenal. In July 1960, the minister for the armed forces presented to Parliament a four-year plan to construct Mirage IV bombers and a nuclear-powered ballistic missile submarine (SSBN) and called for more research into thermonuclear weapons. The first Mirage IV squadron became operational in October 1964 as part of the new nuclear bomber force that now included Boeing C-135F air-to-air refueling aircraft sold to France by the U.S. government. The tankers greatly increased the range of the Mirage IV, thereby increasing the ability of the Mirage to penetrate Soviet airspace. Initially, the French military chose the Mirage IV bomber as its primary nuclear delivery system for the *Force de Frappe*. In 1967, the *Force de Frappe* became operational with 62 aircraft, each capable of delivering a 60-kiloton nuclear bomb.

To save time and money, de Gaulle incorporated U.S.-supplied enriched uranium in the development of the nuclear power plant for France's new submarine fleet. In the period 1966–1970, France financed the construction of two nuclear submarines and a squadron of strategic ballistic surface-to-surface missiles buried in silos on the Plateau d'Albion in Provence. Both forces became operational in 1971. In 1963, de Gaulle also decided that France, like the United States, should procure tactical nuclear weapons to be deployed on Mirage III and Jaguar aircraft and Pluton tactical nuclear missile launchers forward-deployed in West Germany.

Political Rationale for the
Force de Frappe

By 1967, expenditures on the nuclear arsenal had peaked at about 50 percent of France's defense capital expenditures. This proportion steadily decreased during the following years. De Gaulle's nuclear objectives were essentially political. The same considerations prompted him to refuse all proposals to cooperate with NATO in its nuclear war plans: he refused to have medium-range missiles installed on French soil, and he rejected French participation in a NATO multilateral nuclear force. In 1958, he also breached a secret protocol negotiated under the Fourth Republic to begin nuclear cooperation with the Germans and Italians.

However, the general's overriding focus on political ends did not mean that he took no interest in the strategy of deterrence as it applied to France: deterrence of the strong by the weak. What really counted for him was the determination of the "deciding party." He vested sole power to decide the use of France's nuclear arsenal in the Office of the President of the Republic. French doctrine reflects a concept of nonemployment, that is, there is no question of using nuclear weapons in conflicts that do not threaten vital interests. Contrary to the NATO doctrine of flexible response, French doctrine did not incorporate the threat of gradual nuclear escalation to back up conventional deterrence. French nuclear doctrine is instead motivated by the effort to guarantee that France can deter an adversary by inflicting damage that is out of proportion to any benefits that could be achieved by attacking France. The French posture was one of immediate and massive retaliation once French territory was threatened.

Of course, the credibility of the French nuclear deterrent was in the mind of the beholder, but after about 1969, doubts emerged about the ability to make good on these deterrent threats. The ability of the fixed-site ballistic missiles to escape destruction if the Soviets struck first was suspect, and the ability of the Mirage IV to penetrate Soviet air defenses was questionable. French planners recognized these shortcomings and worked diligently to deploy a submarine-based deterrent force. Financial constraints and difficulties in development resulted in delays. In 1971, the first nuclear-armed submarine, *Le Redoutable*, became operational.

During the Euro-missile debate of the early 1980s, French and British officials refused to include their nuclear forces in the superpower Intermediate-Range Nuclear Forces (INF) talks. In the aftermath of the Cold War, French nuclear doctrine began to adjust to new strategic realities. The Mirage IV was retired, the missile field in the Plateau d'Albion was dismantled, and France settled on a dyad of systems to deliver its 290 operationally available nuclear warheads.

Today, the French nuclear deterrent consists of four Triomphant-class SSBNs, 20 Mirage 2000, and 30 Rafale fighter-bombers. Plans also exist to upgrade both the warhead and missile carried by its submarine force.

Gilles Van Nederveen

Further Reading

Fieldhouse, Richard W., Robert Norris, and Andrew S. Burrows, *Nuclear Weapons Databook*, vol. 5, *British, French, and Chinese Nuclear Weapons* (Boulder, CO: Westview, 1994).

Gordon, Philip, "France and Virtual Nuclear Deterrence," in *Nuclear Weapons in a Transformed World*, edited by Michael J. Mazarr (New York: St. Martin's Press, 1997), 219–228.

Hopkins, John C., and Weixing Hu, *Strategic Views from the Second Tier: The Nuclear Weapons Policies of France, Britain, and China* (San Diego: Institute on Global Conflict and Cooperation, University of California, San Diego, 1994).

Norris, Robert S., and William M. Arkin, "NRDC Nuclear Notebook: French and British Nuclear Forces," *Bulletin of the Atomic Scientists* vol 56 issue 5 (September/October 2000): 69–71.

Yost, David, "Nuclear Debates in France," *Survival* vol 36 number 4 (Winter 1994–1995, pp. 113–139). https://www.tandfonline.com/doi/abs/10.1080/00396339408442766. Accessed May 11, 2018.

Fusion

Fusion is the process by which one heavier nucleus is produced from two lighter nuclei. According to Albert Einstein's special theory of relativity, mass and energy are convertible. In fusion, some of the mass of the two lighter nuclei is converted to energy. Fusion reactions power the sun and stars and are responsible for the enormous release of energy from a hydrogen bomb. The use of nuclear fusion reactions as a controlled source of energy is feasible, but there are significant engineering problems still to overcome.

The nucleus of an atom is held together by the strong force. This short-range attractive force acts as a sort of nuclear glue, counteracting the repulsive electrical force between positively charged protons. For fusion to occur, the two light nuclei must be brought into very close proximity. As each nucleus has a net positive charge, the nuclei must overcome a very strong repulsive force, the Coulomb barrier, before they can be brought close enough together to fuse. One way to overcome the Coulomb barrier is to raise the kinetic energy of the particles by increasing their temperature. A high density of light nuclei, along with a long confinement time, will ensure a high probability of collisions and the fusion rate necessary to produce useful amounts of energy. In stars, these conditions exist naturally. To harness fusion power in a reactor, scientists and engineers must recreate the conditions that exist in a star.

Owing to their availability and their interaction probability, the light elements of choice for producing usable energy in a fusion reactor are deuterium and tritium (D-T) in combination. Deuterium can be extracted from seawater, where 1 in 6,500 hydrogen atoms is deuterium. D_2O is known as *heavy water*. Tritium can be created from lithium, which is abundant in the earth's crust. Thus, the fuel for the fusion reaction is considered inexhaustible and accessible.

As the temperature of the D-T mix is raised, a gas-like mixture of electrons and ions, called a *plasma*, is established. The plasma must be heated to nearly 100 million degrees Celsius to give the D-T particles sufficient kinetic energy to overcome the Coulomb barrier. As the electrons and ions have electric charge, the plasma can, in principle, be confined by a magnetic field. The challenge is to confine the plasma in sufficient density long enough for the reactions to take place and for the energy to be extracted.

One method for containing the high-temperature plasma is through use of a magnetic field that is toroidal, or doughnut shaped. In the toroid, the plasma forms a continuous circuit, and the particles are forced to follow a path along the magnetic field lines. The Russian-designed *tokamak* (a toroidal confinement machine) has been the most successful confinement approach. No material can withstand the high temperatures of a fusion plasma. Fusion plasmas cool quickly, however, if they touch the wall of the vacuum chamber. The tokamak uses strong externally applied magnetic fields to contain the plasma and maintain separation from the chamber walls. Among many engineering challenges to be solved before controlled fusion reactions become commonplace is the development of materials that are resistant to high-energy particle bombardment, thermal stresses, and magnetic forces.

As a cost-effective way to further worldwide fusion research, and to demonstrate the essential technologies necessary for the eventual commercial production of fusion power, the international community began building the International Thermonuclear Experimental Reactor (ITER) in 2013 in southern France. The ITER is a power reactor–scale research project that is scheduled to begin deuterium-tritium fusion experiments in 2035.

Brian Moretti

Further Reading

Tipler, P. A., and R. A. Llewellyn, *Modern Physics*, 3rd ed. (New York: W. H. Freeman, 1999).

G

Gun-Type Devices

A gun-type device creates a supercritical mass of fissionable material, uranium 235 (U-235), to produce a nuclear explosion. In this device, conventional propellants or explosives drive a subcritical, fissionable projectile into a second subcritical, fissionable target to achieve a supercritical mass. The technique can also employ more than two subcritical masses that are brought together rapidly to achieve a supercritical mass.

The first nuclear weapon ever used in combat was the gun-type device "Little Boy," the bomb dropped by the United States on Hiroshima, Japan, on August 6, 1945. Its explosive yield was approximately 15,000 tons of TNT. The gun-assembly method of attaining a supercritical mass was considered to be so infallible and highly enriched uranium so valuable that the Little Boy designers chose not to test the bomb prior to its use. In fact, the Little Boy weapon used the entire U.S. stockpile of highly enriched uranium at the time of its construction.

Unlike the implosion technique for attaining a supercritical mass, the gun-assembly method is inefficient because it does not compress the fissionable material to achieve greater density. Although it was an inefficient way to achieve nuclear fission, the United States used the gun-assembly method to develop special-purpose weapons, such as penetration weapons for subsurface detonations and early tactical nuclear weapons, including artillery-fired atomic projectiles (AFAPs). Because of the simplicity of the design, the gun-type device has been used by other countries. It is the weapon design of choice for emerging nuclear weapons states.

History

After the discovery of fission in late 1938, there was much debate about the possibility of harnessing the energy of fission to make a nuclear weapon. Otto Frisch and Rudolf Peierls authored a memorandum in February 1940 that served as the impetus for the development of the gun-type device. In the Frisch-Peierls memorandum, the authors discuss the possibility of constructing a "super bomb" using a "critical size" of pure U-235. They describe how to keep two (or more) subcritical pieces of uranium apart to avoid the possibility of premature detonation due to stray neutrons. They also discuss providing a mechanism to bring the two parts together rapidly to achieve a nuclear explosion. Frisch and Peierls were living in the United Kingdom at the time, and they submitted their manuscript through Mark Oliphant, the director of the physics department at the University of Birmingham, to Henry Tizard, the chairman of a scientific committee devoted to the defense of the United Kingdom.

In April 1940, Tizard formed a separate group, known as the MAUD Committee, to discuss the possibility of building a nuclear weapon. The MAUD Committee's final report, composed before the group disbanded in July 1941, concluded that nuclear weapons were feasible and that the development of this type of weapon could result in decisive victory in World War II. It also provided technical details about the amount of uranium necessary, the expected yield, and the cost estimates to build a nuclear weapon.

Based on the findings of the MAUD Report, President Franklin D. Roosevelt decided to expand support for a U.S. program to develop nuclear weapons. After a slow start, the U.S. nuclear bomb project was consolidated in September 1942 into the Manhattan Project, which was led by Major General Leslie Groves and Professor J. Robert Oppenheimer. Groves and Oppenheimer created a laboratory at Los Alamos, New Mexico. As scientists arrived at Los Alamos, theoretical physicist Robert Serber gave a series of lectures designed to sum up the current knowledge of nuclear weapons design. As part of these lectures, Serber outlined the gun-assembly method of creating a supercritical mass of fissionable material through the use of a cylindrical projectile fired into a spherical target. These lectures were later published as the *Los Alamos Primer* (1992).

The original plan was to use the gun-assembly method to attain a supercritical mass for both uranium 235 and plutonium 239. The Los Alamos Ordnance Division under navy captain William Parsons was in charge of directing gun-type weapons research. Early research focused on developing a gun with a very high velocity, greater than 3,000 feet per second, to assemble a critical mass of plutonium. Plutonium has a high spontaneous fission rate, which means that a high muzzle velocity would be required to assemble a supercritical mass before the plutonium could predetonate, resulting in low or no nuclear yield.

In April 1944, Italian physicist and emigrant Emilio Segré, who was working on the Manhattan Project, measured the spontaneous fission rate of plutonium and found that it was much higher than previously thought owing to the existence of trace amounts of plutonium 240, which contaminated the plutonium. As a result, the plutonium gun-type weapon was abandoned, and the implosion technique would be used to achieve a supercritical mass for a plutonium-based weapon. A crash program to develop the implosion device required a complete reorganization of effort in the Manhattan Project.

In August 1944, navy commander A. Francis Birch was given the responsibility of completing the uranium gun-type weapon dubbed Little Boy. Birch completed testing of the Little Boy gun tube using natural uranium. By May 1945, the design and testing of the weapon were complete; the only component missing was the highly enriched uranium core. In July 1945, approximately 60 kilograms of highly enriched uranium was fabricated into both target and projectile, and the first gun-type weapon was ready for use.

After World War II, several designs of gun-type weapons were developed. The gun-type weapons Mark 8, 10, and 11 were developed as penetrating weapons to be used against armored, reinforced, or underground targets. The first AFAPs were the Mark 9 and Mark 19, which were 11-inch-diameter artillery shells. An 11-inch howitzer had to be designed and built to accommodate these new nuclear weapons, as the largest howitzer in the army at the time was only 8 inches in diameter. Another AFAP was the Mark 23, a 16-inch-diameter projectile designed for naval guns. By the mid-1950s, the Mark 33, a gun-type 8-inch

AFAP, had been designed and tested for the army's 8-inch howitzer.

Technical Details

Timing in a gun-type weapon, as with any nuclear weapon, is critical because it largely determines the amount of energy yield that can be achieved given a specific quantity of fissile material. Each generation of neutrons takes approximately 10 nanoseconds to generate once the supercritical chain reaction is started. The challenge is to create as many generations of neutrons as possible before the device explodes due to the heat and pressures produced by fission. To produce an appreciable yield, it is desirable to hold the supercritical chain reaction together for 50–100 generations, that is, 0.5–1 microsecond. Consequently, there are several basic components to a gun-type device that are necessary for its proper function, in addition to the subcritical fissionable target and projectile.

One basic component is a neutron initiator that must be present to provide a large amount of initial neutrons to generate the explosive chain reaction at the precise time that the mass becomes supercritical. In the case of Little Boy, this initiator consisted of polonium and beryllium. When crushed together, polonium emits a large amount of alpha particles that are energetic enough to separate neutrons from the beryllium. This provides the first generation of neutrons as the supercritical mass begins the explosive chain reaction.

The supercritical mass is usually a sphere. A sphere is used because it has the smallest surface area compared to all other solid shapes from which neutrons can escape. The more neutrons that are available to the supercritical mass, the more fissions will occur, and thereby, more energy will result. Another basic component of a gun-type device is the use of a reflector. A reflector is a metal shield that surrounds the spherical supercritical mass with the purpose of reflecting neutrons back into the core. The material for a reflector should have a high probability of scattering neutrons back into the core; that is, it requires a high scattering cross-section and a low absorption cross-section.

A *tamper* is a layer of heavy metal that surrounds the reflector and fissionable core to contain the core long enough to obtain an appreciable yield of energy. As the explosive chain reaction takes places, the heat and pressure of fission forces the fissionable material apart, thereby stopping the chain reaction. The tamper holds the supercritical mass together long enough to achieve the desired yield.

The Little Boy bomb, an example of early gun-type devices, weighed 8,900 pounds and was 126 inches long and 28 inches in diameter. The main sections of this bomb included the nose section, which contained the fissionable target; a 3-inch-diameter cannon barrel; and the breechblock of the cannon. A 6-inch-thick steel and tungsten carbide tamper weighing 5,000 pounds was in the nose section surrounding the fissionable target. The smooth-bore cannon barrel was 6 feet long, made of steel, and weighed about 1,000 pounds. A hole in the breechblock allowed for the projectile and propellant to be inserted. Later gun-type weapons were improvements to this first weapon in terms of efficiency, yield, size, and weight.

The low efficiency of the gun-type weapon was expected from the Little Boy explosion and illustrates one of the disadvantages of using this method to assemble a supercritical mass: it wastes highly enriched fissionable material. The amount of fissionable material necessary to make a gun-type weapon is two to three times the amount needed to make an implosion weapon. Another disadvantage to using the gun-assembly method is that it is based on a single point detonation device that is not safe in terms of accidental detonation. Implosion devices can be two or more points safe (that is, they can withstand explosive shocks in more than one direction without going supercritical). The timing of the initiator is another drawback to gun devices because the time at which the initiator functions cannot be controlled as precisely as in the implosion technique.

There are distinct advantages to the gun-type devices. The most important advantage is that the simplicity of the device increases its reliability. Early gun-type devices were also smaller and lighter than the implosion devices, making their delivery easier. Finally, as gun-type devices generally have a smaller diameter than implosion devices of the same yield, the gun-assembly method has been used to develop all U.S. weapons specifically designed for subsurface bursts.

Developing Technologies

Emerging nuclear states are more likely to develop nuclear weapons utilizing a gun-type device to create a supercritical mass than they are to develop implosion weapons because the design is simpler and can be developed without testing. Non-state actors, such as terrorist organizations, also may strive to develop gun-type devices for the same reasons. Technology is not a stumbling block in creating a gun-type device. What slows and complicates the construction of this type of weapon is the need for large quantities of highly enriched uranium to create a supercritical mass.

Don Gillich

Further Reading

Bernstein, Jeremy, *Nuclear Weapons: What You Need to Know* (New York: Cambridge University Press, 2008).

Cochran, Thomas B., William M. Arkin, and Milton M. Hoenig, "Chapter Two: Nuclear Weapons Primer," in *Nuclear Weapons Databook*, vol. 1, *U.S. Nuclear Forces and Capabilities* (Cambridge, MA: Ballinger, 1984), 22–36.

Rhodes, Richard, *The Making of the Atomic Bomb* (New York: Simon & Schuster, 1986).

Serber, Robert, *The Los Alamos Primer* (Berkeley: University of California Press, 1992).

H

Halabja Incident

The Iraqi use of chemical weapons on the northern Iraqi village of Halabja in 1988 illustrates the indiscriminate damage such weapons can inflict. On March 16, 1988, to eliminate segments of the Kurdish population that had become an irritant to Saddam Hussein, the Iraqi military launched a three-day artillery and air attack against the Kurdish town of Halabja in northern Iraq, then a town of about 80,000 people. In addition to the nerve agents tabun, sarin, soman, and VX, Iraq employed mustard agent in artillery and aerial munitions against civilian targets. This attack also had a secondary purpose: it was an experiment to study the effects of Iraqi chemical weapons using different nerve agents. Estimates place the number of dead in the immediate aftermath of the chemical attacks at approximately 5,000, with another 20,000 injured. Although Syria has recently used toxic agents against civilians (including sarin in 2013 and 2017), the assault on Halabja remains the largest chemical weapons attack against a civilian population.

The town of Halabja is situated approximately 15 miles west of the border with Iran. At the time, Halabja was home to roughly 8,000 Kurds. As was the case with most of Iraqi Kurdistan, the inhabitants of Halabja supported the Peshmerga. These Kurdish fighters were in a state of perpetual revolt against Saddam Hussein, and they used the town as a safe haven and sometimes as a base of operations for the insurgency against Saddam's Ba'ath regime. Whenever the tide

of battle turned and Iranian forces controlled the region, Halabja was used as a staging area for joint Iranian-Peshmerga operations against nearby Iraqi positions.

On the morning of March 16, 1988, following a successful joint attack between the Peshmerga and the Iranian military on Iraqi outposts surrounding the town, the Iranian Revolutionary Guard infiltrated and passed through Halabja. The town's residents assumed that an Iraqi retaliatory air strike was imminent due to the town's collusion with Iranian Revolutionary Guards, and they began to take cover in cellars and other underground shelters. Eyewitness accounts reported that at approximately 10:30 a.m. an Iraqi helicopter appeared over the horizon, snapping aerial photographs and taking video of the town. Approximately 30 minutes after the helicopter vacated the area, the Iraqi army began an artillery barrage on Halabja from a position in the nearby town of Sayid Sadiq. Shortly after the artillery bombardment began, Iraqi warplanes dropped what is believed to have been napalm near the northern area of the town.

After three hours, the pace of the opening barrage tapered off. As the explosions subsided, a different sound was heard. As one survivor noted, it was like "pieces of metal just dropping without exploding." These were the first of many chemical weapons canisters that were dropped by Iraqi aircraft and helicopters. Another helicopter soon returned to Halabja, this time dropping small pieces of paper. It was later understood that the Iraqis were attempting to assess the wind direction and speed for delivery of their chemical weapons.

Coinciding with the sound of falling metal, survivors described a strange odor filling the air, reminiscent of a cocktail of garbage, eggs, garlic, and apples. As the inhabitants of the town began to panic, they once again rushed to the perceived safety of their cellars and underground bunkers. Tragically, these makeshift shelters quickly filled with the deadly mixture of gases, killing everyone inside.

The chemical cloud engulfed the town, contaminating water, land, and air. Those who ran became disoriented and died in the streets as the wind blew the gas in all directions. Those who stayed behind in the shelters met similarly grisly fates, choked by the invisible fumes.

Each gas attack lasted approximately 45 minutes, with 15 minutes between each wave. The Iraqis made a total of 14 sorties, each using seven or eight warplanes. The attack ended the following day. Iranian forces returned and occupied the town shortly after the attack had subsided, evacuating many of the sick and wounded to hospitals in Tehran.

Iran utilized the event for propaganda purposes, stressing that the atrocity had been committed by Saddam's military. Western observers echoed the sentiment that this chemical attack constituted a crime against humanity. The incident at Halabja nearly led the Reagan administration to impose economic sanctions against Iraq, but it did not cut off all military assistance.

After the Second Gulf War, Ali Hassan al-Majid ("Chemical Ali"), an Iraqi general and cousin of Saddam Hussein, was captured in August 2003. Among many other atrocities, he was charged with having directed the chemical weapons attack on Halabja. An Iraqi court sentenced him to death, and he was hanged for his crimes on January 25, 2010.

Brian L'Italien

Further Reading

Dizaye, Kawa, "Case Report: Victims of the Long Term Effects of Chemical Weapons on Health in Kurdistan of Iraq," *Middle East Journal of Internal Medicine* 5, no. 4 (July 2012): 27–35.

Francona, Rick, *Ally to Adversary* (Annapolis, MD: Naval Institute, 1999), 24.

Hamza, Khidhir, *Saddam's Bombmaker* (New York: Scribner, 2000).

Half-Life

Half-life is the time in which half of the radioactive nuclei in a radioactive substance will disintegrate or decay. A specific rate of radioactive decay is characteristic of each radionuclide. It is the time required for the disintegration of one-half of the radioactive atoms present when measurement starts. It does not represent a fixed number of atoms that disintegrate, but a fraction of the total number of atoms that were present at the initial measurement.

Radioactive elements are unstable and can spontaneously decay, causing them to produce radiation. Half of the residue present in a radioactive substance will disintegrate in another equal period of time and decay into another form. When several half-lives of a radioactive substance occur, only a fraction of the original radionuclides remains. Half-lives can range from a few seconds to hundreds of years, depending on the type of radionuclide.

Laura Fontaine

Further Reading

Brodine, Virginia, *Radioactive Contamination* (New York: Harcourt Brace Jovanovich, 1975).

Hemorrhagic Fever Viruses

Infections with hemorrhagic fever viruses (HFVs) can damage the vascular system and are often (as their name implies) accompanied by uncontrollable bleeding. HFVs can also cause multisymptom syndromes, meaning that multiple organ systems in the body are affected. Based on numerous criteria, HFVs have been identified as biological agents that carry particularly serious risk if used as biological warfare (BW) agents against military personnel or civilian populations.

There are four distinct families of HFVs that have different clinical and epidemiological manifestations. The viruses vary in their transmission, but overall they can be transferred to humans through the bites of arthropods (ticks, mosquitoes); contact with hosts (often rodents) or their droppings; exposure to infected livestock; or sometimes person-to-person contact. With the exception of dengue, all HFVs can be transmitted as aerosols to laboratory animals. It is this feature that makes these viruses attractive as potential BW agents for state-level programs and perhaps terrorist organizations.

History and Background

The Centers for Disease Control and Prevention (CDC) has designated two of the families of HFVs (filoviruses and arenaviruses) as Category A biological agents, meaning that they pose the greatest potential for "adverse public health impact" to the United States. When evaluating the threat from potential disease agents, the U.S. Working Group on Civilian Biodefense also took into consideration previous attempts by the superpowers (including the United States and the former Soviet Union) to weaponize these agents.

State-run programs to research the weaponization of HFVs were known to have existed in the United States, in the former Soviet Union, and in similar programs reported in other states, including North Korea. The United States pursued research on Junin (responsible for Argentinean HF), Hantaan (responsible for Korean HF), Machupo (responsible for Bolivian HF), Lassa, yellow fever, dengue, and Rift Valley fever virus. (Rift Valley fever was tested by the United States as a potential weapon in field aerosol tests, but it was never weaponized.) These programs were discontinued in 1969 when offensive biological weapons research and development was halted by President Richard M. Nixon.

Despite having signed the 1972 Biological and Toxin Weapons Convention, the former Soviet Union continued its own BW program. As far as is known from open sources, Soviet BW scientists successfully weaponized Marburg hemorrhagic fever and conducted research into the weaponization of Ebola (which was less successful) as well as Machupo, Junin, Lassa, and yellow fever. Although research into biological weapons continued until 1992, it is not known whether further HFV research was continued by Russian military scientists.

VHFs are caused by four distinct viral families: *Filoviridae*, *Arenaviridae*, *Bunyaviridae*, and *Flaviviridae*. Marburg and Ebola are the only known members of the *Filoviridae* family thus far identified. The incubation time for Marburg and Ebola ranges from three days to three weeks following exposure.

Marburg virus was first detected in 1967 when laboratory workers in Marburg, Germany, and in Yugoslavia became infected after handling tissue from green monkeys shipped from Africa. Infected individuals can spread the virus through bodily fluids during and after illness, as observed by a transmission occurring through semen up to seven weeks after clinical recovery. There is currently no treatment or approved vaccine for this rare disease, which has a case fatality rate of 23–25 percent.

Ebola HF is one of the most virulent diseases known, with a fatality rate of 40–90 percent of all clinical cases. Ebola was first identified in 1976 outbreaks that occurred in Zaire (now the Democratic Republic of Congo) and Sudan. Two additional subtypes were later identified, Ebola-Reston and Ebola–Ivory Coast, with the former causing disease in primates (but not in humans). In addition to monkeys, bats are also known to be animal reservoirs for Ebola virus. The "patient zero" source case of the 2014–2015 Ebola outbreak in West Africa—which killed an estimated 11,000 people—was ultimately linked to a two-year-old boy in Guinea who had been infected by an Ebola virus–carrying bat in December 2013. Although it has never been directly demonstrated in human cases, airborne transmission of filoviruses like Ebola cannot be ruled out.

While there is still no approved vaccine for Ebola, a number of promising candidates were undergoing phase 2 trials (involving over 5,000 participants) in 2017.

Elizabeth Prescott and Eric A. Croddy

Further Reading

Carroll, Miles W., David A. Matthews, Julian A. Hiscox, et al., "Temporal and Spatial Analysis of the 2014–2015 Ebola Virus Outbreak in West Africa," *Nature* 524, no. 7563 (August 6, 2015): 97–101.

Wojda, Thomas R., et al., "The Ebola Outbreak of 2014–2015: From Coordinated Multilateral Action to Effective Disease Containment, Vaccine Development, and Beyond," *Journal of Global Infectious Diseases* 7, no. 4 (October–December 2015): 127–138.

Highly Enriched Uranium

Highly enriched uranium is a man-made substance used for atomic reactor fuel or nuclear weapons. In nature, uranium consists largely of two isotopes: U-235 and U-238. The production of energy in nuclear reactors results from the fission, or splitting, of the U-235 atoms, a process that releases energy in the form of heat. U-235 is the main fissile isotope of uranium. U-235 and U-238 are chemically identical but differ in their physical properties, particularly their mass. The difference in mass between U-235 and U-238 allows the isotopes to be separated and makes it possible to increase, or enrich, the percentage of U-235. All currently used enrichment processes directly or indirectly make use of this small mass difference. Mined uranium has 0.7 percent U-235. Most power reactors use 3–5 percent enriched uranium, and weapons require 90 percent enriched uranium. U-238 that has extremely low levels of U-235 is known as *depleted uranium* and is considerably less radioactive than even natural uranium.

Enrichment Processes

Although a number of enrichment processes exist, only two, the gaseous-diffusion process and the centrifuge process, are operating commercially. In both of these processes, uranium hexafluoride (UF6) is used as the feed material. Molecules of UF6 with U-235 atoms are about 1 percent lighter than the rest of the feed material, and this difference in mass is the basis of both processes. The gaseous-diffusion process involves forcing uranium hexafluoride gas under pressure through a series of porous membranes. As U-235 molecules are lighter than the U-238 molecules, they move faster and have a slightly better chance of passing through the pores in the membrane. The

UF6 that diffuses through the membrane is thus slightly enriched, and the gas that did not pass through is depleted in U-235 atoms. The process is repeated many times in a series of diffusion stages called a *cascade*. Each stage uses a compressor, a diffuser, and a heat exchanger to remove the heat caused by compression of the gas. The enriched product is withdrawn from one end of the cascade, and the depleted gas is removed at the other end. The gas must be processed through some 1,400 stages to obtain a product with a concentration of 3–4 percent U-235. Existing gaseous-diffusion plants are nearing the end of their design life and are being replaced by centrifuge enrichment technology.

The centrifuge process uses UF6 gas as its feed and makes use of the slight difference in mass between U-235 and U-238. The gas is fed into a series of vacuum tubes, each containing a rotor 1–2 meters long and 15–20 centimeters in diameter. When the rotors are spun rapidly, at 50,000 to 70,000 revolutions per minute (rpm), the heavier molecules with U-238 increase in concentration toward the cylinder's outer edge. There is a corresponding increase in the concentration of U-235 molecules near the center. The enriched gas forms part of the feed for the next stages, and the depleted UF6 gas goes back to the previous stage. Eventually, enriched and depleted uranium are drawn from the cascade at the desired levels of purity. Centrifuge stages normally consist of a large number of centrifuges in parallel. Such stages are then arranged in cascade similarly to those for diffusion. In the centrifuge process, however, the number of stages may only be 10 to 20, compared to 1,000 or more for diffusion.

Use of HEU in Weapons

Uranium gun-assembly weapons are the easiest of all nuclear devices to design and build. It is generally considered impossible to prevent any nation that has the requisite amount of HEU from building a gun-type weapon. The Little Boy bomb dropped on Hiroshima on August 6, 1945, was a uranium bomb. The United States halted HEU production in 1992.

Gilles Van Nederveen

Further Reading

Schaper, Annette, *Highly Enriched Uranium, a Dangerous Substance That Should Be Eliminated*, PRIF Report No. 124 (Frankfurt, Germany: Peace Research Institute Frankfurt, 2013).

Hiroshima

Hiroshima is a major port city in western Honshu, Japan, on the Inland Sea, that was destroyed at the end of World War II by an atomic bomb. Historically a military center, it was the site of a major castle from the shogunate and later of the headquarters for several army elements, including the Second General Army, which was responsible for the defense of the home islands. During World War II, it had a population of about 380,000, which was reduced by evacuations to 255,000. Manufacturing and storage facilities for military materiel were located in Hiroshima, and it was a point of embarkation for troops moving to the South Pacific.

By the summer of 1945, Japan was clearly defeated. The only remaining question was how the emperor's household was going to allow the war to end. Nevertheless, Japanese forces continued to stage a determined defense: the U.S. conquest of Okinawa had cost 49,151 American casualties. The Japanese lost 110,000 men, 7,800 aircraft (1,465 in kamikaze attacks), and 16 ships. The

Japanese civilians had been taught to defend the home islands to the death, so based on the costs of Okinawa, American military planners estimated that a ground invasion to secure surrender could cost 1 million American lives as well as millions of lives of Japanese civilians. The firebombing of Tokyo had already resulted in 125,000 civilian deaths in one night, with no offer of surrender forthcoming from the Japanese.

During the war, U.S. scientists and engineers working on the Manhattan Project had developed and produced three atomic bombs. One was used in the first test at the Trinity Site, and the other two were ready for use in July 1945. Desiring to bring the war to an end without additional American casualties, President Harry S. Truman authorized the use of an atomic bomb against Hiroshima.

The bomb dropped on Hiroshima was "Little Boy," a gun-assembly weapon designed at Los Alamos, New Mexico, with an explosive uranium 235 core using material extracted at the Oak Ridge National Laboratory, Tennessee. A B-29 bomber, the *Enola Gay*, piloted by Colonel Paul W. Tibbets, carried the bomb. It was dropped at 8:15 a.m. on August 6, 1945, on central Hiroshima. The bomb detonated at 2,000 feet, with a force of 12–18 kilotons. Four and three-quarters square miles of the city were completely destroyed by the blast and resulting firestorm. Two-thirds of the buildings within 10 square miles surrounding the detonation were destroyed, including 26 percent of the production facilities in the city. The memorial cenotaph in the city's museum acknowledges that 61,443 people were victims of the bomb, but the United States estimated 71,379 known dead, with almost 70,000 additional people injured. Radiation sickness among the civilian population overwhelmed the surviving medical services. International medical aid did not arrive until September 1945, too late for many of the severe burn victims who needed hydration and supportive therapy.

Ground Zero in Hiroshima is a memorial park that includes the "Atomic Dome," a building preserved in its postbomb state, and other memorials as well as a large museum that describes the bombing from the Japanese perspective. The museum does not include documentation of the events leading to the bombing, information about atrocities committed by the Japanese military during the war, or any acknowledgment of Japan's role in the instigation of the Pacific War. The city of Hiroshima has been rebuilt as a thriving commercial area with a major port.

Frannie Edwards

Further Reading

Sherwin, Martin J., *A World Destroyed: Hiroshima and Its Legacies*, 3rd ed. (Palo Alto, CA: Stanford University Press, 2003).

Hydrogen Bomb

The hydrogen bomb, also known as the H-bomb, the fusion bomb, and the thermonuclear bomb, is based on nuclear fusion, where light nuclei of hydrogen or helium atoms combine together into heavier elements and release large amounts of energy.

On September 23, 1949, President Harry S. Truman announced that the Soviet Union had tested its first atomic bomb. The announcement caused panic in the country and created a flurry of activity in scientific and political circles. On January 31, 1950, in response to the news of the Soviet test, President Truman announced that the United States would undertake a program to develop a hydrogen bomb.

Physicist Edward Teller, mathematician Stanislaw Ulam, and other scientists spent more than a year of research in Los Alamos, New Mexico, solving technical problems involved in producing a hydrogen bomb. On November 1, 1952, the first hydrogen device was detonated at the Enewetak Atoll with an explosive power of 10.4 million tons (megatons) of TNT. It caused an island to disappear and created in its place a crater a mile wide and 175 feet deep. The device was weaponized (turned into a deliverable bomb) and successfully tested in 1954.

The Soviet Union tested its first true fusion bomb on November 22, 1955—a 1.6-megaton device designed by Andrei Sakharov. On October 31, 1961, the Soviet Union detonated a device at its range on the Arctic Ocean island of Novaya Zemyla; it turned out to be history's largest nuclear explosion, the Tsar Bomba, with a yield of 58 megatons.

On May 15, 1957, the United Kingdom successfully detonated a fusion device at Christmas Island with a yield of 200–300 kilotons. In September of that year, it detonated a hydrogen bomb with a yield of 1.8 megatons.

China next entered the hydrogen bomb club on June 17, 1967, when it tested a bomb with a yield of 3.3 megatons that was designed and manufactured with little assistance from the Soviet Union.

France tested its first hydrogen bomb at the Fangataufa Atoll on August 24, 1968. It had a yield of 2.6 megatons. Other nations, such as India, Israel, and Pakistan, have either tested fusion devices or claim to have the capability to produce them.

In September 2017, North Korea conducted an underground nuclear test with a yield probably in excess of 100kt. Although the device probably was not a fusion weapon, it could have involved a "boosted" fission device, whereby hydrogen isotopes are injected into the fissile to accelerate a fission reaction.

The hydrogen bomb is based on the tremendous power of nuclear fusion—the collision of neutrons with the nucleus of an unstable isotope of hydrogen, either deuterium or tritium, under high temperatures. The reason for the power of fusion is originally found in Albert Einstein's famous equation, $E = mc^2$, in which mass and energy are directly related and, under the right conditions, interchangeable. By combining two atoms into one, when the product weighs less than its original components, the excess weight is translated into a tremendous amount of energy.

The hydrogen bomb explosion is actually a chain reaction triggered by a normal fission bomb that produces temperatures and pressure within the thermonuclear device that allow for nuclear fusion. A modern hydrogen bomb has at its center an atomic bomb surrounded by a layer of lithium deuteride (the isotope of hydrogen with a mass number of 2). This is surrounded by a thick outer layer known as the *tamper*, which is often composed of fissionable material and functions to hold the contents together to contain the pressure and heat long enough to obtain a larger explosion. Neutrons from the atomic explosion cause the lithium to fission into helium and tritium (the isotope of hydrogen with mass number 3), producing a tremendous amount of energy. The initial atomic explosion also supplies the heat required for fusion, raising temperatures within the thermonuclear device to as high as 400 million degrees Celsius. Enough neutrons are produced in the fusion reactions to produce further fission in the core and to initiate fission in the tamper.

Like other large nuclear explosions, the hydrogen bomb creates an extremely hot zone near the blast site. Because of the high temperature, nearly all of the matter near the blast site is vaporized. The high pressure generated by such a large blast progresses away from the center of the explosion as a shock wave. It is this wave, containing most of the energy released, that is responsible for most of the destructive kinetic effects of a nuclear explosion. The details of shock-wave propagation and its effects vary depending on whether the burst is in the air, underwater, or underground.

Like other large nuclear blasts, hydrogen bomb blasts can scatter a large amount of radioactive fallout, especially if the nuclear fireball comes in contact with the ground. Even low concentrations of radiation can be lethal, causing death and illness for years after the blast.

Abe Denmark

Further Reading

Rhodes, Richard, *Dark Sun: The Making of the Hydrogen Bomb* (New York: Simon & Schuster, 1996).

Implosion Devices

An implosion device is a nuclear weapon that relies on a spherical compression of fissile material to achieve critical mass. It is more sophisticated and efficient than the gun-type compression system. It was first designed, built, and tested by the Manhattan Project, the World War II program that constructed the first nuclear weapons.

History and Background

During the initial phase of the Manhattan Project, two designs were proposed. One was the gun-type device, which was attractive because of its simplicity, ease of construction and operation, and high reliability. The second design, the implosion device, was also attractive because it offered a more elegant solution to producing nuclear fission and did not require highly enriched uranium, which was very difficult to produce. Using a similar amount of fissile material, an implosion device will produce a far greater explosive yield than a gun device. Serious material and engineering hurdles had to be overcome, however, before an implosion device became a reality. The implosion device required extensive testing using explosives, detonators, triggering mechanisms, and timers to arrive at a design that would work. Therefore, both gun and implosion designs were developed by the Manhattan Project: the gun-type device would be immediately available for wartime use, and the implosion device would be developed to create the next generation of more sophisticated and powerful nuclear weapons.

In the summer of 1944, a new impetus emerged for the development of the implosion device with the discovery that nuclear reactors created an isotopic impurity, plutonium 240, which could not be used in gun-type assemblies. All the plutonium for atomic bombs would have to be made in reactors, so the only way to make use of the plutonium coming from the Hanford, Washington, production reactors built by DuPont was to find a way to perfect implosion.

The Los Alamos National Laboratory organized Division GX (for "gadget explosive") to develop the nuclear and high-explosive components of the implosion device. Dr. Robert Oppenheimer, head of the Manhattan Engineering Project, created the Trinity Project in September 1944. A design team at Los Alamos National Laboratory, New Mexico, arrived at a functional design far ahead of schedule. As a result, the implosion device was constructed simultaneously with the gun-type device. On July 16, 1945, the Trinity implosion device was detonated at the Alamogordo Bombing Range in New Mexico.

The theoretical expectations about the greater efficiency of the implosion device were confirmed by use of both types of weapon in combat. "Little Boy," the gun-type device dropped on Hiroshima, had an estimate yield of approximately 15 kilotons. "Fat Man," the implosion device dropped on Nagasaki, had a yield of approximately 20 kilotons.

Technical Details

The fission implosion device consists of arming and power mechanisms and the physics package (known as the "pit"). The core is usually plutonium 239, with a beryllium casing wrapped with an explosive material. The high-explosive shell is lined by detonators at a predetermined spacing to produce uniform compression of the fissile material and ensure complete, instantaneous detonation. When the explosive is detonated, an inwardly directed implosion wave is produced, uniformly crushing and tamping the fissionable material. The decreased surface volume, plus the increased density, makes the mass supercritical.

In a hydrogen (thermonuclear or fusion) implosion device, the process of creating a nuclear explosion contains several additional steps. The pit must include a neutron source, usually tritium gas. This is surrounded by plutonium 239 (Pu-239), then uranium 235 (U-235), a vacuum, uranium 238 (U-238), a beryllium casing, and an explosive casing. The nuclear explosion depends on fission to release the binding energy in certain nuclei, which is rapid and violent. The fissile materials, such as plutonium and uranium, can be split into two roughly equal-mass fragments when a neutron is forced into them. A self-sustaining chain reaction occurs.

The minimum mass of fissile material for a nuclear chain reaction is called a critical mass. The amount of material needed to create a critical mass depends on the material used as well as on the surrounding material, known as a reflector or tamper. This surrounding material reflects the escaping neutrons back into the critical mass. Until 1994, the Department of Energy stated that 8 kg of plutonium would be needed to make a small nuclear weapon, but later experiments proved that 4 kg would be sufficient. Some scientists believe that 1 kg of plutonium would be adequate in modern designs to create a critical mass.

A second type of hydrogen implosion device, the Teller-Ulam fusion bomb, uses thermal radiation. This type of bomb was created in 1953 at a time when tritium gas was difficult to obtain and store. A fission implosion device is used as the triggering mechanism to release thermal radiation in the form of soft X-rays. The X-rays are directed into the pit, setting off a secondary stage that leads to fusion reaction. The bomb casing includes an implosion fission bomb and a cylinder casing (tamper) of U-238. Within the tamper are lithium deuteride (fuel) and a hollow rod of Pu-239. A shield of U-238 and plastic foam fills the spaces in the bomb casing. When the fission bomb explodes, it gives off X-rays and exerts pressure against the lithium deuterate, causing it to compress thirtyfold and initiate fission in the plutonium rod. The neutrons released in this process go into the lithium deuterate to make tritium, yielding fusion reactions that result in a fusion explosion.

Although implosive devices are fairly simple to design, building one is quite difficult, making them an unlikely initial path for emerging nuclear weapons states. The machining tolerances necessary for the casing, the layering of explosive material, the positions of the detonators, and the design of the triggering mechanism for the detonators are extremely demanding. The manufacture and assembly of a nuclear bomb would require a large organization's financial backing to develop the tools and expertise required. Although basic implosion designs are now the stuff of high school physics, individuals or small terrorist cells continue to lack the ability to manufacture a nuclear weapon that utilizes implosion to create a fission reaction.

Some nations that have developed nuclear weapons, such as South Africa and Pakistan, have only developed gun-type devices. North Korea could easily possess a gun-type device. The United States, Russia, Britain, France, India, and China possess implosion devices.

Dan Goodrich

Further Reading

Brown, Richard K., "Nuclear Weapons Diagrams." http://nuclearweaponarchive.org/Library/Brown/index.html. Accessed October 1, 2003.

Harris, William, Craig C. Freudenrich, and John Fuller, "How Nuclear Bombs Work," HowStuffWorks. http://science/howstuffworks.com/nuclear-bomb.htm.Accessed October 1, 2003.

Mello, Greg, "New Bomb No Mission," *Bulletin of the Atomic Scientists* 53, no. 3 (May/June 1997): 28–32.

Norris, Robert S., "Nuclear Notebook," *Bulletin of the Atomic Scientists* 59, no. 1 (January/February 2003): 74–76.

India

Chemical Weapons

India's first contact with chemical warfare (CW) in the modern era probably began in 1920 with the founding of the Chemical Defence Research Establishment (CDRE) in Rawalpindi. Much of this work in CW was prompted by a requirement for civilian defense and by the need to determine the effects of mustard and other CW agents in warm climates. Mustard agent was apparently brought into India to deal with anticolonial rebels in the northwest, and Winston Churchill called for its use against "uncivilized tribes." Nevertheless, it was only approved for in-kind retaliation.

By the 1930s, chemical weapons–related research under the CDRE involved testing of live chemical agents, specifically mustard, on both British citizens and Indian colonials. Efforts were made to determine differences of its effects among those of various skin colors: for example, Punjabi, Muslamans, Ghurkas, Pathans, Dogras, and Sikh.

Following World War II and Indian independence (1947), little was known about India's offensive CW capability until 1997, when it declared to the Organization for the Prohibition of Chemical Weapons (OPCW) that it possessed chemical weapons. Precursors—chemicals that could be used to make CW agents, such as sulfur mustard—were also declared by India, including chloroethanol. Subsequent to signing on as a state party to the Chemical Weapons Convention (CWC), India was obligated to destroy its entire chemical stockpile, completing the destruction of 1,044 tons of sulfur mustard agent in 2009.

Biological Weapons

India ratified the Biological and Toxin Weapons Convention in 1974. Despite some open-source reports suggesting that India possesses biological weapons, none of these allegations can be confirmed.

During the Indo-Pakistan War in 1965, Indian intelligence agencies became suspicious when they detected an outbreak of scrub typhus in northeast India (caused by the organism *Orientia tsutsugamushi*). Although these cases of scrub typhus occurred during the Indo-Pakistan War, they were undoubtedly a natural consequence produced by the disruption of sanitary measures. Similarly, in 1994, an outbreak of plague in Surat was deemed suspicious. Some Indian security specialists believed that outside actors—perhaps terrorists—may have been responsible for the plague outbreak. Nevertheless, there is no evidence to support such a claim, and it is nearly certain that the Surat plague outbreak was due to natural causes.

There were also unfounded rumors of bioterrorism during the dengue outbreak in 1996 in Delhi. Molecular studies of isolates from this epidemic showed an especially virulent type of the disease, and the director of the Indian Veterinary Research Institute was not willing to rule out a foreign point of origin. This case, however, was also most likely a natural outbreak of dengue.

Like many countries, India conducts research into defenses against biological warfare (BW). Military-related research into possible biological weapon threats is conducted at India's Defense Research and Development Establishment at Gwalior. There is no evidence from open sources, however, that India has ever pursued an offensive BW program.

Nuclear Weapons

In 1964, Indian prime minister Lal Bahadur Shastri promoted research and development into what was called a "Subterranean Nuclear Explosion for Peaceful Purposes." India detonated its first atomic device 10 years later, on May 18, 1974, using fissile material derived from a Canada Deuterium Uranium (CANDU) reactor. Although India had previously claimed its atomic forays were solely for peaceful nuclear purposes, in May 1998—after testing five nuclear devices—India formally declared itself a nuclear weapons state. India is not a member of the Nuclear Nonproliferation Treaty (NPT) of 1968, however, and refuses to join, claiming that the NPT is a discriminatory regime. Over the last 15 years, estimates of the size of India's nuclear arsenal

have stood at about 100 nuclear warheads, although most observers agree that India has enough plutonium on hand to double that arsenal.

In establishing its nuclear command and control organization, India promulgated its own nuclear doctrine in 1999, claiming its policy was "no first use" and that its nuclear forces were intended to provide only a "credible minimum deterrent." The Indian government also claims that it has nuclear devices possessing the capability of low yields to 200 kilotons involving fission, boosted-fission, and two-stage thermonuclear designs. India's nuclear delivery systems were initially composed of fighter-bombers (today about 50 aircraft capable of delivering about 50 weapons). In 2003, India began to deploy land-based ballistic missiles, capable of delivering approximately 50 additional warheads. The Indian Navy also possesses a nascent submarine-based ballistic missile capability and has conducted tests with ship-based missile systems that are apparently capable of delivering a nuclear weapon.

Claudine McCarthy, Eric A. Croddy, and Jolie Wood

Further Reading

Grayzel, Susan M., "Protecting Which Spaces and Bodies? Civil Defence, the British Empire and the Second World War," in *An Imperial World at War: Aspects of the British Empire's War Experience, 1939–45*, edited by Ashley Jackson, Yasmin Khan, and Gajendra Singh (New York: Routledge, 2017), 66–83.

Kristensen, Hans M., and Robert S. Norris, "Indian Nuclear Forces, 2017," *Bulletin of the Atomic Scientists* 73, no. 4 (2017): 205–209.

Sharma, Rohit, "India Wakes Up to Threat of Bioterrorism," *British Medical Journal* 323, no. 7315 (September 29, 2001): 714.

Intermediate-Range Nuclear Forces Treaty

The Treaty Between the United States of America and the Union of Soviet Socialist Republics on the Elimination of Their Intermediate-Range and Shorter-Range Missiles—better known as the Intermediate-Range Nuclear Forces (INF) Treaty—was the first arms control agreement to eliminate an entire class of weapon systems (that is, all U.S. and Soviet intermediate-range and shorter-range ballistic and cruise missiles with a range of 500–5,500 kilometers). It was signed in Washington, D.C., on December 8, 1987, by President Ronald Reagan and General Secretary Mikhail Gorbachev. The treaty entered into force the following year and called for all prohibited items to be eliminated within three years. It also provided for an on-site inspection regime that not only promoted confidence on compliance with the treaty provisions but also served as the model for on-site inspections for subsequent arms control agreements. Additionally, the INF Treaty incorporated asymmetric reductions. The Soviet Union was forced to eliminate significantly more weapon systems than the United States. The INF Treaty includes the basic treaty, a memorandum of understanding, two protocols, and an annex.

Several U.S. missile systems were eliminated by the INF Treaty: the intermediate-range Pershing II ballistic missile, the BGM-109G cruise missile, and the shorter-range Pershing IA, which was not deployed at the time of the treaty signing). In addition, the Pershing IB missile, which had been tested but not deployed, was also banned. The treaty also called for the destruction of the Pershing II launcher and launch pad shelter, the BGM-109G cruise missile launch canister and launcher, and the Pershing IA launcher.

The Soviet systems covered by the treaty included the intermediate-range SS-20; the SS-4; the SS-5, which was not deployed; the shorter-range SS-12; and the SS-23. An advanced cruise missile being developed by the Soviet Union, the SSC-X-4, was also included in the treaty. The SS-20 launch canister, launcher, missile transporter vehicle, and fixed structure for a launcher; the SS-4 missile transporter vehicle, missile erector, launch stand, and propellant tanks; the SS-12 missile launcher and missile transporter vehicle; the SS-23 missile launcher and missile transporter vehicle; and the SSC-X-4 launch canister and launcher were additional Soviet systems that had to be eliminated according to the provisions of the INF Treaty. The INF protocol outlined the specific guidelines and procedures for eliminating each of these treaty-related items.

Although the success of the INF Treaty served to bolster confidence in the arms control process and encourage further negotiations to reduce strategic nuclear arms, the treaty failed to capture Chinese systems, which worked against Soviet/Russian interests. In February 20007, Russian president Vladimir Putin stated that Russia was no longer served by the INF Treaty, especially given U.S. missile defense deployments in Central Europe. In 2012, the United States alleged that the Russians had violated the INF Treaty by developing the R-500 cruise missile and a short-range ballistic missile.

Ken Rogers

Further Reading

Frederking, Brian, *Resolving Security Dilemmas: A Constructivist Explanation of the INF Treaty* (Aldershot, UK: Ashgate, 2000).

Gallagher, Nancy W., *The Politics of Verification* (Baltimore: Johns Hopkins University Press, 1999).

INF Treaty Text. http://www.state.gov/www /global/arms/treaties/inf1.html. Accessed March 1, 2003.

Matlock, Jack F., Jr., *Reagan and Gorbachev: How the Cold War Ended* (New York: Random House, 2004).

Rueckert, George L., *Global Double Zero: The INF Treaty from Its Origins to Implementation* (Westport, CT: Greenwood, 1993).

Woolf, Amy, *Russian Compliance with the Intermediate Range Nuclear Forces (INF) Treaty: Background and Issues for Congress*, CRS Report 7-5700 (December 2017).

International Atomic Energy Agency

The International Atomic Energy Agency (IAEA) is an autonomous organization under the United Nations. Founded in 1957, it promotes and monitors the peaceful uses of atomic energy. Following its statute, the agency seeks "to accelerate and enlarge the contribution of atomic energy to peace, health and prosperity throughout the world" and to "ensure, so far as it is able, that assistance provided by it or at its request or under its supervision or control is not used in such a way as to further any military purpose."

The IAEA was given an enhanced role in promoting worldwide nuclear safety following accidents at Three Mile Island in Pennsylvania and Chernobyl in the Soviet Union. Over time, the agency's emphasis has shifted away from promoting peaceful uses of nuclear power and toward security concerns, such as diversion of atomic material for nuclear proliferation. It has therefore become associated with inspections tied to the 1968 Nuclear Nonproliferation Treaty (NPT) and efforts to prevent proliferation in Iraq and North Korea.

The IAEA's mandate to lead global efforts in three areas of atomic energy—peaceful usage, safety, and limitation of proliferation—has proven challenging. IAEA resources are limited, and these three objectives at times conflict. The IAEA has come under increasing criticism in recent years, especially following the Fukushima nuclear reactor accident in Japan. Some critics have called for enhancing the IAEA's ability to conduct independent assessments of nuclear safety issues worldwide.

President Dwight D. Eisenhower's Atoms for Peace initiative of 1953 was the genesis of the IAEA. Eisenhower joined many scientists and others in suggesting that peaceful uses of atomic energy could play a major role in future human development. The IAEA has a General Conference composed of representatives from all member states. As of 2018, there are 169 member states. The organization also has a 35-member Board of Governors. Some seats on the board are reserved for the 10 states most advanced in nuclear technology, and others are elected by the General Conference.

The IAEA has been a leader in other peaceful uses of nuclear technology. One of the IAEA's original functions, preventing the diversion of nuclear material to military projects, took center stage after the 1968 NPT was signed. In keeping with the provisions of the NPT, nonnuclear weapons states sign "comprehensive safeguard agreements," which cover all declared nuclear material and activities. Nuclear weapons states sign "voluntary offer agreements," which cover only facilities voluntarily submitted by the states, which effectively prohibits monitoring of existing military programs. The IAEA monitors activities by carrying out material accounting and inventory duties, by enforcing containment and surveillance measures at nuclear sites, and by conducting on-site inspections. The agency currently monitors more than 1,000 installations in more than 70 countries.

Some observers have questioned the effectiveness of IAEA monitoring in cases of noncompliant states. These concerns were highlighted and grew more widespread with the IAEA's interactions with both Iraq and North Korea. IAEA inspectors monitored Iraq before the 1991 Gulf War. After the war, however, it became clear that Iraq had a more extensive nuclear program than was realized, that it had been actively concealing information from the inspectors, and that, at times, inspectors had checked on and certified parts of complexes that later turned out to contain other extensive facilities. With these problems in mind, new IAEA safeguard agreements were developed that allowed access to all sites, not just those declared by the state, and that focused less on nuclear material accountancy and more on complete assessments of a state's facilities and intentions.

The IAEA has also played a central role in disputes with North Korea concerning its early efforts to clandestinely develop a nuclear weapons program. Some analysts saw North Korea's removal of IAEA inspectors and monitoring equipment as further proof that the IAEA system only works with countries that already intend to comply. Other observers argue that the strong international reaction in response to these cases of noncompliance show that IAEA goals and inspections have become institutionalized, global norms.

Iraqi, North Korean, and Iranian cases of covert nuclear proliferation have led some to argue that the IAEA is too cautious and slow. Several former IAEA inspectors became well-known critics of the inspection regime. These criticisms flow from three main institutional limitations. First, as the IAEA depends on states for some intelligence information and for enforcement, it can be greatly affected by states' political calculations and efforts at denial and deception. Second, the IAEA's budget and staffing are small compared to its expanded goals and responsibilities—a problem that may worsen as the IAEA takes on new roles and responsibilities in the war on terrorism. Third, the IAEA's main goals of promoting the spread of nuclear energy while maintaining tight restrictions to prevent diversion inherently conflict to some degree.

John W. Dietrich

Further Reading

Busch, Nathan E., and Joseph F. Pilat, *The Politics of Weapons Inspections: Assessing WMD Monitoring and Verification Regimes* (Stanford, CA: Stanford University Press, 2017).

Fischer, David, *History of the International Atomic Energy Agency: The First Forty Years* (Vienna, Austria: International Atomic Energy Agency, 1997).

McGeary, Johanna, "The Trouble with Inspections," *Time* vol 160 no. 25 (December 16, 2002): 36–42.

Scheinman, Lawrence, *International Atomic Energy Agency and World Nuclear Order* (New York: Resources for the Future, 1987).

Iran

Iran has consistently figured prominently as an international threat for the proliferation of weapons of mass destruction (WMD). Unstable relations between Iran and the United States following the Islamic revolution of 1979—and the Iran-Iraq War (1980–1988) that involved the use of Iraqi chemical weapons—have exacerbated concerns about Iranian weapons aspirations.

Following the Iran-Iraq War, Iran's conventional arsenal was largely devastated, and Iran turned to the Soviet Union for assistance in reconstituting its military. The Soviet Union viewed its cooperation with Iran as a means of extending its own influence in the pivotal Persian Gulf region, and it formally agreed in 1989 to bolster Iran's military capacity. Iran has also received extensive military assistance from China and North Korea.

Chemical Weapons

Iran is believed to have initiated a chemical weapons program in the mid-1980s, in response to the use of chemical weapons against it during its war with Iraq. Reportedly, Iran began to stockpile cyanogen chloride, phosgene, and mustard after 1985 and to produce nerve gas in 1994. In 2000, U.S. intelligence analysts assessed that Iran possessed at least several hundred metric tons of weaponized and bulk chemical agents, including nerve, blood, blister, and choking agents, and that it has attempted to obtain weapons-relevant technology, training, and chemicals from China and Russia. Iranian opposition groups have also reported that Iran has produced VX nerve gas and aflatoxin, probably in response to Iraq having developed weapons along these same lines.

Iran signed the Chemical Weapons Convention in 1997 and submitted a declaration of its holdings, as required by its membership. Iran disclosed that it had a chemical weapons program in the final months of the Iran-Iraq War, during which it was exposed to chemical weapons attacks by Iraq, but it has denied all accusations that it has an ongoing program. It has accepted visits from inspectors of the Organization for the Prohibition of Chemical Weapons (OPCW), who have not found evidence of treaty violations.

Biological Weapons

During its war with Iraq (1980–1988), Iran reportedly initiated a biological weapons program. Little information, however, is publicly available about Iran's efforts to acquire biological weapons. Some observers suspect that Iran has a biological weapons laboratory at Damghan and has produced small quantities of biological weapons agents such as anthrax and botulinum toxin. Other locations suspected of biological weapons research and development also include academic research laboratories, including the Imam Reza Medical Center at Mashhad University, and the Iranian Research Organization for Science and Technology. Nevertheless, Iran has denied all allegations about developing or stockpiling biological weapons and maintains that it adheres to the Biological and Toxin Weapons Convention, which it ratified in 1973.

U.S. intelligence agencies have suggested that biomedical research conducted in Iran has been used in support of a biological weapons program and that Iran has received biotechnology from Russian research facilities. Some experts have also suggested that Iran likely accelerated its biological weapons program following revelations about Iraq's biological weapons program in 1995. Press reports have indicated that Iran has recruited Russian weapons scientists to work on its biological weapons programs.

Nuclear Weapons

Beginning in the 1950s, under the U.S. "Atoms for Peace" program, Iran (under the shah) was actively involved in obtaining nuclear energy technology. Despite having ratified the Nuclear Non-Proliferation Treaty in 1968, by 1976, Iran had begun research activities to enrich uranium using laser separation, reportedly to pursue nuclear weapons development. Following the Islamic Revolution in Iran (1979), the theocratic regime reportedly resumed Iran's nuclear weapons program in 1987. Insisting that its interest in atomic energy was solely for peaceful purposes, in the mid-1990s (with Russian assistance), Iran purchased nuclear reactor technology, and it finally completed work at its first operational reactor (Bushehr I) in September 2011.

To rebut reports that Iran was secretly working on a nuclear weapon, in 1992, Iranian authorities invited the International Atomic Energy Agency (IAEA) to visit Iran's nuclear facilities, and the IAEA reported it found no evidence of a weaponization program. Nevertheless, following revelations that Iran was covertly carrying out uranium separation at Natanz and heavy-water production at Arak, the IAEA reported in June 2003 that Iran had failed to meet its safeguards agreement obligations.

Despite a negotiated deal with France, Germany, and United Kingdom that reaffirmed Iran's commitment to only pursue peaceful nuclear energy, in November 2003, the IAEA maintained that Iran was still noncompliant (although it had no evidence that Iran was developing a nuclear weapon). Despite Iran's agreement to allow for more intrusive IAEA inspections, the IAEA concluded in late 2004 that the Iranian government was in breach of its obligations and had undertaken a "pattern of concealment." In 2005, the U.S. intelligence agencies concluded that "Iran conducted a clandestine uranium enrichment program for nearly two decades in violation of its IAEA safeguards agreement, and despite its claims to the contrary, we assess that Iran seeks nuclear weapons."

As Iran's suspicious behavior continued, the U.S. intelligence community began drafting its National Intelligence Estimate (NIE) on Iranian nuclear weapons in 2006. As this new estimate was being prepared, the painful memory of the Iraqi WMD intelligence failure was very much in play. In a painstaking effort to avoid another Iraqi WMD debacle, the U.S. intelligence decided to conduct a "zero-based" (or ground-up) review of Iran's nuclear program and its intent to develop nuclear weapons. In was in this context that the 2007 NIE, a new assessment of Iran, emerged. The 2007 NIE, "Iran's Nuclear Intentions and Capabilities," stated, "We judge with high confidence that in fall 2003, Tehran halted its nuclear weapons program." This contradictory assessment was all the more surprising given Iran's active ballistic missile program, which appeared to be designed to deliver nuclear warheads. Nonetheless, the U.S. intelligence agencies still maintained in 2012 that there was not enough evidence to conclude that Iran was developing nuclear weapons.

To achieve a diplomatic breakthrough and ultimately forestall Iranian nuclear weapons development, in July 2015, President Barack Obama's administration led an international effort to negotiate a Joint Comprehensive Plan of Action (JCPOA), involving France, Germany, the United Kingdom, China, and Russia. In exchange for relief from international sanctions—to include financial transactions, restricted military weapons sales, and bans on sensitive technology imports—Iran agreed to, among other things, intrusive IAEA inspections to ensure its nuclear program remains peaceful in nature. Trumpeting the success of this agreement, President Obama issued the following:

On January 16, 2016, the International Atomic Energy Agency verified that Iran has completed the necessary steps under the Iran deal that will ensure Iran's nuclear program is and remains exclusively peaceful. . . .

And with the unprecedented monitoring and access this deal puts in place, if Iran tries, we will know and sanctions will snap back into place.

Here's how we got to this point. Since October, Iran has:

- Shipped 25,000 pounds of enriched uranium out of the country
- Dismantled and removed two-thirds of its centrifuges
- Removed the calandria from its heavy-water reactor and filled it with concrete
- Provided unprecedented access to its nuclear facilities and supply chain

Because Iran has completed these steps, the U.S. and international community can begin the next phase under the JCPOA, which means the U.S. will begin lifting its nuclear-related sanctions on Iran. However, a number of U.S. sanctions authorities and designations will continue to remain in place. (White House 2016)

Critics of the JCPOA note that by focusing solely on fissile material production—a technology Iran has mastered and could revamp later—it neglected other activities, including ballistic missile development and other testing not covered under the JCPOA, which could enable Iran to develop a nuclear

weapons system quickly. Critics also noted that by allowing Tehran to maintain its controversial nuclear infrastructure, Iran could still have a "breakout" capability to develop a nuclear weapon within a year. Indeed, this was explicitly noted in the White House announcement that celebrated the JCPOA deal:

Before this agreement, Iran's breakout time—or the time it would have taken for Iran to gather enough fissile material to build a weapon—was only two to three months. Today, because of the Iran deal, it would take Iran 12 months or more. (White House 2016).

In late April 2018, Israeli Prime Minister Benjamin Netanyahu delivered an intelligence briefing on global media. After showing previous statements by Iranian Supreme Leader Ali Khamenei, President Hassan Roumani, and Foreign Minister Javad Zarif—all categorically denying that Iran had any interest in developing nuclear weapons—Netanyahu simply concluded that "Iran lied."

According to Israeli intelligence, after having signed the JCPOA in 2015, two years later Iran clandestinely transported truckloads of sensitive documents having to do with its nuclear weapons program to a location then only known to a handful of Iranian officials. In an audacious intelligence operation, Israeli operatives managed to infiltrate this facility (located in the Shorabad district of Tehran) and physically removed some of these hard-copy and electronic media files. After many months of translation and other analysis, Israel concluded that Iran's "Project Amad"—dating back to 1999—was a continuing, dedicated effort to "Design, produce and test . . . 5 warheads, each with 10 kiloton TNT yield, for integration on a missile." Based on these sensitive documents, Iran was shown to have been intent on designing a spherical, implosion-based nuclear warhead using highly enriched uranium-235, to be fitted onto a ballistic missile.

While some observers maintained that Netanyahu's presentation did not explicitly demonstrate that Iran substantially violated the technical terms of the JCPOA, it increased pressure on the United States and other cosignatories to withdraw from the treaty. On May 8, 2018, in a major reversal of U.S. policy, President Trump announced that the United States would no longer be a party to the treaty.

Jacqueline Simon and Eric A. Croddy

Further Reading

Burns, William J., "Iranian-American Negotiations," *Journal of International Affairs* 69, no. 2 (Spring/Summer 2016): 177–183.

Cordesman, Anthony H., *Weapons of Mass Destruction in the Middle East* (Washington, D.C.: Center for Strategic and International Studies, 2002).

Katzman, Kenneth, *Iran: Arms and Technology Acquisitions*, CRS Report RL30551 (Washington, D.C.: Congressional Research Service, 2001).

Landau, Noa, "Netanyahu: Iran Nuclear Deal Is Based on Lies—Here's the Proof," *Haaretz*, April 30, 2018 (online). https://www.haaretz.com/israel-news/pm-expected-to-reveal-how -iran-cheated-world-on-nuke-program-1 .6045300. Accessed May 1, 2018.

Nelson, Richard, and David H. Saltiel, *Managing Proliferation Issues with Iran* (Washington, D.C.: Atlantic Council of the United States, 2002).

Office of the Director of National Intelligence, National Intelligence Council, National Intelligence Estimate (NIE), "Iran: Nuclear Intentions and Capabilities," November 2007. https://www.dni.gov/files /documents/Newsroom/Reports%20and% 20Pubs/20071203_release.pdf. Accessed June 30, 2017.

Rubin, Michael, "Iran's Burgeoning WMD Programs," *Middle East Intelligence Bulletin* (March/April 2002). http://www .washingtoninstitute.org/policy-analysis /view/irans-burgeoning-wmd-programs. Accessed June 30, 2017.

Treverton, Gregory F., *CIA Support to Policymakers: The 2007 National Intelligence Estimate on Iran's Nuclear Intentions and Capabilities* (Washington, D.C.: Center for the Study of Intelligence, Central Intelligence Agency, May 2013). https://www .cia.gov/library/center-for-the-study-of -intelligence/csi-publications/books-and -monographs/csi-intelligence-and-policy -monographs/pdfs/support-to-policymakers -2007-nie.pdf.Accessed June 30, 2017.

White House, "The Historic Deal That Will Prevent Iran from Acquiring a Nuclear Weapon," January 16, 2016. https://obama whitehouse.archives.gov/issues/foreign -policy/iran-deal. Accessed June 30, 2017.

Iraq

During the 1980s and early 1990s, Iraq developed, produced, and used weapons of mass destruction (WMD). Iraqi WMD programs included chemical, biological, and nuclear weapons research and development. With its ramifications being still felt in the region today, Iraq's possession (real or perceived) of WMD led to dramatic changes in the course of modern Middle East history.

Iraq was the first nation to use chemical weapons since Italy's invasion of Ethiopia (Abyssinia) in 1935–1936, and it holds dubious distinction as having been the first military ever to use a nerve agent (GA, or tabun) on the battlefield (in 1984). Having produced large quantities of chemical agents by the mid-1980s, Saddam Hussein's government and military used over 100,000 chemical weapons against Iranian military personnel and against civilians in the ongoing oppression of internal Kurdish and Iraqi Shi'a Muslim opponents (March 1991).

Having instituted a Chemical Corps in the mid-1960s, with fits and starts, Iraq began research and development of chemical warfare (CW) agents in the 1970s. But it was the war with Iran (1980)—especially the problem of dealing with Iranian human-wave attacks—that provided the main impetus for Iraqi development of chemical weapons. A full-scale effort, code-named "Project 922," was formally undertaken on June 8, 1981. The initial requirements for CW agent production (and munitions to carry them) included blister (sulfur mustard); nerve (tabun, sarin, VX); and white phosphorus incendiaries.

Chemical weapons use became a regular part of Iraqi military operations, and these weapons were used for both strategic and tactical effect to offset Iranian numerical superiority. The Iraqi chemical arsenal consisted of CS gas, mustard, and nerve agents. From 1983 to the end of the Iran-Iraq War (August 1988), Iraq used some 19,500 chemical-laden bombs, more than 54,000 chemical artillery shells, and 27,000 short-range chemical rockets, expending 1,800 tons of mustard, 140 tons of tabun, and more than 600 tons of sarin.

First Gulf War, 1991

After Iraq invaded Kuwait (over a border dispute involving oil deposits) in early August 1990, the United States led a multinational coalition to force Saddam Hussein into submission. Following a short but violent military engagement, Kuwait was liberated, and President George H. W. Bush declared a cease-fire on February 28, 1991.

In April 1991, the terms of Iraq's formal cease-fire with Kuwait and coalition nations were determined under United Nations Security Council Resolution 687, which called for the complete destruction of Iraq's weapons of mass destruction, including all of its chemical and biological weapons and the infrastructure supporting them. A United Nations Special Commission (UNSCOM) was set up to oversee the destruction of these weapons and to report this to the UN Security Council. With the establishment of UNSCOM's Chemical Destruction Group (CDG) in 1992, a massive effort was undertaken to destroy all known (declared) Iraqi chemical weapons, including some 30,000 weapons, about 120,000 gallons of CW agents, and 500,000 gallons of CW agent precursors.

UNSCOM's efforts to uncover the full extent of the chemical warfare program and its remaining constituent parts, however, were hampered by Iraqi efforts at denial and deception. When UNSCOM withdrew in December 1998, it could not confirm that it had fulfilled its mandate of destroying the Iraqi program in full. This lack of certainty would play a crucial role in the flawed U.S. intelligence assessment four years later that laid the groundwork for the Second Gulf War in 2003.

Biological Weapons

Initially, Iraq claimed that it had no biological program, and for the first four years of UNSCOM inspections, little was discovered about the Iraqi biological weapons (BW) program. The scope and extent of the various programs was only finally revealed when General Hussein Kamel Hasan defected from Iraq in August 1995. His debriefing revealed many details about various Iraqi programs and led to the subsequent modification of Iraqi denials. It also led the Iraqis to move steadily toward acknowledging the actual scale of the program as the inspectors discovered further details about the various operations. This proved to be a major shock for the international community, which had been close to accepting the Iraqi denials about its chemical and biological programs and to removing economic sanctions as a reward.

The Iraqis had developed a wide-ranging biological weapons program that was based on viruses, bacteria, and fungi in both their living form and their toxin derivatives. These weapons ranged from lethal antipersonnel to anticrop agents, and their delivery means included field artillery, aircraft with tanks, and al-Hussein surface-to-surface missiles (modified Scuds). Subsequent investigations by UNSCOM confirmed that the Iraqis had produced at least 8,500 liters of anthrax and 19,000 liters of botulinum toxin, more than the Iraqis had ever admitted. In addition to these lethal agents, the Iraqi regime reported that it had made weapons out of 1,580 liters (of a total of 2,200 liters produced) of aflatoxin (derived from a fungus). The Iraqi regime also admitted to having conducted research and development tests on a range of agents—*Clostridium perfringens*, ricin, and viruses that included hemorrhagic conjunctivitis, rotavirus, and camel pox—for weapons purposes, plus field trials on an anticrop agent (wheat cover smut).

It was later learned that, prior to Operation Desert Storm (1991), Iraq had accelerated its production of anthrax and botulinum toxin. UNSCOM's executive chairman, Rolf Ekeus, was subsequently informed that authority had been delegated to local Iraqi commanders to use these agents in response to a massive attack on Baghdad. After Iraq's invasion of Kuwait in August 1990, a coalition-bombing raid

destroyed Iraq's prototype aerial spray tanks.

The United Nations Monitoring, Verification, and Inspection Commission (UNMOVIC) replaced UNSCOM in 1999. In 2002, the UN Security Council passed Resolution 1441, giving Iraq a final chance to cooperate. The inspection mission returned to Iraq under the leadership of Hans Blix in late 2002, but it was again withdrawn in March 2003 when a U.S.-led coalition decided to use force against Iraq, arguing that Iraq had again failed to comply fully with the United Nations. A U.S.-led inspection mission looked for evidence of Iraqi weapons of mass destruction for months after the quick victory in April 2003, but little evidence of an ongoing Iraqi WMD program—of any sort—was ever found. What was found in the ensuing years of occupation and surveys were older pre-1991 chemical munitions. Numbering in the hundreds, these weapons included filled and unfilled chemical weapons. For example, in ca. 2006, coalition forces had uncovered 448 battlefield rocket (al Borak) warheads (122 mm), many of which contained sarin nerve agent.

Nuclear Weapons

Iraqi nuclear weapons research and development began in the early 1970s, and although it had ended in 1991 (after the First Gulf War), Saddam Hussein expressed continuing interest in nuclear weapons. Nevertheless, no existing capability in this regard was found after the Second Gulf War (2003, Operation Iraqi Freedom). Initially, Iraq sought plutonium from research nuclear reactors (purchased from France), the largest of which, Osiraq (40 MWt), was destroyed by an Israeli F-16 strike in June 1981, just before becoming operational. Afterward, Saddam Hussein directed that work on nuclear weapons be moved to more concealed areas, and Iraq expanded its routes for obtaining fissile materials to include calutrons (for electromagnetic isotope separation), gaseous diffusion, and centrifuge technology.

After Iraq's invasion of Kuwait (1990), pending intervention by U.S. and coalition military forces, Saddam Hussein decided to harvest weapons-grade uranium from Iraqi research reactors, but coalition air strikes in 1991 prevented this effort from being carried out.

Intelligence Failure: Iraqi WMD

With the end of the war in Iraq (2003), after four months of U.S.-led inspections (under David Kay), the Iraq Survey Group had found nothing of ongoing WMD programs in Iraq. It became apparent that previous assessments of Iraqi WMD by the United States (and other national intelligence agencies) were largely wrong. A fair question to ask is why.

Although Saddam Hussein had done much to invite a military intervention due to his multitude of cease-fire obligations and human rights violations, the George W. Bush administration spent much political capital making the case for invading Iraq squarely on the WMD issue. The first major driver, of course, was the 9/11 attack on New York and the destruction of the World Trade Center. Al Qaeda's success in launching attacks across the Atlantic Ocean brought the global war on terrorism to the U.S. homeland. Then, the U.S. government had to consider the still unresolved issues concerning Iraqi WMD programs (UN and IAEA inspectors had departed Iraq prior to the 2003 assaults) and the potential threat of both regional attacks and the use of Iraqi chemical or biological agents by terrorists. Iraqi nuclear weapons were also considered

a very real near-term (seven months to a year) threat.

In 2002, a year before invading Iraq, the intelligence policy-making community in the United States had its own "concept" of the Iraqi regime's objectives: Saddam Hussein surely would not have given up Iraq's WMD programs or weapons. Ominously, there was the likelihood that Saddam would use them if seriously threatened. Although heavily redacted, the National Intelligence Estimate (NIE) of 2002 included the following language that was not only wildly off the mark but also helps to explain the motivation of the U.S. government in deciding to authorize military intervention, particularly given what had just occurred a year earlier on September 11, 2001: "Saddam, if sufficiently desperate, might decide that only an organization such as al-Qa'ida—with worldwide reach and extensive terrorist infrastructure, and already engaged in a life-or-death struggle against the United States—could perpetrate the type of terrorist attack that he would hope to conduct" (NIE 2002). The 2002 NIE concluded with "High Confidence" that "Iraq is continuing, and in some areas expanding, its chemical, biological, nuclear and missile programs contrary to UN resolutions."

The intelligence failures regarding the status of Iraq's WMD before 2003 rested on a number of analytical errors and misjudgments, as well as bureaucratic fumbles, and were addressed in a 2005 postmortem on U.S. Intelligence Community (IC) assessments of Iraqi WMD: the Commission on the Intelligence Capabilities of the United States Regarding Weapons of Mass Destruction's *Report to the President of the United States*).

The commission's final verdict was damning: "The [U.S.] Intelligence Community, because of a lack of analytical imagination, failed even to consider the possibility that Saddam Hussein would decide to destroy his chemical and biological weapons and to halt work on his nuclear program after the first Gulf War" (Commission 2005).

In fairness, given the extremely tight control and compartmentalization of information held by Saddam Hussein, it may have been impossible to know what was found out after the fact: Iraq had basically eliminated all its WMD programs by the end of 1991. But this reality was not only kept from the prying eyes of the U.S. IC, but even from Saddam's top circle. What's more, Saddam Hussein made no efforts to show that he was complying with the basic requirements of demilitarization. On the contrary, he was purposefully evasive—both to his own people and the international community—to allow everyone to believe he could still have WMD.

With regard to Iraq, its purported WMD, and the intelligence failure to properly categorize it, the following remains valid today: Saddam Hussein himself (who was executed by the Iraqi government by hanging in December 2006) had every intention to restart his WMD programs once the UN-imposed sanctions had been lifted. It is worth considering that, had there been no invasion of Iraq, Saddam Hussein could have outlasted what was already a flagging international sanctions regime. The counterfactual question remains: how would the international community respond to an Iraq armed with chemical, biological, or even nuclear weapons that was led by a despotic regime that had no moral constraints against their use?

Andrew M. Dorman and Eric A. Croddy

Further Reading

Central Intelligence Agency, "Iraq: Biological Warfare Program," October 2002. https://www.cia.gov/library/reports/general-reports-1/iraq_wmd/Iraq_Oct_2002.htm #06. Accessed August 30, 2017.

Central Intelligence Agency, "Iraq's Chemical Warfare Program," 2004. https://www.cia.gov/library/reports/general-reports-1/iraq_wmd_2004/chap5.html#sect6. Accessed August 30, 2017.

Commission on the Intelligence Capabilities of the United States Regarding Weapons of Mass Destruction, *Report to the President of the United States,* March 31, 2005.

Director of Central Intelligence, National Intelligence Estimate (NIE), "Iraq's Continuing Weapons of Mass Destruction Program," (NIE 2002-16HC), October 2002 (redacted, approved for release 2004). http://nsarchive.gwu.edu/NSAEBB/NSAEBB129/nie.pdf. Accessed August 29, 2017.

Drogin, Bob, *Curveball: Spies, Lies, and the Con Man Who Caused a War* (New York: Random House, 2007).

Obeidi, Mahdi, and Kurt Pitzer. *The Bomb in My Garden: The Secrets of Saddam's Nuclear Mastermind* (Hoboken, NJ: John Wiley & Sons, 2004).

Islamic State

The Islamic State of Iraq and Syria (ISIS), also known as the Islamic State of Iraq and the Levant (ISIL) and the Arabic term Daesh, has its origins with the jihadist spiritual leader Abu Mus'ab al-Zarqawi.

Starting out as a basic street thug, al-Zarqawi traveled to Afghanistan to join the mujahideen to fight the Soviets in 1989, but he arrived too late to participate in combat. He was nonetheless adept at forming networks among Levantine jihadis. After being jailed for attempted terrorist attacks in Jordan, his release from prison in 1999 set al-Zarqawi on a path toward extremely violent activity in the name of an extremist and fundamentalist interpretation of Islam.

Later, having founded the original Al Qaeda in Iraq (AQI), the Jordanian al-Zarqawi arose to notoriety with assassinations, massive suicide bombings, and other ruthless killings committed during insurgent attacks in Iraq (2003). Although the majority of terrorist attacks directed by al-Zarqawi (and later ISIS) have employed the typical conventional arsenal of explosives and firearms, in April 2004, Jordanian authorities uncovered a plot by Zarqawi to use a "chemical dirty bomb" to kill thousands of people. The plot involved packing explosives with various toxic chemicals, potassium cyanide being among them. It is unclear what the results of such a chemical blast would have been, but the intent was clearly to devise a weapon of mass destruction (WMD).

Al-Zarqawi was killed by a U.S. air strike in spring 2006. Yet, his ultraviolent jihadi organization continued to increase in strength. Officially marking October 15, 2006, as the formal establishment of the Islamic State of Iraq (ISI), under its new "emir," Abu Umar al-Baghdadi, ISI purported to have a strength of about 20,000 irregular soldiers. By June 2007, ISI was incorporating chlorine in its attacks. Even so, most casualties were likely caused by the explosive charges and not toxic gas.

Syrian Civil War

Just as al-Zarqawi took advantage of the political disorganization in Iraq (May 2003) to gain momentum, the civil uprising and open warfare in Syria (2011) gave the Islamic State a chance to exploit this now very chaotic environment, finding adherents, establishing city strongholds, and eventually occupying territory. By this time, al-Baghdadi's Syrian adventure was called the al-Nusra Front, and it was responsible for, among other things, conducting bombings in Damascus. On April 9, 2013,

Baghdadi officially announced the creation of the Islamic State of Iraq and al-Sham (or Levant; *ad-Dawlah al-Islāmiyah fī 'l-Irāq wa-sh-Shām*).

An official proclamation of the ISIS caliphate was announced at the beginning of Ramadan in 2014 (June 28). At this time, ISIS controlled lands that were the approximate size of Great Britain. More recently, however, under air attack by U.S. forces and Iraqi military campaigns, ISIS has lost control of most of its geographic holdings since 2014.

Still, ISIS remains a significant terrorist threat regionally. Internationally, ISIS was able to coordinate mass terrorist attacks in Europe, most infamously in France (Bataclan 2015), killing 130 people, and suicide bombings at the Brussels airport (March 2016) that killed 30 civilians.

ISIS-affiliated fighters have reportedly used some isolated chemical attacks. Investigators from the Organization for the Prohibition of Chemical Weapons (OPCW) found evidence of mustard agent having been used during an August 21, 2015, ISIS attack on Marea, Syria. But perhaps the more unsettling development was reporting that ISIS-affiliated jihadists were involved in developing biological weapons. In May 2016, Kenyan authorities arrested medical interns at the Wote District Hospital in southeastern Kenya and charged them with planning "to unleash a biological attack in Kenya using anthrax."

As an organization, ISIS has clearly shown interest in using WMD, although thus far its main weapons have been the typical combination of explosives and bullets in carrying out terrorist attacks. The combined military forces of Iraq, regional players, and the United States continue to put pressure on ISIS. Despite its current challenges in Syria, Iraq, and other operating areas, it is not impossible for this terrorist group to acquire chemical, biological, or radiological weapon technologies.

Eric A. Croddy

Further Reading

Fishman, Brian H., *The Master Plan: ISIS, Al-Qaeda, and the Jihadi Strategy for Final Victory* (New Haven, CT: Yale University Press, 2016).

Holbrook, Donald, "Al-Qaeda and the Rise of ISIS," *Survival* 57, no. 2 (April–May 2015): 93–104.

Morell, Michael, with Bill Harlow, *The Great War of Our Time* (New York: Twelve, 2015).

Warrick, Joby, *Black Flags: The Rise of ISIS* (New York: Doubleday, 2015).

Wright, Robin, "After the Islamic State," *New Yorker* 92, no. 41 (December 12, 2016): 30–34.

Isotopes

Isotopes are atoms of the same element that have the same number of protons (atomic number) but different numbers of neutrons in the nucleus. Because different isotopes of the same element have different numbers of neutrons, their atomic mass (the sum of the protons and neutrons) is different. Isotopes are denoted by the element name or symbol and the atomic mass number. As an example, uranium has 92 protons in the nucleus. Uranium 238, which has 146 neutrons in the nucleus, and uranium 235, which has 143 neutrons in the nucleus, are examples of uranium isotopes. An alternative term for *isotope* is *nuclide*.

Most naturally occurring elements have two or more isotopes; just 20 of the 90 elements that occur in nature have only one isotope. Some isotopes are stable, and others are unstable (or radioactive); that is, they may decay into other isotopes or elements. There are 266 stable and 65 unstable naturally occurring isotopes. The latter are also called *radionuclides*.

Bombarding certain elements with other particles, for example neutrons, alpha particles, and protons, can create "man-made" isotopes. More than 2,500 isotopes have been produced through such processes. Many of these nuclides are artificially produced radioactive isotopes.

Because two isotopes of the same element are chemically similar, they are difficult to separate. Due to differences in atomic mass, stability, and other physical characteristics, however, isotopes may be separated by several methods. Separation techniques that are used for uranium enrichment, for example, build on this knowledge and include gaseous diffusion, gas centrifuge, electromagnetic separation, and laser isotope separation.

Don Gillich

Further Reading

Parrington, Josef R., Harold D. Knox, Susan L. Breneman, Edward M. Baum, and Frank Feiner, *Nuclides and Isotopes: Chart of the Nuclides*, 15th ed. (New York: General Electric and KAPL, 1996).

Israel

The creation of Israel, on May 14, 1948, brought with it existential fears. Beginning in 1957, with help from the French, the Israelis constructed their own nuclear reactor at Dimona in the Negev Desert. The Dimona facility served both as a means to establish a nuclear industry and as a production facility of fissile material needed for a nuclear weapons program. By the late 1960s, Israel probably possessed a fission weapon. The nuclear weapons stance that Israel takes is one of ambiguity. It neither confirms nor denies the existence of an Israeli nuclear arsenal. The Israeli government has also pledged that it would not be the first to introduce nuclear weapons into the Middle East.

Chemical Weapons

Israel's history with chemical and biological warfare (CBW) began inauspiciously when Avraham Marcus Klingberg, an Ashkenazi Jew who had been an epidemiologist in the Soviet Red Army, immigrated to Israel in 1948. Under David Ben-Gurion's initiative to recruit personnel with expertise in the biological sciences—both for defense and potential offensive capabilities—Klingberg was originally recruited because of his background in the military health sciences. Klingberg eventually landed at the very sensitive Israel Institute for Biological Research (IIBR) at Nes Ziona and had risen to deputy director by the late 1960s. Feigning chronic illness, Klingberg often traveled to Switzerland for "treatment," but he was in fact meeting with his Soviet KGB handler and likely providing the Soviet Union with everything he knew regarding Israeli work in biological and probably chemical weaponry. His espionage activities, which spanned back to 1950, were finally discovered in 1983. Eventually released from house arrest in 2003, he died in December 2015.

At the time Klingberg's espionage had been uncovered, the U.S. Intelligence Community (IC) had made the following secret assessment of Israeli capabilities in chemical weapons:

Israel, finding itself surrounded by frontline Arab states with budding CW [i.e., chemical warfare] capabilities, became increasingly conscious of vulnerability to chemical attack. Its sensitivities were galvanized by capture of large quantities of Soviet CW-related [defensive] equipment during both 1967 Arab-Israeli and Yom Kippur wars. As a result, Israel undertook a program of chemical warfare preparations in both offensive and protective areas. While we cannot confirm that the Israelis possess lethal [chemical agents], several indicators lead us to believe that they have available to them at least persistent and non-persistent nerve agents, a mustard agent, and several riot-control agents, matched with suitable deliver systems. In late 1982 a probable CW nerve agent production facility and a storage facility were identified at the Dimona Sensitive Storage Area in the Negev Desert. Other CW agent production is believed to exist within a well-developed Israeli chemical industry. Extensive defense exchange agreements with the United States assist the Israelis in achieving their CW development objectives. They nonetheless remain somewhat dependent on Western nations for protective materiel. There are few technological constraints that would prevent them from achieving self-sufficiency in this area. Financial constraints and competing priorities are more likely inhibitors. (U.S. Director of Central Intelligence 1983)

Current Status

Israel signed the Chemical Weapons Convention (CWC) on January 13, 1993, but it awaits wider participation by its neighbors before ratifying the treaty. Although Syria has since joined the CWC, its continued indiscriminate use of chemicals (sarin, chlorine gas) against rebels in a number of cities (e.g., Damascus and Aleppo) obviously run counter to the main objective of the treaty and likely does not inspire confidence in Israel to ratify the CWC in the near term.

Various unconfirmed reports suggest that Israel has at least developed processes to synthesize nerve agents, such as VX, and may have weaponized aerial munitions for delivery by fighter-bomber aircraft. However, Israel has never declared any chemical weapons stockpile, likely relying on strategic ambiguity for deterrence purposes.

Biological Weapons

According to the Israeli scholar Avner Cohen, a biological warfare unit—HEMED BEIT—was formed in February 1948 and moved to "a remote orange grove outside the gown of Ness Ziona" (Cohen 2001). Based on information provided by a military historian, the HEMED BEIT employed typhoid and dysentery bacteria to poison wells in the town of Acre during the Arab-Israeli War (May 1948). It should be noted here that, especially during this time, natural outbreaks of typhoid and other diseases were relatively common and occurred more frequently in times of general conflict and breakdowns in local hygiene.

During the 1950s the IIBR reportedly conducted research on infectious agents as well as disease vectors, including antiagricultural agents. Over the past decades, IIBR has also conducted studies in the causative agents of plague (*Yersinia pestis*) and toxins (e.g., Staphylococcal enterotoxin B (SEB)). Other potential BW agents include typhus (*Rickettsia prowazekii*), anthrax (*Bacillus anthracis*), and botulinum toxin. Although Israel is still not a signatory, such research can be performed under the legal framework of peaceful (defensive) activities under the Biological and Toxin Weapons Convention.

Although Israel is widely suspected to continue research and development of offensive biological weapons, no details are available to substantiate this. As in the case of a potential CW capability, by neither confirming nor denying it has biological weapons, Israel uses this ambiguity for the purposes of strategic deterrence.

Nuclear Weapons

In 1986, revelations made by Mordechai Vanunu to the British press provided tangible evidence of the existence of a sophisticated Israeli nuclear weapons program. There is no clear evidence about the size of the Israeli nuclear arsenal, although some estimates put it at about 400 weapons, which would make it the third-largest arsenal in the world. Israel also possesses a triad of nuclear delivery systems: Dolphin class submarines that carry nuclear-capable cruise missiles; Jericho ballistic missiles, which could be capable of carrying multiple targeted reentry vehicles; and fighter-bombers that might be equipped to carry nuclear weapons. Scholars suggest that the Israeli nuclear doctrine is intended as a response to existential threats and is not part of an integrated conventional nuclear war–fighting strategy.

Eric A. Croddy and James J. Wirtz

Further Reading

Cohen, Avner, "Israel and Chemical/Biological Weapons: History, Deterrence, and Arms Control," *Nonproliferation Review* 8, no. 3 (Fall–Winter 2001): 27–53.

Cohen, Avner, *Israel and the Bomb* (New York: Columbia University Press, 1998).

Friedman, David, Bracha Rager-Zisman, Eitan Bibi, and Alex Keynan, "The Bioterrorism Threat and Dual-Use Biotechnological Research: An Israeli Perspective," *Science & Engineering Ethics* 16, no. 1 (March 2010): 85–97.

U.S. Director of Central Intelligence, *Implications of Soviet Use of Chemical and Toxin Weapons for US Security Interests*, Special National Intelligence Estimate, SNIE-11-17-83, September 15, 1983.

J

Joint Comprehensive Plan of Action

The Joint Comprehensive Plan of Action (JCPOA) was signed by the United States, Germany, Great Britain, France, Russia, and Iran in Vienna on July 14, 2015. The JCPOA is an international treaty meant to ensure that Iran's nuclear program will be exclusively peaceful. The nuclear deal was endorsed by UN Security Council Resolution 2231 and adopted on July 20, 2015. Iran's compliance with the nuclear-related provisions of the JCPOA will be verified by the International Atomic Energy Agency (IAEA) according to certain requirements set forth in the agreement.

October 18, 2015, marked Adoption Day of the JCPOA, the date it went into effect and the participants began taking the steps necessary to implement their JCPOA commitments. January 16, 2016, was Implementation Day of the JCPOA. The International Atomic Energy Agency (IAEA) has verified that Iran has implemented its key nuclear-related measures described in the JCPOA, and the secretary state has confirmed the IAEA's verification. After Iran verifiably met its nuclear commitments, the United States and the European Union lifted nuclear-related sanctions on Iran, as described in the JCPOA.

The agreement caps the number of enrichment centrifuges that Iran is allowed to operate; limits the level of HEU enrichment to 3.67 percent for 15 years; places restrictions on Iran's enrichment facilities; and authorizes the IAEA to inspect, monitor, and verify Iranian compliance with the agreement. In return, the United Nations, the European Union, and the United States agreed to remove sanctions that had been imposed on Iran in prior years, including the return of its significant frozen financial assets. A Special Commission was created that will meet quarterly for 25 years to assess compliance and determine whether to reinstate sanctions in case of violation.

The agreement was considered a significant achievement for President Barack Obama and his administration, but it generated substantial debate and opposition within conservative and anti-Iranian elements in the United States. President Donald Trump called the JCPOA "the worst deal ever" and promised to change or cancel it once in office. After appearing to moderate his views during his first year in office, Trump returned to his campaign promises and withdrew the United States from the treaty on May 8, 2018.

Jeffrey A. Larsen

Further Reading

Davenport, Kelsey, "The Joint Comprehensive Plan of Action (JCPOA) at a Glance," *Arms Control Today,* January 2016. https://www.armscontrol.org/factsheets/JCPOA-at-a-glance. Accessed February 6, 2018.

"Joint Comprehensive Plan of Action," Treaty Text. https://www.state.gov/documents/organization/245317.pdf. Accessed February 6, 2018.

K

Kaffa, Siege of

The Mongolian siege of the Crimean city of Kaffa in 1346 is often cited as one of the first recorded incidents of biological warfare. Although it is unlikely that the Mongolian strategy of hurling corpses over the city walls would have been effective in spreading disease, the outbreak of bubonic plague in and around Kaffa definitely coincided with the spread of Black Death in medieval Europe.

Background

By 1289, as the Mongolian empire expanded, the city of Kaffa (modern-day Feodsijia, Ukraine) fell under the control of the Khan Toqtai (or Tokhta) of the Golden Horde. But the khan allowed the city's Genoese inhabitants substantial autonomy. However, as the major trading hub between Genoa and the Far East, Kaffa's inhabitants and their Mongol khanate overlords were often in conflict. In 1308, Khan Toqtai was displeased by Genoese slave trading, and he conducted a punitive siege of Kaffa. The Genoese responded by setting fire to the city and fleeing. After Toqtai's death, Khan Uzbeg (Öz Beg) allowed the Genoese to return. Genoa rebuilt its trading colony in 1312.

In 1343, a brawl between Christian locals and Muslims in the Italian enclave of Tana in the Crimea brought the ire of the later khanate (Jani Beg). The Italians fled from Tana to Kaffa, leading the khan's army to besiege the city once again. In February 1344, the Italians managed to break the siege, killing 15,000 of the khan's Tartars and destroying their siege machines. Khan

Jani Beg renewed the siege the following year, but with access to the sea for crucial supplies, the residents of Kaffa were able to hold their position.

As the siege of Kaffa continued, in 1346, the khan's army suffered an outbreak of bubonic plague (caused by *Yersinia pestis*). Desperate to break the will of Kaffa's inhabitants, the Tartars catapulted the plague-infected corpses of their dead comrades over the city walls. According to one historical account, the Tartars' tactic finally broke the three-year stalemate; the Genoese were crippled by the plague and fled Kaffa by sea.

A contemporaneous account of the siege was written by Gabriele de' Mussi, a notary of the town of Piacenza, north of Genoa. Written in ca. 1349, the account describes the "mysterious illness" that struck the Tartar army. De' Mussi recounts how the Tartars, desperate from the devastation of the disease on their army, devised to kill the inhabitants of Kaffa with the stench of their diseased dead. According to the de' Mussi account, once the air and water had been contaminated, the people of Kaffa had no hope: only 1 in 1,000 was able to flee the city. Those that did manage to escape took the plague with them as they left.

De' Mussi's account suggests that not only did the Tartars deliberately hurl their diseased dead over the city walls, but those fleeing Kaffa may have brought the disease into the ports of Europe. However, due to the way bubonic plague infects humans (via infected flea bites), it is unlikely the disease was spread from contact with the Tartar dead. The disease, in classic fashion, was most likely brought within the walls of Kaffa by plague-infected rodents. Nonetheless, the deliberate use of infected cadavers as a weapon is certainly an example of the *intent* to use disease as a means of warfare.

Jennifer Lasecki

Further Reading

Benedictow, Ole Jørgen, *The Black Death, 1346–1353: The Complete History* (New York: Boydell Press, 2004).

Cunningham, Kevin, *The Bubonic Plague* (Edina, MN: ABDO Publishing, 2011).

Wheelis, Mark, "Biological Warfare at the 1346 Siege of Caffa," *Emerging Infectious Diseases* 8, no. 9 (September 2002). https://wwwnc.cdc.gov/eid/article/8/9/01-0536_article. Accessed May 1, 2018

Kiloton

A kiloton is a measure of the energy released during a nuclear detonation. A 1-kiloton "yield" is roughly equal to the detonation of 1,000 tons of the high-explosive trinitrotoluene (TNT), which is equivalent to about 4.184 terajoules. This definition refers to all the energy released by a nuclear weapon: radiation, light, heat, and blast. In contrast, a chemical explosion mostly takes the form of blast. Estimates of the yield of the nuclear weapon used against Hiroshima range between 12 and 18 kilotons. Some note that these measures of yield underestimate the destructiveness of nuclear weapons because they fail to account for the full effects (e.g., fire, genetic damage) caused by a nuclear detonation.

Zachariah Becker

Further Reading

Eden, Lynn, *The Whole World on Fire: Organizations, Knowledge, & Nuclear Weapons Devastation* (Ithaca, NY: Cornell University Press, 2004).

L

Libya

Following his successful coup against King Idris in September 1969 and until his death in October 2011, Colonel Muammar Qaddafi ruled as the unchallenged leader of Libya. During Qaddafi's self-styled revolutionary rule, the North African nation gained pariah status among the nations of the world.

Throughout most of Qaddafi's rule, Libya was considered a "rogue nation," developing chemical weapons as well as acquiring delivery systems, such as the Scud B and C missiles. Although a member of the Nuclear Nonproliferation Treaty (NPT) and subject to International Atomic Energy Agency (IAEA) inspections, an unconfirmed report from the 1970s alleged that Libya had attempted—but ultimately failed—to purchase a nuclear device from China. Some earlier reports suggested that Libya may have pursued biological weapons development. There were also rumors that Dr. Wouter Basson, the former director of South African biological weapon activities, covertly assisted Libya in this pursuit during the mid-1990s. However, subsequent reporting indicates Libyan work in biological weaponry never went further than basic research and development.

In addition to gaining relief from sanctions by the international community, the 2003 invasion of Iraq by coalition forces likely incentivized Qaddafi to decide a new course. In a startling announcement made on December 19 of that year, Qaddafi announced that his government would forgo its weapons of mass destruction (WMD) programs, including all activities related to the production of chemical, biological, and nuclear weapons. Furthermore, Libya would subject itself to international inspections, including full disclosure of its nuclear fuel cycle.

Chemical Weapons

Egypt, the former East Germany, and other countries may have shipped chemical munitions to Libya during the 1970s. In its war with neighboring Chad, Libyan troops reportedly used chemical warfare (CW) agents in the late 1980s. As a response, the United States shipped some 2,000 protective masks to Chad. During this same period, Libya established a suspected CW agent production facility at Rabta (Pharma 150) using technology acquired from West Germany. In the early 1990s, after the United States hinted that a preemptive strike against Pharma 150 was possible, Libyan officials decided to build an underground chemical facility. Another suspect facility was located in the remote town of Sebha (Sabha), which had been built in similar fashion to Rabta, and was given the cover moniker Pharma 200. Another facility built inside of a granite mountain at Tarhunah was described by the Central Intelligence Agency (CIA) as the "world's largest underground chemical weapons plant." Qaddafi later announced that he would stop construction at Tarhunah after a diplomatic consultation with Egyptian president Hosni Mubarak. In the summer of 1996, Pentagon sources confirmed that the site appeared dormant. In March 1997, however, Israeli sources reported that construction at Tarhunah had resumed.

After the U.S.-led coalition successfully invaded Iraq in 2003 (and a shipment of centrifuge parts bound for Libya was intercepted), Qaddafi was likely concerned that it could be next, and he agreed to eliminate Libya's WMD programs. Specialists from the United States and the United Kingdom inspected the Libyan facilities and found that Libya had amassed about 25 tons of sulfur mustard and over 3,000 bombs capable of carrying CW agents. In addition, Libya declared about 1,400 tons of nerve agent precursor chemicals.

Because Libya had acceded to the Chemical Weapon Convention (CWC), the Organization for the Prohibition of Chemical Weapons (OPCW) oversaw the elimination of Libyan chemical munitions. By December 2014, using a mobile incinerator, Libyans (trained in Europe and funded by the U.S. government) finally destroyed the last of Libya's sulfur mustard agent. In August 2016, the OPCW declared that all remaining precursor chemicals, including isopropyl and pinacolyl alcohol (sarin and soman nerve agent precursors, respectively), had been removed from Libyan soil.

Nuclear Weapons

Libya had sought to develop nuclear weapons from the time Qaddafi assumed leadership in 1969, and in the 1990s, it had reportedly obtained nuclear device specifications used by Pakistani proliferator Abdul Qadeer (A. Q.) Khan. Progressing toward an enrichment capability to produce weapons-grade uranium, Khan shipped enough equipment for Libya to assemble 20 P1 centrifuges. When components for Libya's centrifuges were intercepted in October 2003, this may have served as another critical decision point for Qaddafi to rethink his WMD program. Qaddafi then finally renounced Libya's special weapons programs, agreed to IAEA oversight, and ultimately revealed the locations of additional nuclear weapons–related facilities.

The civil war in Libya (2011) has since propelled the nation into chaos and led to the killing of Qaddafi on October 20 of that year. As far as is known, the only WMD-related item of consequence is yellowcake (uranium oxide), 6,400 barrels of which remain at the Sebha facility. The ultimate fate of this uranium concentrate was still unclear as of 2017, although the IAEA is expected to address this issue when it is safe on the ground to do so.

Eric A. Croddy

Further Reading

Busch, Nathan E., and Joseph F. Pilat, "Disarming Libya? A Reassessment after the Arab Spring," *International Affairs* 89, no. 2 (March 2013): 451–475.

Newnham, Randall, "Carrots, Sticks, and Bombs: The End of Libya's WMD Program," *Mediterranean Quarterly* 20, no. 3 (Summer 2009): 77–94.

Wiegele, Thomas C., *The Clandestine Building of Libya's Chemical Weapons Factory: A Study in International Collusion* (Carbondale: Southern Illinois University Press, 1992).

Limited Test Ban Treaty

The Limited Test Ban Treaty (LTBT), first signed by the United States, the United Kingdom, and the Soviet Union in August 1963, prohibits nuclear explosions in the atmosphere, underwater, in outer space, or in any other environment if the explosion would disperse radioactive debris outside the border of the state conducting the test. The

LTBT was signed after years of negotiations on a comprehensive nuclear test ban that had primarily been slowed by disputes over verification of underground nuclear tests; in that sense, it represented a practical step forward in arms control and disarmament by not allowing more ambitious goals to stand in the way of what was politically possible.

Once the countries agreed to set aside the underground testing issue, the treaty was negotiated in a matter of weeks. It was also quickly ratified by a vote of 80–19 in the U.S. Senate and came into force in October 1963. The treaty was later opened to other signatories, and 123 countries have now signed. France and China remain formally outside of the treaty but have pledged to adhere to its restrictions. The treaty has helped to protect the global environment from further contamination from radioactive fallout.

Attempts to negotiate an international nuclear test ban began in 1955, but they failed to progress because of U.S. and Soviet efforts to link the test ban to broader arms control measures unacceptable to the other side. Support for a ban grew in both public and government circles as surveys showed increasing global radioactive contamination from atmospheric tests of nuclear weapons. Scientists warned of possible genetic defects and higher cancer rates, and several accidents have exposed civilians to high levels of fallout.

In the aftermath of the Cuban Missile Crisis, President John F. Kennedy and Premier Nikita Khrushchev looked for new ways to reduce tensions and the risk of nuclear war between the superpowers. Officially known as the Treaty Banning Nuclear Weapon Tests in the Atmosphere, in Outer Space and Under Water, the LTBT reflected the slight thaw in the Cold War that occurred following the Cuban crisis.

John W. Dietrich

Further Reading

"Limited Test Ban Treaty," Treaty Text. https://www.state/gov/t/isn/4797.htm. Accessed June 1, 2002.

Loeb, Benjamin S., "The Limited Test Ban Treaty," in *The Politics of Arms Control Treaty Ratification*, edited by Michael Krepon and Dan Caldwell (New York: St. Martin's Press, 1991), 167–228.

Lithium

Lithium (Li) is only about half as dense as water and is the lightest of all metals. It does not occur freely in nature; in compounds, it is found in small units in nearly all igneous rocks and in the waters of mineral springs. Since World War II, the production of lithium metal and its compounds has increased. Lithium is often used in heat transfer applications. It is highly corrosive, however, and requires special handling.

Lithium-6 (Li-6), an isotope, has two nuclear weapons applications: as a reactor target and control rod material for the production of tritium and as a thermonuclear weapons material. Li-6 is a critical material for the manufacture of dry thermonuclear devices that do not require the use of liquid deuterium and tritium as boosters. Li-6 has the special property of being readily transformed into helium 4 and tritium when its nucleus is struck by a neutron. To produce a thermonuclear device, lithium is combined with deuterium to form the compound lithium-6 deuteride. Neutrons from a fission (primary) device bombard the lithium in the compound, liberating tritium that fuses with the deuterium. The alpha particles are electrically charged and at a higher temperature contribute directly to forming the nuclear fireball.

Lithium enriched in the isotope Li-6 is most often separated from natural lithium by the column-exchange electrochemical process, which exploits the fact that Li-6 has a greater affinity for mercury than Li-7. A lithium-mercury amalgam is first prepared using the natural material. The amalgam is then agitated with a lithium hydroxide solution, which is also prepared from natural lithium. The desired Li-6 concentrates in the amalgam, and the more common Li-7 migrates to the hydroxide. A counterflow of amalgam and hydroxide passes through a cascade of stages until the desired enrichment in Li-6 is achieved.

Gilles Van Nederveen

Further Reading

Lide, D. R., ed., *CRC Handbook of Chemistry and Physics, 1999–2000: A Ready-Reference Book of Chemical and Physical Data* (Boca Raton, FL: CRC Press, 1998).

Low Enriched Uranium

Low enriched uranium (LEU) is uranium that is enriched to less than 20 percent of its fissile isotope, uranium 235 (U-235). Most commercial power reactors require low enriched uranium to function. Typical enrichments for these power plants are between 2 percent and 5 percent. However, some fuels in research reactors are enriched to nearly 20 percent to allow for more compact cores.

Low enriched uranium is mainly produced by processing natural uranium at an enrichment plant. Mixing natural uranium with highly enriched uranium is another way to produce LEU.

History and Background

Early in the development of nuclear reactors, it was recognized that U-235 is the only naturally available isotope that is fissile. In its natural form, uranium contains only 0.72 percent U-235, severely limiting the availability of this fuel source. To create a critical mass using natural uranium, moderators with special properties were necessary to slow the neutrons down. Owing to the limited amount of fissile uranium available, moderators had to slow these neutrons without absorbing them, leaving as many neutrons as possible available for fission. This requirement forced scientists and engineers to use graphite and heavy-water moderators in their attempts to build a sustained chain reaction. As the supply of enriched uranium slowly increased, it eventually became feasible to build reactors that used LEU as the fuel source. These reactors could use light water as the coolant/moderator, which greatly reduced reactor construction and operating costs. Most reactors in the world today use LEU as their fuel source.

The enrichment processes that are used to create low enriched uranium are similar to the processes used to create highly enriched uranium. Because the different isotopes of uranium are chemically identical, all enrichment schemes rely on the small mass differences that exist between the isotopes. Gaseous diffusion, gas centrifuge, Becker nozzle, electromagnetic separation, and laser isotope separation are some of the different methods that exploit this mass difference. All these techniques, except laser separation, require a very large multistage cascade system to achieve significant enrichment. These cascade systems require a lot of space and substantial quantities of electrical power.

Another method for creating low enriched uranium is through the process of diluting highly enriched uranium with natural uranium. This is often referred to as *downblending*. The United States and some former Soviet states use this relatively new method to create low enriched uranium because it allows them to dispose of their inventories of highly enriched (weapons-grade) uranium. Low enriched uranium is unsuitable for use in nuclear weapons.

Technical Details

The primary reason that low enriched uranium is the most prevalent fuel in modern reactors is that fuel enriched in U-235 can use light water as a moderator/coolant. In nuclear reactors, neutrons are more easily absorbed after they have slowed down. Slowing neutrons is called *moderation*. To reduce the velocity of neutrons, three tasks must be accomplished. First, nuclei should have low mass numbers so that each scattering event causes the neutrons to lose a large fraction of their energy. Second, the nuclei need to have large probabilities that scattering, and hence energy loss, will occur over short distances. Third, moderating nuclei should have low probabilities for absorption so that when scattering interactions take place, few neutrons are removed from the system. Light water meets these requirements, but it still has a much smaller scattering-to-absorption ratio than either graphite or heavy water. As result, a graphite or heavy-water reactor can use natural uranium as a fuel, but a light-water reactor requires slightly enriched uranium to function.

All current enrichment methods only slightly enrich the uranium as it passes through one of the many stages in the enrichment facility. This process of feeding the material repeatedly through many enrichment stages is referred to as a *cascade system*, and the measure of separation that takes place in each stage is called a *stage separation factor*. For U-235, the stage separation factor is theoretically limited to 1.0043, but it is typically much closer to 1.003. Using the ideal stage separation factor at a gaseous-diffusion plant, at least 1,100 stages are required to enrich uranium to 3 percent by weight. For a gaseous-centrifuge, the separation factor is higher, and as few as 90 stages may be required for the same enrichment.

C. Ross Schmidtlein

Further Reading

Lamarsh, J. R., and A. J. Baratta, *Introduction to Nuclear Engineering*, 3rd ed. (Upper Saddle River, NJ: Prentice-Hall, 2001).

Parrington, Josef R., Harold D. Knox, Susan L. Breneman, Edward M. Baum, and Frank Feiner, *Nuclides and Isotopes: Chart of the Nuclides*, 15th ed. (New York: General Electric and KAPL, 1996).

M

Manhattan Project

The United States initiated the top-secret Manhattan Project in September 1942 to build an atomic bomb before Germany could develop its own nuclear weapon. The undertaking, named for the fact that it was managed out of the Army Corps of Engineers' Manhattan District, was a massive and costly project that engaged many top U.S., Canadian, and British scientists. It benefited from contributions by numerous U.S. corporations and universities. After overcoming substantial scientific, technical, and practical obstacles, the project produced the weapons that were used on Hiroshima and Nagasaki during World War II, leading to Japan's surrender in August 1945. (Germany had surrendered in May 1945, before the bombs were ready.) The use of atomic weapons against these two Japanese cities ended hostilities in the Pacific.

History and Background

The origins of the Manhattan Project were shaped in the crucible of the tumultuous1930s. By 1934, the idea of using nuclear chain reactions to produce an atomic bomb had received a patent in the United Kingdom. Many European scientists who had been active in nuclear physics sought to escape from the reach of the Nazi regime, which targeted "Jewish" (i.e., nuclear) physics because it was populated by many Jewish scientists. A considerable number of these refugees ended up working on the Manhattan Project.

German scientists had split the first uranium atom in 1938, which provided experimental evidence that it was possible to use nuclear fission to produce a very destructive weapon. The next year, Albert Einstein, who in 1933 had left Germany and settled in the United States, was urged by three Hungarian refugee physicists (Leo Szilard, Edward Teller, and Eugene Wigner) to alert U.S. political authorities to the dangers posed by Germany's nuclear research. Einstein signed a letter to President Franklin D. Roosevelt describing German atomic research and the possibility that Hitler could produce an atomic bomb based on that research. Roosevelt responded by creating a special Advisory Committee on Uranium, referred to as "S-1." In June 1940, the committee was placed under the auspices of the National Defense Research Committee (NDRC), led by the Carnegie Institution's director, Dr. Vannevar Bush. It immediately launched a major research program through contracts with universities and other institutions. In November 1941, the S-1 committee was placed under the jurisdiction of the U.S. Office of Scientific Research and Development (OSRD), the parent organization of the NDRC.

Much of the research contracted by the Uranium Committee had been oriented toward using uranium 235 (U-235), a rare isotope constituting less than 1 percent of uranium metal in its natural state, to produce a controlled chain reaction. At the time, it was uncertain whether sufficient quantities of highly refined U-235 could be produced to manufacture an atomic bomb.

A second broad approach to the problem suggested that U-238, more abundant than U-235, could be converted into plutonium, which then could be used as the foundation for the atomic chain reaction.

The Project

On June 17, 1942, Vannevar Bush reported to President Roosevelt that the Uranium Committee's research program had demonstrated that production of fissionable uranium and plutonium could produce an atomic weapon. Roosevelt decided to move the atomic program from the research and development stage to large-scale production. That same month, Roosevelt directed the army to manage this transition, and the task was given to the Army Corps of Engineers, which created a new organization known as the Manhattan Engineer District (MED), located in New York City. The Manhattan Project got under way in September. West Point graduate and army engineer Leslie R. Groves was chosen as its director.

Brigadier General Groves, who had previously supervised construction of the Pentagon, was known for his ability to deliver results. He took on the task somewhat reluctantly, having preferred an assignment in an active theater of operations. He later wrote that his initial reaction was one of "extreme disappointment." Nevertheless, the disappointment was mitigated when he was told that his appointment had been made by the secretary of war and approved by the president. One official told him, "If you do the job right, it will win the war" (Groves 1983, 3–4).

Groves's initial assignment was to organize production of the atomic bomb. It soon became clear that the production effort could not succeed unless ongoing research efforts were focused more effectively on the practical task of producing enough fissionable material to yield several bombs. The Uranium Committee's research programs had focused on five basic ways of producing fissionable material: U-235 could be separated from the parent uranium by using a centrifuge, gaseous diffusion, or an electromagnetic process, or plutonium could be produced by organizing uranium and graphite blocks in a "pile," or reactor, or in a reactor using heavy water instead of graphite to control the chain reaction during the production process. The Uranium Committee decided to move all five approaches from the research stage to the production stage. After examining research into the centrifuge separation method at the University of Virginia and the Westinghouse Research Laboratories in Pittsburgh, Pennsylvania, General Groves decided to drop further work on this method and to concentrate on the other four.

Atomic research was undertaken in a number of locations across the country, but three became critical centers for the transition from research to production. Scientists at Columbia University in New York, under the direction of Professor Harold Urey, concentrated on issues related to using gaseous diffusion to separate out U-235. Scientists at the University of California at Berkeley, led by Professor Ernest O. Lawrence, worked on the process of electromagnetic separation. At the University of Chicago, a team of scientists led by Arthur Compton that included Italian Nobel Prize winner Enrico Fermi and Hungarian expatriate physicists Leo Szilard and Eugene Wigner concentrated on the process of producing fissionable plutonium with the uranium/graphite pile. A critical breakthrough in the research process came in December 1942, when Fermi demonstrated the first self-sustaining nuclear chain reaction at a pile built under a squash court at the University of Chicago.

The scientific challenges posed by the project were considerable, including the seemingly mundane but extremely difficult tasks of developing filters, valves, pipes, and other processing equipment to stand up to demanding production requirements. Equally challenging was the task of building facilities for production processes that were still being developed. In November 1942, a remote and undeveloped site in Los Alamos, New Mexico, was selected as the location for a laboratory where the actual production of atomic bombs would take place. Dr. J. Robert Oppenheimer, from the University of California–Berkeley, was chosen to head the lab.

Also, late in 1942, a large site in Oak Ridge, Tennessee, was selected for construction of what was then called the Clinton Engineer Works, which was renamed after the war as the Oak Ridge National Laboratory. The site became the factory for the production of plutonium in the "Clinton Pile" and for separation of U-235 in gaseous-diffusion and electromagnetic plants. The main production facilities for weapons material were the K-25 gaseous-diffusion plant, the Y-12 electromagnetic plant, and the S-50 thermal-diffusion plant.

A third major facility, the Hanford site, was constructed in Richland, Washington, to produce plutonium. At the peak of the construction effort, some 45,000 construction workers were employed at the Hanford site.

All three facilities were built quickly and without knowing exactly how all the production methods would work. The projects included housing for the construction workers, engineers, and scientists who would construct and operate the facilities. Most of the thousands of engineers, construction workers, and technicians involved had no idea what the facilities would produce. The project relied on contributions from many of America's major companies, including Allis-Chalmers, Celotex, Chrysler, DuPont, Eastman Kodak, Goodyear, IBM, Ingersoll-Rand, International Nickel, Stone and Webster, Union Carbide, and Westinghouse.

As the Manhattan Project approached the point where enough fissionable material was available to produce a few weapons, the war in Europe had moved toward a successful conclusion. The end of the Third Reich and Germany's surrender in May 1945 removed the threat of a German-produced atomic bomb.

Japan, however, remained a stubborn combatant, and President Harry S. Truman, who had succeeded Roosevelt after his death in early 1945, decided to use nuclear weapons against Japanese cities to force a Japanese surrender (the deaths of over 100,000 Japanese civilians in firebombing attacks against Tokyo had not accomplished that goal).

The development of U-235 weapons and those made from plutonium, despite various setbacks along the way, came to fruition at roughly the same time in 1945. The first test of an atomic bomb took place on July 16, 1945, at a remote range in Alamogordo, New Mexico, with Oppenheimer in charge. The weapon was an implosion-type plutonium fission bomb. The test site was code-named "Trinity." With the test's success, two other weapons, code-named "Little Boy" and "Fat Man," were rushed to an air base in the Pacific.

On August 6, 1945, Little Boy, a U-235 weapon, was flown from Tinian, in the Mariana Islands, on a B-29 named *Enola Gay* and dropped on the city of Hiroshima, Japan. Its design had not been tested due to the scarcity of U-235 and because the scientists of the Manhattan Project were certain that its gun-type design would work. Fat Man, a plutonium bomb, was dropped by another B-29, *Bockscar*, on Nagasaki, Japan, on August 9. Japan surrendered soon after, bringing World War II to an end.

Consequences

The overall cost of the Manhattan Project effort was about $20 billion (in 1996 dollars). Despite the extraordinary security that surrounded the Manhattan Project, the Soviet Union managed to obtain critical nuclear secrets from spies inside the project. The acquisition of this information greatly facilitated the development of the Soviet nuclear weapons program.

Stanley R. Sloan

Further Reading

Gosling, Francis G., U.S. Department of Energy, *The Manhattan Project: Science in the Second World War* (Washington, D.C.: U.S. Department of Energy, 1990).

Groueff, Stephane, *Manhattan Project: The Untold Story of the Making of the Atomic Bomb* (Boston: Little, Brown, 1967).

Groves, Leslie M., *Now It Can Be Told: The Story of the Manhattan Project* (New York: Da Capo, 1983).

Rhodes, Richard, *The Making of the Atomic Bomb* (New York: Simon & Schuster, 1986).

Megaton

A megaton is a measure of the energy released during a nuclear explosion. One megaton is equal to 1 million tons of the high-explosive trinitrotoluene (TNT), approximately 4.184 petajoules. This definition refers to all the energy released by the weapon, regardless of the form. When a nuclear explosion occurs, only a small part of the released energy is in the form of explosive energy, whereas the energy of a chemical explosion (e.g., TNT) is mostly released as blast. The largest U.S. nuclear detonation was the thermonuclear Castle/Bravo test in 1954, which had a yield of 15 megatons. The Soviet Union reportedly tested a thermonuclear bomb in 1961 that measured 58 megatons.

Zachariah Becker

Further Reading

Pringle, Laurence, *Nuclear War: From Hiroshima to Nuclear Winter* (Hillside, NJ: Enslow, 1985).

Missile Defense

The term *missile defense* refers to a system or systems designed to defend against ballistic missile attack, including both active and passive measures to detect, identify, assess, track, and defeat offensive ballistic missiles during any portion of their flight trajectory. It most often refers to the use of ballistic missiles to shoot down other ballistic missiles, but it may include other means of interception, such as directed-energy or laser weapons. The term *antiballistic missile* strictly refers to a ballistic missile that intercepts another ballistic missile. The term *ballistic missile defense* is sometimes used interchangeably with *missile defense* and can refer to either defense against ballistic missiles (such as silo-based intercontinental ballistic missiles (ICBMs)) by any means or defense of any potential target by means of antiballistic missiles.

History and Background

Throughout most of the Cold War, missile defenses were divided into two categories. *Theater missile defense* referred to defense against short-, medium-, or intermediate-range ballistic missiles and was associated with the defense of forces deployed to a given theater of combat against ballistic missile attack. *National missile defense* referred to broader defense of the national territory against long-range or intercontinental ballistic missiles. This distinction was institutionalized by the 1972 Anti-Ballistic Missile (ABM) Treaty, which strictly limited the development and deployment of missile defenses against intercontinental missiles but did not limit theater missile defenses.

Following U.S. withdrawal from the ABM Treaty in June 2002, which was partially motivated by the blurring of technological distinctions between systems designed to detect and counter intercontinental ballistic missiles and those designed to detect and counter shorter-range ballistic missiles, the distinction between theater missile defense and national missile defense no longer preoccupied strategists. Missile defense systems are now grouped into three categories: boost phase, the midcourse phase, and the terminal phase, depending on that phase in the trajectory of an incoming missile where interception occurs. Intercepts during each phase presents its own advantages and challenges from the defender's perspective.

During its boost phase, an offensive missile's booster rockets continue to fire, lifting it into a ballistic trajectory. This phase is very short, lasting anywhere from 3 to 10 minutes. The heat generated by the firing rocket plumes create easily detected thermal signatures, facilitating detection, tracking, and identification, especially from space-based infrared sensors. As the missile is traveling relatively slowly in the early stages of boost phase, it may be more easily intercepted by high-acceleration ground- or sea-based interceptors located within range. Decoys or other devices intended to distract or confuse the interceptor missile will not

have been released during this phase, thus easing the problem of discriminating between the warhead and other items traveling through space with it. Missiles launched from deep inside an attacking nation's territory, however, may be difficult to reach by land- or sea-based interceptors. Because this phase is very short, warning and response timelines are extremely compressed, making it challenging to detect and assess a hostile launch and then cue and direct interceptors in time to destroy the attacking missile while it is still in the boost phase of its flight.

During the midcourse phase, the missile's boosters cease firing, and the warheads, and in many cases decoys, separate from the third stage. This phase may last up to 20 minutes, constituting the longest portion of the trajectory, and thus offers the best opportunity for an adversary to track the missile, assess its intended target, and attempt one or more intercepts. The Ground-Based Interceptor system deployed by the United States in Alaska and California is a midcourse interception system. Nevertheless, interception during this phase is challenging because missiles may release multiple warheads or penetration aids, such as decoys or chaff, to complicate targeting.

Lasting for as little as a minute, the terminal phase begins upon a missile warhead's final approach to its intended target. At this point, the warhead is traveling at its fastest speed, which leaves only a slight window for attempting an intercept. The atmosphere, however, strips away decoys and chaff, simplifying targeting. Terminal defense systems can only provide protection for relatively small areas.

Kill Mechanisms

A variety of kill mechanisms have been devised to achieve the destruction of an incoming missile or warhead, though not all have been fully developed or even tested. Blast fragmentation devices are designed to explode in proximity to an incoming warhead or missile and to destroy or damage it through collisions with fragments of the interceptor warhead. This is the mechanism employed by most theater missile defenses, and its shortcomings were highlighted by the partial successes of the Patriot missile defense efforts to shoot down Iraqi Scud missiles during the First Gulf War in 1991.

Early U.S. and Soviet antiballistic missile systems employed nuclear warheads as their primary kill mechanism. The Russian ABM system around Moscow still carries interceptor warheads that rely on nuclear blasts to destroy incoming warheads. In the late 1980s, the United States made a decision to develop kinetic kill mechanisms, or hit-to-kill devices, that use the energy released by direct collisions between interceptors and attacking warheads. Such collisions obliterate both the interceptor and the offensive warhead so thoroughly that any nuclear, biological, or chemical weapon carried by the offensive warhead is incinerated. The U.S. ground-based interceptor uses a kinetic kill vehicle.

Political Considerations

Few issues in the field of foreign and defense policy have been of such enduring controversy and debate as missile defense. This debate, which has raged since the mid-1960s, has revolved around two basic questions: (1) *Could* a truly effective and affordable missile defense system be developed and deployed? And, (2) *should* such a system be developed and deployed, if it is possible to build one? The first question involves issues of technology, the reliability of complex command and control networks, the pros and cons of automated decision making, resilience in the face of countermeasures, and the rigors and "realism" of the testing regime. The second question raises concerns about the impact of missile defense systems on international and regional stability, whether they would provoke action-reaction arms races or whether they would help or hinder efforts to combat the proliferation of weapons of mass destruction.

These same issues were revisited during the course of three successive debates on missile defense. The first started in the 1960s, culminating in the conclusion of the ABM Treaty in 1972, which settled the debate in favor of those opposed to missile defense. The debate was revived in the early 1980s when President Ronald Reagan called for the development of a Strategic Defense Initiative (SDI) to provide a hemispheric shield against a potential attack by thousands of Soviet ballistic missiles. This debate was rendered moot by the dissolution of the Soviet Union, which reduced the sense of urgency behind the missile defense issue.

President Bill Clinton's administration (1992–2000) responded to the fall of the Soviet Union by reconfirming the status of the ABM Treaty as the "cornerstone of strategic stability" and discontinuing negotiations with Russia for a cooperative evolution toward a "Global Protection Against Limited Strikes," or GPALS, system. The GPALS system was aimed at loosening or amending ABM Treaty restrictions on missile defense and would have led to the joint development of a modest capability to intercept missile launches by rogue states in certain regions. During the first Clinton administration, funding for SDI was reduced by nearly 80 percent, for theater missile defenses by nearly 25 percent, and for advanced science and technology research by over 95 percent.

Nevertheless, the debate over missile defense flared up again, for the third time, in the late 1990s in the face of increasing proliferation of ballistic missiles among rogue states and, in particular, by North Korea's test launch of a three-stage missile of apparent intercontinental range in August 1998. The Clinton administration formulated four criteria for evaluating whether to deploy some form of missile defense as a response to the proliferation threat: the degree to which the threat of ballistic missile attack justified such a response; whether a technically feasible system could be developed; the affordability of such a system; and the likely impact of a U.S. decision to deploy missile defenses on the ABM Treaty and other U.S. arms control and nonproliferation objectives. Eventually, in a speech given on September 1, 2000, President Clinton announced his decision to defer deployment of a missile defense system, largely out of concern about its anticipated impact on U.S.-Russian relations and arms control.

Shortly after assuming office in January 2001, President George W. Bush declared that his administration would deploy a limited missile defense as soon as technically feasible. The Bush administration believed that the ABM Treaty had blocked fully exploring all technological avenues of achieving an effective missile defense, that an effective system was affordable, that it was justified by the prospective threat, and that the arms control and international stability ramifications could be managed. In December 2001, President Bush exercised the U.S. right to withdraw from the ABM Treaty on six months' notice, and shortly afterward, he announced a decision to begin deploying a limited missile defense system in 2004.

Each president since has supported the development of a layered U.S. missile defense program. By the end of 2017, approximately 44 ground-based interceptors had been deployed in Alaska and California; sea-based interceptors had been deployed on Aegis ships; and a variety of land-, sea-, and space-based sensors, including upgrades to three existing early-warning radar systems located in Clear, Alaska; Thule, Greenland; and Fylingdales, Great Britain, had been completed.

The end of the ABM Treaty failed to produce the dire consequences predicted by critics, but North Korean nuclear tests and missile tests validate decades-old decisions to move forward on developing a limited missile defense for the United States.

Kerry Kartchner

Further Reading

Butler, Richard, *Fatal Choice: Nuclear Weapons and the Illusion of Missile Defense* (Boulder, CO: Westview, 2001).

Payne, Keith B., *Missile Defense in the 21st Century: Protection against Limited Threats, Including Lessons from the Gulf War* (Boulder, CO: Westview, 1991).

Wirtz, James J., and Jeffrey A. Larsen, eds., *Rockets' Red Glare: Missile Defenses and the Future of World Politics* (Boulder, CO: Westview, 2001).

Missile Technology Control Regime

The Missile Technology Control Regime (MTCR) is a set of guidelines regulating the export of ballistic and cruise missiles, unmanned aerial vehicles (UAVs), and related technology for those systems capable of carrying a 500-kilogram payload at least 300 kilometers.

On April 16, 1987, Canada, France, Germany, Italy, Japan, the United Kingdom, and the United States established the MTCR to govern the export of missiles and related technology. The regime is an informal, voluntary arrangement rather than a treaty or international agreement. It consists of a set of common export policies applied to a list of controlled items. Each member implements its commitments in the context of its own national export laws. In addition to the states that have formally joined the MTCR, a number of countries unilaterally observe or adhere to the guidelines.

The MTCR guidelines cover ballistic missiles, space launch vehicles, sounding rockets, cruise missiles, drones, and remotely piloted vehicles. The guidelines explicitly state that the regime is "not designed to impede national space programs or international cooperation in such programs as long as such programs could not contribute to delivery systems for weapons of mass destruction." When announced in 1987, the regime was only concerned with nuclear-capable delivery systems. In January 1993, however, the adherents extended the guidelines to cover systems capable of delivering all nuclear, biological, and chemical weapons.

The MTCR's annex of controlled equipment and technology includes equipment and technology, both military and dual-use, relevant to missile development, production, and operation. It is divided into Category I and Category II items. Export of Category I items—including complete rocket systems, cruise missiles, and unmanned aerial vehicles; specially designed production facilities for these systems; and certain complete subsystems—is subject to a presumption of export denial. Category II items—such as propellants, structural materials, test equipment, and flight instruments—may be exported at the discretion of the MTCR partner government on a case-by-case basis for acceptable

end uses. They also may be exported after the exchange of government-to-government assurances, which provide that they not be used on a missile system capable of delivering a 500-kilogram payload to a range of at least 300 kilometers.

In 2002, The Hague Code of Conduct was launched. With 119 members, the code calls for participants to restrain proliferation of ballistic missiles capable of carrying weapons of mass destruction. The code has a greater membership than the MTCR, which had 35 members in 2016, but it places more modest restrictions on members' activities.

Tom Mahnken

Further Reading

U.S. Department of State. http://www.state.gov/www/global/arms/np/mtcr/mtcr.html. Accessed January 10, 2018.

Mustard (Sulfur and Nitrogen)

Mustard (U.S. code HD) usually refers to sulfur mustard, a classical vesicant (or blister) agent. It was first used by Germany in World War I, then by Italy during Mussolini's war against Ethiopia (1936), and then by Iraq against Iranian troops in the 1980s.

Although not as toxic as the nerve agents developed in the 1930s, mustard is still regarded as a significant chemical threat due to its ability to cause mass casualties. As a consequence, mustard was once known as the "king" of chemical warfare agents, especially during the World War I era. In Germany, mustard was referred to as "Lost" (from the names of researchers Lommel and Steinkopf, who developed processes for its mass production), and France and Russia named the mustard agent "Yprite" after its initial use at Ypres, Belgium.

Other forms of mustard include the nitrogen-based vesicants, coded HN-1, HN-2, and HN-3. Although the nitrogen mustards differ in some respects from sulfur mustard, the basic mechanism and injuries that result from their exposure are largely the same. There is little information to suggest that nitrogen mustards have ever been used in battle.

The effects of mustard agent reverberate in historical and modern contexts. Since its use in World War I, injuries still occur from old munitions left on battlefields from China to Europe. In 1990, for example, a Frenchman suffered serious mustard burns on his hands and arms after he picked up a mustard shell on the old battlegrounds of Verdun. And in the People's Republic of China (2003), one person was killed and 43 injured when construction laborers unknowingly dug up a leaking World War II–era Japanese mustard agent canister.

Sulfur and nitrogen mustards are toxic via a number of routes, including the skin, eyes, and upper respiratory tract. Mustard, an oily liquid, is also more persistent than other true "gases" that were used in the beginning of World War I. Thus, mustard's effects are insidious. Exposure to mustard results in itchy, painful irritation of the skin and especially the eyes. Very large blisters (vesicles) follow after a considerable delay (up to 24 hours).

The mode of mustard's action is cytotoxic—that is, it kills living cells. After coming into contact with living tissue, the mustard molecule forms a highly reactive ion called a *free radical*. By interfering with DNA synthesis, mustard then destroys cells from the inside. When these cells die, they release enzymes called *proteases*, breaking down tissues into liquid exudate (pus). This is the basic process through which blisters are formed. Being fat soluble, mustard readily penetrates the skin and can also attack vital organs of the body.

History of Sulfur Mustard

The Belgian Cesar-Mansuete Despretz first synthesized sulfur mustard in 1822, but he did not describe its qualities. The British scientist Guthrie repeated Despretz's experiments in 1860, describing the compound as having an odor of mustard and a flavor similar to garlic, but noting that it caused blisters on the skin. At the time, however, this newly discovered compound and its irritating effects did not receive much attention. Independently, the German chemist Victor Meyer synthesized mustard in 1886, first by making thiodiglycol and then reacting this nontoxic chemical with chlorine. Much to his surprise, this small change produced an extremely toxic chemical.

By 1916, both sides in World War I had developed fairly effective defenses against chemical warfare (CW) that predominately consisted of gaseous chemicals, such as chlorine and phosgene. An irritant like mustard agent was found to be the next logical step. Given mustard's high persistency, a half-quart could contaminate nearly 150 square yards of ground for about a week. However, its toxicity was found to be relatively low, and it was not yet made a priority CW agent for the Allied forces.

Germany first used sulfur mustard (Yellow Cross) at Ypres in July 1917. Because of its persistency and its latency period, soldiers exposed to this chemical often did not know they had been contaminated until injuries manifested later. Although Germany had confidence that mustard could help turn the tide in World War I, Fritz Haber—the chief of the German chemical weapons program—warned that the Western militaries would be able to respond using mustard as well.

Although it did not have the lethal effect of phosgene and other gases, mustard agent was the cause of the greatest number of total casualties (80 percent) from chemicals throughout World War I. With advances in protective gear, however, mortality rates due to mustard agent fell from 6 percent to 2 percent by war's end.

In World War II, CW was limited to the Chinese theater of operations during Japan's invasion of East Asia. While the European militaries and the United States refrained from using chemical weapons during the war, Japan employed a large number and variety of CW agents, including mustard, against the Chinese in the 1930s and 1940s.

During the Iran-Iraq War (1980–1988), after having made initial military successes, Iraq soon found itself on the defensive. Early on, Iran had adopted a "revolutionary" battle strategy—basically throwing bodies at the enemy with little equipment or preparation for battle—and Iraq struggled to stave off the mass attacks of Iranian foot soldiers. Knowing that these ill-equipped Iranian troops were extremely vulnerable to chemical agents, in ca. 1984, Iraq thus valued the use of mustard as a key defensive weapon.

It is unknown how many Iranian casualties were caused by CW during the war. Figures of 50,000 or more casualties, mostly inflicted by mustard, are certainly possible. At first, Iraq was able to obtain chemical precursors from Western countries, including Europe and the United States. When it was cut off from these supplies in the mid-1980s, Iraq turned to its domestic petroleum industry for alternative sources. By cracking oil and breaking it down into ethylene, Iraq found a relatively efficient means to produce mustard agent from indigenous materials.

Nitrogen Mustards

Nitrogen mustards were first developed out of research into nitrogen-carbon compounds during the 1920s and 1930s. In 1935, Kyle Ward found that using nitrogen to link chlorinated carbon chains produced a highly potent vesicant. Although the United States Chemical Warfare Service was interested, code-naming the first of these nitrogen mustards as "HN-1," it was not considered to be more effective than sulfur mustard.

At about the same time, the German military found the nitrogen mustards to be of great interest. Variations of nitrogen mustard yielded different analogs, some of which were later coded by the U.S military as HN-2 and HN-3. Germany considered the latter—"nitrogen pyrite" (tris-(2-chloroethyl)-amine)—to be highly effective for contaminating the ground for area denial and harassing the enemy. The German military ultimately produced some 2,000 tons of HN-3 during World War II, but it was never used in battle. Allied forces destroyed these stockpiles at the end of the war in Europe.

Nitrogen mustards are generally more toxic than the sulfur variety, and like sulfur mustard, they are easily manufactured. Both types of mustard cause injury with similar mechanisms, and because of mustard's well-known ability to kill cells, physicians theorized that it could help treat cancer. Experiments found that tumors shrank following treatment with HN-2 nitrogen mustard, variously known as *mustine* (Mustargenor mechloroethamine). The latter, administered in the form of a topical gel, was approved by the U.S. Food and Drug Administration (2013) to treat mycosis fungoides (Alibert-Bazin syndrome), a cutaneous T-cell lymphoma.

Because the mustard agents produce blisters on the skin, casualties are at risk for secondary infections and systemic poisoning. By and large, however, injuries to the skin will heal, although there may be significant scarring due to changes in pigmentation. Exposure to mustard agent is particularly dangerous when its fumes are inhaled. In these cases, dead tissue in the upper airways can form "false membranes" that may block the respiratory system, causing death by asphyxia. Today, the primary defenses against mustard are still those used in World War I: skin and respiratory protection. Medical treatment options are still limited to supportive therapy.

Survivors of single exposures to mustard do not show to have elevated risk of cancer. Repeated contact with the agent, on the other hand, has been shown to be carcinogenic, such as for those who worked in mustard manufacturing during the world wars. Mustard has a severe injurious effect on the eyes, causing at the very least temporary blindness in low concentrations. However, most victims recover from mustard's effects on the eyes, although some may require corrective lenses. In severe cases of exposure, permanent blindness is possible.

Eric A. Croddy

Further Reading

Wachtel, Curt, *Chemical Warfare* (Brooklyn, NY: Chemical, 1941).

Ward, Clyde, "Fritz Haber Said of His Chemical Agents, Especially Mustard Gas, 'It Is a Higher Form of Killing,'" *Military History* 23, no. 3 (May 2006):18–72 (3p).

Mutual Assured Destruction

Mutual assured destruction (MAD) is a situation in which two or more states possess a secure second-strike capability that would allow them to destroy their adversaries even after absorbing a major nuclear attack. During the Cold War, MAD was depicted as a stable deterrence relationship by many theorists who believed that the threat of massive retaliation could prevent each side from initiating a surprise nuclear first strike. They therefore recommended having enough survivable nuclear weapons to assure the adversary's destruction as a modern society in a retaliatory response. These theorists often assumed that such a second strike would target cities in a strictly punitive retaliation with no specific military objective other than the complete annihilation of the attacker's nation. Many believed that the possession of a secure second-strike capability was the only sure means of deterring a surprise nuclear attack and that MAD was thus the inescapable basis of crisis stability in a Cold War environment dominated by two heavily armed superpowers. The acronym became an ironic metaphor for the belief that the destructiveness of war has reduced the danger of war.

MAD did not describe the actual targeting strategy followed by either the United States or the Soviet Union, both of which pursued more operationally oriented counterforce targeting strategies, although U.S. war plans called for withholding a "strategic reserve," and the strike plans for these reserves came close to resembling a MAD targeting doctrine. Nevertheless, many believed that MAD described a reality that neither superpower could transcend regardless of targeting strategy, as long as the opponent retained a significant retaliatory force following a nuclear attack.

Most criticisms of MAD revolved around its credibility, or lack thereof. Some asserted that no one would actually believe that either side was politically capable of unleashing an all-out attack against urban-industrial centers, especially if it came in the aftermath of a series of nuclear exchanges that had already left most of both sides in ruins. Moreover, religious authorities noted that it was not morally sustainable to threaten to do what one was morally forbidden to do and that a strategy of assured destruction violated the most fundamental precepts of the just war tradition.

Despite these criticisms and the end of the Cold War, many continue to believe that as long as the United States and Russia maintain large residual nuclear arsenals, a condition of MAD will exist between them, and that such a condition could come to include China in the near future.

Kerry Kartchner

Further Reading

Enthoven, Alain C., and K. Wayne Smith, *How Much Is Enough?: Shaping the Defense Program, 1961–1969* (New York: Harper and Row, 1971).

Martel, William C., and Paul L. Savage, *Strategic Nuclear War: What the Superpowers Target and Why* (New York: Greenwood, 1986).

N

Nagasaki

Nagasaki is a commercial port city on the southern Japanese island of Kyushu and was the site of the second U.S. atomic attack against Japan on August 9, 1945, three days after the first nuclear bomb ever used in warfare was dropped on Hiroshima. On September 2, 1945, Japan surrendered, ending World War II.

Nagasaki was the site of the first European influence in Japan. Portuguese traders and missionaries established a community there in the late 1500s. Even during the shogunate period of "enclosure," Nagasaki remained open to foreigners for trade. Because of its clay deposits, the area has long been a center for ceramics, including pottery and fine china. Its commercial port made Nagasaki a more cosmopolitan area than many other parts of Japan.

During World War II, the U.S. Manhattan Project developed two types of atomic bombs: a gun-type device that used uranium to create a critical mass and an implosion device that used plutonium as its fissile material. By the summer of 1945, one bomb of each type was available for use against Japan.

U.S. war plans had included an invasion of the Japanese home islands as a means to force the surrender of the Japanese government. Kyushu was slated for invasion by 190,000 U.S. troops. It was estimated that the invasion of Kyushu would produce hundreds of thousands of U.S. and Japanese casualties. President Harry S. Truman decided to delay the invasion of the home islands and instead use aerial atomic bombing to shock Japan into surrendering, thereby saving the lives of both U.S. troops and Japanese civilians.

Nagasaki was not among the original cities selected as a potential nuclear target. It was substituted for Kyoto when Secretary of War Henry L. Stimson moved to protect Kyoto's antiquities. Nagasaki was selected because of its large commercial harbor and four large Mitsubishi war production plants.

The bomb dropped on Nagasaki was "Fat Man," an implosion weapon that used plutonium 239 (Pu-239) that had been produced at nuclear reactors in Hanford, Washington It was dropped from a B-29 named *Bockscar*. Due to weather problems, the original commercial target site was missed, and the bomb was dropped over Nagasaki's industrial center. The plutonium bomb created a blast equivalent to 20,000 tons of TNT, more powerful than the gun-type device dropped on Hiroshima. The hills surrounding Nagasaki concentrated the blast produced by the bomb, leaving about 25 percent of the population dead or injured. The hills also served to protect some of Nagasaki's population from radiant heat and ionizing radiation.

The area of total destruction covered about one and a half square miles. About 50,000 people were immediately killed or injured by the detonation. The topography prevented a firestorm from developing and localized the direct effects of the blast, resulting in less public panic than in Hiroshima. The industrial damage was high: 68 percent of the nondockyard industrial production in Nagasaki was destroyed.

The area of the explosion has been rebuilt as a modern city center. There is a museum and park memorializing the lives lost in the attack. With descriptive materials confined to the events in Nagasaki, the museum is less politicized than the larger and more well-known museum in Hiroshima,.

Frannie Edwards

Further Reading

Bauer, E., *The History of World War II* (New York: Military Press, 1984).

Napalm

Napalm is an incendiary, that is, a weapon designed for destroying targets with a very high-temperature flame. Napalm falls under the rubric of a weapon of mass destruction (WMD) due to its widespread and indiscriminate effects.

Napalm is basically a jellified liquid containing a fuel, such as kerosene, combined with other components to give it persistence. By thickening flammable liquid in such a manner, napalm (or similar mixtures) becomes more practical to use in aerial munitions and in flamethrowers. The physical properties of napalm enable it to adhere to surfaces, be they materiel or individual soldiers. When delivered from combat aircraft—as demonstrated in World War II and the Korean and Vietnam Wars—napalm proved to be devastating against troop concentrations caught in the open.

Napalm was first conceived as a jellied mixture of gasoline and rubber in 1942 when Professor Louis Fieser of Harvard produced a soap combining aluminum naphthenate and aluminum palmitate. This formula gave the world the name *napalm*. The first use of napalm by the U.S. military was during the Sicilian campaign in 1943.

Ultimately, about 80,000,000 pounds of napalm were produced by the United States during World War II for incendiary bombs and flamethrowers.

In response to the tenacity of Japanese soldiers—who also employed flamethrowers against American troops in the Philippines (1942)—U.S. soldiers increasingly relied on napalm used from the air and in flamethrowers during the later island-hopping campaign in the Pacific. During the latter stages of the campaign against Japan, American bombers used napalm bombs, such as the M-47, against Tokyo in March 1945. The M-47 was a device with napalm that was ignited by white phosphorus surrounding a high-explosive charge. By the end of May 1945, the widespread use of this incendiary weapon had ignited firestorms that ultimately consumed over 50 square miles of Tokyo, and at least 100,000 civilians had been killed. In the Korean War (1950–1953), plastic canisters, each containing 90–100 pounds of napalm, were dropped on North Korean and Chinese positions from the air.

Later, isobutyl methacrylate polymers were employed as thickeners to produce napalm. From 1965 to 1969, Dow Chemical mixed a polystyrene-gasoline-benzene fuel that was primarily used during the Vietnam conflict. Other applications for napalm included explosive devices attached to 55-gallon drums containing napalm, called *fougasse* (from the French *fougade*, referring to a type of land mine). These were employed in Vietnam for tripwire perimeter security at military bases.

The use of napalm was often a target of Vietnam War protesters during the 1960s, and it was often mentioned by international critics of U.S. policy in Southeast Asia. A now-famous photograph of a young Vietnamese girl (Kim Phúc), who had been severely burned by a U.S. napalm strike, captured for many not only the unpopularity of the Vietnam War, but also the inhumane use of napalm as a weapon.

In 1998, the United States undertook to destroy some 23 million pounds of stockpiled napalm, and in 2001, the remaining napalm stores in the United States had been destroyed or recycled into furnace fuel. Although other incendiaries, such as fuel-air (thermobaric) munitions, have been used and developed for special combat roles, napalm is no longer included in U.S. military planning.

Eric A. Croddy

Further Reading

Neer, Robert M., *Napalm: An American Biography* (Cambridge, MA: Belknap Press of Harvard University Press, 2013).

Nerve Agents

A nerve agent can be described as any chemical compound that poisons the mammalian system by moderating the body's nervous system impulses. In addition to the toxic organophosphates (those chemicals combining phosphorous with a carbon-based structure), other chemical classes, such as the carbamates and various cyclic compounds, could also potentially be used as nerve agents. Thus far, however, only organophosphorus (OP) compounds have been used as chemical warfare (CW) nerve agents.

During the 20th century, nerve agents such as tabun (GA), sarin (GB), soman (GD), and VX (or the Russian V-gas) were weaponized in large quantities. During the Cold War, both the United States and the Soviet Union maintained thousands of tons of nerve agents in stockpiles. These included sarin, soman, and VX (the Soviet version, VR, being a slightly different analog than the U.S. formula). The U.S. chemical weapons program was halted in 1969, but it was revived temporarily in the mid-1980s by the Reagan administration as a counter to Warsaw Pact forces in Europe. Although several weapons systems were developed in the 1980s, the United States primarily integrated the binary 155-mm (GB) shell and the VX Bigeye glide bomb. By 1989, however, the United States and the former Soviet Union had come to an understanding to disarm their respective chemical inventories. The 1993 Chemical Weapons Convention (CWC) later cemented this agreement in a multilateral disarmament treaty.

Nerve compounds are extremely toxic. In animal studies, the average lethal dose is used as a means for comparing the relative toxicities. The dose required to kill 50 percent of a given population is termed the LD_{50}. It takes more than a teaspoon of the blister agent sulfur mustard, for example, to produce an LD_{50} for skin exposure (percutaneous). The nerve agent VX, by comparison, is about 700 times as toxic as mustard. Nerve agents also have liquid properties that make them more suitable for fill in artillery shells, rockets, and missile warheads.

Depending on the operational mission, one nerve agent may be more effective against unprotected troops (e.g., sarin), while another excels at creating highly toxic contaminated areas that can prevent troop movement or deny forces access to materiel or logistics (e.g., VX). For example, sarin forms toxic vapors at room temperature and can be applied grossly on targets, allowing its volatile fumes to do the rest of the work. A more persistent nerve agent, VX, does not create appreciable amounts of vapor under normal conditions. However, its dermal (skin) activity and high persistency both make it a prime candidate for rendering areas uninhabitable for troops. The rapid percutaneous action of VX agent was recently highlighted by North Korea's assassination of Kim Jong-un's half-brother, Kim Jong-nam, at Malaysia's Kuala Lumpur International Airport in February 2017. Operatives sent by the North Korean government applied VX nerve agent to Kim Jong-nam's face. Despite having received emergency medical intervention, Kim Jong-nam died on the way to the hospital.

In 1984, Iraq became the first to employ tabun (GA) nerve agent during the Iran-Iraq War (1980–1988). Iraqi military units, including its air forces, also mixed a precursor chemical (DF) with cyclohexanol and isopropyl alcohol, forming roughly an equal mixture of sarin and cyclosarin (GF) for use in aerial bombs. Iraq used tabun, sarin, VX, and soman against Kurdish populations in the northern part of Iraq in the late 1980s. Most notoriously, in 1988, Iraq military forces killed at least 5,000 civilians in a chemical attack on Halabja.

Background: Toxic Organophosphorus (OP) Compounds and Nerve Agents

In the mid-1850s, research chemists Wurtz and Clermont reported on their work with tetraethyl pyrophosphate (TEPP). Marketed under the German trade name Bladan, TEPP was the first widely used OP insecticide. In the 1930s, the large German chemical firm I.G. Farbenindustrie undertook research into phosphorus-based compounds. In 1937, a laboratory team led by Gerhard Schräder synthesized tabun, an extremely toxic OP compound that had more relevance to military chemistry than agriculture. During its initial synthesis in the laboratory, tabun vapors produced characteristic symptoms of nerve agent poisoning among Schräder's laboratory staff. Later, another nerve agent analog, sarin, was discovered by the same German chemists. Due to the laws in effect at the time, these formulas were dutifully provided to the Nazi authorities for possible military use.

At about the same time, research performed in England in 1941 also characterized the toxic nature of diisopropyl fluorophosphate (DFP). Although not nearly as poisonous as other nerve agents, it nonetheless had the same properties. In addition to possibly using DFP as a CW agent, Allied military chemists saw that it could be mixed with sulfur mustard to lower mustard's freezing point, allowing the agent to remain liquid even at low temperatures for winter combat.

Tabun was manufactured by the German military during World War II at the Dyhernfurth plant in Silesia. Although Germany produced large quantities of tabun (as well as relatively limited amounts of sarin), none of these stocks were used in World War II. Soman, the more toxic of the so-called G-series of nerve agents, was synthesized by Richard Kuhn in 1944.

By the early 1950s, DDT (dichlorodiphenyltrichloroethane) was the most successful insecticide ever used. But pests (especially lice) also became more and more resistant to chlorinated pesticides. With a market ever widening for substitutes, Ranajit Ghosh, a British chemist at Imperial Chemical Industries, patented a number of new and promising OP compounds. Using a combination of phosphorus, sulfur, and nitrogen, Ghosh synthesized a chemical that was so toxic to mammals that that only the military would have any use for his discovery. Variations on Ghosh's formula would form the most toxic nerve agent to have been weaponized: VX.

There also exist many more known and as of yet undiscovered analogs of the traditional OP nerve agents that could be developed by militaries or terrorist organizations. Of these, in the late 1980s, the former Soviet CW program (Foliant) developed Novichok (new guy), a nerve agent similar in structure to VX but 5–7 times as lethal and reported to be more difficult to treat with standard drug interventions.

Nerve Agent Toxicity

All known nerve agents possess similar toxicological properties. The OP molecule acts upon human enzymes, the one of most concern being acetylcholinesterase (AChE). The enzyme AChE normally functions as a regulator of the neurotransmitter acetylcholine, thus its name (-ase indicates an enzyme). The OP-based nerve agents inhibit the normal activity of AChE. By attaching itself to the enzyme, like a key fitting into a lock, the nerve agent stops the action of AChE. The body therefore loses its capacity to break down acetylcholine. This, in turn, brings about a crisis, because nerve receptors are now constantly being stimulated by ever-rising acetylcholine levels. This ultimately generates life-threatening effects on the respiratory system as well as the central nervous system. Outward symptoms include miosis (constricting of the pupils) and twitching (fasciculation) of the skeletal muscles. The constant stimulation of glands by high levels of acetylcholine results in copious amounts of secretions in the upper airways. These fluids can asphyxiate victims of nerve agent exposure. Depending on dose and route of exposure, these effects can occur within a matter of minutes.

Nerve agent exposures can be treated with (1) drug pretreatment (carbamates), (2) counteraction of increased acetylcholine levels (atropine), and (3) restoration of impaired enzymes with oximes (e.g., 2-PAM chloride). Drug pretreatment involves ingestion of the drug before possible nerve agent exposure. In the West, pyridostigmine bromide (PB) has traditionally been used to prepare soldiers for combat in chemical warfare environments. Although they are a mild, reversible inhibitor of AChE, carbamates such as PB are essentially nerve agents as well, holding AChE temporarily in reserve. Following nerve agent exposure, the reactivated enzyme then aids in the treatment and recovery of nerve agent casualties.

Eric A. Croddy

Further Reading

Kosolapoff, Gennady M., *Organophosphorus Compounds* (New York: John Wiley & Sons, 1950).

Moshiri, Mohammd, Emadodin Darchini-Maragheh, and Mahdi Balali-Mood, "Advances in Toxicology and Medical Treatment of Chemical Warfare Nerve Agents," *DARU Journal of Pharmaceutical Sciences* 20, no. 81 (2012): 1–24.

Shih, Tsung-Ming, John A. Guarisco, Todd M. Myers, Robert K. Kan, and John H. McDonough, "The Oxime Pro-2-PAM Provides Minimal Protection against the CNS Effects of the Nerve Agents Sarin, Cyclosarin, and VX in Guinea Pigs," *Toxicology Mechanisms and Methods* 21, no. 1 (January 2011): 53–62.

Wise, David, *Cassidy's Run: The Secret Spy War over Nerve Gas* (New York: Random House, 2000).

Neutron Bomb (Enhanced Radiation Weapon)

The enhanced radiation weapon is a specialized thermonuclear weapon that produces minimal blast and heat but releases a large amount of lethal radiation. It is a third-generation nuclear device (after fission and fusion bombs). Third-generation nuclear weapons are fusion devices that transform, select, or direct their energy in some unique way. The definition includes inertial confinement fusion, X-ray lasers, nuclear explosion–powered directed-energy weapons, nuclear kinetic-energy weapons, and enhanced microwave devices.

Based on work conducted by U.S. weapons laboratories in the 1950s, weapons designers discovered that by removing the uranium casing on a hydrogen bomb, neutrons could travel farther, and the lethal effects of high-energy neutrons produced by the fusion of deuterium and tritium could be maximized. A 1962 test demonstrated the viability of the concept.

The destructive power of nuclear weapons depends on the combination of different effects. Typically, the energy released by a fission-type explosion consists of 50 percent blast, 35 percent thermal radiation, 5 percent prompt radiation, and 10 percent residual radiation. If a pure fusion weapon were possible, then the proportions might be 20 percent blast and thermal energy and the majority, 80 percent, of the energy released as prompt radiation. Such a pure fusion weapon would produce very little residual radiation. Research aimed at altering the balance between the fission trigger and the fusion element of the bomb, however, only managed to increase the percentage of a weapon's yield that takes the form of radiation by a small margin. Used over a battlefield, a 1-kiloton neutron bomb would kill or incapacitate people over an area twice as large as the lethal zone of a 10-kiloton standard nuclear weapon, but with a fifth of the blast.

This third-generation nuclear weapon also prompted a surge in nuclear protest movements in the late 1970s and early 1980s,

because many believed that the enhanced radiation weapon lowered the nuclear threshold, making nuclear weapons use more likely. Others pointed to the relative absence of long-term weapons effects (fallout) that would make the weapons appear to be more usable on battlefields adjacent to urban areas. The debate became quite shrill, with German socialist politicians referring to enhanced radiation weapons as immoral and the "perversion of humanity."

Supporters believed that the enhanced radiation weapon offered a significant improvement in the credibility of the nuclear deterrent posed by the North Atlantic Treaty Organization (NATO). The prompt radiation produced by the neutron bomb could disable troops, even in tanks, while reducing the risk of collateral damage and long-term radiation. By the late 1970s, NATO was preparing to deploy the neutron bomb in the form of artillery shells and Lance warheads in West Germany.

The weapon that killed humans but spared buildings unleashed a political firestorm of protest throughout Western Europe in 1977. These weapons were never deployed to Europe but were stockpiled in the United States. By the late 1990s, the United States had dismantled its stockpile of enhanced radiation weapons.

Gilles Van Nederveen

Further Reading

Wasserman, Sherri, *The Neutron Bomb Controversy: A Study in Alliance Politics* (Westport, CT: Praeger, 1984).

New START Treaty

The New Strategic Arms Reduction Treaty (New START) was signed April 8, 2010, in Prague by Russia and the United States and entered into force on February 5, 2011. New START replaced the 1991 START I treaty, which expired December 2009, and superseded the 2002 Strategic Offensive Reductions Treaty (SORT), which terminated when New START entered into force.

New START continues the bipartisan process of verifiably reducing U.S. and Russian strategic nuclear arsenals begun by Presidents Ronald Reagan and George H. W. Bush. New START was the first verifiable U.S.-Russian nuclear arms control treaty to take effect since START I in 1994.

Seven years after entry into force, the treaty limits accountable deployed strategic nuclear warheads and bombs to 1,550. Each heavy bomber is counted as one warhead. Deployed intercontinental ballistic missiles (ICBMs), submarine-launched ballistic missiles (SLBMs), and heavy bombers assigned to nuclear missions are limited to 700. Deployed and nondeployed ICBM launchers, SLBM launchers, and bombers are limited to 800. This number includes test launchers and bombers and Trident submarines in overhaul. The ceiling of 800 is intended to limit the ability to "break out" of the treaty by preventing either side from retaining large numbers of nondeployed launchers and bombers.

New START does not limit the number of nondeployed ICBMs and SLBMs, but it does monitor them and provide for continuous information on their locations and on-site inspections to confirm that they have not been added to the deployed force. Nondeployed missiles must be located at specified facilities away from deployment sites and labeled with "unique identifiers" to reduce concerns about hidden missile stocks.

For deployed ICBMs and SLBMs, the number of warheads counted is the actual number of reentry vehicles (RVs) on each missile. START I did not directly count RVs, but instead counted missiles and bombers that were "associated with" a certain number of warheads. New START does not prohibit either side from deploying conventional warheads on long-range ballistic missiles. Such deployments would be counted under the warhead and missile limitations of the treaty.

The treaty's duration is 10 years from entry into force (February 2021), unless it is superseded by a subsequent agreement, and it can be extended for an additional five years. As in START I, each party can withdraw if it decides for itself that "extraordinary events related to the subject matter of this treaty have jeopardized its supreme interests." The treaty would terminate three months after a notice of withdrawal.

New START was politically difficult to confirm in the U.S. Senate, requiring a commitment by President Obama that he would carry out the second half of his Prague Speech, which called for the modernization of the U.S. nuclear arsenal.

Jeffrey A. Larsen

Further Reading

Reif, Kingston, "New START at a Glance," Arms Control Association Online, August 2012. https://www.armscontrol.org/factsheets/NewSTART. Accessed January 20, 2018.

Woolf, Amy F., "The New START Treaty: Central Limits and Key Provisions," CRS Report 7-5700, Congressional Research Service, October 5, 2017. https://fas.org/sgp/crs/nuke/R41219.pdf. Accessed January 20, 2018.

North Korea

More than half a century after the Korean War (1950–1953) was suspended by a ceasefire, the Korean Peninsula remains a volatile place. Since the 1990s, WMD programs in the Democratic People's Republic of Korea (DPRK) have been a focal point of international security concerns.

Chemical Weapons

Although concerns about WMD in North Korea highlight its nuclear weapons program, the country probably possess a longstanding chemical weapons (CW) program and large chemical weapon stockpiles. The Korean People's Army organized chemical and biological units and received sarin nerve gas from the Soviet Union in the 1950s. The Soviet Union also reportedly provided small quantities of mustard and nerve agents to the DPRK in 1966. South Korean sources assert that the North Koreans augmented these acquisitions in the late 1970s with domestic production of mustard and tabun chemical agents. By the late 1970s, North Korea probably fielded significant offensive chemical capabilities.

Between 2003 and 2017, U.S. Intelligence Community estimates of the North Korean stockpile of nerve, blister, and blood agents have ranged between 2,500 and 5,000 tons. North Korean officials have not only rejected these estimates but also the very existence of a North Korean chemical arsenal.

In a 1999 white paper, South Korea alleged that North Korea maintains 8 chemical weapons production facilities, 4 research sites, and 6 storage facilities. In 2009, according to the Republic of Korea (ROK) Research Institute of Chemical Technology, Pyongyang operated a network of 11 chemical weapon facilities that produced and stored CW agents, with an additional 13 research and development (R&D) laboratories dedicated to chemical weapons development.

North Korean expertise in CW agents was demonstrated in February 2017, when operatives (possibly from the notorious Office 35, Pyongyang's premier covert intelligence and sabotage operations organization) assassinated Kim Jong-un's half-brother, Kim Jong-nam, with topical application of VX nerve agent while he was in transit at Malaysia's Kuala Lumpur International Airport. Although some reports suggested that the assassins literally mixed binary components of VX on Kim Jong-nam's face, it is more likely the operatives received the chemical premade and that it was delivered to the Malaysian-based operatives via diplomatic pouch.

Biological Weapons

According to a variety of sources, including North Korean defectors, the DPRK undertook biological weapons (BW) R&D as early as the 1960s. The DPRK began production of biological weapons agents, including anthrax, botulinum toxin, and possibly bubonic plague bacteria, in the 1980s. Although it acceded to the Biological and Toxin Weapons Convention in 1987, North Korea is reported to maintain a rudimentary offensive biological weapons program.

For its part, in 1993, Russian intelligence (which likely has better access to North Korea than most Western countries) reported that Pyongyang has funded research for the military application of anthrax, cholera, and plague bacteria as well as smallpox virus.

At the Fifth Review Conference of the Biological Weapons Convention in 2001, the United States accused North Korea of violating its obligations under the treaty, a charge that North Korea has denied. South Korea's Defense Ministry has more recently suggested that North Korea has acquired several additional biological agents, including smallpox, and that it has an ongoing program to weaponize a variety of pathogens. According to the ROK Ministry of National Defense (2012), North Korea had the capability to develop a number of other BW agent candidates, including tularemia (*Francisella tularensis*) and hantavirus (Korean hemorrhagic fever virus).

Nuclear Weapons

Following more than 50 years of effort and significant international opposition, North Korea's nuclear weapons program had hit its stride by 2017, achieving significant weaponization milestones at an alarming rate. The 1994 Agreed Framework—probably the last best hope to decelerate the North Korean weapons program—disintegrated in 2002. At about the same time, Pakistan admitted that Pyongyang had gained access to nuclear technologies through clandestine trade, and in 2003, North Korea withdrew from the Non-Proliferation Treaty. In 2005, Pyongyang announced it was closing its nuclear weapons program and admitted that it had produced a nuclear weapon.

In 2006, North Korea conducted its first nuclear test, a sub-kiloton underground blast. By the end of 2017, North Korea had undertaken its fifth underground test, which produced a yield of about 25 kilotons. Pyongyang also bragged about developing a thermonuclear weapon, a claim discounted by experts. Nevertheless, it did test an intercontinental ballistic missile capable of reaching the United States. A particularly alarming development was Pyongyang's announcement that it might load a warhead aboard a long-range missile to conduct an atmospheric nuclear test over the Pacific Ocean.

Since the turn of the century, North Korea's nuclear weapon's technology has progressed from barely functional gun-type fission devices to experimentation with boosted-fission weapons. Its missile delivery systems have also progressed from short- and medium-range weapons to intercontinental-range ballistic missiles. The regime in Pyongyang still confronts system-integration problems that probably preclude it from fielding weapons that can be delivered at intercontinental ranges. Weapons have to be miniaturized and packaged to fit inside reentry vehicles—three technological achievements that remain beyond Pyongyang's grasp. Nevertheless, reports emerged in 2017 that North Korea probably overcame these system integration problems for its medium-range missile force. North Korea is working quickly to develop a nuclear arsenal and ballistic missiles to hold targets in the United States at risk.

Jacqueline Simon, Eric A. Croddy, and James J. Wirtz

Further Reading

Bennett, Bruce W., "The Challenge of North Korean Biological Weapons," Testimony before the Committee on Armed Services Subcommittee on Intelligence, Emerging Threats and Capabilities, United States House of Representatives, October 11, 2013. http://www.rand.org/content/dam/rand/pubs/testimonies/CT400/CT401/RAND_CT401.pdf. Accessed May 1, 2018.

Bermudez, Joseph S., Jr., *The Armed Forces of North Korea* (New York: I.B. Tauris, 2001).

Cordesman, Anthony H., *Proliferation in the "Axis of Evil": North Korea, Iran, and Iraq* (Washington, D.C.: Center for Strategic and International Studies, 2002).

Niksch, Larry, *North Korea's Nuclear Weapons Program,* Issue Brief for Congress (Washington, D.C.: Congressional Research Service, 2002).

Oh, Kongdan, and Ralph C. Hassig, *North Korea through the Looking Glass* (Washington, D.C.: Brookings Institution Press, 2000).

Nuclear Fuel Cycle

The nuclear fuel cycle describes the transformation of uranium (U) into either enriched uranium or plutonium (Pu) fuel for use in nuclear energy production or in a nuclear weapon. The cycle is dual-use in nature: materials can be diverted for use in nuclear weapons development at any stage of the cycle.

Uranium is a naturally occurring element, but plutonium must be created through a nuclear reaction. Uranium can either be enriched to concentrate its fissionable isotopes, or it can be transformed into plutonium in a reactor. Both materials can be used in power-generating nuclear reactors and in the manufacture of nuclear weapons.

Depending on the type of fuel and the purpose of the reactor, there are two main routes uranium can thus follow through the nuclear fuel cycle: natural uranium reactors and enriched uranium reactors. Both routes have consequences for nuclear weapons proliferation.

The Cycle

The nuclear fuel cycle is complex. The first stage of the fuel cycle involves the geological exploration of uranium reserves followed by the mining of the raw material, uranium ore. Because percentages of uranium in ore are very low, large amounts must be mined to obtain material for use in a reactor. Uranium can be extracted through in situ leaching or traditional mining. Traditional mining involves blasting and digging the uranium ore rock from the earth. The ore is separated from the rock and then purified and refined into a powdery yellow substance called *yellowcake*. Yellowcake is also referred to as *natural uranium*. In situ leaching involves pumping a leaching liquid, such as ammonium carbonate or sulfuric acid, into the ground and extracting the fluid. A processing plant separates the leaching liquid from the uranium. The extracted uranium is then purified and refined into yellowcake.

Before being usable in a reactor, yellowcake must be further refined, converted, and fabricated into fuel. It is converted through a multistep chemical process into uranium metal or the gas uranium hexafluoride (UF6) to be used as feedstock for enrichment. Fuel fabrication produces fuel assemblies that are composed of tubes of fuel pellets called *fuel rods*. In a nuclear reactor, the fuel rods are bombarded with neutrons to cause a nuclear reaction that releases heat that can be converted into electricity. A certain percentage of the rods are also transformed into materials that could be used in the nuclear weapons production process.

Natural uranium–fueled reactors, such as heavy-water reactors, graphite-moderated reactors, and some research reactors, use uranium that has not had its isotope level enriched. Moderators are used to slow the bombardment of neutrons at the fuel long enough to allow the nucleus of the uranium-235 (U-235) to split. These reactors are particularly dangerous in terms of weapons proliferation. They produce material that does not require an enrichment capability to produce plutonium, a by-product of the nuclear reaction and a fuel for nuclear weapons. As part of the energy production process, the fuel rods in these natural uranium–fueled reactors are irradiated, and as the uranium absorbs neutrons, it becomes plutonium. This plutonium requires reprocessing before it can be used as fuel for a nuclear weapon.

Natural Uranium Reactors

Several types of reactors are used to produce electricity. Heavy water (deuterium oxide), a moderator, allows for the fission of natural uranium, making uranium enrichment unnecessary, and thus bypassing a difficult step of the fuel process. This feature makes heavy-water production highly desirable for nations seeking an indigenous nuclear infrastructure. Tritium, used as a neutron source to boost the explosive power of a nuclear weapon, can be produced from heavy water. Some reactors use graphite as a moderator. Reactor-grade graphite also allows for the fission of natural uranium, making uranium enrichment unnecessary, thereby bypassing a difficult step of the fuel process.

Uranium Enrichment

The enrichment of uranium involves the separation of the uranium into U-238 and U-235 atoms. U-235 atoms are fissionable. By concentrating U-235 atoms, it is possible to produce a nuclear reaction. Uranium can be enriched to different concentrations. An enrichment level less than 20 percent U-235 is considered low enriched uranium (LEU); greater than 20 percent U-235 is considered highly enriched uranium (HEU); and weapons-grade uranium is enriched to greater than 90 percent. To produce 25 kilograms of weapons-grade uranium requires approximately 5,000 kg of natural uranium.

There are several methods of uranium enrichment. The gas-centrifuge method can produce large amounts of weapons-grade uranium quickly. In this method, uranium hexafluoride is spun in cylinders so that centrifugal force moves the heavier U-238 atoms to the outer edges of the cylinder. The concentrations of U-238 are then removed, and repeated iterations continue to increase the ratio of U-235 atoms to U-238 atoms until the desired concentration of U-235 is reached.

Gaseous diffusion is the most common enrichment method. It requires large amounts of electricity, however, which makes it difficult to undertake clandestinely. At one time, gaseous diffusion cascades in the United States consumed a significant percentage of the electricity produced in the country.

Gaseous diffusion involves the transfer of uranium hexafluoride through a series of membranes. The membranes create a separation between a high- and low-pressure environment. The change in pressure causes the atoms to move from the high-pressure side, through the membrane, to the low-pressure side. The lighter U-235 atoms are collected as they move through the membranes faster than the U-238 atoms. As in the gas-centrifuge method, in gaseous diffusion multiple iterations are required to reach higher and higher concentrations of U-235 atoms. Approximately 4,000 iterations are required to enrich uranium to weapons grade.

Enriched Uranium Reactors

Light-water reactors (LWR) fueled with LEU are less of a proliferation threat than heavy-water reactors (HWR) fueled with natural uranium. The spent fuel rods from light-water reactors contain plutonium that requires reprocessing to be usable in a nuclear weapon. By contrast, the spent fuel rods from HEU-fueled research and fast reactors contain weapons-grade plutonium. Breeder reactors are designed to produce more fuel than they consume.

Spent Fuel Storage, Use, and Waste

It is necessary to store fuel leaving a reactor in pools of water to reduce its radioactivity before it is reprocessed for plutonium retrieval. It also has to cool before being sent to a permanent waste disposal facility.

Despite the presence of plutonium in spent fuel, the risk of diversion of material at this stage is very low because of the dangers of handling it.

After fuel rods are kept for several months in storage ponds, they can be reprocessed to extract the plutonium from the uranium. The plutonium is then ready to be converted for use as reactor fuel or as fissile material in a nuclear weapon. Although the extraction method is fundamentally a chemical one—involving chopping the material, stripping the cladding, and using chemical solvents such as nitric acid to extract radioactive isotopes—facilities must be very carefully constructed to handle nuclear materials. Reprocessing is done with remote manipulators behind heavy shielding (called *hot cells*) for safety reasons.

Waste from the nuclear fuel cycle is considered high-level waste and must be stored in a way that protects the environment against radioactivity and toxicity of the substances for an extremely long time. Advanced waste storage includes sealing waste in an insoluble glass-like material and deep-mine disposal.

Jennifer Hunt Morstein

Further Reading

Gardner, Gary T., *Nuclear Nonproliferation: A Primer* (Boulder, CO: Lynne Rienner, 1994).

Walker, P. M. B., ed., *Chambers Nuclear Energy and Radiation Dictionary* (New York: Chambers, 1992).

Nuclear Nonproliferation Treaty

The Nuclear Nonproliferation Treaty (NPT) opened for signature on July 1, 1968, and came into force on March 5, 1970. The treaty was the result of several years of negotiations involving nuclear weapons states (NWS) and nonnuclear weapons states (NNWS). It is intended to prevent the spread of nuclear weapons, weapons materials, and technology to additional countries, to promote cooperation among nations in the peaceful uses of nuclear energy, and to achieve global nuclear disarmament.

The NPT is the pivotal component of the nuclear nonproliferation regime, which comprises a set of norms, principles, treaties, and procedures through which countries pledge not to obtain nuclear weapons or help other states acquire a nuclear arsenal. International and bilateral safeguards verify national commitments and thereby prevent defection and cheating. The International Atomic Energy Agency (IAEA), which administers the NPT's safeguards system, is the chief institutional component of the regime. The main principle of the regime is that the spread of nuclear arms is a threat to international security, and its underlying norm is that nonnuclear members of the regime should not develop nuclear weapons and no member should help another nation to build such weapons.

The NPT is governed by two principles: that the spread of nuclear weapons undermines international peace and security and that the peaceful application of nuclear energy should be made available to all parties of the treaty. The treaty contains 11 articles. Article I calls upon all NWS parties to the treaty not to transfer nuclear weapons or nuclear explosive devices directly or indirectly or encourage NNWS to manufacture such devices. Article II stipulates that NNWS will not undertake weapons programs or receive transfers of nuclear weapons or assistance in their manufacture. Under Article III, each NNWS party to the treaty undertakes to accept IAEA safe-guards, as negotiated with the IAEA, on their nuclear facilities. It also requires NNWS not to provide fissionable materials to other states without safeguards. Article IV reassures all NNWS of their inalienable right to peaceful nuclear energy research and development, and Article V offers the potential benefits of peaceful nuclear explosions, made available through appropriate international procedures. Article VI requires NWS to pursue negotiations in good faith on effective measures relating to the cessation of the nuclear arms race at an early date and the conclusion of a treaty on general and complete disarmament under strict and effective international control. Article VII states that nothing in the treaty shall prevent any group of states from concluding regional treaties. Article VIII discusses the amending procedure, and Article IX identifies the signature and ratification procedures. Article X guarantees the sovereign right of each party to withdraw from the treaty if it decides that extraordinary events have jeopardized its supreme national interests. And Article XI discusses the depository procedures.

Article VI was crucial for many NNWS to agree to sign the treaty. This article remains the only binding commitment to nuclear disarmament in a multilateral treaty on the part of the NWS. The treaty defines a NWS as one that had manufactured and exploded a nuclear weapon or other nuclear explosive device prior to January 1, 1967. All other states are considered NNWS. Under this criterion, only the United States, the Soviet Union (Russia), the United Kingdom, China, and France are legally allowed to keep nuclear weapons.

With the end of the Cold War in 1991, remaining opposition to the treaty waned. Several previous opponents to the treaty signed the NPT, including Argentina (1995), Brazil (1996), and South Africa (1991, after dismantling the seven nuclear devices it had built). The three successor states of the Soviet Union that had inherited Soviet nuclear weapons based on their soil, Ukraine, Kazakhstan, and Belarus, also joined the treaty in the mid-1990s.

The cap on the so-called nuclear club makes the treaty unamendable because there is no room for a future nuclear weapons state to emerge with international legitimacy. Unless the treaty is modified, India and Pakistan, which both detonated nuclear weapons in 1998, will remain outside the treaty.

Technical Details

The NPT was initially intended to be in force for a 25-year period. In 1995, however, the members agreed to extend it in perpetuity. Since 1975, the parties have held review conferences every five years. In addition, PrepCom (Preparatory Committee) meetings are held periodically to review the global efforts at nuclear nonproliferation. The IAEA is the chief organization verifying NPT compliance by member states. It conducts periodic safeguard inspections of the member states' nuclear facilities to make sure no violation takes place (that is, it verifies that nuclear materials or technology are not being diverted to military purposes). It also acts as the organization responsible for helping to transfer nuclear materials and technology for peaceful purposes. These IAEA safeguards are technical means of verifying a state's fulfillment of its commitments to the peaceful uses of nuclear energy. In the event of violation by the signatory, the IAEA will refer the matter to the UN Security Council, which has the ultimate authority to determine what sanctions are to be authorized to force compliance.

Current Status

As of 2018, there were 190 states parties to the treaty. The only states outside the treaty are India, Israel, Pakistan, and South Sudan. North Korea officially withdrew from the treaty in March 2003. This was the first withdrawal by a signatory state.

T. V. Paul

Further Reading

Nuclear Nonproliferation Treaty (NPT). Treaty Text. http://disarmament.un.org/wmd/npt. Accessed March 1, 2002.

Paul, T. V., *Power versus Prudence: Why Nations Forgo Nuclear Weapons* (Montreal: McGill-Queen's University Press, 2000).

Rauf, Tariq, and Rebecca Johnson, "After the NPT's Indefinite Extension: The Future of the Global Non-Proliferation Regime," *Nonproliferation Review* 3 issue 1 (1995), pp. 28–42.

Nuclear Posture Review

In 1994 2001, 2010, and 2018, the U.S. Defense Department published comprehensive Nuclear Posture Reviews (NPR) outlining the future of U.S. nuclear forces. Although some of these reports remain classified, these reports are linked to various planning documents, such as the National Security Strategy and the Quadrennial Defense Review. Although the 1994 review was generally welcomed for calling for a reduction in nuclear force structure following the end of the Cold War, subsequent reviews have been more controversial.

The 2001 NPR called for a new strategic "triad" made up of conventional and nuclear offensive forces, missile defenses, and a robust nuclear infrastructure. It downplayed the role of Russia in U.S. strategic planning and nuclear force sizing and highlighted the need to deter and preempt emerging state and nonstate actors armed with weapons of mass destruction. The 2001 NPR called for a range of conventional and nuclear deterrence options to provide a credible deterrent across a wide range of scenarios. The secret 2001 NPR failed to generate congressional support.

The Barack Obama administration benefited from the George W. Bush administration's experience: the 2010 Nuclear Posture Review was a public document that was released with much fanfare. The two documents had other commonalities. The Obama administration announced its commitment to the new strategic triad, while also reducing the role of nuclear weapons in U.S. military strategy. The administration also intended to maintain strategic stability with Russia and to continue the arms control process. Additionally, the Obama administration made a commitment to bolster the U.S. nuclear infrastructure, operational forces, and command and control structure so that the United States can maintain a safe and effective nuclear deterrent for the foreseeable future. The 2010 NPR, however, laid down a revolutionary benchmark for U.S. nuclear policy. The United States adopted nuclear abolition as the ultimate goal of U.S. nuclear strategy. Nuclear deployment, employment, procurement and declaratory policy would now be developed with this ultimate goal in mind.

The 2018 NPR reflects a return of sorts to the 2001 review, calling for new types of nuclear weapons to support tailored deterrence approaches to key nuclear adversaries. Nuclear disarmament does not take center stage in the review. The 2018 review also places renewed emphasis on revitalizing the U.S. nuclear weapons infrastructure and delivery systems, sectors of the U.S. defense establishment that have been in steady decline since the end of the Cold War. Time will tell, however, whether Congress will support the nuclear programs outlined by the Donald J. Trump administration.

James J. Wirtz

Further Reading

U.S. Defense Department, "Nuclear Posture Review Report," April 2010. https://www.defense.gov/Portals/1/features/defenseReviews/NPR/2010_Nuclear_Posture_Review_Report.pdf. Accessed February 1, 2018.

U.S. Defense Department, "2001 Nuclear Posture Review Report," December 31, 2001. Classified. See "Foreword" at https://fas.org/sgp/news/2002/01/npr-foreword.html. Accessed May 12, 2018.

U.S. Defense Department. "2018 Nuclear Posture Review," February 2018. https://media.defense.gov/2018/Feb/02/2001872886/-1/-1/1/2018-NUCLEAR-POSTURE-REVIEW-FINAL-REPORT.PDF. Accessed May 12, 2018.

U.S. Defense Department, "1994 Nuclear Posture Review," December 1994. Classified. See discussion at http://nukestrat.com/us/reviews/npr1994.htm. Accessed May 12, 2018.

Nuclear Taboo

The nuclear taboo is a norm that makes the leaders of nuclear-armed states almost unthinkingly rule out the employment of nuclear weapons. Perhaps the most notable characteristic of nuclear weapons is that they have not been used in conflict since the United States dropped two atomic bombs on Japan to end World War II. Why no nuclear weapons have been used in combat since 1945 is a matter of controversy. Several conditions could explain the nonuse of nuclear forces: deterrence, lack of suitable targets, availability of other military options, constraints created by public opinion, luck, or a normative inhibition against inflicting nuclear devastation. The last factor is called the *nuclear taboo.*

The armed forces of all nuclear weapons states plan and train to use nuclear forces under certain contingencies, but the use of these weapons has been most seriously considered only a few times, such as during the Korean War and or to relieve the French defenders during the Viet Minh siege of Dien Bien Phu. After considerable debate, U.S. officials ruled out nuclear use during these crises, mainly out of fear of provoking direct military conflict with the Soviet Union, although moral and political considerations also mattered. In the aftermath of these episodes, U.S. policy makers made it a priority to avoid circumstances in which the president would have to contemplate nuclear use.

It is difficult to know just how strong and universal the nuclear taboo has become. The normative constraint against nuclear use probably grows stronger with the passage of time since the last nuclear detonation. The next use of nuclear weapons, particularly if that use is deemed effective, however, could seriously erode the taboo and make the possession of nuclear weapons more desirable and their use more thinkable.

Peter R. Lavoy

Further Reading

Paul, T. V., *The Tradition of Non-Use of Nuclear Weapons* (Stanford, CA: Stanford University Press, 2009).

Quester, George, "The End of the Nuclear Taboo?," in *On Limited Nuclear War in the 21st Century*, edited by Jeffrey A. Larsen and Kerry M. Kartchner, chapter 8 (Palo Alto, CA: Stanford University Press, 2014), pp. 172–190.

Tannenwald, Nina, *The Nuclear Taboo: The United States and the Non-Use of Nuclear Weapons since 1945* (Cambridge: Cambridge University Press, 2004).

Nuclear Weapons Ban Treaty

On July 7, 2017, 122 states adopted the Treaty on the Prohibition of Nuclear Weapons in the General Assembly of the United Nations. The treaty was opened for signature on September 20, 2017. This was a high-water mark for the nuclear abolition movement, led in this case by the International Campaign to Abolish Nuclear Weapons (ICAN), a loose collection of international organizations that seek the elimination of nuclear weapons. ICAN was awarded the 2017 Nobel Peace Prize for its leadership of the campaign.

Resolution 71/258 of the UN General Assembly convened a United Nations conference to negotiate a legally binding instrument to prohibit nuclear weapons, leading toward their total elimination. The assembly encouraged all member states to participate in the conference, with the participation and contribution of international organizations and civil society representatives.

The Treaty on the Prohibition of Nuclear Weapons prohibits states parties from developing, testing, producing, manufacturing, acquiring, possessing, or stockpiling nuclear weapons or other nuclear explosive devices. Signatories are barred from transferring or receiving nuclear weapons and other nuclear explosive devices, from control over such weapons, and from any assistance with activities prohibited under the treaty. States are also prohibited from using or threatening to use nuclear weapons and other nuclear explosive devices. Finally, states parties cannot allow the stationing, installation, or deployment of nuclear weapons and other nuclear explosive devices in their territory.

The treaty had its origins in the Humanitarian Initiative, a group of nonnuclear weapons states that sought to push nuclear disarmament forward by focusing on the severe humanitarian consequences of nuclear war. Although 160 states endorsed the Humanitarian Initiative at the 2015 NPT Review Conference, the conference failed to adopt a consensus final document. For many advocates of nuclear disarmament, the UN General Assembly was a preferable negotiating forum, as it reaches decision by a majority vote of member states rather than consensus.

The debates and final vote were boycotted by all nuclear weapons–possessing states, most NATO countries, and many military allies of nuclear weapons states. Proponents of the treaty have hailed it as an important step in delegitimizing nuclear weapons and reinforcing the norms against their use, while opponents have criticized the treaty as political grandstanding that could undermine the Nuclear Nonproliferation Treaty.

The treaty does not contain a verification regime. Each state party must maintain its existing safeguards agreements with the International Atomic Energy Agency (IAEA). The treaty will enter into force 90 days after the ratification by 50 states. As of early 2018, only 3 states had ratified the treaty.

Jeffrey A. Larsen

Further Reading

"Treaty on the Prohibition of Nuclear Weapons," Nuclear Threat Initiative, October 6, 2017. http://www.nti.org/learn/treaties-and-regimes/treaty-on-the-prohibition-of-nuclear-weapons. Accessed February 20, 2018.

Nuclear-Weapons-Free Zone

Nuclear-weapons-free zones (NWFZs) are based on treaties that prohibit member states from manufacturing, producing, possessing, testing, acquiring, receiving, and deploying nuclear weapons. They also include provisions for security assurances from nuclear weapons states to treaty members. In April 1999, the United Nations Disarmament Commission recommended a set of guidelines for the establishment of NWFZs: states should freely arrive at an agreement, and agreements should be undertaken only by the states; nuclear weapons states should be consulted to facilitate their acceptance of the arrangement; and zones should not inhibit peaceful uses of nuclear energy.

There are seven NWFZs in the world today, and Mongolia's nuclear-free status has been internationally recognized. The Antarctic Treaty was the first regional treaty banning nuclear weapons; it opened for signature on December 1, 1959, and entered into force on June 23, 1961. The treaty covers everything south of the latitude 60°S. The Treaty for the Prohibition of Nuclear Weapons in Latin America (and the Caribbean), also known as the Tlatelolco Treaty, was signed on February 14, 1967, and entered into force on April 22, 1968. Cuba became the final Latin American state to ratify the treaty on October 23, 2002.

The South Pacific Nuclear Free Zone Treaty, also known as the Treaty of Rarotonga, was signed on August 6, 1985, and entered into force on December 11, 1986. Thirteen states are full members to this treaty: Australia, Cook Islands, Fiji, Kiribati, Nauru, New Zealand, Niue, Papua New Guinea, Samoa, Solomon Islands, Tonga, Tuvalu, and Vanuatu. The five nuclear weapons states (China, France, the Russian Federation, the United Kingdom, and the United States) are all adhering to the treaty's protocols.

The Treaty on the Southeast Asia Nuclear Weapon Free Zone, also known as the Bangkok Treaty, was signed on December 15, 1995, and entered into force on March 28, 1997. This NWFZ covers Brunei, Darussalam, Cambodia, Indonesia, Laos, Malaysia, Myanmar, the Philippines, Singapore, Thailand, and Vietnam. It also includes all their continental shelves and maritime exclusive economic zones. The Treaty for the Nuclear Weapons Free Zone in Africa is known as the Pelindaba Treaty. It covers the continent of Africa, island states members of the Organization of African Unity (OAU), and all islands considered by the OAU to be part of Africa. The treaty was signed on April 11, 1996. Along with the provisions similar to those set forth in other regional treaties, the Pelindaba Treaty prohibits any armed attack on nuclear installations. It calls for the Organization of the African Commission on Nuclear Energy as the mechanism for compliance. The members to the treaty report to the commission and engage in exchanges of information.

The most recent NWFZ is the Treaty on a Nuclear-Weapon-Free Zone in Central Asia (CANWFZ). The treaty opened for signature on September 8, 2006, and entered into force on March 21, 2009. Kazakhstan, Kyrgyzstan, Tajikistan, Turkmenistan, and Uzbekistan are states parties to the treaty.

Kimberly L. Kosteff

Further Reading

United National Office for Disarmament Affairs, "Nuclear-Weapon-Free Zones." https://www.un.org/disarmament/wmd/nuclear/nwfz/. Accessed May 12, 2018.

Nuclear Winter

Nuclear winter refers to the environmental disaster that some scientists believe would occur following a nuclear war. According to the nuclear winter theory, the cumulative effects of extreme heat, blast, radiation, and dust thrown into the air in such a major exchange would destroy the ozone layer and block the sunlight needed to warm the earth. The effect would be global and perhaps result in the extinction of most forms of life on Earth.

Several studies on the possibility of nuclear winter were conducted in the 1970s and 1980s, the most famous being the 1983 TTAPS (Turco, Toon, Ackerman, Pollack, and Sagan) study. This study incorporated factors such as forest fires, burning fossil fuels, and intense smoke covering the earth for periods lasting for weeks or months. The authors of the study further postulated that a period of darkness would exist that could plunge average temperatures by as much as 40 degrees Fahrenheit (thus, the term *nuclear winter*).

Many scientists disputed the idea of a nuclear winter, saying that it did not follow normal meteorological processes and that the smoke would quickly disperse. In 1990, a more detailed study (TTAPS 1990) incorporated extensive meteorological modeling. Although the new study revealed that 10–25 percent of the ejected soil would fall to the ground by immediate precipitation (black rain, such as was seen at Hiroshima), it also showed that the smoke would spread through different hemispheres, reducing temperatures within one to two weeks. The long-term effects of a nuclear winter could last from one to two years and kill an estimated 1–2 billion people.

Since the fall of the Soviet Union and the slashing of strategic arsenals, nuclear winter studies have become passé. Almost all of them were based on a nuclear exchange in the 5,000-megaton range, which now seems both politically implausible and beyond the deployed nuclear capability of Russia and the United States. It is now believed by many that nuclear exchanges in the 21st century would involve considerably less explosive power and relatively small nuclear weapons that would be targeted with great precision—perhaps fewer than 10 weapons of 100 kilotons or smaller. Although these would have devastating local effects, they would have no significant impact on global weather patterns.

One area where the TTAP studies have made a lasting useful impact is in the study of effects from an asteroid impact on Earth. The impact of a large asteroid on Earth would not generate residual radiation, but the widespread fires and dust ejected into the atmosphere could easily exceed the nuclear winter effect created by a large-scale nuclear exchange.

Zachariah Becker

Further Reading

Sagan, Carl, and Richard Turco, *A Path Where No Man Thought: Nuclear Winter and the End of the Arms Race* (New York: Random House, 1990).

Turco, R. P., O. B. Toon, T. P. Ackerman, J. B. Pollack, and C. Sagan, "Climate and Smoke: An Appraisal of Nuclear Winter," *Science* 247 (1990): 166–176.

Turco, R. P., O. B. Toon, T. P. Ackerman, J. B. Pollack, and C. Sagan, "Global Atmospheric Consequences of Nuclear War," *Science* 222 (1983): 12–83.

P

Pakistan

Today, Pakistan most likely relies on its nuclear weapons arsenal for strategic deterrence, and it is not known to have either offensive chemical or biological warfare capabilities. Pakistan ratified the Biological and Toxin Weapons Convention (BWC) in 1972 and the Chemical Weapons Convention (CWC) in 1997. Pakistan has not declared any chemical warfare (CW) agent, nor any chemical munition stockpiles. Generally speaking, Pakistan has the technical capability to develop basic biological and chemical weaponry, but the same can be said for many nations of similar industrial development.

In 1987, India charged Pakistan with having used (unspecified) chemical warfare agents against Indian military forces on the Siachen glacier. A decade later, Pakistan alleged that India used, or intended to employ, chemical weapons during the 1999 Kashmir crisis. There is no supporting documentation or other reliable data to support either story.

According to the U.S. Department of State in 2015, "Pakistan's biotechnology infrastructure continued . . . to pursue a range of biological research and development activities. Information available . . . did not indicate that Pakistan is engaged in activities prohibited by the BWC" (U.S. Department of State 2015).

Nuclear Weapons

Pakistan tested a handful of nuclear weapons and declared itself a nuclear weapons state in May 1998. These tests brought to fruition a secret nuclear bomb production program that began soon after Indian troops defeated Pakistani forces in a 1971 war that saw Bangladesh (formerly East Pakistan) emerge as an independent state. Pakistan's initial motive for acquiring nuclear weapons was Prime Minister Zulfiqar Ali Bhutto's desire to have a way to ensure Pakistan's national security against an increasingly powerful adversary without having to rely on Western military assistance, which had proved to be unreliable. Especially after India tested its first nuclear explosive device in 1974, Bhutto and senior Pakistani military officials believed that nuclear weapons could help Pakistan's armed forces overcome the growing disparity in conventional military capabilities with India. Nuclear weapons were also attractive because they could largely be developed indigenously, with some financial support from Saudi Arabia and Libya and technical assistance from China and North Korea (the Koreans helped Pakistan build the Ghauri, Pakistan's first ballistic missile).

Pakistan initially attempted to acquire the facilities needed to produce weapons-grade plutonium. But when U.S. nonproliferation diplomacy blocked these efforts, Islamabad redirected its focus to produce gas-centrifuge machinery to enrich uranium for nuclear weapons. In 1976, Abdul Qadeer Khan, a Pakistani metallurgist working for the European nuclear consortium Urenco, managed to flee Europe with stolen centrifuge designs and a list of 100 companies that supplied centrifuge parts and materials. He soon set up a uranium enrichment plant at Kahuta, and by the mid-1980s, he had navigated his way through the international export controls of the nuclear nonproliferation regime to produce enough bomb-grade material for a few nuclear weapons.

Sometime in the 1980s, Khan turned from recipient to supplier of nuclear technology. He was still bringing in material and components for Pakistan's nuclear bomb–making program, but he had ordered more material than Pakistan needed. At the same time, Khan Research Laboratories (KRL) was maturing. KRL scientists published papers starting in 1987 on the construction of more difficult centrifuges made of maraging steel, rather than the earlier aluminum-based designs. Both trends— overordering and technological evolution— left Khan with excess inventory. During the 1990s, Khan became the world's most notorious nonstate exporter of nuclear material, selling nuclear technology, materials, and, in at least one case, even bomb designs, to Iran, Libya, and North Korea.

Today, Pakistan possesses stockpiles of nuclear weapon components and could assemble and deploy nuclear weapons within a few days to a week. Although Islamabad refuses to reveal information about the size, composition, and operational status of its nuclear arsenal, a rough estimate can be calculated from publicly available information. Given its plutonium and HEU inventories, Pakistan could possess enough fissile material to fabricate 100–200 weapons.

The Pakistan Air Force flies two kinds of aircraft that are probably capable of nuclear weapons delivery: U.S.-supplied F-16s and JF-17s, coproduced with China's Chengdu Aircraft corporation. Land-based nuclear systems include Babur cruise missiles; liquid-fueled Ghauri missiles, developed with North Korean assistance; and solid-fueled Shaheen 1 and 2 missiles, developed with Chinese assistance, which probably would be employed to deliver Pakistan's nuclear weapons. Pakistan has adopted a first-use nuclear doctrine to deter India from using its conventional superiority to defeat Pakistan.

Eric A. Croddy and Peter R. Lavoy

Further Reading

Lavoy, Peter R., "Managing South Asia's Nuclear Rivalry: New Policy Challenges for the United States," *Nonproliferation Review* 10, no. 3 (Fall–Winter 2003): 84–94.

Peters, John E., James Dickens, and Derek Eaton, *War and Escalation in South Asia* (Santa Monica, CA: RAND Corporation, Project Air Force, 2005).

U.S. Department of State, "2015 Report on Adherence to and Compliance with Arms Control, Nonproliferation, and Disarmament Agreements and Commitments," June 5, 2015. https://www.state.gov/t/avc/rls/rpt/2015/243224.htm#Pakistan. Accessed June 15, 2017.

Phosphorus

Phosphorus (P) is an element found in numerous applications that apply to weapons of mass destruction (WMD). These include, among others, the toxic organophosphates (i.e., nerve agents) and military incendiaries (e.g., napalm). Organic phosphorus compounds also play key roles in uranium and plutonium processing.

In 1669, the German alchemist Hennig Brand was the first to have isolated phosphorus from urine by heating it and reducing the phosphate to elemental phosphorus. This new curious substance glowed in the dark and burst instantly into flame, and Brand became wealthy by marketing it (e.g., Phosphorus Mirabilis, Brand's Phosphorus, inter alia). A hundred years later, Swedish chemists (Gahn and Scheele) discovered a more efficient method of deriving phosphorus from bones. Finally, by the early 19th century, processing calcium phosphate in rock was found to be the most economical source of phosphorus.

White phosphorus (P_4)—which has also been referred to as yellow phosphorus—was once used as a rodenticide. In 1830, a French chemist (Sauria) found that white phosphorus made an excellent source of ignition ("strike anywhere") for matches. Unfortunately, there is a major hazard in the manufacture of white phosphorus (WP), as its toxic vapors caused "phossy jaw." Workers suffering from phossy jaw developed painful teeth abscesses and rotting mandibular bone that would become exposed to the air and glow in the dark. Red phosphorus (discovered in 1845) is a nontoxic elemental form and is now used in matchstick heads.

Incendiaries

During the Napoleonic Wars, the German chemist Frederick Accum proposed for the British navy a type of munition that would use phosphorus as an incendiary. And, almost as a prelude to the development of napalm in the 20th century, in 1855, an Englishman by the name of John McIntosh patented an incendiary composed of "coal-tar naphtha mixed with phosphorus and bisulphuret of carbon, with bursting powder sufficient to open the shells." But the British Admiralty had no interest in either of these schemes.

White phosphorus ("Willie Pete" (WP)) has been used for incendiary attacks against personnel, and it is especially useful in laying down screening smoke for military operations. In 2005, for example, the U.S. military employed WP during combat in Fallujah, Iraq.

Toxic Phosphorus Compounds

The toxicity of a phosphoric ester, triorthocresol phosphate (TOCP) was belatedly discovered in the early 1930s. Because of Prohibition in the United States, to get around the restrictions on the sale of alcoholic beverages, unscrupulous venders sold medicinal tonics that contained high amounts of alcohol. One of these, Ginger Jake, was adulterated with TOCP as a cheaper alternative. Unfortunately, TOCP was found to cause neuromuscular deficits, especially of the extremities. As a result, at least 60,000 people in the United States were poisoned and suffered permanent disability, commonly referred to as "Jake Leg Paralysis."

About the same time the toxicity of TOCP was recognized in the United States, in 1934, German investigators (I.G. Farben) were researching organophosphates as potential insecticides. In 1944, Germany marketed Bladan (later determined to contain tetraethyl pyrophosphate) to be used against aphids. It was this development of organophosphate insecticides that led to the discovery of the classic nerve agents: tabun (GA), sarin (GB), and soman (GD). Toward the end of World War II, Germany had built a tabun nerve agent plant capable of manufacturing 100 tons per month.

Almost simultaneously (1941), British investigators (Adrian, Feldberg, and Kilby) discovered the highly toxic nature of some organophosphate, including diisopropyl fluorophosphate (DFP), as did their German counterparts. It was quickly recognized that DFP had potent anticholinesterase activity. In 1958, Ranajit Ghosh (Imperial Chemical Industries) patented (no. 797,603) a family of organophosphate compounds incorporating sulfur, that is, (RP-(O)(OR) SR'), that could have pesticide applications;

the highly toxic VX nerve agent was later derived from this research.

The industrial processes for manufacturing phosphorus-containing chemicals often begin with phosphorus trichloride (PCl_3). Not surprisingly, this is a very useful starting material for the manufacture of toxic organophosphate compounds (e.g., nerve agents). As such, PCl_3 is a regulated Schedule 3 chemical under the Chemical Weapons Convention and is also export controlled under the Australia Group.

Other

Phosphine (PH_3) is an industrial gas used in the semiconductor industry that is highly toxic. During World War II, German sailors were sometimes poisoned from phosphine gas that was generated from the calcium phosphide used in torpedoes.

Nuclear industry

Organic phosphates are commonly used in the purification and separation of uranium and plutonium metal. Traditionally, impure uranium oxide, after being dissolved in nitric acid, is purified using tributyl phosphate (TBP) in kerosene. Going back to the 1950s, the PUREX method employs TBP as a solvent in the fuel reprocessing and separation of uranium and plutonium.

Eric A. Croddy

Further Reading

Benedict, Manson, and Thomas H. Pigford, *Nuclear Chemical Engineering* (New York: McGraw-Hill Book Company, 1957).

Miles, Wyndham, "The History of Dr. Brand's Phosphorus Elementaris," *Armed Forces Chemical Journal* 12 (November–December 1958): 24–25.

O'Brien, Richard D., *Toxic Phosphorus Esters* (New York: Academic Press, 1960).

Pit

"Pit" is a slang term used to describe the "trigger" inside the physics package of a nuclear bomb. The term was first used by scientists to describe the radioactive materials at the heart of the Trinity device tested at White Sands and the "Fat Man" bomb dropped on Nagasaki, Japan. It has since been used by the Department of Energy to identify the main fissile material package of a nuclear weapon.

The term is used to differentiate the radioactive core of a nuclear weapon from the arming and power mechanisms that are part of the device. The specific composition of the pit varies from one type of device to another. In an implosion device, the pit is a ball-shaped piece of radioactive metal surrounded by conventional high explosives, with detonators spaced at specific intervals. This produces an even compression of the materials contained inside the pit and ensures simultaneous detonation of all explosive materials. A typical implosion-device pit consists of a core of radioactive material (such as uranium-235 (U-235) or plutonium-239 (Pu-239) encased in a shell (beryllium, for example) surrounded by high explosives. The conventional explosion compresses the pit and creates a fission reaction in which an atom is split into two smaller fragments with a neutron. This method usually involves isotopes of uranium (U-235, U-233) or Pu-239.

The pit is subject to decomposition over time owing to breakdown of both the fissile and explosive materials. Routine inspection is therefore required to ensure that the physics package (i.e., the pit) remains functional. The only way to conduct the inspection is through disassembly in a controlled environment. In the United States, this inspection routine is supervised by the Department of Energy.

Dan Goodrich

Further Reading

Freudenrich, Craig C., "How Nuclear Bombs Work," HowStuffWorks. https://science. howstuffworks.com/nuclear-bomb.htm. Accessed October 1, 2002.

Plague

Plague is one of the oldest diseases known to humankind. The first documented bubonic plague epidemic occurred in 542 BCE in Egypt; the deadly disease spread worldwide within four years. Lasting some 50–60 years, this pandemic probably led to the death of 100 million people. During the siege of Kaffa (1346 CE), Mongolians laid siege to the medieval trading port and hurled dead bodies over the walls. Although it was not an effective means of delivery, the intent was certainly to spread plague disease among the Genoese inhabitants. Thereafter, the disease spread throughout Europe. This second plague pandemic (ca. 1347–1356) caused 20–30 million deaths.

During the 17th century, a lesser-known but more sophisticated attempt at biological warfare was concocted by the Venetians at Candia (modern-day Heraklion, Greece). Under attack by the Ottomans, and during the longest known siege recorded (1648–1669), Venetian intelligence operators recommended harvesting body fluids from infected bodies (using the "spleen, buboes, and carbuncles of the plague ridden") and employing this noxious extract against the Turks. One scheme involved contaminating Albanian fez cloth and distributing the textile among Ottoman soldiers. This plan—which was relatively sophisticated given the time period—was ultimately never carried out.

The most recent (third) plague pandemic began in 1894 and lasted roughly to 1950; it started in Yunnan province, China, and spread to Hong Kong and India as well as other regions of the globe, causing at least 10 million deaths.

The common name of the plague is *black death* because cyanosis (a bluish or purplish discoloration due to lack of oxygen in the blood) causes the victim's skin to darken during the terminal stage of the sickness. There are two forms of the disease found in humans as well as animals: classic bubonic plague and pneumonic plague, the inhalation form of the disease. Bubonic plague occurs from an infectious flea bite, while person-to-person spread of plague is possible through infectious aerosols (such as those produced by coughing or sneezing). Plague still remains an infectious disease problem, resulting in thousands of infections worldwide every year. In a biological warfare context, pneumonic plague—due to the contagious nature of person-to-person transmission and its high mortality rate—would present the greatest threat. According to a World Health Organization (WHO) estimate, for example, there would be 5 million people infected and 150,000 deaths if only 50 grams of *plague bacteria* were disseminated as an aerosol over a major metropolitan city.

The bacterium that causes plague is *Yersenia pestis* (formerly *Pasteurella pestis*). Virulent plague bacteria secrete a variety of substances that protect them against the body's defenses and are triggered by the elevated temperature found in the body (37 degrees Celsius). In classic bubonic plague, the disease begins with a flea and host life cycle. Fleas feed on infected animals, taking in a blood meal. Infectious material containing *Y. pestis* bacteria clogs the upper gut (proventriculus) of the flea. When this occurs, the flea can no longer take in nourishment. Now desperately hungry, it attempts to bite other animals, including those not typically associated with fleas (including humans). In the course of biting, the flea may disgorge the bacteria-laden material into the wound, infecting the animal. When a host (such as a rat) dies, its infected fleas move to other living rats and pass the disease along.

When infected fleas bite a human, bacteria enter the dermal lymphatics (the draining system that handles foreign matter, including pathogens). The plague bacteria eventually reach the nearest lymph node, frequently in the groin (due to the fact that fleas often bite at the lower extremities). This route of infection results in classic bubonic plague, presenting with swelling of the lymph nodes, such as those in the groin, after a one- to eight-day incubation period. (The term *bubonic* comes from the Latin and Greek derived term for groin, *bubo*.) However, bites that occur in other parts of the body may result in swelling of the nodes found in the armpit or neck. Headache, chills, sudden fever, and vomiting often follow. Without medical treatment, bubonic plague has a mortality rate of 50 percent. Left untreated, bubonic plague may develop into systemic infection of the blood, and then to the pneumonic form. In the latter case, bacteria seed the lung, forming infectious material that can be exhaled as aerosolized particles.

Plague can be treated with antibiotics. Without treatment, the pneumonic plague mortality rate is almost 100 percent; thus, early treatment is especially critical for pneumonic plague. Bubonic plague usually responds well to antibiotic treatment. It is important to prevent the spread of plague at the source, notably through control of rodents—a very difficult task in dense urban environments—and the use of insecticides to kill fleas. Although recent research (2015) has shown some promising results using a genetically altered bacteria related to plague (*Y. pseudotuberculosis*), there still is no effective plague vaccine available to the public.

Plague as a Biological Weapon

Yersenia pestis is among the main candidates for use in biological weapons because it is relatively easy to culture and therefore could be mass produced. Additionally, *Y. pestis* can form infectious aerosols, causing the deadliest form, pneumonic plague.

From the 1930s until 1945, the Japanese Unit 731, under the command of General Shiro Ishii, developed plague as a biological weapon. They devised a porcelain bomb that contained tens of thousands of infected fleas. When the bomb hit the ground, the porcelain shell shattered, and the fleas were released into the surrounding environment to spread the disease. According to some reports, these bombs offered an 80 percent survival rate for the fleas loaded inside the munition. It is unknown how many Chinese died of plague, either naturally caused or due to Unit 731 forays in biological warfare.

Until President Richard Nixon announced the termination of biological weapon preparation in 1969, the United States was engaged in defensive as well as offensive research of plague as a biological weapon, but it was never successful in developing an effective plague weapon formulation. In contrast, during the former Soviet era, several thousand scientists were involved in a plague project at 10 different institutes, and by the 1980s, the Soviet Union had weaponized a so-called super plague.

Nation states—or plausibly terrorist organizations—could bioengineer plague bacteria to make them resistant to antibiotics and able to lodge deeper in the lungs, making the new strains more lethal than the normal plague. With the advancement of biotechnology, it is also possible to make antibiotic-resistant plague by inserting antibiotic-resistant genes into the plague bacteria.

Anthony Tu and Eric A. Croddy

Further Reading

Benedictow, Ole Jørgen, *The Black Death, 1346–1353: The Complete History* (New York: Boydell Press, 2004).

Cunningham, Kevin, *The Bubonic Plague* (Edina, MN: ABDO Publishing, 2011).

Thalassinou, Eleni, Costas Tsiamis, Effie Poulakou-Rebelakou, and Angelos Hatzakis, "Biological Warfare Plan in the 17th Century—The Siege of Candia, 1648–1669," *Emerging Infectious Disease* 21, no. 12 (December 2015): 2148–2153.

Plutonium

Plutonium (Pu) is a man-made radioactive element, the 94th in the periodic table. Its radioactivity, toxicity, and explosive yield have made it one of the most feared elements in history. Plutonium is a by-product of the fission process that takes place in nuclear reactors and results from neutron capture by uranium-238 (U-238), in particular. The process of separating and extracting Pu from U-238 consumes large amounts of energy. All plutonium isotopes are radioactive. Plutonium-239 (Pu-239) is fissionable, has a long half-life (24,360 years), and can be readily produced in large quantities in breeder reactors by neutron irradiation of plentiful, but nonfissile, U-238. The metal has a silvery appearance and takes on a yellow tarnish when exposed to air. It is chemically reactive. A relatively large piece of plutonium is warm to the touch because of the energy given off in alpha decay.

Critical mass (the amount that will spontaneously explode when brought together) becomes a safety consideration when handling quantities of plutonium in excess of 300 grams. The critical mass of Pu-239 is only about one-third that of U-235, hence its utility in weapons design. The element was first detected in 1940 as the isotope Pu-238 by Glenn Seaborg, Joseph Kennedy, and Arthur Wahl, who produced it in Berkeley, California, by deuteron bombardment of U-238.

Pu-238, Pu-240, and Pu-242 emit neutrons as their nuclei spontaneously fission. They also decay, and the decay heat of Pu-238 enables it to be used as an electricity source in the radioisotope thermoelectric generators (RTG) of some cardiac pacemakers, space satellites, and navigation beacons. Plutonium is toxic in a chemical sense, and its ionizing radiation also makes it a radiation hazard. The main threat to humans from plutonium comes from inhalation. Although it is very difficult to create airborne dispersion of a heavy metal, in the case of plutonium, particles the size of 10 microns or less are hazardous because they enter the lungs. The alpha particles have a high rate of emission, and the element is absorbed on bone surfaces and collected in the liver; thus, plutonium and other transuranic elements are radiological poisons and must be handled with special equipment and precautions. Plutonium in liquid solution is more likely to become critical than solid plutonium.

Plutonium is also a fire hazard, especially finely divided material. Its chemical reaction with oxygen and water may result in an accumulation of plutonium hydride, a pyrophoric compound (that is, a material that will burn in air at room temperature). Plutonium expands considerably in size as it oxidizes and thus may break its shipping container if oxidation begins. Magnesium oxide sand is the most effective material for extinguishing a plutonium fire.

Plutonium is produced in two industrial stages. The first involves the irradiation of uranium fuel rods by neutrons in nuclear reactors. The second involves the chemical separation of plutonium from the uranium, transuranic elements, and from fission products contained in discharges or irradiated fuel. These techniques are usually referred to as *reprocessing* when applied commercially and *plutonium separation* when undertaken to recover fissile material used in nuclear weapons. It takes about 10 kilograms of nearly pure Pu-239 to make a nuclear bomb. Producing this amount would require 30 megawatt-years of reactor operation, with frequent fuel changes and reprocessing of hot fuel rods.

During the Cold War, the Z plant, or plutonium finishing plant at the Hanford nuclear complex, converted liquid plutonium nitrate from the PUREX Plant into solid, disc-shaped metal buttons the size of hockey pucks. The machined plutonium was then shipped to the Rocky Flats Plant, Colorado, to be turned into nuclear weapon components. Since the end of the Cold War, the United States and Russia have been converting some of their excess plutonium stockpiles to mixed oxide fuel, where uranium and plutonium are blended so that they can be used to fuel commercial electrical power reactors. The only remaining facility that utilizes plutonium to refurbish and remanufacture fissile "pits" in the United States is located at Los Alamos National Laboratory, New Mexico.

Gilles Van Nederveen

Further Reading

Institute for Energy and Environmental Research, "Physical, Nuclear and Chemical Properties of Plutonium." https://ieer.org/resource/factsheets/plutonium-factsheet. Accessed September 17, 2002.

Von Hippel, Frank N., "Plutonium and Reprocessing of Spent Nuclear Fuel," *Science* 293, no. 5539 (September 28, 2001): 2297–2398. http://www.princeton.edu/~globsec/publications/pdf/Sciencev293n5539.pdf. Accessed September 17, 2002.

Prague Agenda

On April 5, 2009, President Barack Obama delivered a major speech on nuclear disarmament in Prague, Czech Republic. In that speech, he laid out his vision for a world without nuclear weapons, one we should aspire to but which, he acknowledged, was unlikely to occur in his lifetime. Nonetheless, this speech inspired many in the global disarmament community to renew their efforts to control and secure nuclear weapons, delivery vehicles, fissile materials, and related items. That same year, the Nobel Committee awarded Obama the Nobel Peace Prize for restating the goal of achieving nuclear disarmament.

The Prague Agenda launched by President Obama had multiple effects. The Obama administration led a series of Nuclear Security Summit meetings, beginning with the first in Washington, D.C., one year after the speech. These summits resulted in many countries surrendering their stocks of highly enriched uranium and plutonium, mostly used for civil power or research reactors, to international control or to the states where the materials originated. It led, six years later, to the Joint Comprehensive Plan of Action with Iraq. It led to increased emphasis within the International Atomic Energy Agency (IAEA) on safeguards, safety, and security of fissile materials. It led to the creation of a U.S.

Department of Energy Fuel Bank for down-blending material from nuclear weapons for use in civil power plants. It helped energize negotiators on both sides to conclude the New Strategic Arms Reduction Treaty in 2010. In an effort to increase transparency, in 2010, the U.S. Department of Defense released historical stockpile numbers for the first time.

One could argue that momentum from Prague led to the creation of the International Campaign to Ban Nuclear Weapons, whose efforts resulted in a United Nations vote approving a Nuclear Weapons Ban Treaty in July 2017—although all nuclear states and all but one member of NATO abstained from voting. The ICAN movement was awarded the 2017 Nobel Peace Prize.

Obama's speech, however, stated that as long as nuclear weapons exist in the world, the United States would possess a nuclear arsenal second to none to ensure deterrence for itself, its allies, and its friends and partners. This required a significant investment in the modernization and recapitalization of the long-ignored U.S. nuclear weapons infrastructure and the commitment to replace all three legs of the American nuclear triad (land-based missiles, sea-based missiles, and manned bombers). The U.S. Congress ratified the 2010 New START Treaty only on condition that the ongoing nuclear modernization program was endorsed by the president. The forecast is for these new weapons to enter the inventory in the mid-2020s through the 2030s.

Jeffrey A. Larsen

Further Reading

Mason, Shane, "In Defense of Obama's Prague Agenda," *National Interest*, April 22, 2016. http://nationalinterest.org/feature/defense-obamas-nuclear-record-15879. Accessed February 22, 2018.

Office of the Press Secretary, the White House, "Remarks by President Barack Obama in Prague as Delivered," April 5, 2009. https://obamawhitehouse.archives.gov/the-press-office/remarks-president-barack-obama-prague-delivered. Accessed February 22, 2018.

The White House, "Fact Sheet: The Prague Nuclear Agenda," January 11, 2017. https://obamawhitehouse.archives.gov/the-press-office/2017/01/11/fact-sheet-prague-nuclear-agenda. Accessed February 22, 2018.

Primary Stage

The primary stage of a thermonuclear warhead is a fission device that creates the necessary conditions for a subsequent fusion reaction. Modern thermonuclear warheads use both fission and fusion reactions, traditionally referred to as the primary and secondary stages, to produce explosive yield.

When the warhead is detonated, chemical explosives compress the primary stage, which is often composed of plutonium 239. Because of the high temperatures and pressures generated by the chemical explosives, the plutonium splits into new types of atoms. These new atoms have a collective weight less than the weight of their original components; the remaining mass is released as energy and neutrons. The energy is what makes up the power of an atomic blast, and the additional neutrons perpetuate the fission chain reaction.

In modern thermonuclear warheads, this primary mechanism is surrounded by a layer of lithium deuteride, which is in turn encased in a thick outer layer known as the *tamper*, which is often composed of fissionable material and functions to hold the contents together to contain the pressure and heat needed to generate a fusion explosion.

Neutrons from the atomic explosion cause the lithium to fission into helium and tritium (the isotope of hydrogen with the mass number 3), which yields a tremendous amount of energy.

The primary stage generates the conditions required for fusion, raising temperatures within the warhead to as high as 400 million degrees Celsius. The majority of the overall energy, or yield, released by a two-stage nuclear warhead is derived from the secondary (fusion) stage.

Abe Denmark

Further Reading

Rhodes, Richard, *Dark Sun: The Making of the Hydrogen Bomb* (New York: Simon & Schuster, 1996).

Psychoincapacitants

In chemical warfare (CW), psychoincapacitants are designed to render military personnel and other targeted individuals incapable of performing even the most basic tasks. The ideal psychoincapacitant does not cause death or permanent damage and has temporary effects, lasting just long enough for the attacker to achieve tactical advantage on the battlefield. In the U.S. chemical weapons arsenal, the compound called BZ (3-quinuclidinyl benzilate) was the only psychoincapacitant standardized by the U.S. military (1962). Other militaries, including Iraq and the former Yugoslavia, are also suspected of having developed BZ or similar agents. (The Iraqi version was called Agent-15.) In 1989, the United States destroyed all remaining stocks of BZ munitions.

Background

Examples of the use of psychoincapacitating agents in war go back almost 1,000 years. In his study on atropine—a belladonna plant–derived chemical long known for its effects on both mind and body—a U.S. Army chemical researcher, E. Goodman (1961), found that in 1040 CE Scottish armies had poisoned wine with belladonna nightshade and given it to Norwegian troops. History also describes a battle during which belladonna was used by the bishop of Müenster during a 1672 siege of Gröningen. Delivered by grenades and other pyrotechnic projectiles, unfavorable winds caused the belladonna to blow back against attacking forces. Other examples from modern military history include the inadvertent consumption of jimsonweed, a plant that also has belladonna-like effects (e.g., scopolamine), which caused extensive (albeit transient) delirium among the troops.

From 1953 to 1973, the U.S. Army investigated the use of a number of chemicals that had potent but largely transient effects on human cognition and behavior, including the following:

- depressants (barbiturates, opiates)
- diliriants (BZ, other belladonna-like drugs)
- stimulants (amphetamine derivatives, nicotine, etc.)

At first, lysergic acid diethylamide (LSD-25) seemed a promising psychoincapacitant because it had a thousandfold spread between what was needed for incapacitation and the lethal dose. However, its effects on the enemy would be unpredictable, and in ways that may have been undesirable. For example, would enemy soldiers not only manage to fire their weapons under the effects of LSD but also become better shots?

Other chemicals investigated as possible psychoincapacitants in warfare or sabotage have included MDMA (popularly known on the street as "ecstasy"); phencyclidine (PCP or "angel dust"); and tetrahydrocannabinol (THC, the active ingredient in marijuana).

BZ: The Only Weaponized Psychoincapacitant in the U.S. Chemical Arsenal

During the Cold War, the U.S. Army, after researching these and many other potential candidate psychoactive chemicals, finally settled on BZ (agent "buzz"). But even this compound had its limitations. Its effects were by no means immediate, requiring up to a few hours to manifest themselves following exposure. And similar to other psychoactive compounds under study, BZ was delivered as an aerosol, similar to military-type CS tear gas (riot control agent). This generated a large pall of smoke that was clearly visible to the enemy, and thus little tactical surprise could be achieved. Although it was decidedly less deadly than other CW agents in the U.S. arsenal, the side effects from large doses of BZ could be very dangerous in the field.

Generally, the delirium induced by BZ involves hallucinations, including impairment of perception in terms of size and shapes; delirious "woolgathering" behavior (the pulling at clothing, real or imagined); and delusions (*folie à deux*) played off on others affected by the drug. The psychological impact can be long-lasting (a day or longer), but it generally resolves on its own. As with the other belladonna drugs, widened pupils, rapid heartbeat, flushed skin tone, and visual impairment are hallmarks of BZ intoxication. Administering a carbamate (e.g., physostigmine) can at least temporarily diminish the effects of belladonna-induced delirium.

Modern Uses of Psychoincapacitants

In the 21st century, the potential always exists for the use of psychoincapacitants in warfare. Iraq admitted to producing a version of BZ, called "Agent 15," in significant quantity before eliminating its offensive chemical weapons in ca. 1991. We have no evidence that Iraq ever used this compound. In ca. 1995–1999, Serbian armed forces allegedly used BZ against Bosnian Muslims; this allegation has also yet to be fully evaluated.

Syria may have employed something similar in one of the first reported uses of chemical weapons on December 23, 2012. In this attack by Syrian forces against probable rebel-held neighborhoods in Homs, seven people were killed. Reportedly, the Assad regime may have used Agent 15 or something similar. Those affected suffered from flaccid musculature, blurry eyesight, and nausea (among other symptoms), falling into a spectrum of possible effects from exposure to an anticholinergic agent like BZ.

The 1993 Chemical Weapons Convention (CWC) clearly prohibits the use of psychoincapacitants in warfare; BZ, for example, is a proscribed chemical (Schedule 2A) under the CWC lists of toxic chemicals.

Eric A. Croddy

Further Reading

Gardner, John H., *Covert Use of Psychochemicals and Other Agents to Influence National Policy* (Chevy Chase, MD: Johns Hopkins University, 1956).

Ketchum, James S., *Chemical Warfare Secrets Almost Forgotten: A Personal Story of Medical Testing of Army Volunteers* (Santa Rosa, CA: ChemBooks, 2007).

Khatchadourian, Raffi, "Operation Delirium," *New Yorker* 88, no. 40 (December 17, 2012): 46–65.

Q

Q Fever

Q fever is a common global disease of wild animals and domestic livestock, especially sheep, cattle, and goats. Caused by the bacterium *Coxiella burnetii*, humans are usually infected with *C. burnetii* by direct contact or inhalation of aerosols from infected animal products or dust particles (fomites). During recent outbreaks in the Netherlands (2007–2010), for example, over 4,000 people became ill with Q fever (25 of these cases being fatal). Significantly, a large proportion of these Q fever infections were caused via aerosol transmission and were traced to a nearby farms where goats had been infected with *C. burnetii*. Thus, the capacity for *C. burnetii* to infect humans by airborne route makes it a prime candidate for a biological warfare agent.

When disease develops, Q fever has both acute and chronic forms, and the predominant clinical symptoms vary widely, making diagnosis difficult. The onset of acute Q fever usually takes 10–40 days following exposure and typically begins with sudden high fever and flulike symptoms. Rarely, a few individuals develop a chronic illness with liver or heart complications, and in such cases, Q fever is often fatal.

Background and Military Applications
Q fever (named after "query" fever when the cause of the unknown disease was first being investigated) was first described as a blood-transmissible disease in Queensland in 1937 by Edward H. Derrick, who was investigating a cluster of febrile illnesses of unknown origin among Australian abattoir workers. At about the same time, researchers in the Rocky Mountain Laboratory in Montana were studying a febrile illness transmitted by ticks. The causative agent, *Coxiella* (formerly *Rickettsia*) *burnetii*, was named for both MacFarlane Burnet (Melbourne, Australia) and Herald R. Cox (U.S. Public Health Service), who isolated and characterized the new pathogen in the late 1930s. Q fever is colloquially known in different parts of the world as "nine mile fever," "north Queensland fever," and "the Balkan grippe."

The U.S. Army studied experimental *C. burnetii* infections in soldiers, using vaccines, antibiotic treatment, and prophylaxis protocols in the mid-1950s and 1960s. The exceptional infectivity of *C. burnetii* aerosols was observed in volunteers in open-air tests at Dugway Proving Ground, Utah. Inhalation of a single organism could cause infection in a susceptible person 40 days after exposure. According to Bill Patrick (d. 2010), who was a primary scientist involved with offensive biological weapons, U.S. plans included the use of Q fever (as well as Venezuelan equine encephalitis) as an incapacitating agent during the 1962 Cuban Missile Crisis.

Generally, the *C. burnetii* organism is hardy and survives in the environment in a spore form that allows significant spread of the agent by wind. A World Health Organization (WHO) committee estimated in 1970 that if 50 kilograms (110 pounds) of a virulent *C. burnetii* strain were released upwind of a city of 500,000, it could incapacitate 125,000 people and kill 150.

Biological weapons stockpiles, including Q fever bacteria, were destroyed by the United States upon signing the Biological and Toxin Weapons Convention of 1972. The Soviet Union, however, continued biological weapons development into the early 1990s, including work with the Q fever agent. The Japanese religious cult Aum Shinrikyo attempted to weaponize the agent in the mid-1990s. (Several cult members were reported to have been infected by the agent as they worked on it.) In 1999, due to increasing concerns regarding bioterrorism, the United States made Q fever a notifiable disease to public health authorities.

Medical Aspects

C. burnetii is carried by a variety of birds, ticks, and mammals, including wild goats, cattle, sheep, kangaroos, wallabies and bandicoots, and other domestic and wild animals. Although it can cause abortion and stillbirth in goats and sheep, most animals infected with *C. burnetii* are healthy (asymptomatic). The organism may be transmitted by aerosols from animal excretions, contaminated straw, wool, hides, and clothing; ingestion or inhalation of raw milk or goat cheese; blood transfusions; and tick bites.

Early acute Q fever is often characterized by a sudden onset of high fever (up to 105°F), with or without a flulike illness, pneumonia, or hepatitis. The most common symptoms are high fever, chills, sweating, severe headache, and malaise. Patients also frequently complain of muscle pain, fatigue, anorexia, weight loss, chest pain, and cough.

The disease normally resolves on its own without medical intervention, lasting up to three weeks. Up to 15 percent of patients may develop a post–Q fever chronic fatigue syndrome lasting many months. Most people will recover within 60 days, even without treatment. However, prompt antibiotic treatment with a tetracycline can be helpful. Only 1–2 percent of people with acute Q fever die of the disease, and recovery usually confers lifelong immunity against reinfection.

Amy E. Krafft

Further Reading

De Rooij, Myrna M. T., Floor Borlée, Lidwien A. M. Smit, Arnout de Bruin, Ingmar Janse, Dick J. J. Heederik, and Inge M. Wouters, "Detection of *Coxiella burnetii* in Ambient Air after a Large Q Fever Outbreak," *PLoS ONE* 11, no. 3 (March 18, 2016): 1–15.

Maurin, M., and D. Raoult, "Q Fever," *Clinical Microbiology Reviews* 12, no. 4 (1999): 518–553.

R

Radiation

Ionizing radiation is one of the three principal effects produced by a nuclear explosion, along with blast and thermal radiation. It is composed of alpha particles, beta particles, gamma rays, X-rays, neutrons, high-speed electrons, high-speed protons, and other particles capable of producing ions. Radiation, as used in this context, does not include nonionizing radiation.

All material is composed of atoms. Atoms, in turn, are composed of a nucleus, which contains minute particles called *protons* and *neutrons* and an outer shell made up of particles called *electrons*. The nucleus carries a positive electrical charge, and the electrons carry a negative charge. As electrons are bound to the nucleus of the atom, so are the particles within the nucleus. These forces work toward a strongly stable balance. The process by which the nuclei of atoms work toward becoming stable is to shed excess energy. Unstable nuclei may emit a quantity of energy, or they may emit a particle. This emitted atomic energy or particle is called *radiation*.

A nuclear explosion produces ionizing radiation. The process by which atoms gain or lose electrons is called *ionization*. In ionizing radiation, the energy from the radiation is sufficient to remove electrons from atoms, leaving two positively charged particles (ions) behind. Some forms of radiation, such as visible light, microwaves, or radio waves, do not have sufficient energy to remove electrons from atoms. They are called *nonionizing radiation*. A nuclear explosion creates four kinds of radiation—alpha, beta, gamma, and neutron. Only three of these are significant to this discussion: alpha, beta, and gamma.

Alpha radiation has low penetrating power and a short range (a few centimeters in air). Because of this short range, the danger to the external surface of the human body is negligible. The most energetic alpha particle will generally fail to penetrate the dead layers of cells covering the body and can easily be stopped by a sheet of paper. Alpha particles, however, are hazardous if allowed to enter the body through a break in the skin, ingestion, or the respiratory tract. Once inside the body, the alpha particles, with their high ionizing ability, will expend their energy into a single group of cells. This causes a high degree of localized tissue damage. Alpha emitters present an internal hazard 20 times as great as beta or gamma emitters.

Even though airborne beta particles can travel significant distances, solid materials will stop them. Beta emitters present two potential external radiation hazards: the beta particles themselves and the X-rays they can produce when they strike certain materials, such as lead. Although beta particles can travel significant distances in air, materials such as aluminum, plastic, or glass provide appropriate shielding.

Gamma radiation does not consist of particles, it has no electrical charge, and science has demonstrated that it has no mass. Gamma radiation is far more dangerous than alpha or beta because its rays are more penetrating and harmful. Protection depends on the type, density, and thickness of the shielding. As the thickness of the shielding increases, the penetration of the gamma radiation decreases. Higher-density materials, such as lead, tungsten, concrete, and steel, can shield against gamma emissions.

Although radiation is perhaps the best-known effect of nuclear weapons, it accounts for only 15 percent of the energy released by the explosion. This includes initial radiation (neutrons and gamma rays), which is emitted within the first minute after detonation, and residual nuclear radiation, which is emitted after the first minute.

Approximately 5 percent of the energy released in a nuclear burst is transmitted in the form of initial neutron and gamma radiation. The neutrons result almost exclusively from the energy produced by the fission and fusion reactions. The initial gamma radiation arises from these reactions as well as from the decay of short-lived fission products. The intensity of the initial nuclear radiation decreases rapidly with distance from the point of burst. The character of the radiation received at a given location also varies with distance from the explosion. Near the point of the explosion, the neutron intensity is greater than the gamma intensity, but it diminishes quickly with distance. The range for significant levels of initial radiation does not increase markedly with weapon yield. Therefore, initial radiation actually becomes less of a hazard with increasing yield, as individuals close enough to be significantly irradiated are killed by the blast and thermal effects.

Residual radiation from a nuclear explosion accounts for 10 percent of the energy released and is primarily distributed as fallout. Fallout is created when a nuclear weapon surface burst vaporizes large amounts of earth or water because of the heat of the fireball. This debris is drawn up into the radioactive "mushroom" cloud, especially if the explosive yield exceeds 10 kilotons. This material becomes radioactive and will eventually settle to earth as fallout. The area and intensity of the fallout is strongly influenced by local weather conditions. Much of the material is simply blown downwind, forming a plume-shaped pattern on the ground. Rainfall can also have a significant influence on how fallout is deposited, as rain will carry contaminated particles to the ground. The areas receiving such contaminated rainfall become hot spots of greater radiation intensity than their surroundings.

Severe local contamination can extend far beyond the limits of the blast and thermal effects, particularly in the case of high-yield surface detonations. The danger from fallout lessens with time. This lessening is called *decay*. In technical terms, radioactive decay is the process by which large unstable atoms become more stable by emitting radiation. The radiation can be in the form of a positively charged alpha particle, a negatively charged beta particle, or gamma rays.

Jeffrey A. Adams

Further Reading

Adams, Jeffrey A., and Stephen Marquette, *First Responders Guide to Weapons of Mass Destruction (WMD)* (Alexandria, VA: American Society for Industrial Security, February 2002).

U.S. Army Field Manual (FM) 4-02.283. *Treatment of Nuclear and Radiological Casualties* (Washington, D.C.: Headquarters, Department of the Army).

Radiological Dispersal Device

Radiological dispersal devices (RDDs) cause contamination and health risks by dispersing radioactive substances into a populated area. The most spectacular type of RDD is the so-called dirty bomb. In a dirty bomb, radioactive material is wrapped around a conventional explosive and detonated, contaminating the surroundings. Unlike nuclear weapons, dirty bombs do not involve a nuclear chain reaction; they rely on the innate radioactivity of the materials released to cause injury.

Radioactive substances are widely available in society because of their use in industry, medicine, and research. Substantial contamination would require highly radioactive materials that are difficult to procure and to handle. The amount of radioactive material used, dispersal effectiveness, exposure time, and exposure patterns would all influence the risk of acute death from a dirty bomb, but the risk of lethal exposure from an RDD is generally low. The danger to health and life is thus primarily due to long-term effects (for example, increased cancer risks). The use of RDDs could create a strong psychological impact and widespread panic.

Terrorists could spread radioactive substances simply by pouring out or dispersing the material in high-traffic areas. Decontamination could be difficult, time-consuming, and expensive. Food and drinking water could also be contaminated and introduced into commercial distribution. More sophisticated perpetrators could use sprayers to contaminate the air with radioactive dust.

In 1995, Chechnyan rebels threatened to blow up several dirty bombs in Moscow, but the threats were never carried out. Although government officials across the globe are concerned that terrorists will employ a dirty bomb against a civilian target, their worst fears have not yet become a reality.

Morten Bremer Maerli

Further Reading

Radiation Emergency Medical Management, "Radiological Dispersal Devices (RDDs)," U.S. Department of Health & Human Services. https://www.remm.nlm.gov/rdd.htm. Accessed January 12, 2004.

Reprocessing

Reprocessing is the industrial process of removing plutonium from spent nuclear reactor fuel. When uranium fuel rods are put into a reactor and irradiated, they are described as *spent fuel*. Irradiated fuel has to be removed from a reactor's core when only about 3 percent of its uranium has been burned, if plutonium recovery is the goal. Weapons-grade plutonium is produced when special rods are used to convert uranium-238 (U-238) into plutonium in a so-called target. Irradiated fuel and special weapons targets from production or power reactors are chemically processed to separate and recover fissile uranium and plutonium.

Reprocessing plants consist of heavy reinforced-concrete structures to provide shielding against the intense gamma radiation produced by the decay of short-lived isotopes in the spent fuel rods. The most challenging technical component of a reprocessing plant is the separation system (consisting of mixers/settlers, extracted columns, or centrifugal contractors). Flow rates through the reprocessing plant require precise monitoring, the chemistry must be exact, and any accumulation of radioactive products large enough to reach critical mass leading to massive radioactive release must be prevented.

Radioactive isotopes can also be recovered for special radiochemistry purposes. These include plutonium-238, strontium-90, cesium-137, and krypton-85 as well as the by-product transuranic elements neptunium, americium, curium, and californium. Spent fuel from reactors is stored in water ponds from six months to four years to allow for a decrease in radioactivity. This permits short-lived, highly radioactive isotopes to decay. Reprocessing involves removing the metal casing from around the fuel (decladding) and dissolving the fuel in hot concentrated nitric acid. The most common method for chemically processing irradiated fuel is the PUREX (plutonium-uranium extraction) process.

Two early methods for separating plutonium—the bismuth phosphate process and the Redox process—are historically important, but they are no longer used. The bismuth phosphate process was developed during World War II at the Metallurgical Laboratory at the University of Chicago. In 1942, it was used to separate the first plutonium that had been produced in a cyclotron. The bismuth phosphate process was then developed on an engineering scale and demonstrated at the Oak Ridge, Tennessee, X-10 plant in 1944. It was put into full operation at Hanford, Washington, to separate plutonium from production fuel. After the fuel elements were dissolved in nitric acid, bismuth nitrate and sodium phosphate were added to the solution, and plutonium was then removed. This method created a large amount of hot radioactive waste that is still stored at Hanford. The bismuth phosphate process recovered plutonium but was unable to separate and recover any uranium from the irradiated fuel. This was a serious disadvantage, as it meant that half of the reusable isotopes from the fuel rods was wasted.

The Redox process was the first countercurrent process used in the United States for large-scale extraction of plutonium and uranium from irradiated fuel. Unlike the bismuth phosphate process, it could operate continuously rather than in batches (when the reactor fuel was cool and ready for processing). In the Redox process, plutonium, uranium, and fission products were recovered and discharged in separate streams. After spent fuel was dissolved in nitric acid, an aqueous solution of uranyl nitrate, plutonyl nitrate, and fission product nitrates remained. This was followed by the introduction of an organic solvent, hexone, in which the uranyl and plutonyl nitrates concentrated. Fission product nitrates were left in the liquid phase. In three subsequent steps, the fission products were first removed and then plutonium was chemically reduced and removed as plutonium nitrate. The bismuth phosphate process was in use from 1944 until 1956, the Redox process from 1956 until 1968. The Redox process recovered both plutonium and uranium and thus was a more efficient means of producing weapons fuel.

In the PUREX process, the irradiated fuel is dissolved in an aqueous solution of nitric acid, and the desired chemical elements are extracted in a series of steps with an organic solvent. Fuel rod elements are cut into smaller pieces to expose the fuel material for subsequent acid leaching. Fuel cladding is frequently not soluble in nitric acid, so the fuel rod itself must be opened to allow chemicals to reach the fuel inside. Developed in 1954, the PUREX process was used at both Hanford and the Savannah River, South Carolina, production sites. The aqueous solution contains uranyl nitrate, plutonium nitrate, and other fission product nitrates. The liquid solution is then fed into a solution extraction contractor.

The uranium and plutonium are separated from each other in further extraction steps. Plutonium is then converted to a solid oxide or metal form before it is shipped or stored. Uranium is generally converted to uranium trioxide.

Although all nuclear weapons states have operated reprocessing facilities, most have ended or vastly curtailed operations. Reprocessing has produced vast amounts of radioactive waste for 50 years. Everything that comes into contact with spent fuel is radioactive and must be disposed of in special storage sites. Some items will be radioactive for tens of thousands of years. The discharges by these plants into the atmosphere, water, and ground are frequently cited by Greenpeace in its reports about the most contaminated places on earth.

Gilles Van Nederveen

Further Reading

Von Hippel, Frank N., "Plutonium and Reprocessing of Spent Nuclear Fuel," *Science* 293, no. 5539 (September 28, 2001): 2297–2398. http://www.princeton.edu/sgs/publications/articles/Sciencev293n5539.pdf .Accessed September 20, 2003.

Ricin

Ricin is a highly lethal proteinaceous toxin found in the seeds of the castor bean plant, *Ricinus communis*. Upon entering the body, the toxin is strongly cytotoxic, killing most cells that it contacts by rapidly and irreversibly inhibiting protein synthesis. Ricin's effects vary by route of entry: injection, ingestion, or inhalation.

Based on an historical case study, *injection* of a lethal dose causes generalized weakness, fever, vomiting, dysphonia (difficulty speaking), and swelling of lymph nodes proximal to the site of injection within 24 hours, followed by symptoms of shock over the next 1–2 days and ultimately ending in circulatory collapse, diffuse hemorrhaging, and death on day 3.

Following *ingestion*, symptoms of abdominal pain, vomiting, and (at times bloody) diarrhea appear within a few hours. Severe dehydration ensues over the next several days, leading to decreased urine output and blood pressure. Death can result in 3–5 days due to massive gastrointestinal hemorrhaging.

Inhalation of a lethal dose leads to symptoms of cough, difficulty breathing, nausea, and muscle aches within approximately 3 hours. Death occurs 36–48 hours after initial exposure, as a result of either respiratory failure or circulatory collapse.

In addition to its high lethality, ricin is relatively inexpensive and easy to acquire and produce; it is therefore considered by many analysts to be the present-day biological weapon of choice for actors with limited funds or technical expertise. Ricin is listed in Schedule 1 of the Chemical Weapons Convention (CWC), meaning it is a toxic chemical banned by international law, and it is listed as a weapon of mass destruction (WMD) according to U.S. federal statute (Biological Weapons Anti-Terrorism Act of 1989).

Military History

Ricin was investigated by the U.S. Army's Chemical Warfare Service (CWS) late in World War I, but the toxin was never deployed. During World War II, the United States, along with Canada and Great Britain, took another look at ricin as a potential biological warfare (BW) agent. Called Agent W, by the end of the war, more than 1,700 kilograms of the toxin had been produced. The toxin was processed into a liquid suspension and then incorporated into high-explosive shells, cluster bombs, and plastic containers specially designed for its dispersal. Dubbed the "W bomb," each cluster was composed of 500 pounds of independent 4-pound bomblets.

Field testing suggested that, under appropriate weather conditions, the contents of just one W bomb distributed over 80 percent of a target area 100 by 100 yards would kill more than half of the area's population. Ricin's lack of odor also suggested that its detection would be difficult, and its low persistency made it unlikely to hinder Allied advances after its delivery. While the Allies considered using ricin against Japan, it was never deployed during World War II.

Japan

Human experimentation with ricin was performed within the confines of Japan's biological weapons (BW) program during World War II. Castor beans were placed in food that was then provided to prisoners of war over two-week periods. These test subjects invariably died as a result of their involvement in the experiments.

Soviet researchers have performed similar experiments since World War II. Varied amounts of ricin and other poisons were added to the food of unsuspecting prisoners at Laboratory No. 1, a covert KGB facility. If the amount given did not prove lethal, more was injected with a syringe until death occurred.

In September 1978, Bulgarian dissident Georgy Markov was assassinated with ricin. While Markov awaited a bus on Waterloo Bridge in London, a Bulgarian secret service agent covertly fired a steel pellet filled with the toxin through the tip of a pneumatic umbrella into Markov's leg. Markov died three days later. A second Bulgarian, Vladimir Kostov, was targeted with a similar device in Paris but survived. Both the toxin and the umbrella designs used against Markov and Kostov had been provided for the operation by the former Soviet KGB.

Following the First Gulf War (1991), it was learned that Iraq had considered ricin as a potential BW agent in 1989 and had produced approximately 10 liters of concentrated ricin solution. All of this was consumed during field tests of 122-millimeter artillery shells, according to Iraqi declarations to the United Nations Special Committee (UNSCOM).

Ricin and Terrorism

In March 1991, four members of the Minnesota Patriots Council, an American anti-government group, purchased castor beans through the mail. Upon receiving the beans, and despite a lack of higher education and technical expertise, these men were able to extract 0.7 grams of 5 percent ricin. Having plotted to kill law enforcement officials with the toxin, they were discovered before they could carry out their plan. In 1994 and 1995, they became the first persons to be convicted under the U.S. Biological Weapons Anti-Terrorism Act of 1989.

The extraction process for ricin for assassination purposes is described in the Al Qaeda training manual, and the Kurdish group Ansar al-Islam, which has known ties to Al Qaeda, reportedly tested the toxin on animals and possibly a human subject in northern Iraq. During the post-9/11 U.S. military action, instructions for the preparation of ricin were discovered in the basements of two Arab doctors connected to Al Qaeda, and trace amounts of ricin were detected at 5 or 6 of the approximately 110 sites searched throughout Afghanistan.

In January 2003, the search by authorities of a London apartment uncovered castor beans and equipment for the extraction of ricin, leading to multiple arrests. Subsequent forensic analysis identified traces of ricin itself. Allegedly, four of the men arrested in the sweep—one of whom had been in contact with persons employed on a British military base—were linked to Al

Qaeda. And in March 2003, two vials of ricin were discovered in a locker at the Gare de Lyon railway station in Paris. To date, no arrests have been made in the case.

More recently, a man was indicted for possession of ricin after checking himself in at a local hospital on February 2, 2017. William Christopher Gibbs, from Morganton, Georgia, was concerned that he may have exposed himself to ricin, and he was arrested after authorities found residues of ricin in his car.

Ricin poisoning is very difficult to treat and is mostly limited to supportive care. In March 2017, a biopharmaceutical firm, Soligenix, announced that its developmental vaccine (RiVax) showed 100 percent protection in monkeys challenged with ricin aerosol challenge tests.

Rich Pilch and Eric A. Croddy

Further Reading

Moshiri, Mohammad, Fatemeh Hamid, and Leila Etemad, "Ricin Toxicity: Clinical and Molecular Aspects," *Reports of Biochemistry & Molecular Biology* 4, no. 2 (April 2016): 60–65.

Russian Chemical and Biological Weapons

When the Soviet Union disintegrated on December 25, 1991, Russia possessed the largest stockpile of chemical and biological agents and nuclear weapons in the world. Even after signing the Chemical Weapons Convention (CWC) and the Biological and Toxin Weapons Convention (BTWC), Russia continued to develop chemical and biological weapons in secrecy. In 1992, President Boris Yeltsin claimed that the chemical and biological warfare (CBW) programs in Russia had been abandoned

and that Russia was committed to destroying its stockpiles of chemical and biological weapons and operating within the framework of the CWC and the BTWC. Some observers believe, however, that Russia still has an offensive CW and BW program today, despite promises to the international community that its research and development in this area are strictly for defensive purposes.

Russian CBW programs were an even more closely kept secret than their nuclear program; Soviet offensive CBW programs were well hidden behind legitimate bioscience and chemical industry covers. Most of what is known about their efforts comes from former Russian scientists like Ken Alibek, who immigrated to the United States after the end of the Cold War. He was the former deputy director of Biopreparat, the principal Soviet government agency responsible for biological weapons research and development.

Chemical Weapons

The first major chemical assault in modern warfare took place against Russian troops during World War I at Bolimow, Poland. The German military filled 15 cm high explosive shells with a lacrimator (tear agent), xylyl bromide (T-Stoff), and these were brought to the Eastern Front. But despite concentrated attacks using T-Stoff artillery shells against Russian troops on January 3, 1915, the cold weather prevented the agent from becoming volatile, and it ultimately had no impact.

In World War I, the Soviet Union reportedly suffered nearly 500,000 chemical casualties, more than any country involved in the conflict. But with a backward industrial base, the Soviets were only able to produce relatively small amounts of offensive CW agents. Beginning in the 1920s, the

Military Chemical Complex (MCC) of the Soviet Union secretly developed, produced, and stockpiled chemical weapons. There are unconfirmed reports that the Soviets (under the leadership of Mikhail Tukhachevsky) used toxic gases to suppress peasant uprisings, especially the one that occurred in Tambov in 1921.

During the Cold War, the Soviet Union produced thousands of tons of chemical weapons at multiple facilities. The Soviet arsenal included nerve (sarin, soman, and Russian V-agent) and blister agents (mustard and lewisite, usually in mixtures). Vil Mirzayanov, eventually a Russian émigré to the United States, had worked for more than 25 years in the Soviet chemical weapons program and helped develop a new series of extremely lethal third-generation nerve agents under the Foliant program. These were binary agents—nontoxic by themselves but lethal when mixed together. He also worked to develop agents that were not detectable by Western early-warning systems.

Under the Soviet system, chemicals were divided into three categories based on their combat effectiveness. First-generation chemical weapons were those World War I vintage agents, including persistent toxic chemicals that produce a skin-blistering or general toxic effect (mustard, for example); nonpersistent toxic chemicals (such as phosgene); and irritants (riot control agents) such as adamsite. Second-generation chemical weapons were toxic organophosphates (nerve agents), including tabun (GA), sarin (GB), soman (GD), and Soviet V-gas (VR). Sarin, soman, and Soviet "VR"—the latter basically an analog of VX nerve agent— were produced on a large scale to be included in the army arsenal. Third-generation chemical weapons encompassed new types of toxic chemicals and more effective

means of delivery during combat. The Foliant program produced several of these agents, of which A-232 and novichok-5 were produced for combat operations. Not much is known about these third-generation chemical weapons, and Russia continues to deny they ever existed.

Soviet chemical weapons designers conducted open-air field testing near the Caspian Sea, near Lake Baikal, and even in cities close to Moscow. Some of the most prominent testing facilities were Kuzminki and Kuntsevo in Moscow, Shikhany Central Military Chemical Proving Grounds on the banks of the Volga River, and Nukus, located on the Ustyurt Plateau in Karakalpakia, Uzbekistan. Until the early 1980s, chemicals were even tested during training exercises and on humans, although it is not known whether these tests were performed with the consent of the participants. The Soviet program has received much domestic criticism because of the legacy of reported environmental damage produced by CW agent testing, although the type and extent of this purported damage are still unclear.

Although chemical weapons production facilities were numerous, they were concentrated in the Volga basin. The experimental plant Volsk, for example, produced various toxic chemicals and their precursors, including irritants and incapacitants. The S. M. Kirov Chemical Plant in Stalingrad produced large-scale quantities of mustard ("yperite") and phosgene gas. Nerve (VR) and other toxic agents were produced near the city of Novocheboksarsk, on the southern bank of the Volga.

Under the U.S.-Soviet Wyoming Memorandum of 1989, in which the United States and the USSR exchanged information on their military chemical facilities, the Soviet Union identified locations where chemical weapons were stored. Some of the storage sites include the Shikhany Central Military Chemical Proving Grounds, Gornyy, and Kambarka. Under the CWC, Russia has since made further declarations that included civilian entities; however, there are still questions as to whether full declarations and disclosures have been made by Russia.

After considerable delays due to financial, logistical, and other reasons, on October 11, 2017, the Organization for the Prohibition of Chemical Weapons (OPCW) certified that Russia had completely destroyed its declared chemical weapons stockpile. Once totaling some 40,000 tons, the stockpile had included lewisite-mustard mixtures as well as sarin, soman, and VR nerve agents.

Novichok: Attempted Assassination in the United Kingdom

On March 4, 2018, Sergei Victorovich Skripal, a former Russian military intelligence officer, who had defected to Great Britain, and his daughter Yulia were found unresponsive on a park bench in Salisbury, England. British experts from the Defence Science and Technology Laboratory at Porton Down later determined that Sergei and Yulia Skripal were poisoned by a Novichok-type nerve agent. In addition, a detective sergeant was also poisoned when he responded to the scene. While all three survived, Skripal spent months recovering in hospital. The attempted assassination of these two Russian émigrés was likely carried out by Russian intelligence operatives, who may have used as much as 100 grams of the Novichok agent against the Skripals. Two months of decontamination operations later, areas in and around Salisbury were finally reopened for public access. The United Kingdom, United States, and NATO all accused Russia of this crime, but Moscow denied any involvement and claimed that Britain had perpetrated the crime using nerve agent produced at Porton Down. This event marked the first time a nerve agent has ever been used in Europe.

Biological Weapons

The Soviet BW program involved thousands of personnel from the military, education, and civilian sectors. The Soviets compartmentalized sensitive aspects of the program so that few people had knowledge of the program as a whole or its intended military applications. Although the Soviet Union produced tons of agents, such as anthrax (*Bacillus anthracis*), smallpox, plague (*Yersinia pestis*), tularemia, glanders, Venezuelan equine encephalitis (VEE), Q-fever (*Coxiella burnetii*), and Marburg virus, research was also conducted on more types of organisms for antipersonnel and antiagricultural biological weapons.

The Soviets were developing biological weapons by the 1930s, but progress was slowed—perhaps even halted—due to Stalin's purges. Later, however, knowledge of Japanese BW efforts during World War II spurred the Soviets to reenergize their own biological weapons research. Soviet scientists used data culled from germ warfare documents taken from the Japanese in Manchuria, including personnel from the notorious Unit 731 at Pingfang, Harbin.

A bacteriological facility was built at Kirov in 1953, where a subsequent leak released anthrax bacteria into the city's sewer system. The West remained unaware of this incident, but according to Ken Alibek, a rodent was found a few years later in the sewer system carrying a more virulent form of anthrax bacterium typed "836." The Soviets used this strain in its offensive biological munitions. Soviet Union also conducted research and development (R&D) on botulinum toxin, which reportedly had been weaponized by the mid-1960s.

Sverdlovsk, a "Biological Chernobyl"

Sverdlovsk was home to a secret Soviet government facility known as Compound 19 that manufactured weapons-grade anthrax and other biological agents. Although U.S. intelligence long suspected the existence of the Sverdlovsk biological research facility, it held no corroborating evidence to prove its suspicions that Compound 19 served as a biological weapons facility.

Originally built as a biological laboratory in 1949 at the former grounds of a military school, it grew to become a large BW complex. The facility was subordinate to the 15th Directorate of the Soviet Army, the military organization in charge of biological weapons. By the 1960s, it was producing tons of anthrax bacteria. Using a formulation that is still unknown, bioengineers at Sverdlovsk devised a technique to produce anthrax spores in such a way that they formed very fine, highly infectious particles for aerosolized delivery.

On April 2, 1979, after turning off the driers used to process anthrax spores, workers removed air filters for routine examination. Observing that the filters were defective, the staff did not replace them, leaving a note for the nighttime production staff to not operate the driers. Unfortunately, the next shift did not get the word, and when they turned on the drying equipment, up to two pounds of particles containing anthrax spores were released in the atmosphere. Prevailing wind currents carried the escaped spores through a narrow zone extending from Compound 19 all the way to the southernmost part of the city. Those in the immediate path of the spore cloud were at the greatest risk, having been exposed to the highest concentration of spores. As the spore cloud dissipated, its strength dwindled. Cattle as far away as 30 miles south of the city, however, were still found dead due to anthrax exposure, a testament to the efficiency with which the agent dispersed.

According to official Soviet accounts, this accidental release of a highly contractible aerosolized strain of anthrax claimed the lives of at least 68 men and women in the spring of 1979. Some reports place the number of fatalities at closer to 100, and some earlier intelligence estimates placed casualty estimates in the thousands.

The source of the Sverdlovsk outbreak became a matter of intense international debate. Authorities knew that if the outbreak were proven to be of other than natural origin, it would be evidence of actions prohibited by the 1972 Biological and Toxin Weapons Convention. In 1990, several articles about the epidemic surfaced that challenged the original Soviet explanation of the outbreak. As pressure mounted on the new postcommunist Russian government, President Boris Yeltsin (who, in 1979, was the chief Communist Party official for the Sverdlovsk area) directed his counselor for ecology and health to determine the origin of the epidemic. In May 1992, Yeltsin was quoted as stating, "The KGB admitted that our military developments were the cause."

Yeltsin's admission notwithstanding, the Russian government has provided no further information regarding the outbreak. Subsequently, the chairman of the committee to oversee biological and chemical disarmament expressed doubt that the biological agent originated at Compound 19. The committee then conducted its own investigation into the outbreak, but it has yet to provide the results of its investigation.

In 1994, Russia officially returned to the bogus explanation that the anthrax outbreak was due to consumption of infected meat and has refused to provide any further explanations. Furthermore, under the leadership of President Vladimir Putin, the Russian Federation also denies that any offensive biological weapons program was undertaken either by the former Soviet Union or modern-day Russia, only that defensive research had taken place.

While Russia continues to dispute clear evidence that offensive BW work was being done at Sverdlovsk, in 2015, genetic testing of samples from autopsies from victims of the 1979 outbreak showed the bacteria to have been the anthrax "836" strain—the same strain that was employed for the Soviet biological weapons program.

Recent BW Activities and Doctrine

Subsequent Western focus on the incident at Sverdlovsk meant that continued operations there would be difficult. Four facilities had originally been established under the Ministry of Defense; however, research and development was carried out within institutions under the MOD, Ministry of Agriculture, Ministry of Health, Academy of Sciences, and Biopreparat. Eventually, between 40 and 50 different institutions were involved in some aspect of the BW program. Not all were engaged in microbiology or weapons R&D, however. Some were cover operations to further secure the covert nature of the program. Others supported fermenter design and the construction of test chambers. Because of its geographic isolation in the Aral Sea, Vozrozhdeniye Island (in Kazakhstan) was used as a test site where open-air testing of BW agents took place.

Biopreparat took advantage of the pressure that was put on the MOD and became the main developer of new biological weapons using agents such as *Francisella tularensis*, the causative agent of tularemia. Because Biopreparat was ostensibly a civilian organization, it was easier to conceal its activities from the West under the guise of anodyne medical research. The MOD, the Military Industrial Commission, and other state organs, all the way up to the Central Committee and the Office of the President, ultimately controlled the programs undertaken by Biopreparat. Eventually, all biological weapons–making equipment and materials were transferred to Stepnogorsk, Kazakhstan, a Biopreparat-controlled research facility. The first mission of Stepnogorsk was to take the virulent "Anthrax 836" strain and develop a technique for reproducing it on a massive scale, creating an assembly line for mass production of weaponized anthrax.

The continued development and modernization of its BW program led the Soviet Union to develop a coherent biological weapons doctrine. Biological weapons were divided into two categories. Strategic agents were to be targeted against the continental United States, and operational agents were to be used against North Atlantic Treaty Organization (NATO) staging and logistic areas in the event of war in Europe. Strategic agents were typically lethal and included smallpox, anthrax, and plague. Operational agents, on the other hand, such as the causative agents of tularemia and glanders (*Burkholderia mallei*) were intended to incapacitate enemy soldiers and overwhelm their medical services. The overall goal of Soviet doctrine was to create mass casualties and disrupt critical civilian and military infrastructures.

Soviet biological weapons R&D and production were concealed within the legitimate biotechnology and pharmaceutical industries. Genetic engineering produced a new generation of BW agents. Chimeric agents were developed, a genetic alteration of infectious organisms that caused victims to display symptoms of several infectious organisms. Chimeric agents also shortened the time between infection and the onset of symptoms and caused symptoms to reveal themselves at noncharacteristic times. What resulted were biological agents with increased virulence, improved resistance to antibiotics, longer shelf life, and more ease of dissemination. The new agents could survive environmental effects that greatly reduced the virulence of naturally occurring organisms.

Two biological agents within the Russian arsenal, smallpox (*Variola major*) and Marburg viruses, were especially menacing in terms of their potential effect on global populations. The World Health Organization (WHO) announced in May 1980 that smallpox had been eradicated from the planet. When the WHO named the Centers for Disease Control and Prevention in Atlanta, Georgia, and the Ivanovsky Institute of Virology in Moscow as the only two sites where limited stockpiles of smallpox could be held for research purposes, Moscow saw this as an opportunity to exploit smallpox as a weapon. In the 1981–1985 Five-Year Plan, Moscow listed smallpox as a virus targeted for improvement for military purposes. The Soviet program worked to shorten the time it takes smallpox symptoms to occur and to strengthen its virulence so that any vaccine would be ineffective. This was quite different from the West's policy, which limited its weaponized agents to those having a cure and which are noncommunicable. According to Dr. Ken Alibek, the Soviet Union stockpiled smallpox in the tons to be readied for delivery via intercontinental ballistic missile warheads. A strong and stable strain

of Marburg was also produced by Soviet researchers. The Soviet Union/Russia continued on this path into the early 1990s.

Equally important to the Russian BW program was the development of effective mechanisms for delivery of biological agents. At the Institute of Ultra-Pure Biopreparations, one of the major projects was the modification of cruise missiles to deliver BW agents. Soviet SS-11 and SS-18 missiles were equipped with biological weapons to attack strategic targets within the United States.

Russia, under the leadership of Vladimir Putin, has been no more transparent about its past work in BW and has even intimated continued interest in biological weapons. While continuing to deny any involvement in offensive BW research, in early 2012, Putin promulgated requirements for future needs in terms of weaponry to include those "based on new physical principles: radiation, geophysical, wave, *genetic*, psychophysical, etc." This reference to a "genetic" type of weaponry has brought renewed focus on Russia and potential biological weapons development.

Stephanie Fitzpatrick and Eric A. Croddy

Further Reading

Alibek, Ken, and Stephen Handelman, *Biohazard: The Chilling True Story of the Largest Covert Biological Weapons Program in the World* (New York: Random House, 1999).

Davies, Gareth, "Police Lift Cordon at Every Salisbury Site Linked to the Skripal Poisoning Apart from Spy's House," *The Telegraph*, May 8, 2018 (online). https://www.telegraph.co.uk/news/2018/05/08/salisbury-given-clear-open-every-site-linked-skripal-poisoning. Accessed May 8, 2018.

Davis, Christopher J., "Nuclear Blindness: An Overview of the Biological Weapons Programs of the Former Soviet Union and

Iraq," *Emerging Infectious Diseases* 5, no. 4 (July–August 1999): 509–512.

Federov, Lev, *Chemical Weapons in Russia: History, Ecology, Politics* (Moscow: Center of Ecological Policy of Russia, 1994).

Leitenberg, Milton, and Raymond A. Zilinskas, with Jens Kuhn, *The Soviet Biological Weapons Program* (Cambridge, MA: Harvard University Press, 2012).

Monterey-Moscow Study Group on Russian Chemical Disarmament, Monterey Institute of International Studies, *Eliminating a Deadly Legacy of the Cold War: Overcoming Obstacles to Russian Chemical Disarmament* (Monterey, CA: Center for Nonproliferation Studies, 1998).

National Research Council, *The Biological Threat Reduction Program of the Department of Defense from Foreign Assistance to Sustainable Partnerships* (Washington, D.C.: National Academies Press, 2007).

Shoham, Dany, and Ze'ev Wolfson, "The Russian Biological Weapons Program: Vanished or Disappeared?" *Critical Reviews in Microbiology* 30, no. 4 (October–December 2004): 241–261.

Russian Nuclear Forces and Doctrine

After the detonation of the first Soviet atomic device in 1949 and the Soviet hydrogen (fusion) device in 1953, the Soviet military went about acquiring the world's largest arsenal of nuclear weapons. In addition, the Soviets introduced ballistic and cruise missiles, satellites, and computers into their arsenal. Soviet military writings since the late 1950s asserted that there had been a revolution created by the introduction of nuclear weapons and long-range, high-speed delivery systems. In Soviet defense publications, these inventions were referred to as a "revolution in military affairs." Soviet writers believed that nuclear

weapons altered the nature and methods of armed struggle on the strategic level because they could accomplish the military's strategic tasks without operational art or tactics. According to Soviet military theory, this revolution fundamentally altered the character of any future war by increasing the importance of the opening moments of a conflict. It changed the relationship between strategic and nonstrategic forces. It also created the requirements for a new force posture, geared to a new tempo, scope, and scale of nuclear operations at the continental and intercontinental ranges. The heart of this force posture and associated doctrine was developed in the 1960s and recorded in Marshal Vasily Sokolovsky's three editions of *Military Strategy* (published in 1962, 1963, and 1968).

In the Soviet Union, where strategy is considered a science and the special province of the military, nuclear weapons were not held to be *absolute*. The idea of mutual deterrence was never accepted. Soviet theorists rejected the idea that technology determines strategy and instead adapted nuclear weapons to their traditional Clausewitzian view of war as an extension of politics (based on the well-known military concepts of Carl von Clausewitz (1780–1831)). Transition to a nuclear strategy began in the mid-1950s, when Soviet military thinkers recognized the importance of surprise and the first stages of a war and sought to use nuclear strikes to determine the course and outcome of battle. This concept stressed the importance of preemption—striking before the enemy could strike the Soviet heartland or other socialist countries.

The increased mobility of the Red Army, the traditional battlefield force, and the power of nuclear weapons allowed the Soviets to explore deep offensive operations. They concluded that their political objectives and their views on war dictated a force posture that would enable them to take the offensive from the outset of a war, thereby setting the conditions in the initial period, which would determine the course and outcome of the conflict. Their strategy also held out the promise that some level of damage limitation to the Soviet Union could be achieved if hostile offensive forces could be destroyed before they could be employed. As a result, the Soviets required reliable forces able to destroy distant targets quickly; intercontinental ballistic missiles (ICBMs) were the ideal delivery system to fulfill their military strategy.

The first formal Soviet doctrine for the nuclear age was that of Nikita Khrushchev's "one-variant war." According to this view, a future war would be extremely short and swift and would have an initial period of hostilities that would decide the course and outcome of the entire war. Consequently, Soviet nuclear strategy emphasized mass nuclear strikes and dismissed Western notions of escalation thresholds or limitations to the character and size of nuclear operations. These strikes were best characterized as *countervalue*, as counterforce targeting required accuracies in missile systems that did not exist until the early 1970s. Because an advantage would accrue to the side that struck first, and because Soviet strategic offensive forces in the 1960s were relatively unreliable, inflexible, and vulnerable, Soviet nuclear strategy focused on obtaining strategic warning of an impending war.

The drawbacks to the one-variant war concept soon became apparent to Soviet political and military leaders. The threat of massive retaliation served only to deter direct, massive attacks on the Soviet homeland; it was of doubtful utility in responding to less-than-all-out attacks. Furthermore,

the Khrushchevian strategy offered no prospect for Soviet survival in the event of a general nuclear war. Soviet strategists realized that a more robust strategic force posture was required to meet Soviet political and military options. Although the means for preemptive counterforce operations were unavailable in the 1960s, the Soviets set about to create the desired force structure.

By the late 1970s, the Soviets began to acknowledge that even successful preemption was unlikely to determine the outcome of a nuclear war. Initial strikes by land-based ballistic missiles, it was said, would have a decisive impact on the initiation and course of hostilities but could not determine the outcome. This was the signal that the Soviets believed that more than a single massive nuclear salvo was required for victory. Such formulations also gave an increasing role to other Soviet nuclear forces, the submarine-launched missiles and bombers, in determining the course and outcome. The targeting objectives for the fleet ballistic submarine force suggest that although the use of submarine-launched ballistic missiles (SLBMs) in initial strikes was contemplated, the majority of the SLBMs at sea would be withheld to conduct follow-on strikes that could determine the overall course of the war.

Discussions of the prospects for victory in a strategic nuclear war appeared to turn on judgments regarding the ability of Soviet offensive and defensive forces to avoid suffering a preemptive attack and to destroy the opponent's nuclear forces to limit damage to the Soviet homeland. Despite the attainment of strategic parity in the mid-1970s, the continued production of nuclear weapons by itself was seen as providing no enduring advantages to the Soviet Union. Chief of General Staff Marshal Nikolay Ogarkov made a number of provocative statements between 1982 and 1985 about the paradox existing between the continued acquisition of nuclear weapons and their inability to achieve decisive victories against opponents of the Soviet Union.

Brezhnev and Nuclear Parity

During the Leonid Brezhnev era, the Soviet Union achieved strategic "parity"—a rough equivalence in strategic nuclear capability—with the United States. Second-generation Soviet systems, created in the second half of the 1960s, included permanently fueled missiles with a very high level of readiness. These second-generation systems also were deployed in hardened single silo launchers. The deployment of single silo launchers in a wide crescent, stretching from the Ukraine into Kazakhstan along the trans-Siberian railroad, improved the survivability of the missile force. Second-generation solid-fuel Soviet ballistic missiles could now be kept on a high state of alert, increasing their survivability. The SS-11 became the main component of the land-based nuclear deterrent, with a force of 990 deployed missiles. The SS-9, a heavy ICBM capable of lofting a 10-megaton warhead against U.S. ICBM complexes, was also deployed. The USSR eventually deployed 308 of these heavy ICBMs.

U.S.-Soviet arms control negotiations during the Brezhnev era often highlighted the fact that Soviet planners failed to accept the situation of mutual assured destruction (MAD) as an unalterable fact. Soviet military writings, political statements, and force structure suggested to many Western observers that Soviet planners believed they could benefit from the early and massive use of nuclear weapons in any serious conflict with the West. In the 1970s, a Soviet conventional and theater nuclear force buildup was accompanied by redoubled civil defense measures and preemptive nuclear doctrines. Observers suggested that the Soviets had adopted a policy of "deterrence by denial," that is, their notion of deterrence was based on the ability to fight and win a nuclear war. Soviet officials, however, probably never believed that they could actually use nuclear war as an instrument of policy or that victory in an all-out nuclear war was really within their reach.

By the early 1980s, the Soviets began deploying a third generation of strategic systems that bolstered their nuclear war-fighting capabilities. The SS-18 emerged to replace the SS-9, and the SS-17 and SS-19 replaced the SS-11 force. Soviet ICBMs also were equipped with multiple independently targetable reentry vehicles (MIRVs), which increased the overall prompt hard-target kill capability of the Soviet nuclear arsenal. The SS-20, a MIRVed, road-mobile intermediate-range ballistic missile (IRBM), and the Tu-22M Backfire bomber were also deployed during this period and greatly increased the ability of Soviet forces to hold theater targets at risk with nuclear weapons.

Soviet Strategy at the End of the Cold War

Fourth-generation Soviet strategic forces were entering service by 1991, just as the Cold War was ending. Soviet planners had begun to increase the survivability of their land-based missile force by deploying rail-mobile (SS-24) and land-mobile (SS-25) ICBMs. As the range of Soviet submarine-launched ballistic missiles increased, they began to deploy their fleet ballistic missile submarines in bastions operating close to Soviet bases. These were heavily defended by the Soviet Navy and land-based aviation. The culmination of Soviet ballistic missile submarine development was the Typhoon class, which had a unique hull configuration and was equipped with a new MIRVed missile. Each Typhoon could carry up to 200 nuclear warheads. The Soviets also began to produce an intercontinental jet bomber, the Blackjack. But by 1989, only 16 of these expensive bombers had been built.

Russian Nuclear Doctrine Today

As the Soviet empire slipped away, Russian nuclear force modernization slowed to a snail's pace as Russian officials, in conjunction with their U.S. counterparts, greatly reduced the size of their strategic nuclear arsenal. For more than 15 years following the end of the Cold War and the dissolution of the Soviet Union, Russia struggled to maintain a professional, modern, and efficient strategic force. In addition, from Moscow's perspective, the former military competition now seemed to focus on nonproliferation efforts and arms control, all of which seemed to undermine Russian strength.

Russia accepted Western help and funding to find, return, and secure its far-flung nuclear arsenal when the USSR became 15 independent republics in 1991. Russia joined several U.S.-sponsored programs to help it secure its warheads and nuclear infrastructure, including the Cooperative Threat Reduction Program, Nuclear Cities Initiative, and Nuclear Materials Control and Accountability program. It was a beneficiary of the 2002 G20 global partnership against the spread of WMD. It accepted funding to modernize and secure its nuclear infrastructure, including such big-budget items as the construction of the Mayak nuclear warhead storage facility near Moscow.

But by the end of the first decade in the new century, under the long tenure of President Putin, attitudes and policies changed. Russia embarked on an across-the-board modernization program for its strategic weapons and delivery systems, it modified its national security strategy to enhance the requirement for nuclear weapons, and, in 2014, it brazenly began violating the sovereignty of its neighbors by invading Ukraine to capture Crimea and foment civil war in the Donbas region while threatening the Baltic and Scandinavian states and making nuclear threats against specific NATO members. For many in the West, the Cold War appeared to be returning, led by Russia and its nuclear forces.

The Russians have stated that they still contemplate the first use of nuclear weapons in response to various strategic threats; the emergence of a Russian "escalate-to-de-escalate" doctrine that emerged in 2015 was deemed highly provocative by Western observers. In 2018, Russia continues its long-standing nuclear force modernization program that will replace all remaining Soviet-era missiles, on a less than one-for-one basis, with newer types by 2020. Russia retains about 7,000 nuclear weapons in its operational and reserve arsenal.

Gilles Van Nederveen, James J. Wirtz, and
Jeffrey A. Larsen

Further Reading

Garthoff, Raymond L., *Deterrence and Revolution in Soviet Military Doctrine* (Washington, D.C.: Brookings Institution, 1990).

Herspring, Dale, *The Soviet High Command, 1967–1989: Personalities and Politics* (Princeton, NJ: Princeton University Press, 1990).

Kristensen, Hans M., and Robert S. Norris, "Russian Nuclear Forces 2017," *Bulletin of the Atomic Scientists* 73, no. 2 (2017), https://thebulletin.org/2017/march/russian-nuclear-forces-201710568. Accessed May 21, 2018.

Lasconjarias, Guillaume, and Jeffrey A. Larsen, eds., *NATO's Responses to Hybrid Threats* (Rome: NATO Defense College, 2015).

Lynn-Jones, Sean, Steven Miller, and Stephen Van Evera, eds., *Soviet Military Policy* (Cambridge, MA: MIT Press, 1989).

Podvig, Pavel, ed., *Russian Strategic Nuclear Forces* (Cambridge, MA: MIT Press, 2001).

Scott, Harriet Fast, and William Scott, eds., *The Soviet Art of War: Doctrine, Strategy, and Tactics* (Boulder, CO: Westview, 1982).

Scott, Harriet Fast, and William Scott, *Soviet Military Doctrine: Continuity, Formulation, and Dissemination* (Boulder, CO: Westview, 1988).

Turbiville, Graham, ed., *The Voroshilov Lectures: Materials from the Soviet General Staff Academy*, 3 vols. (Washington, D.C.: National Defense University Press, 1989).

Zaloga, Steven J., *The Kremlin's Nuclear Sword: The Rise and Fall of Russia's Strategic Nuclear Forces, 1945–2000* (Washington, D.C.: Smithsonian Institution Press, 2002).

S

Smallpox

Smallpox is a highly contagious viral disease of humans that causes death in about 30 percent of its victims. The last case of smallpox in the United States occurred in 1949; worldwide, the last naturally occurring case of smallpox was in Somalia (1977). The World Health Organization (WHO) undertook a worldwide vaccination campaign that continued through the 1970s. In 1980, the WHO officially certified the elimination of smallpox from the globe. Although the disease was declared eliminated, concerns have emerged about state or terrorist use of smallpox as a weapon. It is known that the Soviet Union ran a program to weaponize smallpox. In addition, terrorists are known to be interested in biological weapons, with smallpox being a potential candidate.

Medical Aspects

The variola virus, a member of the poxvirus family, causes smallpox, and it can take two forms: variola major, the predominant form, and variola minor, a less common and less severe form that causes death in less than 1 percent of cases.

A variola major infection can manifest in four ways. In 90 percent or more of cases, patients experience "ordinary" infection (see below). Other types include modified (a milder infection that normally occurs in previously vaccinated individuals), a malignant form (flat), and hemorrhagic, a particularly dreadful outcome involving bleeding in skin tissues. Both the malignant and hemorrhagic forms of smallpox are nearly always fatal. As with many viruses, there is no specific treatment for smallpox, although prompt administration of vaccine before symptoms appear can prevent the disease.

In the past, natural smallpox was usually spread through close contact of less than six feet, with an infected individual spreading aerosolized viral particles, or through contaminated clothing or bed linens. There were occasional cases of transmission over greater distances. The average patient (ordinary infection) developed a fever, experienced severe aches, and became completely exhausted within 12–14 days (within a range of 7–17 days after infection). One to three days after the onset of fever, a rash consisting of small, solid raised lesions developed on the face and extremities and, to a lesser extent, on the trunk. As the rash progressed, the small blisters filled with fluid and became inflamed. Eventually, the lesions crusted over and formed scabs, which often scarred the patient severely. Death generally occurred during the second week in about 20–30 percent of cases, depending on the strain and quality of supportive care.

Smallpox as a Weapon

In the second half of the 20th century, the United States experimented with smallpox (or simulants) for the purpose of developing defensive measures, but the Soviet Union took the extra step of actually weaponizing variola major. The Soviets chose smallpox as a viable biological weapon because it is a hardy virus, is highly infectious as an aerosol, and can survive explosive delivery. One strain chosen by the Soviets, known as India 1967, was particularly virulent. It killed more than 30 percent of those infected, retained virulence when stored for long periods, and was extremely stable in aerosol form. Additional stabilizers, filling agents, and chemicals extended the shelf life of weaponized smallpox.

Complications in the Event of an Attack

Recognition and diagnosis of smallpox in the modern context may be difficult because many health care workers have little experience with smallpox. Furthermore, its symptoms can be confused with other disease processes, and it has been confused with chicken pox in the past. Smallpox lesions develop on the same time line and appear identical on all parts of the body at a given time; however, they are deeper than chicken pox lesions, and smallpox typically appears on the face and extremities, whereas chicken pox lesions are usually concentrated on the trunk.

Smallpox vaccination side effects can be severe, and because the risks of a natural outbreak of smallpox are negligible, routine administration of Vaccinia is only given to U.S. military personnel and certain health care professionals. (Between 2002 and 2014, about 2.4 million individuals in the U.S. armed forces were vaccinated for smallpox.) The smallpox vaccine is made up of live Vaccinia virus. This virus is not normally harmful in humans, but because the vaccine virus is alive, it can cause severe complications. On the positive side, immunization before exposure and up to five (or possibly seven) days after exposure will almost certainly prevent death, and early vaccination—within one to four days following exposure—will prevent the

fulminant disease. A more recent formulation, ACAM2000, Smallpox (Vaccinia) Vaccine, is a live preparation that was approved by the U.S. Food and Drug Administration in 2007.

The Threat

Although there is great concern about a potential smallpox attack, the likelihood of a smallpox attack by terrorists or a state is extremely low—although certainly not zero. Currently, the virus causing smallpox is very difficult to obtain. Starting in 1975, the Smallpox Eradication Unit of the WHO attempted to identify all laboratories that held samples of smallpox by (1) contacting every country and territory and requesting a list of laboratories that maintained stocks of the virus, (2) searching the literature, and (3) contacting laboratories directly. As a result, there are only two remaining known stocks ,of smallpox in the world. One is located at the Centers for Disease Control and Prevention (CDC) outside of Atlanta, Georgia (450 isolates), and the other is at the State Research Institute of Virology and Biotechnology (VECTOR) near Novosibirsk in Russian Siberia (about 120 different strains). While the World Health Organization (WHO) has periodically deliberated whether remaining smallpox virus stocks should be destroyed, as of 2018, there is no consensus on this issue.

Jennifer Brower and Eric A. Croddy

Further Reading

Babkin, Igor V., and Irina N. Babkina, "The Origin of the Variola Virus," *Viruses* 7, no. 3 (2015): 1100–1112.

Berche, Patrick, "The Threat of Smallpox and Bioterrorism," *Trends in Microbiology* 9, no. 1 (January 2001): 15–18.

Meltzer, Martin I., Inger Damon, James W. LeDuc, and J. Donald Millar, "Modeling

Potential Responses to Smallpox as a Bio-terrorist Weapon," *Emerging Infectious Diseases* 7, no. 6 (November–December 2001): 959–969. http://www.cdc.gov/ncidod/EID/vol7no6/meltzer.htm. Accessed May 1, 2018.

Tucker, Jonathan B., *Scourge: The Once and Future Threat of Smallpox* (New York: Atlanta Monthly Press, 2001).

South Africa

Toward the end of 1981, the South African regime established a covert chemical and biological weapons program code-named "Project Coast" (later "Project Jota"). The project, ostensibly created for defensive purposes, was in response to reports that government and Cuban military forces in Angola were using chemical weapons against South African Defense Force (SADF) troops and their allies. The program, however, also included offensive capabilities. The apartheid-era government viewed itself as the target of a "total onslaught" by Soviet-backed Marxist guerrillas and regimes in neighboring states as well as by black nationalists at home, and to meet this all-encompassing "red-black danger," it was willing to use any means at its disposal to defend itself. It was in this highly charged political and military context that Project Coast was secretly initiated under the aegis of SADF Special Forces.

Project Coast, like the foreign CBW programs upon which it was supposedly modeled, included both a chemical warfare (CW) component and a biological warfare (BW) component. Both the CW and BW programs in South Africa consisted of one principal production facility and several other facilities that, for administrative, security, or technical reasons, carried out specialized research, testing, or production

tasks. The primary CW facility was Delta G Scientific (Delta G), a large research and production complex located in Midrand. Its staff of about 120 had the ability to make virtually any synthetic chemical, but their efforts were focused on various military projects geared toward the preservation of public order. These included (1) the large-scale production of chemical irritants and incapacitants used for crowd control, such as CS and CR tear gas; (2) the relatively small-scale production of various illegal mind-altering narcotics in an effort to develop and test their potential viability as "calmatives"; (3) a peptide (complex of amino acids) synthesis program, which was apparently working to enhance the physiological effects of bioregulators, novel agents that could induce dramatic changes in victims; and (4) a CW research and analysis program, which manufactured small quantities of toxic substances on demand.

The main BW facility was Roodeplaat Research Laboratories (RRL), a large, sophisticated research, testing, and production complex located north of Pretoria. Its staff of around 70 primarily worked on three types of military projects: (1) a toxin R&D program, whose goal was to develop and test lethal BW and CW agents that were untraceable; (2) a fertility program, whose purpose may have been to limit the growth of the black population; and (3) a BW program linked to new developments in the genetic engineering field, whose aim was to develop antibiotic-resistant strains of pathogens.

Although there was no large-scale production or weaponization of either offensive CW agents at Delta G or offensive BW agents at RRL, a plethora of toxic substances were acquired, researched, tested, or prepared at these facilities. At Delta G, these substances included the psychoincapacitant BZ, mustard agent, and a wide array of other toxic chemicals. At RRL they studied anthrax bacterium, botulinum toxin, *Brucella* bacteria, cholera bacterium, *Clostridium perfringens*, *Escherichia coli*, plague bacterium, *Salmonella* bacteria, HIV-infected blood, and snake venom. Some of the two firms' products were then reportedly tested at the pyrotechnical labs at Special Forces headquarters, the South African Police's Forensic Sciences Laboratory, or other facilities at various state companies, partially state-run companies, private companies, and universities.

The apex of the official chain of command for both the CW and BW components of Project Coast was the president of the republic himself, P. W. Botha, who, under the militarized National Security Management System established in August 1979, exercised his authority primarily through the State Security Council rather than the cabinet. The project officer was Dr. Wouter Basson.

On the verbal instructions of Dr. Basson, RRL's research and development director secretly transferred a host of highly toxic chemicals and freeze-dried pathogens that had been produced at either Delta G or RRL—and thereafter stored in a refrigerator inside a fireproof and bomb-proof walk-in safe in his own office—to military and police personnel through various channels. The actual substances included lethal chemicals and biological agents such as anthrax spores, botulinum toxin, *Brucella* bacteria, *Salmonella* bacteria, mamba venom, and bottles of cholera bacterium, as well as a wide variety of foodstuffs, beverages, household items, and cigarettes that had been contaminated with these poisons. The evidence suggests that several of these toxic materials, items, or devices were used to murder or sicken troublesome prisoners,

guerrillas in neighboring countries, untrustworthy members of the security forces, or activists in the African National Congress (ANC) and other South African opposition groups.

Later, in the course of the extraordinary political transition of the early 1990s during which the apartheid regime reluctantly but peacefully ceded power to a new ANC-led government, the activities of Project Coast were gradually phased out and exposed. In January 1997, Basson was arrested in a sting operation for possessing thousands of capsules of the illegal drug MDMA (ecstasy) that had apparently been manufactured at Delta G, ostensibly for use as a potential "calmative." Following Basson's arrest, the police discovered several trunks full of project documents that he had secretly whisked away and stashed with friends or in storage facilities. Basson was indicted by the state for murder and a host of other crimes that he had allegedly committed during the period when he served as project officer for Project Coast. During the course of this trial, as well as at the earlier hearings held by the Truth and Reconciliation Commission, a wealth of detailed information emerged regarding the true scope and nature of South Africa's CBW program. To the astonishment of most observers, however, Basson was acquitted in April 2002 of all the charges filed against him.

While some analysts regard South Africa as a model for other states that might decide to dismantle their WMD programs, the termination of the country's CBW program was by no means as transparent as that of its nuclear program.

Nuclear

South Africa was a secret nuclear weapons state in the 1980s and 1990s, until unilaterally renouncing its program and destroying its six warheads in 1994. Readily available South African sources of yellowcake had helped to fuel the nuclear industry in the United States immediately after World War II. Reciprocally, South Africans were trained in the United States, which later provided South Africa with a nuclear research reactor. This arrangement operated under a safeguards agreement between the International Atomic Energy Agency (IAEA), the United States, and South Africa. In 1957, the United States signed a bilateral nuclear cooperation agreement with South Africa that committed Washington to supply enriched uranium to the regime in Johannesburg.

Although South Africa had signed the 1963 Limited Test Ban Treaty, it refused to sign the 1968 Nuclear Nonproliferation Treaty (NPT). In 1971, South Africa began investigations into building a nuclear device. This initiated deep suspicion over South Africa's long-term intentions, especially because the country faced growing international isolation over its policy of apartheid. Three years later, the South African government authorized a nuclear program and began secret work on a nuclear test site in the Kalahari Desert.

Notwithstanding efforts to use its strategic location to impress its importance to the West, pressure on South Africa over both apartheid and its nuclear program had increased by the mid-1970s. The Jimmy Carter administration was especially active in the quest to end apartheid. Although Washington opposed a complete ban on nuclear cooperation with South Africa, the 1978 U.S. Nuclear Non-Proliferation Act (NNPA) ended the possibility for the re-export of enriched uranium (even of South African origin) to South Africa to fuel a French-built nuclear power station. In response, South Africa set out to develop local alternatives by constructing a plant to produce highly enriched uranium (HEU) on an industrial scale.

In August 1977, the Soviets detected preparations for a "cold test" at the Kalahari facility. Setting aside ideological differences, the superpowers pressured South Africa not to go forward with its nuclear program. Two years later, however, the United States detected a low-yield, high-altitude nuclear explosion off South Africa's southern coast. What happened remains a mystery. The possibility of nuclear cooperation with Israel remains the most plausible explanation of the event. In 1977, South Africa was removed from its seat on the IAEA board of governors and replaced by Egypt; two years later, it was denied participation in the IAEA General Conference. South Africa also might have sold enriched uranium to Iraq in the late 1980s.

The end of apartheid broke the impasse over South Africa's nuclear program. In early July 1991, South Africa acceded to the NPT, and it completed its IAEA safeguards agreement three months later. In March 1993, South Africa's last minority-elected president, F. W. de Klerk, announced the unilateral dismantling of its six nuclear weapons. Some believe that the decision was made to prevent technology from falling into the hands of a "black government" or to halt the possible transfer of weapons-grade uranium to Libya, Cuba, or the Palestine Liberation Organization. The country's majority-elected government has also followed a nonnuclear policy.

South Africa joined the Zangger Committee in 1994 and the Nuclear Suppliers Group in 1995. Its officials were instrumental in winning indefinite extension of the NPT in 1995 and played a leading role in the successful conclusion of the 2000 NPT Review Conference as a member of the New Agenda Coalition.

The termination of these nuclear programs was never transparent. Assurances that the remaining stocks of Project Coast–related CW and BW agents were destroyed were never independently verified. The South Africans also destroyed much associated documentation when they disbanded their nuclear program, leaving scholars to wonder whether remnants of their program sit long forgotten in some warehouse.

Jeffrey M. Bale and Peter Vale

Further Reading

Burger, Marléne, and Chandré Gould, *Secrets and Lies: Wouter Basson and South Africa's Chemical and Biological Warfare Programme* (Cape Town, South Africa: Zebra, 2002).

Burgess, Stephen, and Helen Purkitt, *The Rollback of South Africa's Biological Warfare Program* (Colorado Springs, CO: U.S. Air Force Institute for National Security Studies, 2001).

Dunn, Kate, "Biological Horrors: Revelations before South African Commission Leave Country Reeling," *Southam News* (Ottawa, Canada), (June 22, 1998): A18.

Gould, Chandré, and Peter Folb, *Project Coast: Apartheid's Chemical and Biological Warfare Programme* (Geneva, Switzerland: United Nations Institute for Disarmament Research, 2002).

Paul, T. V., *Power versus Prudence: Why Nations Forgo Nuclear Weapons* (Montreal: McGill-Queen's University Press, 2000).

Purkitt, Helen E., and Stephen F. Burgess, *South Africa's Weapons of Mass Destruction* (Bloomington: Indiana University Press, 2005).

Staphylococcal Enterotoxin B

The bacterium *Staphylococcus aureus* produces a number of exotoxins, so named because they are excreted from the cell. These proteins generally act on the intestines and are thus also referred to as *enterotoxins*. Natural exposure (such as food poisoning) to *Staphylococcus* toxins generally results in illness, ranging from mild (e.g., vomiting) to very severe (including death). Due to their profound effect on the immune system, these proteins are commonly referred to as *super antigens*.

Of these toxic proteins, staphylococcal enterotoxin B (SEB) is the most studied for its ability to achieve the desired effect at very low quantities. The offensive biological weapons program of the United States pursued SEB as an incapacitant in the 1960s. SEB proved to be stable, easily aerosolized, and able to cause systemic damage, including multiple organ failure. Furthermore, the agent was more attractive than chemical equivalents because a smaller amount was necessary to get the desired effect. Although exposure to this agent most frequently results in a temporary incapacitating illness, inhalation of very high doses could very well lead to shock or death.

In the 1960s, research was conducted by the United States at Camp Detrick (now Fort Detrick), Maryland, to develop SEB (code-named "PG") as an incapacitant. These stockpiles were destroyed between May 1971 and May 1972. It has been reported that Russian biological weapons programs also researched SEB as a toxic warfare agent.

Technical Details

Staphylococcal toxins cause classic food poisoning. When ingested, the toxins are usually confined to the intestines and cause diarrhea and vomiting. If present systemically, toxic shock syndrome can result.

SEB is classified as an incapacitating agent, as most cases are not lethal but cause profound illness within a short incubation time. The incubation time after ingestion of SEB varies from 1 to 8 hours (rarely, up to 18 hours) and results in the abrupt onset of acute salivation, intense nausea, vomiting, cramping abdominal pain, and diarrhea. These symptoms are usually self-limiting and resolve in about 8–24 hours, but high levels of exposure can lead to septic shock and death if left untreated. Treatment consists of administration of antihistamines, and antibodies (gamma globulin) may also increase survivability.

Aerosol exposure manifests itself in a different manner. The incubation time from airborne exposure is 1–6 hours. After 3–12 hours, a high fever (103–106°F), chills, headache, myalgia (muscle aches), and nonproductive cough may appear. Shortness of breath and chest pains may appear in some patients. The fever can last two to five days, and the cough may persist up to four weeks.

Diagnosis of SEB exposure can be challenging, as the early symptoms mimic many naturally occurring diseases, such as influenza, adenovirus, or parainfluenza. Additionally, early clinical manifestations can be similar to those of inhalation anthrax, tularemia, plague, or Q fever.

Treatment for enterotoxin exposure is limited. Generally, supportive care and close attention to oxygenation and hydration are adequate. In severe cases, breathing assistance may be necessary. No approved vaccine is available.

An attack with an aerosolized SEB weapon would be unlikely to lead to significant mortality, but 80 percent or more of those exposed to the toxin could be incapacitated for one to two weeks. This ability to cause casualties, even if nonfatal, makes the toxin a candidate for weaponization. Additionally, SEB could be used to sabotage food or small-volume water supplies.

Elizabeth Prescott

Further Reading

Lindsay, Christopher D., and G. D. Griffiths, "Addressing Bioterrorism Concerns: Options for Investigating the Mechanism of Action of *Staphylococcus aureus* Enterotoxin B," *Human & Experimental Toxicology* 32, no. 6 (June 2013): 606–619.

Stockpile Stewardship Program

The cessation of underground nuclear testing in the early 1990s created a major challenge for the U.S. Department of Energy (DOE): how could it continue to certify the safety and readiness of its nuclear weapons without this key aspect of the annual certification program. Nuclear testing was the core activity that allowed the DOE to certify to the president on an annual basis that the stockpile remained safe and capable. The replacement for the underground nuclear test program is the Stockpile Stewardship Program (SSP).

In 1995, President Bill Clinton announced that the United States would pursue a comprehensive nuclear test ban. The president also directed that necessary programmatic activities be developed to ensure stockpile safety and reliability in the absence of nuclear testing. The DOE Stockpile Stewardship Program was the response to this directive. In 1996, the president signed the Comprehensive Test Ban Treaty to end all nuclear testing. Although the U.S. Senate failed to ratify the treaty on November 10, 1999, the United States continues to abide by a unilateral moratorium on nuclear testing.

The DOE's Stockpile Stewardship Program relies on experiments and simulations to predict, detect, evaluate, and correct problems affecting nuclear weapons without nuclear testing. Critical to meeting this challenge is the development of higher-resolution computer models of the performance of nuclear weapons and the conditions that affect weapon safety. This replaces the previous demonstration-based program with a science-based one that focuses on the implications to performance of an aging stockpile.

The elements of SSP are located at the Lawrence Livermore, Los Alamos, and Sandia national laboratories. The first annual certification of the stockpile under the SSP was signed on February 7, 1997.

Don Gillich

Further Reading

Lawrence Livermore National Laboratory, "Stockpile Stewardship Program," UCRL-LR-129781, October 6, 1998.

Strategic Arms Limitation Talks (SALT I and SALT II)

The Strategic Arms Limitation Talks (SALT) were bilateral discussions between the United States and the Soviet Union on limiting the nuclear arms race. SALT I (November 1969 to January 1972) yielded two agreements, the Anti-Ballistic Missile (ABM) Treaty and the Interim Agreement on the Limitation of Strategic Offensive Arms. SALT II (September 1972 to January 1979) resulted in the Vladivostok Accord and the SALT II Treaty.

History and Background

At the July 1968 signing of the Nuclear Nonproliferation Treaty (NPT), President Lyndon B. Johnson announced that an agreement had been reached with the Soviet Union to begin discussions on limiting strategic nuclear weapons delivery systems and defense against ballistic missiles.

In addition to the issues of trust and hostility that burden adversarial relationships,

negotiations were complicated by the different objectives embraced by each side. The Soviet Union was contiguous with its principal allies, but the United States was geographically separated from its allies in Western Europe and Japan. The Soviets wished to limit all missiles capable of hitting the other side's territory—which would have included Western weapons in Western Europe, including those launched from bombers and aircraft carriers—whereas the United States desired to include only intercontinental ballistic missiles.

Designing a verification regime was also a difficult task because neither side would permit the other free access to its territory, let alone access to military facilities. Eventually, they agreed to use "national technical means of verification" (mainly, satellites deployed in orbit) and promised not to use deliberate concealment to impede verification. Neither of these measures proved satisfactory, however, and both sides routinely accused the other of cheating throughout the life of the SALT treaties. Although the Interim Agreement expired after five years, the ABM Treaty was of "unlimited duration" but granted each party the right to withdraw six months after giving notice if it determined that the strategic situation had changed to the point where adhering to the treaty put its vital interests in danger. The United States activated this clause in December 2001 and withdrew from the ABM Treaty in May 2002.

Negotiations on SALT II began in November 1972 with the aim of creating a permanent framework to replace the Interim Agreement. At a meeting in Vladivostok, Siberia, in November 1974, President Gerald Ford and General Secretary Leonid Brezhnev agreed to a Basic Framework for the SALT II agreement: an equal aggregate limit of 2,400 strategic nuclear delivery vehicles (ICBMs, submarine-launched ballistic missiles (SLBMs), and heavy bombers); deployment of up to 1,300 multiple independently targetable reentry vehicles (MIRVs); a ban on construction of new land-based ICBM launchers; and limits on the deployment of new types of strategic offensive arms. They agreed that these limits would last through 1985. Negotiations stalled in early 1975 owing to disagreements over whether the new Soviet bomber known as "Backfire" would be considered a heavy bomber and therefore included in the 2,400 aggregate, the MIRV verification process, missile throw weight ceilings, and the status of cruise missiles.

Talks were renewed during the administration of President Jimmy Carter. Ultimately, the parties agreed to defer resolution of the sticking points until SALT III (which never occurred). The SALT II Treaty was signed by President Carter and General Secretary Brezhnev in Vienna on June 18, 1979, and transmitted to the Senate for ratification four days later. On January 3, 1980, following the Soviet invasion of Afghanistan, President Carter requested that the Senate shelve discussion of the treaty rather than allowing it to be voted down by the U.S. Senate.

Although the treaty was never formally ratified, both sides were bound under international law to comply with its broad outlines until they formally announced their intention to withdraw from the agreement. Carter pledged to allow the terms to remain in force as long as the Soviet Union reciprocated, and Brezhnev made a similar statement. President Ronald Reagan initially pledged to abide by the terms of the treaty when he took office in 1981. He declared in 1984, and again in 1985, that the Soviets had violated several provisions but that the United States would nonetheless continue to work within SALT II constraints. On May 26, 1986, however, he submitted three detailed reports to Congress describing major violations by the Soviets and announced that the United States would henceforth base decisions about its strategic force structure on the nature and magnitude of the threat posed by Soviet strategic forces and not on the limits outlined by the SALT structure. Ultimately, the Reagan administration did not increase strategic force levels beyond SALT II levels and, finding a more cooperative government under Soviet president Mikhail Gorbachev, obviated the treaty by negotiating two agreements that actually further reduced nuclear force levels on both sides: the Intermediate-Range Nuclear Forces (INF) Treaty and the Strategic Arms Reduction Treaty (START I).

Status

SALT I and II are no longer in force. SALT I's Interim Agreement was for a period of five years and thus expired in 1979. SALT II was never ratified by the U.S. Senate, although its provisions were informally adhered to by successive presidential administrations until the treaty was eventually rendered moot by START I and II. The United States announced its withdrawal from the ABM Treaty on December 13, 2001.

James Joyner

Further Reading

Goller-Calvo, Notburga K., and Michel A. Calvo, *The SALT Agreements: Content, Application, Verification* (New York: Kluwer Law International, 1988).

Smith, Gerard, *Doubletalk: The Story of SALT I* (Lanham, MD: University Press of America, 1985).

Talbott, Strobe, *Endgame: The Inside Story of SALT II* (New York: Harper and Row, 1979).

Strategic Arms Reduction Treaty (START I)

The Strategic Arms Reduction Treaty (START I), officially the Treaty on the Reduction and Limitation of Strategic Offensive Arms, was an agreement between the United States and the Soviet Union signed by Presidents George H. W. Bush and Mikhail Gorbachev in Moscow on July 31, 1991. It entered into force on December 5, 1994. START I was a product of nine years of negotiations. Its terms provided for reductions in strategic offensive arms to equal aggregate levels to be carried out in three phases over seven years. There were specific, equal interim levels for agreed categories of strategic offensive arms by the end of each phase. At the end of the seven-year period, central limits included 1,600 strategic nuclear delivery vehicles (SNDVs), 6,000 accountable warheads, and 4,900 ballistic missile warheads. The Soviets were also limited to 1,540 warheads on 154 heavy intercontinental ballistic missiles (ICBMs). Although the treaty allowed for existing equipment to be modernized or replaced, it banned the production, flight testing, and deployment of new or modified ICBMs and submarine-launched ballistic missiles (SLBMs) with more than 10 warheads. Under START I, U.S. long-range nuclear weapons were cut by 15 percent, and Soviet/Russian strategic forces were cut by 25 percent.

On March 31, 1982, during his first prime-time news conference, President Reagan invited the Soviet Union to join the United States in negotiations to reduce the size of both nuclear arsenals. START negotiations began in Geneva on June 29, 1982. By the end of 1989, many of the treaty's basic provisions had been developed. The Reykjavik Summit meeting of October 11–12, 1986; the foreign ministers meeting of September 15–17, 1987; the Washington Summit meeting of December 7–10, 1987; and the Wyoming Foreign Ministers meeting of September 22–23, 1989, led to agreement on most of the provisions. Important progress was made at the Wyoming foreign ministers meeting. U.S. negotiators were able to prevent any linkage between reductions of strategic offensive nuclear weapons and the Reagan administration's plan to pursue space-based defenses against ballistic missiles. In addition, the Soviet Union agreed to dismantle, without preconditions, the phased-array Krasnoyarsk radar, which violated the 1972 Anti-Ballistic Missile (ABM) Treaty.

Other issues that had previously defied solution at the negotiating table, however, had to be addressed in the treaty. Negotiators had to determine counting rules for heavy bombers carrying nuclear-armed air-launched cruise missiles (ALCMs), a sublimit on ICBM warheads, sublimits on warheads on mobile ICBMs, and counting rules for nondeployed missiles. They had to resolve problems concerning the modernization of heavy ICBMs and determine how to address nuclear sea-launched cruise missiles (SLCMs), telemetry encryption, and cuts in Soviet missile throw weight. They also had to design an effective verification regime to monitor treaty compliance.

After nine years of negotiations, the START team experienced a frenetic pace of activity in the six weeks before it was signed. During this time, negotiators came to an agreement on the three remaining issues: warhead downloading, accountability for new types of missiles, and data denial. Conclusive negotiations centered on counting rules within agreed limits and sublimits for both nuclear delivery vehicles and warheads. The agreement represented the first time in U.S.-Soviet arms control history that the two nations decided to make deep cuts in their respective nuclear arsenals. Unlike the Intermediate-Range Nuclear Forces (INF) Treaty of 1987, however, START I did not require elimination of an entire category of nuclear weapons. At the Group of Seven Summit in London on July 17, 1991, Presidents George H. W. Bush and Mikhail Gorbachev announced that START was ready to be signed at a U.S.-Soviet summit in Moscow by the end of that month.

The Lisbon Protocol and Ratification Issues

Following the end of the Soviet era in December 1991, nuclear arms were still deployed in some ex-Soviet republics. Four "new" states now had nuclear weapons based on their territories—Russia, Belarus, Kazakhstan, and Ukraine. The three republics and the Russian Federation undertook to make arrangements among themselves for the implementation of the treaty's provisions at a May 23, 1992, ministerial meeting in Lisbon, Portugal. The United States, Russia, Belarus, Kazakhstan, and Ukraine signed a protocol to the treaty known as the Lisbon Protocol, making all five countries signatories of START I. Under the protocol, Belarus, Kazakhstan, and Ukraine agreed to eliminate all nuclear weapons on their territory and to join the 1968 Nuclear Nonproliferation Treaty (NPT) as nonnuclear weapons states (NNWS). Russian ratification of START I hinged on this pledge. Thus, though START I was initially a bilateral treaty between the Soviet Union and the United States, the Lisbon Protocol transformed it into a multilateral treaty that was later ratified as a bilateral treaty between Russia and the United States.

START I was ratified by the U.S. Senate on October 1, 1992. The Russian Parliament ratified it on November 4, 1992; Kazakhstan ratified it on July 2, 1992, and deposited the instruments of accession to the NPT on February 14, 1993. Ukraine became the last former Soviet republic to ratify the treaty on November 18, 1993. The Ukrainian Parliament approved a resolution on November 16, 1994, to accede to the NPT as a nonnuclear weapons state. President Leonid Kuchma of Ukraine deposited the NPT instruments of ratification at a ceremony on December 5, 1994, held at the Conference on Security and Cooperation in Europe summit meeting in Budapest, Hungary, paving the way for a second ceremony on the same day where leaders of the five Lisbon Protocol signatory countries signed a protocol exchanging the START I instruments of ratification. Baseline inspections began on March 1, 1995, when three 10-member teams from the United States arrived in Russia to visit 71 weapons facilities in Belarus, Kazakhstan, Russia, and Ukraine.

Results

On December 5, 2001, seven years after the accord had entered into force, the United States and Russia completed their weapons reductions as provided for by the terms of START I, thus completing the largest arms control reductions in history. The treaty remained in effect until December 5, 2009, but Russia and the United States agreed to continue to abide by its terms until the New START Treaty went into force on January 26, 2011. During this time, the treaty parties could request challenge inspections of suspect activity.

Kalpana Chittaranjan

Further Reading

Kartchner, Kerry M., *Negotiating START: Strategic Arms Reduction Talks and the*

Quest for Strategic Stability (New Brunswick, NJ: Transaction, 1992).

"Strategic Arms Reduction Treaty (START I)," Treaty Text. https://www.state.gov/t/avc/trty/146007.htm. Accessed July 15, 2003.

Strategic Arms Reduction Treaty (START II)

The Strategic Arms Reduction Treaty (START II), officially titled the Treaty on Further Reduction and Limitation of Strategic Offensive Arms, is an agreement between the United States and Russia signed by Presidents George H. W. Bush and Boris Yeltsin in Moscow on January 3, 1993. START II reduced the deployed strategic nuclear forces of both nations to 3,000–3,500 warheads (down from 6,000 warheads allowed under START I). Additional limits included a ban on multiple independently targetable reentry vehicles (MIRVs) on intercontinental ballistic missiles (ICBMs), the elimination of all SS-18 "heavy" missiles, a sublimit of 1,700–1,750 submarine-launched ballistic missile (SLBM) warheads (about one-half the SLBM warheads authorized for the United States under START I), and the freedom to "download" (remove) warheads from strategic missiles to meet required reductions (this could be done by "deMIRVing" ICBMs). START II also allowed no discount for heavy bomber weapons (accountable numbers were the number of weapons they were actually equipped to carry). The treaty, however, did give the parties the right to "reorient" bombers capable of carrying nuclear weapons to conventional missions (and thus exempt them from the overall limits). Up to 100 heavy bombers could be transferred to conventional

missions, provided they had never been equipped to carry long-range nuclear air-launched cruise missiles (ALCMs).

Phase I of the treaty was to be implemented within seven years of the entry into force of START I, and Phase II was to be implemented by January 1, 2003. These deadlines were extended to December 31, 2004, and December 31, 2007, by a protocol to the treaty signed by U.S. and Russian representatives on September 27, 1997.

After START I, critics charged that the main shortcoming of the treaty was that it tended to place a floor, not a ceiling, on force size. Thus, efforts were made to reach more comprehensive arms reductions between the United States and Russia. President George H. W. Bush's State of the Union address to the U.S. Congress on January 28, 1992, contained a proposal for a new agreement requiring far deeper cuts than those required by the provisions of START I. In a statement of what was to become the basic provisions of START II, the president said,

> I have informed President Yeltsin that if the [former Soviet republics] will eliminate all land-based multiple warhead ballistic missiles . . . [w]e will eliminate all Peacekeeper missiles. We will reduce the number of warheads on Minuteman missiles to one, and reduce the number of warheads on our sea-based missiles by about one-third. And we will convert a substantial portion of our strategic bombers to primarily conventional use.

Yeltsin responded the next day with a proposal of his own, in which he suggested that the two sides cut their strategic nuclear warheads to 2,000–2,500 each.

Ministerial meetings between Secretary of State James Baker and his Russian counterpart, Foreign Minister Andrei Kozyrev, were held to discuss these proposals in

February, March, May, and June 1992. These negotiations paved the way for Presidents Bush and Yeltsin to hold a summit meeting on June 16–18, 1992, in Washington, D.C. At the summit, the two presidents developed the framework for a follow-on Strategic Arms Reduction Treaty (START II), symbolized by their Joint Understanding on Further Reductions in Strategic Offensive Arms. This agreement included numerical ceilings and a time frame for reductions. The Joint Understanding called for elimination of all MIRVed ICBMs, a limit of 1,750 on SLBM warheads, counting rules whereby bombers count as "the number of warheads they are actually equipped to carry," and reductions by both sides to between 3,000 and 3,500 warheads by 2003.

Telephone calls exchanged between Bush and Yeltsin on December 20 and 21, 1992, produced more progress on an agreement, and a team of U.S. and Russian specialists met in Geneva on December 22–24 to work on specific points of disagreement. At high-level meetings in Geneva on December 28 and 29 between the U.S. secretary of state and Russian foreign and defense ministers, the last issues were finally resolved. When Bush and Yeltsin signed the START II agreement on January 3, 1993, they concluded the most sweeping nuclear arms reduction agreement in history and the first post–Cold War arms control treaty between the United States and Russia.

On January 26, 1996, the U.S. Senate approved a resolution of ratification of START II by a vote of 87–4. Russian ratification of the treaty, however, was a long-drawn affair. U.S. secretary of defense William Perry visited Moscow to address the Duma on October 17, 1996, in an attempt to persuade Russian legislators to ratify START II. But his words apparently had little impact on the Russian lower house. On April 9, 1997, the Russian Duma voted to postpone debate over ratification of the treaty.

Although the treaty remained unratified, both U.S. and Russian officials continued to update its provisions to better meet changing circumstances. In the Helsinki Summit held on March 21, 1997, for instance, President Bill Clinton and President Yeltsin issued a Joint Statement on Parameters on Future Reductions in Nuclear Forces in which, regarding START II, they agreed to extend the elimination deadline for strategic nuclear delivery vehicles from January 1, 2003, to December 31, 2007, and to immediately deactivate all strategic nuclear delivery vehicles scheduled for elimination by December 31, 2003. On September 27, 1997, the extension of these time frames was incorporated into a protocol, which was signed by representatives from both countries.

Political disputes related to the various global events further delayed Russian ratification of the treaty. The Duma postponed its planned ratification vote of START II in December 1998 to signal displeasure with U.S. and British air strikes against Iraq. Air strikes again emerged as a stumbling block to Russian START II ratification when the start of the North Atlantic Treaty Organization's campaign against Yugoslavia forced Russian prime minister Yevgeny Primakov, on March 26, 1999, to ask the Duma to postpone consideration of the treaty yet again.

On April 14, 2000, the Duma finally ratified START II (but with crucial reservations) by a vote of 288–131. Under Article II of the Duma's ratifying legislation, deputies approved motions that allowed Russia to abandon its arms control agreements if the United States violated the ABM Treaty by deploying national missile defenses. The

Duma vote also required the U.S. Senate to approve several additional documents as part of the START II package before instruments of ratification could be exchanged and the treaty could enter into force. These documents included two controversial additional protocols on the issue of the demarcation of theater missile defense and national missile defense interceptors. The Russian upper house of Parliament supported the Duma's resolution 122–15. Russian president Vladimir Putin signed this legislation on May 4, 2000, to ratify the treaty.

As a response to the U.S. withdrawal from the ABM Treaty on June 13, 2002, Russia declared the next day that it would no longer be bound by the START II nuclear arms reduction agreement. Following the collapse of START II, the George W. Bush administration quickly "moved beyond" the agreement with the signing of the Moscow Treaty of May 24, 2002. The Moscow Treaty committed each country to limiting its deployed strategic nuclear forces to fewer than 2,200 warheads by the end of 2012.

Kalpana Chittaranjan

Further Reading

"Strategic Arms Reduction Treaty II (START II)," Arms Control Association. https://www.armscontrol.org/treaties/strategic-arms-reduction-treaty-ii. Accessed July 15, 2003.

Strategic Offensive Reductions Treaty

The Strategic Offensive Reductions Treaty (SORT) between the United States and Russia, also known as the Moscow Treaty, was signed in Moscow on May 24, 2002. It is only two pages in length, the shortest bilateral arms control treaty ever signed. Presidents George W. Bush and Vladimir Putin agreed on the principal elements of the treaty at the Crawford, Texas, summit in November 2001. The treaty committed both parties to continued reductions in their strategic nuclear arsenals, with a target of 1,700–2,200 deployed strategic warheads by 2012. There were no provisions for verification, inspections, or compliance, nor does the treaty require the parties to destroy the warheads they remove from deployed status. This treaty essentially took the place of a third Strategic Arms Reduction Treaty (START III).

Jeffrey A. Larsen

Further Reading

"Treaty between the United States of America and the Russian Federation on Strategic Offensive Reductions," Treaty Text. https://www.fas.org/nuke/control/sort.htm. Accessed January 15, 2018.

Syria

Prior to 2013, Syria possessed an active chemical warfare (CW) program and perhaps a limited biological warfare (BW) program. Although having pledged to give up its chemical stockpiles—some 1,300 tons of CW agent and precursor chemicals have been destroyed under international auspices—Syria continued to use both sarin and chlorine gas against rebel-held civilian targets as recently as 2018. And, at least until Israel destroyed its Al Kibar nuclear facility in early September 2007, Syria had also been working toward nuclear weapons development.

Going back to the 1970s, the Syrian Scientific Research Center—*Centre D'Etudes et de Recherches Scientifiques* (CERS), located in Damascus—has been the locus for

WMD-related research, including chemical, biological, nuclear, and missile technologies. Syria has had an uncertain number—numbering at least in the hundreds—of tactical ballistic missiles, with 100 km to 600 km maximum ranges, and since 2011, it has launched dozens of these against rebel targets in the civil war. According to some reports, Syria only has 10 percent remaining in its ballistic missile inventory. Thus far, none have been reported to have been fitted with CW agents.

Syria's initial interest in chemical and biological weapons probably dates back to the 1970s. There had been persistent rumors that the thousands killed in Hama at the hands of the Syrian military in February 1982 was due to the use of chemical weapons, possibly hydrogen cyanide. However, it appears more likely the thousands (as many as 20,000, or even more) were killed by conventional weapons, such as artillery, used during the near monthlong siege. Since the demise of the Soviet Union (1991), Damascus has placed even greater emphasis on the development and acquisition of unconventional weapons to make up for the loss of Soviet military support.

Now going into its seventh year of a devastating civil war that began in 2011, estimates vary as to the numbers killed in the ongoing Syrian conflict. While hard numbers are difficult to come by, as of 2016, estimates were that nearly 500,000 Syrians had been killed, with another 5 million refugees. Given a starting population of 21.5 million people (2010), if true, these horrific statistics reveal nothing less than a demographic catastrophe. And if we estimate some 5,000 people died (thus far) in Syria from chemical weapons attacks—mostly by the Assad regime but also some attributed to the Islamic State of Iraq and Syria (ISIS)—these represent 1 percent of the overall mortality rate due to the use of chemicals. This small percentage, horrific as it is, is in keeping with the overall low mortality rate (3%) due to gas warfare in World War I.

Chemical Weapons

During the 1990s, it was suspected that Russian general Anatoly Kuntsevich, himself a CW expert, had been actively assisting Syria with its chemical weapons, specifically the synthesis and manufacture of VX nerve agent. (General Kuntsevich died en route to Syria on April 3, 2002.)

The U.S. Central Intelligence Agency assessed that in 2003 Syria continued to seek CW-related expertise from foreign sources. Syria's motivation to acquire chemical warfare agents and ballistic missiles appears to be a response to Israel's superior conventional military capabilities. In January 2004, Syrian president Bashar Assad came close to tacitly admitting to a WMD program during an interview with *The Telegraph*. On the heels of Libyan dictator Muammar Gaddafi having given up his WMD program in late 2003, Assad was defiant, essentially saying that Syria maintained the right to have chemical and biological weapons so long as Israel maintained its nuclear arsenal. Although Assad backtracked somewhat on his comments less than two weeks later (when he realized it was politically inexpedient), it was clear that Syria likely had some WMD program underway.

On July 23, 2012, Assad's Foreign Ministry made the following announcement: "Any stocks of W.M.D. or any unconventional weapon[s] that the Syrian Arab Republic possess would never be used against civilians or against the Syrian people during this crisis." He further said that "all the stocks of these weapons that the Syrian Arab Republic possess are monitored and guarded by the

Syrian Army. These weapons are meant to be used only and strictly in the event of external aggression against the Syrian Arab Republic" (*New York Times* 2012).

In the midst of the violent civil war underway in Syria, the U.S. government made proclamations in response, particularly with regard to the prospect of chemical weapons being used by the Assad regime. On August 20, 2012, President Barack Obama made a now famous statement that the Syrian use of chemical weapons would constitute a serious provocation that would be the basis for a significant response by the U.S. military: "We have been very clear to the Assad regime, but also to other players on the ground, that a red line for us is we start seeing a whole bunch of chemical weapons moving around or being utilized. That would change my calculus. That would change my equation" (The White House 2012).

Four months later, seven people in Homs died from exposure to what may have been a psychoincapacitant. According to the U.S. State Department, the Syrians may have used a version of BZ (3-Quinuclidinyl benzilate), which was known as Agent 15 by the Iraqis. Syria continued to use other unidentified chemical agents, leading to at least dozens of deaths. On March 20, 2013, in response to questions at a press conference with Israeli prime minister Benjamin Netanyahu, President Obama reiterated his concern regarding Syria's use of chemical weapons, saying, "Once we establish the facts, I have made clear that the use of chemical weapons is a game changer." By mid-June 2013, the U.S. government had "high confidence" that, indeed, Syria had been using chemical weapons against rebel forces, including those in civilian areas.

Ghouta Chemical Attacks

Reports on August 21, 2013, indicated that Syrian military forces used sarin-filled battlefield rockets (140 mm and 330 mm) in an attack against 12 areas in and around the Ghouta area, focusing on both contested areas and neighborhoods held by opposition forces, killing at least 1,400 people. On August 30, the White House issued the following statement:

> The United States Government assesses with high confidence that the Syrian government carried out a chemical weapons attack in the Damascus suburbs on August 21, 2013. We further assess that the regime used a nerve agent in the attack. These all-source assessments are based on human, signals, and geospatial intelligence as well as a significant body of open source reporting. (The White House, August 30, 2013)

Following the August sarin attack, a number of countries including the United States and France discussed military options to at least constrain Assad's chemical warfare. While previously having been reluctant to take such initiatives, French president François Hollande was adamant that force would be needed, having stated in late August that "the chemical massacre of Damascus cannot and must not remain unpunished."

Facing a potential military strike by U.S. and Western European forces, Russia intervened by brokering Syrian capitulation to accede to the Chemical Weapons Convention (CWC). This led to the Framework for Elimination of Syrian Chemical Weapons on September 14, 2013.

The characterization of Syria's chemical weapons arsenal was reportedly provided by French intelligence in September 2013. It was said to include sulfur mustard (several hundreds of tons), VX nerve agent (several tens of tons), and sarin nerve agent, the major percentage of the total stockpile (several hundreds of tons). The precursors included DF, the significant component for manufacturing nerve agents (e.g., sarin or soman) isopropyl alcohol (used in sarin manufacture); and hydrogen fluoride. By June 23, 2014, Syrian had declared chemical warfare agents and precursors totaling about 1,300 tons. This declared inventory was then removed for disposal, and Syrian chemical weapons facilities shut down. As of August 2014, the OPCW reported that all of Syria's Category 1 chemicals (i.e., CW agents) had been completely destroyed. The first of 12 declared chemical weapons sites, an underground facility, was destroyed under the supervision of the Organization for the Prohibition of Chemical Weapons (OPCW) on January 31, 2015, with three remaining to be eliminated as of spring 2017.

Despite the apparent success of the demilitarization of Syrian chemical weapons—the OPCW was awarded the Nobel Peace Prize for its efforts in October 2013—continued Syrian use of chlorine gas against rebel-controlled areas led to numerous civilian deaths. Throughout the beginning of 2017, Syrian forces continued to employ chlorine in barrel bombs against rebel-held regions, including major cities (Damascus and Aleppo, among others), causing at least hundreds of deaths.

Idlib Province, Khan Sheikhoun Sarin Gas Attack

Again, and despite the reported success in the elimination of Syria's declared chemical weapons stockpile, on April 4, 2017, Syrian air forces carried out a chemical weapons assault against the town of Khan Sheikhoun, located in the northern Idlib province, killing at least 70 civilians. Victims—many of them children—displayed classic nerve agent intoxication, including salivary exudate from the mouth and involuntary defecation. Two days later, having determined that Syria had indeed used sarin nerve agent in this attack, President Trump ordered an air strike using 59 Tomahawk cruise missiles against Al Shayrat airfield, the facility that based the Syrian aircraft that had carried out the Idlib chemical weapons attack. As of mid-2017, reporting indicates Syria still maintains at least a few tons of chemical agents.

In April 2018, Syria conducted a chemical attack on a neighborhood in Ghouta, killing dozens of people. This led to another round of missile strikes by combined U.S. and French military forces against known Syrian chemical weapons facilities.

Biological Weapons

In 2014, James Clapper, the director of national intelligence (DNI), submitted an unclassified assessment of Syrian biological weapons capability:

We judge that some elements of Syria's biological warfare (BW) program might have advanced beyond the research and development stage and might be capable of limited agent production, based on the duration of its longstanding program. To the best of our knowledge, Syria has not successfully weaponized biological agents in an effective delivery system, but it possesses conventional weapon systems that could be modified for biological-agent delivery. (U.S. DNI 2014)

Syria signed the Biological and Toxin Weapons Convention in April 1972, but since that time, it has refused to ratify the treaty and has given no indication that it might do so in the near future.

Peter R. Lavoy and Eric A. Croddy

Further Reading

Central Intelligence Agency (CIA), "Unclassified Report to Congress on the Acquisition of Technology Relating to Weapons of Mass Destruction and Advanced Conventional Munitions, January 1 through June 30, 2003," 2003. https://fas.org/irp/threat/cia_jan_jun2003.htm. Accessed May 1, 2018.

Eshel, David, "Syria's Chemical Weapons Proliferation Hydra," *Military Technology* 31, no. 11 (November 2007): 7.

Organization for the Prohibition of Chemical Weapons (OPCW), "First of 12 Chemical Weapon Production Facilities in Syria Destroyed," February 3, 2015. https://www.opcw.org/news/article/first-of-12-chemical-weapon-production-facilities-in-syria-destroyed.Accessed May 1, 2018.

U.S. Director of National Intelligence (DNI), James R. Clapper, "Statement for the Record: Worldwide Threat Assessment of the US Intelligence Community," Senate Select Committee on Intelligence, January 29, 2014. https://www.dni.gov/index.php/newsroom/testimonies/203-congressional-testimonies-2014/1005-statement-for-the-record-worldwide-threat-assessment-of-the-us-intelligence-community. Accessed May 1, 2018.

T

Tactical Nuclear Weapons

Nonstrategic nuclear weapons have gone by various names. Primarily stationed in Europe, the Far East, and at sea, they have been known at different times as battlefield nuclear weapons, nonstrategic nuclear weapons (NSNW), theater nuclear weapons, theater nuclear forces (TNF), intermediate-range nuclear forces (INF), short-range nuclear forces (SNF), long-range theater nuclear forces (LRTNF), substrategic nuclear weapons, and tactical nuclear weapons (TNW). Tactical nuclear weapons were a central military and political concern during the Cold War.

It is difficult to define exactly what constitutes a nonstrategic nuclear weapon. Traditional attempts at delineating between types of nuclear weapons—range, delivery vehicle, explosive power, and the like—are overly simplistic and outmoded approaches that miss many of the nuances that surround the deployment and use of these weapons. Some definitions of tactical weapons list them as low-yield, short-range weapons for use on the battlefield rather than against countervalue targets such as cities. The best way to define them may be "by exclusion." That is, anything not captured by strategic arms control negotiations is, by default, nonstrategic. Another perspective holds that *any* nuclear weapon must be strategic, given its potential for physical devastation and political chaos. A third view suggests that only one's adversary can define whether a weapon is strategic or nonstrategic, based on its perceived use.

The key purpose of TNW, from a U.S. perspective, is to deter coercion and aggression against the United States and its allies. To do this, the United States built a massive arsenal during the Cold War, eventually numbering more than 20,000 tactical nuclear weapons in addition to some 15,000 strategic warheads. The Soviet Union had even more nonstrategic nuclear weapons in its arsenal.

The second cornerstone of U.S. TNW policy was to provide a nuclear presence in Europe to support the North Atlantic Treaty Organization (NATO) as the essential link between the European and North American allies. These weapons were part of NATO's "triad" of conventional forces, tactical nuclear weapons in theater, and U.S. and British strategic nuclear systems. NATO's strategic concept still calls for the continued presence of such weapons in Europe to maintain the transatlantic deterrent link to the United States and for purposes of creating political and military uncertainty in the mind of any potential opponent.

Their third purpose became evident in the 1990s: to deter the use of weapons of mass destruction (WMD) more broadly. During the First Gulf War, and again in the first years of the 21st century, the U.S. government made it clear that any WMD use by an adversary would result in a "prompt, devastating retaliatory blow" in which no weapons would be ruled out. It was widely understood by both sides in the First Gulf War that this meant nuclear weapons, although some U.S. officials denied they meant to threaten Iraq with nuclear retaliation.

Historically, nuclear arms control has focused on long-range strategic systems, but the Soviet Union always tried to include U.S. TNW in arms control talks. From the Soviet perspective, nuclear weapons stationed in Europe and aimed at Russian soil should not be considered "nonstrategic." The United States, by contrast, consistently rejected that position, and tactical nuclear forces were largely left off the negotiating table until the 1987 Intermediate-Range Nuclear Forces (INF) Treaty.

The United States has substantially reduced its reliance on these weapons since 1991, although that may change under a Trump administration. Russia is adjusting its national security doctrine to place even greater emphasis on nuclear weapons—including smaller "tactical" warheads. With thousands of these warheads and several delivery systems for them, Russia has a large asymmetrical advantage in numbers of TNW and has been unwilling to implement the 1991 Presidential Nuclear Initiatives (which eliminated most U.S. tactical nuclear weapons) or to discuss TNW in a separate formal arms control forum. Yet, the 1997 Helsinki Agreement indicated that Russia was willing to talk about TNW to the degree that it benefits them or is linked to broader strategic issues. Russia's huge arsenal of tactical nuclear weapons is particularly unsettling given worries about Russia's future and the possibility of the loss or sale of these weapons.

Presidential George H. W. Bush's nuclear initiatives in the fall of 1991 called for the withdrawal and eventual elimination of most U.S. TNW around the globe, including the cancellation of all related research and development programs. The Clinton administration furthered this decision by eliminating naval nuclear capabilities on surface ships entirely. In its 2010 Nuclear Posture Review (NPR), the Obama administration retired the nuclear Tomahawk Land-Attack Missiles (TLAM-Ns) delivered by submarine. America's remaining nonstrategic capabilities are now limited to gravity bombs delivered by tactical aircraft. Precise numbers of warheads are classified, but the total U.S. force of bombs has been drastically reduced since the Cold War. A significant proportion of these remaining weapons are still based in Europe, and several European states maintain nuclear delivery plans in their NATO war orders that would depend on U.S. warheads.

Key issues for the existing nonstrategic nuclear weapons force posture include deciding whether the United States should keep its current levels of TNW, reduce the numbers further, or reinstate certain types of weapons, such as TLAM-N; determining the purposes for these remaining weapons; and deciding where to station them. The perceived battlefield use and utility of these weapons has dropped significantly since the end of the Cold War. Nevertheless, the U.S. government maintains the policy that it must be able to deliver on its threat to use nuclear weapons in dire circumstances. And there exist some military operations that can only be accomplished using the particular effects that nuclear weapons provide. For those reasons, the U.S. military maintains a small arsenal of tactical nuclear weapons and the plans for their use. The 2001 Nuclear Posture Review, in fact, called for continued research and development efforts on smaller, more usable nuclear weapons, a perspective that was echoed in the 2018 NPR.

One of the biggest challenges to planners in today's increasingly complicated world is determining whether nuclear weapons are appropriate in response to enemy chemical or biological weapons use. The maintenance of a nuclear force projection capability also requires the platforms, support infrastructure, and trained and certified crews to be available or maintained at an appropriate level of readiness.

Jeffrey A. Larsen

Further Reading

Alexander, Brian, and Alistair Millar, eds., *Tactical Nuclear Weapons: Emergent Threats in an Evolving Security Environment* (Dulles, VA: Brassey's, 2003).

Foradori, Paolo, ed., *Tactical Nuclear Weapons and Euro-Atlantic Security: The Future of NATO* (London: Routledge, 2013).

Larsen, Jeffrey A., and Kurt J. Klingenberger, eds., *Non-Strategic Nuclear Weapons: Obstacles and Opportunities* (Colorado Springs: USAF Institute for National Security Studies, 2001).

Triad

Coined in the early 1960s, the term *triad* referred to the maintenance of three types of nuclear delivery systems in the United States: intercontinental ballistic missiles (ICBMs), submarine-launched ballistic missiles (SLBMs), and long-range bombers. Each leg of the triad was supposed to be capable of surviving a Soviet first strike and inflicting a retaliatory strike called for by U.S. nuclear war plans.

During the 1950s, American strategic doctrine assumed that U.S. nuclear threats were highly credible. Several academic strategists, such as Albert Wohlstetter at the RAND Corporation, however, believed that the so-called balance of terror was fragile because it rested not on a U.S. first strike but on the ability to launch a second strike after absorbing a Soviet nuclear attack. Concerns were raised about a potential "nuclear Pearl Harbor"—a disarming surprise first strike by Soviet forces that would destroy the United States but leave Russia intact. Wohlstetter and his contemporaries began suggesting that it was not the overall size of the U.S. nuclear arsenal that was important but the forces that would survive a Soviet first strike.

To achieve this secure second-strike capability, and to ensure that it would be available under all circumstances, planners and analysts quickly recognized the benefits provided by a nuclear triad. Each leg of the triad would be able to inflict "assured destruction" of the Soviet Union in a second strike, which was defined by Secretary of Defense Robert McNamara as a strike that killed 30 percent of the Soviet population and destroyed 70 percent of its industry. Deploying the U.S. nuclear arsenal would complicate Soviet attack options and prevent the loss of the entire deterrent force due to a Soviet defensive breakthrough, a security compromise, or a catastrophic failure across an entire type of weapons system. The assured destruction criteria articulated by McNamara also allowed him to cap the size of the U.S. strategic triad; meeting second-strike assured destruction criteria helped to answer "how much is enough" to deter Soviet aggression.

Only the United States and Russia continue to maintain a traditional triad of nuclear delivery systems. The triad concept was redefined in the 2002 Nuclear Posture Review (NPR), and elements of this new concept were retained in the 2010 Nuclear Posture Review. The "new triad" consists of offensive nuclear forces (which encompasses the "old" triad), long-range conventional precision-strike systems, and missile defenses, all supported by a defense infrastructure capable of ensuring a nuclear arsenal for the indefinite future.

Andrew M. Dorman and James J. Wirtz

Further Reading

U.S. Department of Defense, "Excerpts of Classified Nuclear Posture Review/S," 2001. http://www.imi-online.de/download/Nuclear_Posture_Review.pdf. Accessed January 7, 2018.

U.S. Department of Defense, "Nuclear Posture Review Report," 2010. https://www.defense.gov/Portals/1/features/defenseReviews/NPR/2010_Nuclear_Posture_Review_Report.pdf. Accessed January 7, 2018.

Tritium

Tritium is an unstable isotope of the element hydrogen that has one proton and two neutrons. On a geologic time scale, tritium has a short half-life and therefore is not found in nature. It has nuclear properties that are very useful in the nuclear industry and in facilitating fusion reactions, and its phosphorescent qualities make it a useful material as a radioactive tracer and in night and compass sights. In a nuclear detonation, tritium plays a part in both the primary and secondary stages of the weapon. Its name comes from the Greek word *tritos* (third).

In 1934, E. Rutherford, M. L. E. Oliphant, and P. Harteck bombarded deuterons with neutrons and produced the new isotope. Tritium is unstable and undergoes beta decay. It has a half-life of 12.32 years. Tritium is primarily used in fusion reactions with deuterium. Deuterium and tritium collisions have the highest probability of undergoing fusion in most conventional fusion systems. In a nuclear weapon's primary stage, a small quantity of deuterium and tritium gas is used to boost the yield through fusion reactions. Tritium is a product of fission reactions and is produced in an exothermic reaction from lithium by neutron bombardment. These are the primary production reactions that take place in the second stage of a thermonuclear weapon.

Tritium was produced for U.S. military uses at the Savannah River Plant in South Carolina. That facility is now closed. Nevertheless, tritium will remain important for civilian nuclear fusion systems and for commercial phosphorescence applications. In addition, because of its short half-life, tritium will continue to be needed by the United States to ensure that the primary stage of its nuclear weapons perform as expected. Along with deuterium, it will serve as the primary fuel for most magnetic and inertial confinement fusion systems.

C. Ross Schmidtlein

Further Reading

Parrington, Josef R., Harold D. Knox, Susan L. Breneman, Edward M. Baum, and Frank Feiner, *Nuclides and Isotopes: Chart of the Nuclides*, 15th ed. (New York: General Electric and KAPL, 1996).

Tularemia

Tularemia is an infectious disease of small mammals caused by the bacterium *Francisella tularensis*. Humans usually acquire *F. tularensis* from the bite of an infected insect or from contact with infected wild animals. Less often, tularemia can result from inhalation or ingestion of contaminated dusts, food, or water.

The onset of tularemia in humans is usually three to five days following exposure, and the disease usually begins with fever and flulike symptoms, including headache, chills, fever, and cough. Multiple tularemia syndromes can occur, including pneumonia and "typhoidal" tularemia (an infection throughout the body), which can be fatal. About 75 percent of all tularemia cases present with skin lesions and swollen lymph nodes (ulceroglandular), and 4 percent of these patients die without treatment. The remaining 25 percent, typhoidal, has a mortality rate of about 35 percent without treatment. With the use of antibiotics, the disease (encompassing both syndromes) has a death rate of 1–2.5 percent. As of 2017, no licensed vaccine is available for tularemia.

Francisella tularensis is dangerous because it can be released as an aerosol to cause large tularemia epidemics in both human and animal populations. In particular, *F. tularensis* is extremely infectious in humans, requiring inhalation of only 10–50 organisms to cause severe, incapacitating, and sometimes fatal results. A World Health Organization (WHO) committee estimated in 1970 that if 50 kilograms (110 pounds) of a virulent strain of the bacterium were sprayed over a metropolitan area with a population of 5 million, it could incapacitate 250,000 people and kill 19,000. Respiratory failure or shock would cause most of the fatalities.

Historical Background

Research on the military use of *F. tularensis* to spread disease began in the 1930s in Japan and Russia. During World War II, the U.S. War Research Service noted the extremely high infectivity of this organism and developed the highly virulent Schu-4 strain for weaponization (U.S. code: UL). The Soviet Union acquired the Schu-4 strain in the 1950s (apparently obtained from the United States) for its own biological weapons program. Its high infectivity via inhalation made *F. tularensis* one of the more potent germ warfare agents. In the U.S. biological warfare (BW) program, tularemia bacteria were freeze-dried and milled to a fine consistency to deliver as an aerosol.

Biological weapon stockpiles, including tularemia bacteria, were destroyed by the United States upon signing the Biological and Toxin Weapons Convention of 1972. The Soviet Union, however, continued its biological weapons development well after signing the accord and further increased its range of biological warfare agents. As of 2018, it is unknown whether Russia still maintains an offensive BW program.

Background

Tularemia was first described in Japan in 1837 and in Russia in 1926. The organism, renamed *Francisella tularensis* in 1974, was originally isolated in 1911 from ground squirrels with a plague-like illness in Tulare County, California. It was not until 1921 that Dr. Edward Francis of the U.S. Public Health Service established that the bacterium was the cause of deerfly fever. Tularemia is also colloquially known in different parts of the world as rancher's fever, hare plague, lemming fever, and rabbit fever in Japan.

The potential for tularemia epidemics became known in the 1930s when large waterborne outbreaks occurred in Europe. Outbreaks of tularemia in wild animals are often harbingers of outbreaks in humans. In Sweden and the former Soviet Union, human outbreaks of tularemia have been linked to ground vole (small rodent) die-offs. Tularemia is predominantly a rural disease, and large outbreaks occurring in war zones are associated with the breakdown of public health and with surging rat populations that carry the disease.

During World War II, a tularemia epidemic affected many thousands of German and Russian soldiers on the European Eastern Front at the Battle of Stalingrad (1942–1943). The former Soviet biological weapon scientist Ken Alibek has raised the possibility that this epidemic may have resulted from intentional dissemination of *F. tularensis* by the Russians against

German troops. A more mundane explanation is likely, however: Tularemia was already widespread in the local populace of the Volga region well before German armies arrived. The intense fighting prevented the harvesting of crops, and public health services were largely nonexistent. As vermin consumed this uncut grain, the rodent population subsequently exploded, widening the locus of disease. Together, these circumstances cleared the way for an epidemic. Many infections among Russian and German troops occurred from inhaled dust from straw used for bedding.

Sharing some of the same circumstances as Stalingrad, an outbreak of the disease was reported in Kosovo during 1999–2000, totaling over 300 cases. This outbreak was linked to an increase in the population of infected rats as a result of the breakdown of garbage collection after the war of separation from Yugoslavia.

The mortality rate for severe untreated infections (including all cases of untreated tularemia pneumonia and typhoidal tularemia) is about 35 percent. In the United States, recent mortality rates have been 1–2.5 percent with treatment. Poor outcomes are often associated with long delays in diagnosis and treatment. Early antibiotic therapy is effective, and if started within 24 hours of exposure, it may even prevent disease.

Vaccines to prevent tularemia were developed and used in humans in the Soviet Union in the 1940s and 1950s. A live, attenuated vaccine using a *F. tularensis* type B strain called Live Vaccine Strain (LVS) is currently available as an Investigational New Drug from the U.S. Army Medical Research Institute of Infectious Diseases (USAMRIID). Although still not approved by the U.S. Food and Drug Administration (as of 2017), the LVS was demonstrated to protect human volunteers against an aerosol attack with virulent *F. tularensis.*

Amy E. Krafft and Eric E. Croddy

Further Reading

Croddy, Eric, and Sarka Krcalova, "Tularemia, Biological Warfare (BW), and the Battle for Stalingrad (1942–1943)," *Military Medicine* 166, no. 10 (October 2001): 837–838.

Oyston, C. F., Anders Sjostedt, and Richard W. Titball, "Tularemia: Bioterrorism Defence Renews Interest in *Francisella tularensis*," *Nature Reviews Microbiology* 2, no. 12 (December 2004): 967–978.

Sjöstedt, Anders, "Tularemia: History, Epidemiology, Pathogen Physiology, and Clinical Manifestations," *Annals of the New York Academy of Sciences* 1105 (2007): 1–29.

U

United Kingdom

The United Kingdom's chemical, biological, and nuclear warfare programs developed in response to the perceived threat posed by other nations' efforts to develop weapons of mass destruction. The development of British chemical weapons, for example, followed German attacks in 1915. The biological program started shortly after the beginning of World War II in response to concerns about possible Nazi interest in germ warfare. Similarly, in response to concerns that the Nazis might acquire a nuclear weapon, Britain collaborated with the United States in the research and development of atomic weapons during World War II as part of the Manhattan Project.

Chemical Warfare

During World War I, chemical agents—sulfur mustard, chlorine, phosgene, and chloropicrin—were developed and manufactured at a new facility at Porton Down, and substantial progress was being made in protection against chemical attack through the development of gas masks. In addition to the battlefields of the Western Front, German cities were also considered as targets for chemical attacks. Nevertheless, the British limited their use of chemical weapons to the Western Front. British military forces suffered about 185,000 casualties from gas attacks during World War I.

During the interwar period, British opposition to the use of chemical and biological weapons grew. Successive British governments supported the idea of banning chemical weapons, and Great Britain signed the 1925 Geneva Protocol upon its conception, ratifying it in 1930. Britain, however, refused to abandon its chemical warfare capabilities; it accepted in principle the no-first-use concept while insisting on maintaining an in-kind deterrent. In the years preceding World War II, extensive preparations were made for civil defense based on the assumption that Germany, Italy, and Japan were likely to use chemical weapons, and these threatened not only Britain's civilian population but its colonial subjects as well (e.g., India).

In World War II, research at Porton Down was expanded, and production was increased to ensure that sufficient chemical deterrent stocks were available in all theaters of war. In addition to experiments with the new insecticide DDT, the British discovered the toxic organophosphate nerve compound diisopropyl fluorophosphate (DFP), and, although less deadly than tabun or sarin, it significantly enhanced the effect of mustard gas when the two were mixed together. The new compound produced a dual effect from both blister and nerve agents in terms of causing casualties, and the mixture could remain a liquid under colder temperatures than mustard agent alone. Although the U.S. and European armies used no chemical weapons during World War II, Axis and the Allied production of chemical weapons was considerable. The British were prepared to use mustard and other chemicals against German cities by 1944, especially in retaliation if German V1 and V2 ("Vengeance") cruise missiles and ballistic rockets were used to deliver chemical agents against London.

During the Cold War, the British cooperated with the United States and Canada by pooling their knowledge of the German nerve gases tabun, sarin, and soman and conducting tests with these agents. With funds short, however, the British government placed greater emphasis on its nuclear and biowarfare programs and less on its chemical program. Having decided in 1956 to renounce the offensive use of chemical weapons under any circumstances, the United Kingdom never went into full-scale production of the new nerve agents. Since that time, British chemical warfare research has focused on developing defensive equipment. The United Kingdom has become a world leader in protective gear, including the use of ion mobility spectroscopy—the use of measuring ionized particles to determine the identity of a substance—in handheld chemical agent detection systems. The United Kingdom also signed the 1993 Chemical Weapons Convention (CWC) as part of general efforts to eliminate chemical arsenals worldwide.

More recently, and over a 10-year period, Great Britain's Porton Down specialists painstakingly uncovered and destroyed some 4,000 of its legacy chemical weapons dating back to both world wars. Many of these were found rusting but still holding dangerous CW agents; all were finally destroyed in 2007.

Biological Warfare

In Britain, fears about biological warfare first became public in 1934 in the Wickham Steed Affair, when claims were made that German spies had tested biowarfare agents on the London Underground and Paris Metro. Within a year of the outbreak of World War II, a new biology department was set up at the chemical warfare establishment of Porton Down to develop a bioweapon that could be used to retaliate against a German biological weapons attack. The department focused its efforts on anthrax bacterial spores and botulinum toxin (derived from *Clostridium botulinum* bacteria).

Two weapons were developed. The first consisted of 5 million linseed cattle feed cakes filled with a slurry of anthrax spores and stockpiled as an antilivestock weapon ("Operation Vegetarian"). These cakes were to have been dropped over livestock grazing areas in Germany by aircraft, but the operation was never carried out. The second weapon was a prototype antipersonnel anthrax bomb that was tested on Gruinard Island, off the coast of Scotland. After 50 years of isolation due to safety concerns about the possibility of lingering anthrax spores, this island has now been decontaminated and returned to its previous owner.

With the end of World War II, the government gave the biowarfare program equal priority with the atomic program, and a series of tests were undertaken with the pathogens responsible for diseases such as brucellosis, tularemia, and plague. British interest in biowarfare receded with Britain's first atomic test in 1952. In 1972, the United Kingdom signed the Biological and Toxin Weapons Convention, ending research into offensive biological warfare. A pool of British scientists, however, remains engaged in developing protective equipment and treatments for defense against biological attack.

Nuclear Program

When the United States passed the McMahon Atomic Energy Act (1946) forbidding the transfer of nuclear weapons technology to other nations, Britain boosted its efforts at the Atomic Weapons

Establishment (Aldermaston, Berkshire) for an independent nuclear weapons program. It made the decision in 1947 to build and test an atomic weapon. Through agreement reached with Australia, Britain successfully tested its first 25-kiloton nuclear device aboard a ship moored off the northwest coast of Australia, near the Monte Bello Islands, on October 3, 1952. This was followed by Britain's first hydrogen bomb test in 1957 in the Pacific Ocean. Renewed collaboration with the United States led to the transfer of nuclear propulsion technology for submarines. Subsequent joint U.S.-U.K. nuclear warhead tests continued between 1962 and 1991.

The British independent nuclear deterrent initially consisted of free-fall gravity bombs delivered by the V-force bombers (Valiant, Victor, Vulcan). The introduction of the Tornado aircraft into Royal Air Force (RAF) service in 1978 continued this doctrine, with eight operational squadrons of multirole, dual-capable Tornado GR.1/1A aircraft, until the withdrawal of the last remaining WE177 bombs from operational service in March 1998. This terminated the Tornados' nuclear role, bringing to an end a four-decade history of RAF aircraft carrying nuclear weapons. By the end of August 1998, all remaining WE177 bombs had been dismantled.

Today, Britain's nuclear deterrent consists of four Vanguard Class Submarines. Following the 2010 Strategic Defense Review, these submarines will each carry 8 missiles and 40 nuclear weapons, giving Britain an operational nuclear force of about 120 weapons. An operational goal is to keep one of these submarines on patrol at all times. In July 2016, Parliament endorsed construction of Dreadnought-class ballistic missile submarines, which are scheduled to enter service in the 2030s to extend Britain's nuclear deterrent well beyond midcentury. Britain's deployed nuclear weapons are detargeted and require hours to be brought up to full operational status.

Andrew M. Dorman and James J. Wirtz

Further Reading

Balmer, Brian, *Britain and Biological Warfare: Expert Advice and Science Policy, 1930–65* (Basingstoke: Palgrave Macmillan, 2001).

Carter, G. B., *Chemical and Biological Defence at Porton Down, 1916–2000* (London: Stationery Office, 2000).

HM Government, United Kingdom, *National Security Strategy and Strategic Defence and Policy Review 2015: A Secure and Prosperous United Kingdom* (London: Her Majesty's Stationery Office, November 2015).

Norris, Robert S., and Hans Kristensen, "The British Nuclear Stockpile, 1953–2013," *Bulletin of the Atomic Scientists* 69, no. 4 (2013): 69–75.

Sampson, Ben, "Bombs Away!" *Professional Engineering* 20, no. 8 (April 25, 2007): 27–28.

Uranium

Uranium is the heaviest naturally occurring chemical element. It is a dense, heavy metal that contains 92 protons and, in its natural state, is weakly radioactive. Refined uranium is a silvery-white metal that is toxic if inhaled or ingested in other than very small quantities.

Uranium is found throughout the world in minute quantities in most plants, animals, water, soil, and rock. In nature, it is about as abundant as tin or tungsten. Major sources of recoverable uranium can be found in in Canada, Australia, Kazakhstan, Niger, South Africa, Namibia, Brazil, Russia, the United States, and Uzbekistan. Canada, the world's greatest uranium producer, mines approximately 30 percent of the world's supply, and Australia mines about 20 percent.

Enriched uranium is used as fuel for nuclear reactors and weapons. Depleted uranium, which contains less of the isotope uranium 235 than in nature (generally less than 0.2 percent), serves many military purposes, including use as armor-piercing ammunition, protective shielding, wing components for helicopters, and counterweights in airplanes. Depleted uranium also has industrial uses, including use as reinforcement in building materials such as concrete.

When bombarded with neutrons, uranium produces manmade isotopes such as plutonium, which is another type of fuel used in nuclear reactors and weapons.

History and Background

German chemist Martin Heinrich Klaproth is credited with the discovery of uranium in 1789. Klaproth actually discovered uranium oxide, which he believed to be pure uranium, in the mineral pitchblende. Pitchblende is a naturally occurring mineral that is a mix of uranium oxides. He named the new element after the recently discovered planet Uranus.

In 1841, French chemist Eugene-Melchoir Peligot isolated pure uranium metal. In 1896, French physicist Antoine Henri Becquerel discovered that uranium was radioactive. While Becquerel was investigating the fluorescence of uranium salt, he inadvertently discovered radioactivity. In 1903, he won the Nobel Prize in Physics for his discovery of spontaneous radiation.

Natural uranium was used in the first experimental nuclear reactor, designed and built on December 2, 1942, by Italian physicist Enrico Fermi at Stagg Field Stadium in Chicago. Fermi achieved the first nuclear chain reaction with this reactor. The *pile* consisted of approximately 40 tons of uranium oxide and 6 tons of uranium metal intermingled with 385 tons of pure graphite that moderated, or slowed, neutrons to limit thermal energies produced by the nuclear chain reaction.

Approximately 60 kilograms of highly enriched uranium were used to build "Little Boy," the first nuclear weapon dropped by the United States on Hiroshima, Japan, on August 6, 1945. Construction of the Little Boy weapon exhausted nearly the entire stockpile of highly enriched uranium in the United States at the time.

Uranium is also used to produce the manmade element plutonium. Approximately 200 tons of uranium metal was bombarded with neutrons in the first "breeder" reactor at the B Reactor at Hanford, Washington, to produce plutonium for nuclear weapons. This plutonium was used to fuel the first nuclear device, the "Gadget," tested on July 16, 1945, at the Trinity Site near Alamogordo, New Mexico, as well as for the nuclear weapon "Fat Man" dropped on Nagasaki, Japan, on August 9, 1945.

Technical Details

Natural uranium is composed of approximately 99.27 percent of the isotope uranium-238 and 0.72 percent of uranium-235. The isotope uranium-234 also naturally occurs in very small quantities (approximately 0.0055 percent) as a decay product of uranium-238. Natural uranium has an atomic weight of approximately 238.0508. Uranium is an actinide, chemically similar to actinium, with a density of approximately 19.1 grams per cubic centimeter. Uranium-238 has a half-life of approximately 4.68 billion years, and uranium 235 has a half-life of approximately 703.8 million years.

Uranium-238 is fissionable material. The U-238 nucleus may fission, or split into two smaller nuclei, if it absorbs a fast, or high-energy, neutron. A U-238 nucleus releases approximately 2.6 additional neutrons when it fissions. U-238 is also a fertile material, that is, it generally does not fission upon absorption of a thermal neutron but may be converted into fissile material through neutron bombardment. When bombarded with thermal neutrons, U-238 may be changed by neutron capture into plutonium, a fissile material.

Uranium 235 is fissile material, which means that it will likely undergo fission when it absorbs a thermal, or low-energy, neutron. Upon absorption of a neutron, U-235 will almost immediately fission, or split into two smaller nuclei. In the fission process, U-235 emits not only energy but also an average of approximately 2.4 neutrons, which may cause additional fission events. If there are enough U-235 atoms present in the material, these additional neutrons may result in a chain reaction.

Additional artificial isotopes of uranium can be made through various processes. Uranium-233, for example, is made through neutron bombardment of the element thorium-232. Uranium-233 is another fissile material that may be used as fuel for reactors. Another example, uranium-239, is a short-lived isotope that has a half-life of about 23 minutes. It decays into neptunium- 239, which will further decay into plutonium-239.

Some types of nuclear reactors, such as the Canada Deuterium Uranium (CANDU) Reactor, use natural uranium as fuel. Nevertheless, uranium is generally enriched from its natural state to be used as fuel for nuclear reactors and weapons. Enriching uranium involves increasing the amount of the isotope U-235 present in the material.

Reactors in the United States generally require uranium fuel that is enriched to approximately 3–5 percent U-235. The U.S. Department of Energy defines highly enriched uranium (HEU), as any uranium that is enriched to 20 percent or higher of U-235. Nuclear weapons generally require *weapons-grade* HEU, which is uranium that is enriched to approximately 90 percent or higher of U-235.

Various forms of uranium are used during most enrichment processes. One such form of uranium is known as *yellowcake*, which is a highly concentrated (approximately 70 percent or higher by weight) uranium oxide (U_3O_8). Another form of uranium, which becomes a gaseous compound at temperatures above 133 degrees Fahrenheit, is uranium hexafluoride (UF_6). This gaseous compound is the form of uranium used to enrich to higher levels of the isotope U-235. Hex is the form of uranium critical to both of the widely used enrichment techniques, the gaseous-diffusion and gas-centrifuge methods. Following enrichment processes, uranium is converted to uranium dioxide (UO_2) to be used as fuel for reactors.

Current Status

HEU is an internationally controlled material by nuclear nonproliferation treaties. The International Atomic Energy Agency (IAEA) helps to monitor and safeguard the world's supply of HEU. As the world's nuclear watchdog, the IAEA monitors uranium enrichment facilities and the capabilities of the international community.

One of the current issues pertaining to uranium is the use of depleted uranium (DU) as armor-piercing ammunition for conventional military weapons. Because depleted uranium is nearly two and a half times denser than steel, it is used to gain greater momentum to penetrate armor by the military. As a heavy metal, DU is toxic if inhaled in sufficient quantities. The prolific use of DU by the United States during Operation Desert Storm in 1991 and subsequent operations caused public concern about the health hazard to soldiers and civilians who breathed DU dust.

Don Gillich

Further Reading

Garvin, Richard L., and Georges Charpak, *Megawatts and Megatons: A Turning Point in the Nuclear Age* (New York: Knopf, 2001).

U.S. Chemical and Biological Weapons Programs

During the 20th century, the United States amassed one of the largest arsenals of chemical and biological weapons in the world. Since the ratification of the 1975 Biological and Toxin Weapons Convention (BTWC) and the 1993 Chemical Weapons Convention (CWC), the United States has demilitarized its biological and chemical weapons programs. By 2015, the United States had destroyed some 90 percent of the more than 30,000 tons of legacy chemical warfare (CW) agents and munitions, and it expects to complete total demilitarization of its chemical stocks by 2023.

Chemical Warfare

The potential use of chemical agents, in the form of poisonous gases or substances to contaminate water wells, was considered very early on in U.S. history. In 1862, during the Civil War, an American engineer by the name of John W. Doughty wrote to the U.S. Secretary of War, suggesting that chlorine be used in artillery shells. He believed that the introduction of chemical weapons on the battlefield would lead to more decisive results. His ideas were not well received. Other ideas included the use of cayenne pepper (an early introduction of pepper spray), chloroform, and veratria, that is, irritating alkaloid compounds derived from the seeds of the sabadilla plant (cevadilla; *Schoeno-caulon officinale*).

But the United States did very little in terms of chemical weapons development until 1915, when chemicals were used on a large scale for the first time in World War I. Because the United States had yet to become involved in the European hostilities, however, its efforts in "gas warfare" were mostly limited to the manufacture of protective equipment, especially gas masks.

When U.S. troops entered the combat of World War I in 1917, it became clear that the American Expeditionary Forces were woefully unprepared for the chemical battlefield. In May 1917, the CWS Research Division—in coordination with American industrial entities that included Goodyear Rubber, American Can Company, and the General Chemical Company—undertook a crash development program to supply the first 20,000 gas masks to U.S. forces. When full-scale production was achieved, more than 40,000 masks could be produced in a single day, and eventually 5.7 million gas masks were manufactured by the end of World War I. By early September 1917, a "Gas Service" had been established as a separate branch of the AEF in France, and the U.S. Chemical Warfare Service (CWS), led by Major General William L. Siebert, was founded on June 29, 1918.

The U.S. military began filling chemical shells under the auspices of the Trench Warfare Section of the Ordnance Department. The Offense Research Section of the

CWS selected certain substances for their possible use in combat. Approximately 250 chemicals were researched and evaluated for their suitability as chemical weapons for the Western Front. Although chemical weapons used by U.S. forces in the European theater were initially provided by the European allies of the United States, phosgene, mustard, and lewisite (blister agent and irritant) production facilities were built in the United States from 1917–1918. (Lewisite was a late entry into the U.S. chemical arsenal, and although it was shipped to Europe, it was never used in World War I.) Because of its isolated location and ready access to shipping via the Chesapeake Bay, "Gunpowder Reservation," 20 miles east of Baltimore, Maryland, was chosen in December 1917 to be the site for producing toxic agents and filling chemical shells and bombs. On May 4, 1918, the 3,400-acre district was officially renamed Edgewood Arsenal. By war's end, Edgewood Arsenal had filled and shipped more than 150,000 mustard shells of 75-millimeter caliber to the Western Front. Despite these efforts, none of the gas projectors or chemical artillery shells arrived in Europe before the fighting ended.

In the late 1920s, the U.S. chemical arsenal consisted mostly of mustard, chloroacetophenone (CN), phosgene, lewisite, chloropicrin, and chlorine. In 1928, the M1 4.2-inch chemical mortar became the standard chemical delivery system in the U.S. arsenal. It was also used to deliver obscurant smokes and high-explosive shells. But with defense spending cut by the Great Depression, preparations for CW took a low priority for the U.S. War Department.

In 1937, as war loomed once again on the European continent, the United States revamped its offensive chemical weapons program, adding production capacity at Edgewood Arsenal, primarily mustard and phosgene. In contrast to the groundbreaking work in military chemistry going on in Germany and elsewhere, the United States had only a limited chemical warfare capability when it declared war on Germany and Japan.

Especially in light of the Japanese military's use of CW against China in the 1930s, a sense of urgency prevailed to increase the U.S. offensive chemical stockpile. From 1940 to 1945, the United States ramped up its chemical production capacity, producing nearly 150,000 tons of CW agents. In addition to artillery, the U.S. Army Air Corps standardized aerial munitions, including 1,000-pound bombs containing phosgene, cyanogen chloride, and hydrogen cyanide. Substantial chemical weapons were deployed to European staging grounds.

In June 1943—reflecting the general disapproval of chemical warfare by the American public—President Franklin D. Roosevelt categorically stated that the United States would not use chemical weapons unless struck first by enemy forces. By 1945, however, public mood had shifted: 40 percent of the people responding to one survey were in favor of using chemicals against the Japanese, versus 23 percent just a year before. Pitched battles in the Pacific island campaign had resulted in horrendous U.S. casualties, not to mention the massive loss of civilian life during the Okinawa campaign. This no doubt added to the public's acceptance of offensive CW. Defending from heavily fortified redoubts, Japanese troops rarely surrendered and fought ferociously to the very end. It was at this point that the U.S. assistant secretary of war, John J. McCloy, reconsidered the use of chemical weapons.

As plans were being drawn to invade the Japanese mainland, General "Vinegar Joe" Stilwell and General George C. Marshall suggested the use of gas. But the logistics and preparation for such CW would have conflicted with the shipment of sorely needed conventional materiel. Other influential decision makers within the military, notably Admiral William D. Leahy, thought it appalling that the employment of chemical weapons was even being considered.

The postwar discovery of Germany's nerve agent munitions—including 750 tabun artillery shells that were captured in Germany—were a shock to Allied CW experts. By the 1950s, sarin nerve agent and VX were produced in large quantity by the United States at Muscle Shoals, Alabama, and Newport, Indiana, respectively.

By 1954, the M34 and M34A1 chemical cluster munitions were designed to drop sarin on targets. Little progress was made in delivering VX nerve agent, however, until the 1960s. Longer-range systems, including the Honest John (16-mile range) rocket and the Sergeant rocket were fitted with chemical warheads. During the 1960s, unmanned aerial vehicles (UAVs)—more accurately described as drone aircraft—were developed to deliver both chemical and biological agents. An accident on Okinawa, Japan, involving sarin nerve agent, however, led to a halt to both biological and chemical weapons production by the United States in 1969.

The aftermath of the 1973 Yom Kippur War in the Middle East served as yet another wake-up call for the U.S. Chemical Corps. Israeli forces, which barely prevailed after Egypt and Syria launched a surprise attack, discovered Soviet armored vehicles that were equipped to survive in contaminated chemical environments. This spurred the United States to rethink its approach to defensive and offensive CW. More advanced designs for chemical munitions, including the M-687 binary shell, were integrated into U.S. chemical weaponry in 1976.

In the 1980s, President Ronald Reagan revitalized U.S. offensive chemical weapons production. The M-687 and the VX binary bomb (Bigeye) went into full production. Although these and other chemical weapons were available by the First Gulf War in 1990–1991, they played no role in planning for retaliation in the event that Iraq introduced chemical weapons on the battlefield.

Having first signed a memorandum of understanding with the former Soviet Union in 1989, the United States was set on a course to demilitarize its chemical arsenal, culminating in its ratification of the Chemical Weapons Convention in 1997. As of 2004, about 28,000 tons of chemical agent in bulk and weaponized form awaited their final destruction in the United States. In the face of technical hurdles, environmental concerns, and other practicalities, 90 percent of U.S. chemical weapons were destroyed by 2015, with 2023 set for eliminating what remains.

Biological Warfare

Before the renunciation of biological warfare by President Richard M. Nixon in 1969, the United States had developed a series of weaponized BW agents. These included the causative agents of anthrax, brucellosis, tularemia, Venezuelan equine encephalitis, and Q fever, as well as the toxin staphylococcal enterotoxin B. Anticrop agents were also produced in significant quantity to target the wheat and rice crops of the Soviet Union and China. A number of other BW agents, including smallpox, Rift Valley fever virus, and Rocky Mountain spotted fever bacteria were also investigated. All offensive biological weapon stores were destroyed by 1972, and some toxins (such as saxitoxin) were redirected toward peaceful medical research.

Background

Referring to a League of Nations committee formed on the subject, the U.S. Chemical Warfare Service wrote in its 1926 annual report that biological warfare (BW) would be largely ineffective, given the availability of protective measures, such as masks. In the 1930s, however, prewar intelligence reports indicated that Japan and Germany had undertaken research into offensive BW. In September 1939, American military scientists decided to reexamine the problem of BW.

The Chemical Warfare Service reported that nine diseases could be potential BW agents: yellow fever, the dysenteries, cholera, typhus, bubonic plague, smallpox, influenza, tetanus, and sleeping sickness (*Trypanosoma brucei*, via the tsetse fly). These agents were of great interest because they could be spread by insects and because they required neither existing skin lesions nor another agent to enter the human body.

In 1941, the U.S. Chemical Warfare Service began BW-related research, and by mid-1942, George W. Merck, the president of Merck & Company, a large pharmaceutical company, had become the chairman of the War Research Service, which had been established to oversee U.S. BW-related activities. The CWS was given the responsibility of building and operating laboratories and production facilities.

In March 1942, the CWS suggested that, in addition to work conducted by civilian research scientists in biological weapons defense, the following BW agents should be studied in an offensive context:

- antipersonnel agents: coccidioidomycosis, psittacosis, plague, typhoid and paratyphoid, cholera, typhus, yellow fever, and anthrax

- antianimal agents: rinderpest, foot-and-mouth disease, and fowl plague
- anticrop agents: late blight of potato, rice fungi, wheat rusts , and South American rubber leaf blight

By 1944, this list had grown by adding the following agents:

- antipersonnel agents: tularemia, brucellosis, glanders, and melioidosis
- anticrop agent: sclerotium rot

In 1942, the CWS began construction of a BW facility at Camp Detrick. Operational in 1943, the facility at Camp Detrick employed approximately 4,000 people. Other BW-related facilities included a 250-acre site near Dugway Proving Grounds, Utah, and a 2,000-acre facility at Horn Island in Pascagoula, Mississippi, both of which were used for open-air testing.

Meanwhile, cooperation among the United States, Canada, and Great Britain continued in offensive BW research. In 1943, it was learned from tests conducted by the British at Gruinard Island (off the coast of Scotland) and Penclawdd (on the coast of Wales) that loading anthrax into bomblets arranged into cluster munitions was the most feasible method of agent delivery. In one experiment, sheep were placed at various distances from a bomb loaded with anthrax fill. The reach of the deadly spores was such that animals placed 250 yards downwind received a lethal dose of anthrax. Despite these impressive results, cluster-type munitions using anthrax were never supplied to Allied forces in World War II.

In the period following World War II, U.S. BW production capacity was gradually reduced to laboratory-scale research and development. Between 1947 and 1949, small-scale, open-air testing of BW simulants *Bacillus globigii* (BG) and *Serratia marcescens* (SM) was carried out at Camp Detrick. Pathogen tests began at Camp Detrick in 1949 in an enclosed, 1-million-liter steel sphere called the "eight ball."

During the Korean War, the United States expanded its BW program. The government established the Pine Bluff Arsenal BW agent production facility in Arkansas, and it also expanded major research facilities at Camp Detrick. By 1951, the program developed, tested, and produced a variety of BW anticrop agents for military purposes and the bombs capable of delivering such agents. Spending on BW-related research and development amounted to more than $345 million during fiscal years 1951–1953.

During the 1950s, the U.S. military conducted a number of secret tests to assess the vulnerability of the American mainland to BW attack and to test the effectiveness of BW agent delivery methods. Exercise Brown Derby was carried out November 7–20, 1953, by the Chemical Corps and U.S. Air Force to assess the ability of the United States to produce and transport BW weapons overseas. The exercise showed that an attack using BW could be launched within several days of the initial order.

A series of at least three or four "Bellwether" tests, conducted beginning in the late 1950s, studied the biting behavior of mosquitoes. Bellwether 1, for example, was a study conducted in September–October 1959, during which uninfected female *Aedes aegeypti* mosquitoes were released in 52 field trials, and the number of mosquito bites on laboratory animals and humans were counted.

Scientists from Fort Detrick also secretly performed animal studies at remote desert sites and on barges near Johnston Atoll in the Pacific Ocean. Between 1949 and 1968, the U.S. government also surreptitiously dropped BW simulants (such as *Serratia marcescens*) over a number of American cities, including San Francisco and New York City, to assess urban vulnerability to biological attack and to experiment with potential weapons and delivery systems. Simulants such as *Serratia marcescens* (SM) could be cultured at various points distant from release to determine length of travel. In 1955, American scientists and military experts began using human volunteers to test the effect of various BW simulants, including the anthrax simulant *Bacillus globigii* (BG; *B. atrophaeus*). These tests were intended to help scientists learn how to strengthen American BW defenses as well as to evaluate means to carry out a biological attack.

In 1956, further attention was brought to chemical and biological warfare, particularly as a result of the looming threat from the Soviet Union. In that year, Soviet defense minister Georgi Zhukov's speech to the Twentieth Congress of the Soviet Communist Party in Moscow contained references to "weapons of mass destruction," including chemical weapons in future wars. The wording of the speech was used as support for the argument that a Soviet chemical threat existed, and by extension a threat from biological weaponry as well. A December 1958 meeting of the U.S. Defense Science Board recommended developing new unconventional weapons, expanding research, and placing greater resources into public relations. These recommendations, in turn, were supported by the Joint Chiefs of Staff in 1959. They emphasized the need for stockpile modernization and increased research and development funding.

Despite increasing public interest in chemical and biological weapons disarmament during the 1960s, the American BW program continued to grow. The development of large-scale freeze-drying and spray-drying systems was undertaken to improve the ability of biological weapons agents to survive and remain potent during an offensive attack. Research using arthropods was conducted to deliver certain BW agents. By 1966, government facilities at Pine Bluff Arsenal and Fort Detrick had already mass-produced several BW agents, filling several types of biological munitions.

By the time the U.S. BW program was terminated in 1969, American BW scientists had seven standardized biological weapons. In the lethal category, the U.S. Army had weaponized the bacterial agents that cause anthrax and tularemia. For incapacitating agents, the causative agents of brucellosis, Q fever, and Venezuelan equine encephalitis (VEE) were weaponized. Toxins that were developed into validated weapons systems were the lethal toxin botulinum and the incapacitant staphylococcal enterotoxin B (SEB).

In 1969 and 1970, President Richard Nixon renounced all offensive development and production of microbial and toxin agents in National Security Directives 35 and 44, respectively. By 1972, all U.S. antipersonnel BW agent stocks and munitions had been destroyed. The United States also terminated all offensive research, closed or cleaned up all offensive facilities, and turned those facilities over to other government agencies for other research. The American BW defense program was subsequently moved to Fort Detrick, Maryland. The unilateral disarmament initiated by President Nixon's directives set the stage for the 1972 Biological and Toxins Weapons Convention (BTWC). On January 22, 1975, the United States ratified the BTWC, which prohibited the development, production, and stockpiling of bacteriological and toxin weapons.

Eric A. Croddy

Further Reading

Cochrane, Rexmond C., *History of the Chemical Warfare Service in World War II*, vol. 2, *Biological Warfare Research in the United States* (Fort Detrick, MD: Historical Section, Plans, Training and Intelligence Division, Office of Chief, Chemical Corps, 1947).

Fries, Amos A., and Clarence J. West, *Chemical Warfare* (New York: McGraw-Hill, 1921).

Hasegawa, Guy R., "Proposals for Chemical Weapons during the American Civil War," *Military Medicine* 173, no. 5 (May 2008): 499–506.

Regis, Ed, *The Biology of Doom* (New York: Henry Holt, 1999).

Utgoff, Victor A., *The Challenge of Chemical Weapons: An American Perspective* (New York: St. Martin's Press, 1991).

U.S. Nuclear Forces and Doctrine

Early U.S. nuclear doctrine was embedded in the broader strategic bombing doctrine that was refined in combat during World War II: attack military targets located in urban areas using precision bombing wherever possible. *Precision* was, of course, relative to the technology of the times and, especially in the Japanese campaign, was abandoned in favor of broad-area firebombing because of operational considerations. Scholars of military history now know that had the Japanese not surrendered after Nagasaki, the next several nuclear weapons probably would have been used tactically against massed Japanese forces opposing a U.S. land-air-sea invasion of Japan as U.S. firebombing raids destroyed remaining Japanese cities and a naval blockade isolated the Japanese mainland. Then, as now, technology, policy, and the circumstances of battle interacted to shape doctrine.

U.S. nuclear forces and doctrine developed slowly after 1945, owing to budget constraints, the primitive nature of nuclear weapons at that time, uncertainties about U.S. global strategy and the type of military forces needed to support that strategy, and the soon-to-commence negotiations in the newly formed United Nations to try to control and perhaps even ban nuclear weapons. From the beginning, nuclear weapons were placed by U.S. authorities in a special category. Explicit presidential authorization was required for developing, testing, deploying, and using atomic bombs. This special status was recognized in early presidential directives.

The Growth of Nuclear Forces

As the Cold War unfolded and the imperative of deterring Soviet aggression became paramount, nuclear weapons moved to the heart of U.S. military strategy. U.S. nuclear forces and doctrine evolved accordingly. With the advent of the North Atlantic Treaty and the Soviet test of its first nuclear bomb in 1949, the U.S. deterrent strategy became more complicated, and new target categories were added to the strategic air offensive annexes of its contingency war plans. In the late 1940s, strategic air plans continued to rely heavily on conventional as well as nuclear weapons.

In 1950, before the outbreak of the Korean War, President Harry S. Truman approved a major expansion of the nuclear stockpile. He also approved development of the thermonuclear (hydrogen) bomb ("H-bomb"). NSC-68, one of the first major reviews of U.S. national security strategy, was launched in response to the H-bomb decision. In 1950, the U.S. nuclear stockpile numbered some 300 bombs that were still large devices close to the designs of the original nuclear weapons. By the end of the decade, the robust production and development program launched by President Truman had produced a stockpile of more than 12,000 nuclear weapons (and a number of new, more sophisticated designs) deployed not only on large strategic bombers but with U.S. tactical air, sea, and land forces.

The Korean War marked a major turning point for the United States. It confirmed the priorities and tensions of a Europe-first grand strategy that continued until the end of the Cold War. It demonstrated the difficulty of using the nuclear shadow to affect conflicts fought on the margins of the major East-West confrontation. And, notwithstanding the desperate nature of the Korean crisis, the fact that the United States did not use nuclear weapons reinforced the evolving norm that nuclear weapons were tools of last resort, reserved for the most strategically threatening occasions. During the Korean War era, the world also entered the thermonuclear age. There was now no apparent limit to the destructiveness that could be packaged in a single thermonuclear device.

When President Dwight D. Eisenhower took office in January 1953, his highest priorities were to end the Korean War, to anchor the United States to the North Atlantic Treaty Organization (NATO), and to translate what he and his advisers saw as an inchoate containment and deterrence strategy into a coherent grand strategy attuned to the needs of a long, inconclusive struggle conducted in the shadow of the bomb's ability to threaten apocalyptic destruction. U.S. nuclear forces, still heavily centered around the long-range bombers of Strategic Air Command, were at the heart of this endeavor. NSC-162/2, adopted in late 1953, offered a strategy that linked nuclear weapons and deterrence to the long-range mission of containing the Soviet Union.

During the 1950s, the East-West nuclear arms race accelerated. The United States developed a wide range of nuclear weapons deployed on a number of strategic and tactical platforms. Nuclear doctrine evolved to reflect this capability, albeit with final authority for using nuclear weapons reserved to the president or, in the event of his incapacitation, his designated successors (called the National Command Authority). Although Congress exercised indirect influence on the nuclear programs through its budgeting authority, fundamental decisions on U.S. doctrine and on the size, composition, deployment, and use of nuclear forces remained with the executive branch. Also during the 1950s, the imperative of being able to survive a surprise nuclear attack and respond with a substantial "second strike" became a key element of U.S. nuclear doctrine.

Although missile programs had begun both in the United States and in Russia during World War II, and had become more important with the advent of the German V-1 and V-2 systems, missiles developed slowly during the 1950s. Thus, U.S. strategic offensive and defensive nuclear doctrine remained focused on bomber aircraft. The United States constructed a large air defense network during these years and could explore preemptive options for striking Soviet nuclear bomber bases in the face of an imminent Soviet attack. The Soviets progressed quickly with their missile programs, however, and whatever prospect there had been of entertaining the idea of a preemptive nuclear first strike in U.S. strategic doctrine faded.

The shock of Sputnik—the first artificial Earth-orbiting satellite—on the United States and its allies cannot be overstated. It immediately contributed to the development of a NATO nuclear stockpile with nuclear sharing arrangements for otherwise nonnuclear NATO partners and accelerated work on missiles. When President Eisenhower turned over the reins of government to President John F. Kennedy in 1961, the basic structure of the Cold War U.S. nuclear posture and a number of its supporting processes were in place. Strategic nuclear forces consisted of a "triad" of long-range bombers, intercontinental ballistic missiles (ICBMs), and submarine-launched ballistic missiles (SLBMs). Tactical nuclear weapons were deployed with a wide range of forces. A large design and production complex was in place to refurbish the U.S. stockpile, and a large industrial complex supported production and development of new generations of strategic delivery systems. Command and control and intelligence, surveillance, and reconnaissance systems were likewise under continual development and refinement. The Joint Strategic Target Planning Staff (JSTPS) had been created in Omaha, Nebraska, to develop the Single Integrated Operational Plan (SIOP), and the U.S. strategic war plan was beginning to be coordinated with NATO nuclear planning.

Flexible Response and Arms Control

During the Kennedy and Lyndon B. Johnson administrations, the United States moved from a doctrine of "massive retaliation" to one of "flexible response." The new Kennedy administration moved to try to create more strategic nuclear options for the president in the event of an emergency. It also sought to recentralize NATO nuclear decision making in U.S. hands and to seek means of delaying the need to cross the nuclear threshold. Notwithstanding the public manifestations of the Kennedy strategy—for example, Secretary of Defense Robert McNamara's Ann Arbor speech in

1962, where he tried to entice the Soviets to a counterforce doctrine, the "new" NATO strategy unveiled in MC-14/3 in 1967—the United States and its allies remained heavily dependent on early resort to nuclear weapons in any major military confrontation with the Soviet Union. Nuclear options continued to be quietly explored for non-central confrontations such as Vietnam, and to be rejected.

During the early 1960s, U.S. nuclear doctrine and force planning began to interact more deeply with arms control theories that stressed the need to stabilize the nuclear confrontation. After the Cuban Missile Crisis in late 1962, the Americans and their British allies undertook a major initiative to reinvigorate the on-again, off-again nuclear testing talks that had begun in the 1950s, resulting in the Limited Test Ban Treaty in 1963. U.S. authorities were also exploring ways of beginning strategic arms control talks. Moreover, a newly forming nonproliferation agenda became serious after the Chinese detonated their first nuclear weapon in 1964, and the prospect of major deployments not only of missile forces but also of antiballistic missile systems emerged. In 1965, President Johnson committed the prestige of his presidency to seeking a Nuclear Nonproliferation Treaty (NPT), and his administration quietly began reviewing ways to initiate strategic arms talks (something derailed by the Soviet invasion of Czechoslovakia in 1968) when the NPT was opened for signature.

The Richard M. Nixon administration took office in 1969 at the height of the Vietnam War. The backlash from this war spilled over into the strategic weapons debate, leading indirectly to the early demise of America's first operational anti-ballistic missile (ABM) system. Meanwhile, President Nixon and his national security team adjusted to the pace of the missile race. In 1965, the Soviets had slightly more than 200 ICBMs and fewer than 100 SLBMs. By 1969, Soviet missile forces were growing at the rate of 200–300 missiles annually and were projected to equal if not surpass U.S. numbers by 1971.

In this context, the new Nixon administration commenced the Strategic Arms Limitation Talks (SALT), which resulted in the Anti-Ballistic Missile (ABM) Treaty and the interim agreement on offensive arms in 1972. The ABM Treaty in effect codified the doctrine of assured destruction that had been embraced by the Kennedy administration after the short-lived effort to entice the Soviets to adopt a purely counterforce strategy, leading to a situation of mutual assured destruction (MAD). Also in 1972, the Nixon administration began a review of its nuclear policy that resulted in National Security Decision Memorandum (NSDM) 242 in 1974—a policy that reprioritized the targets to be held at risk with strategic nuclear weapons toward industrial targets, called for even more options in the nuclear war plan, created a secure reserve force, and sought ways to further refine escalation control should deterrence fail. A document called the Nuclear Weapons Employment Policy (NUWEP), first issued in 1974, conveyed the new guidance, and on this basis, the JSTPS restructured the SIOP into major attack options (MAOs), selective attack options (SAOs), and limited attack options (LAOs). U.S. strategic bombing doctrine during and after World War II had centered on a number of target sets that now were formalized into the primary categories of military forces (subdivided into nuclear and nonnuclear forces), war-supporting economic and other industrial targets, and leadership and command and control.

The Countervailing Strategy

After conducting an initial review of national security strategy, the Carter administration began a concentrated study on nuclear targeting policy led by Leon Sloss. This study concluded that the United States needed to adjust its nuclear deterrent strategy and doctrine to reflect how the Soviets approached war planning by placing greater emphasis on holding at risk Soviet military forces and the Soviet military command structure. These studies formed the basis for Presidential Directive (PD) 53, which reinvigorated programs for ensuring that American strategic command and control could survive a nuclear attack and continue to function, and for PD-59—a new nuclear policy that, among other things, shifted targeting priorities away from industries and the concept of impeding industrial recovery and provided for a more robust secure reserve force. PD-59 was unveiled publicly by Secretary of Defense Harold Brown and identified for public diplomacy purposes as the "countervailing" strategy. The concept was to seek to ascertain the war aims of the enemy and to then hold at risk assets critical to the success of those aims, thus denying victory to the enemy. The concept of punishment did not disappear as an element of deterrence, but at least for the moment, the concept of denial gained a more prominent role in U.S. nuclear doctrine.

Although highly critical of formal arms control, the newly elected Ronald Reagan administration bowed to European sentiment when it resumed theater nuclear force talks in 1981 under the new name of intermediate nuclear forces (INF). In 1981, the new administration conducted its own nuclear targeting review and reaffirmed PD-59 guidance. The administration also conducted a Damage Criteria Study (DCS) to facilitate translating nuclear targeting objectives into a more coherent target and attack criteria framework. In late 1981, the Reagan White House issued National Security Decision Directive (NSDD) 13, which superseded but did not significantly change PD-59. In 1982, President Reagan also approved the commencement of negotiations for a Strategic Arms Reduction Treaty (START). START, unlike SALT, sought actual reductions in nuclear weapons. By this time, the Reagan administration had set in motion a major rearmament program to challenge the Soviets across the board. In 1983, in announcing the Strategic Defense Initiative (SDI), the president increased this pressure.

The End of the Cold War

After World War II, U.S. nuclear doctrine and forces had evolved as part of a broader national security strategy centered around the concept of containing and deterring the Soviet Union until Soviet domestic change might make possible a dramatically different strategy. Few sensed in the early 1980s that this kind of change was on the horizon. The United States built up its military forces and, in 1986, finally abandoned SALT II. Other arms control talks proceeded slowly. After three leaders in three years, in 1985, the Soviets undertook the bold step of promoting a young, dynamic politician, Mikhail Gorbachev, to the center of their decision-making apparatus. In the face of the failing Soviet economy and the pressures of the Reagan rearmament plan, Gorbachev undertook a number of initiatives, some of which centered on arms control and some of which centered on domestic political reform, that—within a few short years—resulted in the unexpected end of the Cold War and the equally unexpected collapse of the Soviet empire. Along the way, NATO displayed solidarity in proceeding with the deployment of new theater nuclear systems—the American Pershing II intermediate-range ballistic missile (IRBM) and the ground-launched cruise missile (GLCM)—notwithstanding a massive Soviet diplomatic campaign to mobilize European opposition.

The Soviets broke off arms control talks after the NATO deployments, but (with Gorbachev now in power) a way was found to resume talks. In December 1987, Reagan and Gorbachev signed the INF Treaty banning all U.S. and Soviet land-based ballistic missiles and GLCMs in the 500- to 5,500-kilometer range. This was in effect the first nuclear disarmament treaty because it required the destruction and future prohibition of an entire range of nuclear delivery systems. The Threshold Test Ban Treaty and the Peaceful Nuclear Explosions Treaty of the 1970s, which had never entered into force because of verification concerns, now acquired verification protocols that allowed them to take effect.

President George H. W. Bush came to office as the Cold War was ending. He and his national security team presided over the reunification of a German state that retained membership in NATO, the largely peaceful withdrawal of Soviet forces from their external empire, and—in the face of attempted coups—the largely peaceful collapse of communism in the Soviet Union. While this was going on, the First Gulf War also began to reorient U.S. nuclear doctrine toward an existing but now more pressing threat—the proliferation of weapons of mass destruction (WMD) to regional states such as Iraq, North Korea, and Iran.

New Roles for Nuclear Weapons
By the early 1990s, the United States was reorienting its nuclear forces and beginning

to explore how to redirect its nuclear doctrine in the face of the new geopolitical circumstances. The process was messy, with a number of forces intervening. For instance, the new environmental awareness that had developed since the 1940s foreshadowed the closing of the plutonium production facilities at Rocky Flats in Colorado in 1992. In the early 1990s, the United States pursued what to many appeared to be a largely piecemeal nuclear agenda to adjust to the new security environment. START I negotiations proceeded to closure in 1991, but the collapse of the Soviet Union delayed its entry into force while the issue of nuclear succession was resolved. Eventually, Ukraine, Belarus, and Kazakhstan agreed to give up nuclear weapons and to join the NPT as nonnuclear weapons states. The United States undertook unilateral actions to further stabilize the dangerous transition period, hoping to assure Moscow and to elicit stabilizing actions from its former adversary. U.S. strategic bombers were taken off alert, the production of a number of nuclear systems was terminated, Strategic Air Command was dissolved and its forces transferred to several U.S. Air Force commands, and the Joint Strategic Planning Staff was replaced with a new unified command—U.S. Strategic Command. And, as an initiative that began in Congress, the United States entered a nuclear testing moratorium in 1992 while it pursued a formal Comprehensive Test Ban Treaty.

President Bill Clinton took office in 1993 in the midst of these changes. Later that year, the Defense Department announced the counterproliferation initiative to complement traditional U.S. nonproliferation strategy. The new administration also shifted emphasis to theater missile defense while essentially channeling the national missile defense effort into research and development. Congressional politics intervened, however, as the Republicans took control of both chambers of Congress in the 1994 election, and national missile defense again became an issue. In 1994, the first Nuclear Posture Review (NPR) was conducted. U.S. nuclear forces and doctrine remained largely intact as a result of this review, hedging against the uncertainties of the Russian transition to democracy.

The United States was the first to sign the recently completed CTBT in September 1996. On the road to this agreement, the Clinton administration had decided it would support a truly "zero-yield" outcome and, as part of the bargain in the arrangement, began constructing a Stockpile Stewardship Program (SSP) to explore how the safety and reliability of the U.S. nuclear stockpile might be retained in the absence of nuclear testing. Despite the rejection of the CTBT by the Senate in 1999, the United States continues to observe a self-imposed nuclear testing moratorium.

President George W. Bush won the 2000 elections and, notwithstanding a narrow mandate, set out to transform U.S. military forces. One of the early priorities of the new Bush administration was to terminate the ABM Treaty to allow the deployment of ballistic missile defenses aimed at "rogue" states such as North Korea. A Quadrennial Defense Review (QDR) and Nuclear Posture Review (NPR) were underway when the terrorist attacks of September 11, 2001, took place—an event that was as important as Pearl Harbor had been in 1941 in shifting U.S. national security strategy.

The new NPR announced in January 2002 took account of the importance of the supporting infrastructure and of strategic defenses as part of the overall U.S. deterrent, moved unilaterally to reduce U.S. strategic nuclear forces to a level of 1,700–2,200 operationally deployed warheads by 2012, and continued the emphasis in seeking new conventional means to hold at risk targets once considered possible targets for nuclear weapons. To support his 2009 Prague Agenda, the Barack Obama administration's 2010 NPR took the unprecedented step of announcing that nuclear disarmament was the long-term goal of U.S. nuclear policy, while taking steps to bolster the U.S. nuclear infrastructure to maintain a nuclear deterrent until that day arrived. The administration also signed a New START Treaty with the Russians in 2010 that limited accountable deployed strategic nuclear warheads and bombs to 1,550 for each side.

Looking Ahead

The Donald J. Trump administration issued its own NPR in 2018, which reasserted the role of nuclear weapons in U.S. defense policy. Harkening back to the 2002 Bush administration NPR, the 2018 NPR calls for a revitalization of the U.S. nuclear force with specific strategies and force structure tailored to emerging nuclear states, that is, North Korea, and nascent great power competitors Russia and China. The world had reached an inflection point in the history of nuclear weapons. But now it appears as if the pendulum is slowly swinging back from disarmament toward a situation in which nuclear rearmament and modernization is the dominant trend in world politics. One wonders if more could have been done when conditions were permissive, or if North Korean nuclear and missile tests would have inevitably increased the salience of nuclear weapons in various national defense strategies.

Since the United States dropped the atomic bombs on Hiroshima and Nagasaki, nuclear weapons have not been used in combat. They have become powerful political instruments instead of warfighting weapons. But that does not mean they never will be used again, nor that deterrence in the future will resemble deterrence in the past. U.S. nuclear forces and doctrine have evolved enormously and continue to evolve in a world where nuclear weapons remain a currency that must be managed.

Michael Wheeler

Further Reading

Bowie, Robert H., and Richard H. Immerman, *Waging Peace: How Eisenhower Shaped an Enduring Cold War Strategy* (Oxford, UK: Oxford University Press, 1998).

Brodie, Bernard, *Strategy in the Missile Age* (Princeton, NJ: Princeton University Press, 1959).

Bundy, McGeorge, *Danger and Survival: Choices about the Bomb in the First Fifty Years* (New York: Random House, 1988).

Bunn, George, and Christopher F. Chyba, eds., *US Nuclear Weapons Policy: Confronting Today's Threats* (Washington, D.C.: Brookings Institution Press, 2006).

Freedman, Lawrence, *The Evolution of Nuclear Strategy*, 3rd ed. (New York: Palgrave Macmillan, 2003).

Larsen, Jeffrey A. and Kerry Kartchner, *On Limited Nuclear War in the 21st Century* (Palo Alto, CA: Stanford University Press, 2015).

Roberts, Brad, *The Case for US Nuclear Weapons in the 21st Century* (Palo Alto, CA: Stanford University Press, 2015).

V-Agents

The name *V-agents* is a shortened form of "venomous" agents. The category includes those organophosphate (OP) compounds that share similar structural and toxic properties to those of the G-series nerve agents but possess even higher toxicity. Included in this category are VX, the former Soviet "V-gas," and other toxic analogs: VG (Amiton), VM, VE, and VS.

As with other nerve agents, the toxic principle of the V-agents is the inhibition of the enzyme acetylcholinesterase (AChE), the key to normal nerve impulse transmission at the molecular level. The resulting increased levels of the neurotransmitter acetylcholine produce exaggerated levels of bodily secretions and muscular twitching as well as pronounced effects on the cardiovascular and central nervous systems. Death from respiratory paralysis can occur as a consequence. Victims are also prone to asphyxiation due to excess mucous and salivary excretions from the upper respiratory tree.

The toxicity of VX nerve agent via inhalation is three times that of sarin, and VX is 100–400 times as toxic as sarin when absorbed through the skin. Pure VX has no color, is odorless, and at room temperature is a free-flowing oily liquid. In cases of skin exposure, symptoms can appear five to seven minutes following skin absorption. The percutaneous action of VX was demonstrated by the February 2017 assassination of Kim Jong-nam, the half-brother of North Korean leader Kim Jong-un. While transiting through Malaysia's Kuala Lumpur airport, operatives applied VX to Kim Jong-nam's face; he died soon afterward on the way to the hospital.

Background

The discovery of VX—one of the most potent military nerve agents ever developed—had its start in the Korean War. In early 1951, U.S. Army hygienists noted strong resistance in lice to DDT when delousing North Korean prisoners and refugees. In response, chemical firms such as Bayer and Imperial Chemical Industries sensed that the market was especially ripe for new and better replacements.

In 1952, the British company Imperial Chemical Industries patented some novel OP compounds that would later form the basic structure for VX. Although their goal was to develop safe and effective insecticides, one of his new inventions was found to be quite toxic to mammals as well. These toxic chemicals had no apparent commercial value, but it was thought that they could be of interest to the military. The formula and sample of the toxic OP compound were handed over to the defense laboratories of Porton Down in the United Kingdom. But during the 1950s, the British military had already decided to adopt one of the G-series nerve agents for use and was in the process of building a chemical arsenal consisting of either tabun (GA) or sarin (GB). The British government gave the formula to the United States in 1953, and in 1955, these chemicals were coded *V-agents* due to their "venomous" nature. After some molecular changes made at the U.S. Edgewood Arsenal laboratories, one analog was coded VX and standardized in the U.S. military in December 1957.

A facility formerly known as the Dana Heavy Water Plant in Newport, Indiana, was converted to produce VX for the U.S. chemical weapons arsenal in 1960. Production of VX in the United States continued through the 1960s. In 1968, while training with a VX aerial munition near Dugway Proving Grounds, Utah, a U.S. military aircraft accidentally released about 20 pounds of VX in an open field. There were no human casualties, but at least 3,000 sheep died as a result. In November 1969, President Nixon ended production of chemical warfare (CW) agents, following an earlier decision to renounce offensive biological warfare. In 2008—after numerous delays—the United States finally completed the destruction of more than 1,200 tons of VX nerve agent.

Eric A. Croddy

Further Reading

O'Brien, Richard D., *Toxic Phosphorus Esters* (New York: Academic Press, 1960).

W

Wassenaar Arrangement

The Wassenaar Arrangement is a voluntary export control regime that was created in 1996. Most of the world's leading arms exporters participate in the arrangement. The regime seeks to prevent destabilizing accumulations of arms anywhere in the world, and its members consult on arms deals with non-Wassenaar states. The 42 members of the arrangement meet annually in a plenary session.

The agreement calls upon members to subject small arms and light weapons to national export controls, using guidelines drawn up based on best practices that specify criteria to be used when assessing a possible arms sale. For example, a sale should be avoided if the members believe the weapons could end up in the hands of terrorists or organized crime. Members exchange reports every six months on exports of dual-use goods and technologies as well as on seven categories of conventional weapons: battle tanks, armored combat vehicles, large-caliber artillery, military aircraft and unmanned aerial vehicles, military and attack helicopters, warships, and missiles or missile systems.

Jeffrey A. Larsen

Further Reading

Wassenaar. http://www.wassenaar.org Accessed February 21, 2018.

Weapons of Mass Destruction

Although the term *weapon of mass destruction* (WMD) has been in use for more than 45 years, it has no widely accepted definition. Only one international agreement uses the term: the 1967 Outer Space Treaty bans "nuclear weapons or any other kinds of weapons of mass destruction" from Earth orbit or on celestial bodies The term *WMD* is sometimes used to identify weapons considered beyond civilized norms that should be banned or at least internationally controlled.

Most definitions of WMD list biological, chemical, radiological, or nuclear weapons. These four types of weapons can affect large areas and large numbers of people, especially in comparison with conventional weapons targeted at specific soldiers, vehicles, or buildings. In addition, all four can produce effects that spread far beyond their original target area, producing long-lasting contamination over large areas.

WMD Effects

There are significant differences among the four kinds of WMD in terms of effects, difficulty of acquisition and delivery, and expectations about use. Nuclear weapons are the only type of WMD that cause physical destruction. It is not possible to shield a population from nuclear blast effects.

Pound for pound, biological weapons can theoretically produce more casualties than nuclear weapons, but the impact of biological weapons is difficult to calculate in advance because environmental conditions and demographic factors shape their effectiveness. With sufficient warning, military forces can protect themselves against biological weapons; treatments might also be available for civilian populations once an attack is discovered. Biological agents do not usually produce instant death or even incapacitation; they often take hours or days to produce effects. Chemical weapons must be delivered in vast quantities to cause massive casualties on the battlefield; however, if employed in a densely populated confined space (e.g., a sporting arena), a relatively small amount of agent could produce devastating results. When warned, military authorities can have troops use protective gear and antidotes to reduce the number of casualties suffered during a chemical weapons attack. When not protected, however, exposed individuals may experience a nearly instant agonizing death from just drops of certain chemical agents.

Radiological weapons are more likely to produce panic than high numbers of radiation deaths. Nevertheless, conventional explosives laced with fissile material might spread radioactive debris over a large area. The effects of radiological weapons can be minimized with protective clothing and expensive decontamination efforts.

Acquisition and Delivery

Nuclear weapons are probably the most difficult type of WMD to acquire because specialized equipment and knowledge is required to develop and test them. Nuclear weapons production relies on complex and unique equipment and the procurement of weapons-grade fissionable materials. Meeting the requirements to construct nuclear weapons is a challenge for nations and may be beyond the ability of nonstate groups.

Terrorist groups, however, may be able to acquire a weapon on the black market or through theft.

In contrast, biological weapons can be created using commercial equipment in a relatively small facility, and even small amounts can be deadly. They can be distributed easily, as shown in the U.S. anthrax attacks that occurred in the fall of 2001. Production of chemical weapons in quantity requires chemical engineering expertise and chemical production facilities on a scale similar to that of petroleum refineries. Aircraft sprayers and artillery delivery are preferred for battlefield use, but pressurized tanks can serve as a simple way to deliver agent.

Radioactive material suitable for radiological weapons is readily available given its widespread use in medical and research applications. Delivery of radiological weapons by means of aerial dusting would affect the largest possible area, but recent concern has centered on the possible terrorist employment of so-called dirty bombs, that is, conventional explosive devices used for dispersing nuclear material. Explosive dispersal is unlikely to produce many deaths from radiation, but it could require an expensive and time-consuming decontamination cleanup effort to make the area safe for human occupation.

Roy Pettis

Further Reading

Cordesman, Anthony H., *Terrorism, Asymmetric Warfare, and Weapons of Mass Destruction* (New York: Praeger, 2001).

Tucker, Jonathan, *Toxic Terror: Assessing Terrorist Use of Chemical and Biological Weapons* (Cambridge, MA: MIT Press, 2000).

Weapons-Grade Material

The acquisition of weapons-grade material—nuclear material considered most suitable for making nuclear weapons—is the most formidable obstacle to the manufacture of nuclear weapons. The primary weapons-grade materials are uranium enriched to 90 percent or greater uranium 235 (U-235) or plutonium with greater than about 90 percent plutonium 239 (Pu-239). These elements are called "fissile" because they can be split into two roughly equal-mass fragments when struck by a neutron of even low energy. When a large enough mass of either material is assembled, a self-sustaining chain reaction is produced after the first fission. For the nuclear explosive to obtain a significant nuclear yield, sufficient neutrons must be present within the weapon core at the right time. If the chain reaction starts too soon or too late, the result will be only a "fizzle" yield or no yield at all.

Plutonium is used by all the current nuclear weapons states: the United States, Russia, Great Britain, France, China, Israel, India, Pakistan, and North Korea. (South Africa built six nuclear weapons in the 1980s and early 1990s using U-235, but it subsequently destroyed these weapons and dismantled its weapons program.) Pu-239 does not occur in nature. It can be made only in quantities sufficient for constructing a weapon in a nuclear reactor. It must be "bred," or produced, one atomic nucleus at a time by bombarding U-238 with neutrons to produce the isotope U-239, which, as it beta-decays, emits an electron to become the radioactive neptunium 239 (Np-239). The neptunium isotope again beta-decays to become Pu-239. The only proven and practical source for the large quantities of neutrons needed to make plutonium at a reasonable speed is a nuclear reactor in which a controlled but self-sustaining U-235 fission chain reaction takes place. The plutonium then must be extracted chemically in a reprocessing plant, making this route to nuclear weapons production difficult to conceal.

U-235 is the other significant weapons-grade material. The only naturally occurring fissile isotope, natural uranium contains only about 0.7 percent U-235, the rest being largely the less fissionable isotope U-238 (which cannot sustain a chain reaction). To use uranium either as a fuel for nuclear reactors or as the explosive charge of a nuclear weapon, U-235 must be separated from the rest of the uranium by a process known as *enrichment*.

The first nuclear weapons the United States developed contained a hollow ball of plutonium surrounded by conventional explosives. When these explosives were detonated, the resulting force, focused inward, compressed the plutonium, thereby initiating a chain reaction. The United States first detonated this kind of bomb during the Trinity test near Alamogordo, New Mexico, on July 16, 1945, and then it dropped another, called "Fat Man," on Nagasaki, Japan, a few weeks later, on August 9. These two devices were implosion devices. The nuclear bomb the United States dropped on Hiroshima, "Little Boy," on August 6, detonated when one chunk of U-235 was fired down a tube into another piece of U-235. This type, known as a gun-assembly device, is the easiest of all nuclear devices to design and build and does not require testing. It is generally believed to be impossible to prevent any nation having the requisite amount of enriched uranium from building one or more gun-type weapons. Therefore, the acquisition of significant quantities of U-235 or a facility in which to separate the fissile material is an indicator that a state could be in the process of gaining a rudimentary nuclear capability.

Peter R. Lavoy

Further Reading

GlobalSecurity.org, "Introduction to Special Weapons." http://www.globalsecurity.org /wmd/intro. Accessed December 10, 2003.

Office of Technology Assessment, *Technologies Underlying Weapons of Mass Destruction* (Washington, D.C.: U.S. Government Printing Office, 1993). http://www.wws .princeton.edu/~ota/ns20/topic_f.html. Accessed December 10, 2003.

Y

Yellow Rain

A large number of toxic fungal by-products (i.e., mycotoxins) have been implicated in adverse health effects in humans and domestic animals. Fungal growth on hay, rice, wheat and other cereal grains, cotton, and other agricultural products has been demonstrated to produce significant concentrations of mycotoxins. Of the many mycotoxins known to cause tissue damage in animals, the trichothecene family—produced in the *Fusarium* species of fungus—contains several toxic compounds, among which the T-2 mycotoxin is particularly harmful to humans and domestic livestock.

The term *yellow rain* referred to a family of chemically related toxins purportedly making up the active ingredient in a biological toxin weapon. These fungal toxins (mycotoxins) were allegedly weaponized by the Soviet Union and were reportedly used in Cold War conflicts such as those in Afghanistan, Laos, Cambodia, and possibly Vietnam. The material, yellow in color, was purportedly dispersed in droplet or aerosol form from aircraft, hence the term *yellow rain*.

Technical Details

Trichothecenes effectively inhibit protein synthesis in a large number of cell types and are particularly toxigenic (poisonous) in rapidly proliferating host tissues. Trichothecenes, in particular T-2, are biologically active upon the skin, oral ingestion, or inhalation. This is unique among known biological agents, and thus T-2 is a serious candidate for weaponization and employment in an unconventional setting.

Yellow Rain Allegations

Rumors of the use of mycotoxins by the Soviets had circulated in the international community since the early 1970s, and Alexander Haig, the U.S. secretary of state, made an emphatic allegation of Soviet use of yellow rain at a press conference in Berlin in September 1981. In March of the following year, Secretary Haig issued a written report formally accusing the Soviet Union and its client states of using mycotoxins against human targets in Southeast Asia and in Afghanistan.

The United States maintained its claims that from 1974 to 1981, the Soviets (or Soviet client states) used yellow rain in Southeast Asia and Afghanistan. Evidence compiled by U.S. intelligence analysts cited epidemiological support for intelligence estimates of the biological warfare use of trichothecenes. Specific among these allegations were a series of attacks against Hmong villagers in the Laotian highlands in 1975–1981 and Khmer Rouge troops in North Vietnam and Laos (1979–1981). Follow-on scientific investigations, however, failed to provide unequivocal proof that trichothecenes were employed as biological warfare agents by the Soviets or the Laotian military.

Despite the apparent lack of a smoking gun, considerable circumstantial and empirical findings strongly supported the allegations of use. The United States and its allies, for example, recovered and identified trichothecenes from both human and environmental specimens.

In 1983, the Central Intelligence Agency (CIA) issued a "Special National Intelligence Estimate" (SNIE) that provided background to the yellow rain allegations, insisting that the charges of toxin warfare against the Soviet Union (and its clients) had merit.

Yellow Rain from Natural Causes

Since the original yellow rain allegations were made, the passage of time, questionable investigation practices, disingenuous political influence—and a general disintegration of the military threat once posed by the Soviet Union—have made the original charges questionable at best. In retrospect, the yellow rain incidents were more likely due to naturally occurring fusarium in the environment and which is commonly found in Southeast Asia. This, in concert with other natural phenomena—such as clouds of orange-tinged bee feces (during "cleansing flights" from their hives)—combined to create what appeared to be biological toxin warfare.

J. Russ Forney and Eric A. Croddy

Further Reading

Meselson, Matthew, and Julian Perry Robinson, "The Yellow Rain Affair: Lessons from a Discredited Allegation," in *Terrorism, War, or Disease?: Unraveling the Use of Biological Weapons*, edited by Anne L. Clunan, Peter R. Lavoy, and Susan B. Martin (Stanford, CA: Stanford University Press, 2008), 72–96.

Tucker, Jonathan B., "The 'Yellow Rain' Controversy: Lessons for Arms Control Compliance," *Nonproliferation Review* 8, no. 1 (Spring 2001): 25–42.

U.S. Department of State, *Chemical Warfare in Southeast Asia and Afghanistan: Report to the Congress from Secretary of State Alexander M. Haig, Jr.*, Special Report No. 98, March 22, 1982.

U.S. Director of Central Intelligence, *Implications of Soviet Use of Chemical and Toxin Weapons for US Security Interests*, Special National Intelligence Estimate, SNIE-11-17-83, September 15, 1983.

Yield

Yield refers to the energy released in a nuclear detonation. Although this energy takes the form of blast, thermal and nuclear radiation, and electromagnetic pulse, yield usually refers only to the blast produced by a weapon. It is commonly expressed in terms of kilotons (thousands of tons) or megatons (millions of tons) of the equivalent quantity of trinitrotoluene (TNT) required to produce the same amount of energy.

The highest-yield device tested by the United States was approximately 15 megatons. The former Soviet Union tested a device that produced a yield in excess of 50 megatons.

Albert Einstein's mass-energy equivalence equation ($E = mc^2$) implies that mass can be converted into energy. The energy released in the mass conversion in fission and fusion is thousands to millions of times greater than that released in a chemical process. The yield of a weapon is determined by the amount of nuclear fuel available and its efficiency, that is, how much of the available fuel actually undergoes fission or fusion. A higher yield generally produces greater destructive effects.

Don Gillich

Further Reading

Glasstone, Samuel, and Philip J. Dolan, eds., *The Effects of Nuclear Weapons* (Washington, D.C.: U.S. Government Printing Office, 1977).

Primary Documents: Chemical and Biological Weapons

Biological and Toxin Weapons Convention (1972)

Convention on the Prohibition of the Development, Production and Stockpiling of Bacteriological (Biological) and Toxin Weapons and on their Destruction

The States Parties to this Convention,

Determined to act with a view to achieving effective progress towards general and complete disarmament, including the prohibition and elimination of all types of weapons of mass destruction, and convinced that the prohibition of the development, production and stockpiling of chemical and bacteriological (biological) weapons and their elimination, through effective measures, will facilitate the achievement of general and complete disarmament under strict and effective international control,

Recognising the important significance of the Protocol for the Prohibition of the Use in War of Asphyxiating, Poisonous or Other Gases, and of Bacteriological Methods of Warfare, signed at Geneva on 17 June 1925, and conscious also of the contribution which the said Protocol has already made and continues to make, to mitigating the horrors of war,

Reaffirming their adherence to the principles and objectives of that Protocol and calling upon all States to comply strictly with them,

Recalling that the General Assembly of the United Nations has repeatedly condemned all actions contrary to the principles and objectives of the Geneva Protocol of 17 June 1925,

Desiring to contribute to the strengthening of confidence between peoples and the general improvement of the international atmosphere,

Desiring also to contribute to the realization of the purposes and principles of the Charter of the United Nations,

Convinced of the importance and urgency of eliminating from the arsenals of States, through effective measures, such dangerous weapons of mass destruction as those using chemical or bacteriological (biological) agents,

Recognizing that an agreement on the prohibition of bacteriological (biological) and toxin weapons represents a first possible step towards the achievement of agreement on effective measures also for the prohibition of the development, production and stockpiling of chemical weapons, and determined to continue negotiations to that end,

Determined, for the sake of all mankind, to exclude completely the possibility of bacteriological (biological) agents and toxins being used as weapons,

Convinced that such use would be repugnant to the conscience of mankind and that no effort should be spared to minimize this risk,

Have agreed as follows:

Article I

Each State Party to this Convention undertakes never in any circumstances to develop, produce, stockpile or otherwise acquire or retain:

(1) microbial or other biological agents, or toxins whatever their origin or method of production, of types and in quantities that have no justification for prophylactic, protective or other peaceful purposes;

(2) weapons, equipment or means of delivery designed to use such agents or toxins for hostile purposes or in armed conflict.

Article II

Each State Party to this Convention undertakes to destroy, or to divert to peaceful purposes, as soon as possible but not later than nine months after the entry into force of the Convention, all agents, toxins, weapons, equipment and means of delivery specified in Article I of the Convention, which are in its possession or under its jurisdiction or control. In implementing the provisions of this Article all necessary safety precautions shall be observed to protect populations and the environment.

Article III

Each State Party to this Convention undertakes not to transfer to any recipient whatsoever, directly or indirectly, and not in any way to assist, encourage, or induce any State, group of States or international organizations to manufacture or otherwise acquire any of the agents, toxins, weapons, equipment or means of delivery specified in Article I of the Convention.

Article IV

Each State Party to this Convention shall, in accordance with its constitutional processes, take any necessary measures to prohibit and prevent the development, production, stockpiling, acquisition or retention of the agents, toxins, weapons, equipment and means of delivery specified in Article I of the Convention, within the territory of such State, under its jurisdiction or under its control anywhere.

Article V

The States Parties to this Convention undertake to consult one another and to co-operate in solving any problems which may arise in relation to the objective of, or in the application of the provisions of, the Convention. Consultation and co-operation pursuant to this Article may also be undertaken through appropriate international procedures within the framework of the United Nations and in accordance with its Charter.

Article VI

(1) Any State Party to this Convention which finds that any other State Party is acting in breach of obligations deriving from the provisions of the Convention may lodge a complaint with the Security Council of the United Nations. Such a complaint should include all possible evidence confirming its validity, as well as a request for its consideration by the Security Council.

(2) Each State Party to this Convention undertakes to co-operate in carrying out any investigation which the Security Council may initiate, in accordance

with the provisions of the Charter of the United Nations, on the basis of the complaint received by the Council. The Security Council shall inform the States Parties to the Convention of the results of the investigation.

Article VII

Each State Party to this Convention undertakes to provide or support assistance, in accordance with the United Nations Charter, to any Party to the Convention which so requests, if the Security Council decides that such Party has been exposed to danger as a result of violation of the Convention.

Article VIII

Nothing in this Convention shall be interpreted as in any way limiting or detracting from the obligations assumed by any State under the Protocol for the Prohibition of the Use in War of Asphyxiating, Poisonous or Other Gases, and of Bacteriological Methods of Warfare, signed at Geneva on 17 June 1925.

Article IX

Each State Party to this Convention affirms the recognised objective of effective prohibition of chemical weapons and, to this end, undertakes to continue negotiations in good faith with a view to reaching early agreement on effective measures for the prohibition of their development, production and stockpiling and for their destruction, and on appropriate measures concerning equipment and means of delivery specifically designed for the production or use of chemical agents for weapons purposes.

Article X

(1) The States Parties to this Convention undertake to facilitate, and have the right to participate in, the fullest possible exchange of equipment, materials and scientific and technological information for the use of bacteriological (biological) agents and toxins for peaceful purposes. Parties to the Convention in a position to do so shall also co-operate in contributing individually or together with other States or international organisations to the further development and application of scientific discoveries in the field of bacteriology (biology) for the prevention of disease, or for other peaceful purposes.

(2) This Convention shall be implemented in a manner designed to avoid hampering the economic or technological development of States Parties to the Convention or international co-operation in the field of peaceful bacteriological (biological) activities, including the international exchange of bacteriological (biological) agents and toxins and equipment for the processing, use or production of bacteriological (biological) agents and toxins for peaceful purposes in accordance with the provisions of the Convention.

. . .

Article XIII

(1) This Convention shall be of unlimited duration.

(2) Each State Party to this Convention shall in exercising its national sovereignty have the right to withdraw from the Convention if it decides that extraordinary events, related to the subject matter of the Convention, have jeopardised the supreme interests of its country. It shall give notice of such withdrawal to all other States Parties to the Convention and to the United Nations Security Council three months

in advance. Such notice shall include a statement of the extraordinary events it regards as having jeopardised its supreme interests.

Source: United Nations Office for Disarmament Affairs. Opened for signature April 10, 1972. Entered into force March 26, 1975. Available online at http://disarmament.un.org/treaties/t/bwc/text. Accessed April 30, 2018.

Chemical Weapons Convention (1993)

ARTICLE I

GENERAL OBLIGATIONS

1. Each State Party to this Convention undertakes never under any circumstances:
   (a) To develop, produce, otherwise acquire, stockpile or retain chemical weapons, or transfer, directly or indirectly, chemical weapons to anyone;
   (b) To use chemical weapons;
   (c) To engage in any military preparations to use chemical weapons;
   (d) To assist, encourage or induce, in any way, anyone to engage in any activity prohibited to a State Party under this Convention.
2. Each State Party undertakes to destroy chemical weapons it owns or possesses, or that are located in any place under its jurisdiction or control, in accordance with the provisions of this Convention.
3. Each State Party undertakes to destroy all chemical weapons it abandoned on the territory of another State Party, in accordance with the provisions of this Convention.
4. Each State Party undertakes to destroy any chemical weapons production facilities it owns or possesses, or that are located in any place under its jurisdiction or control, in accordance with the provisions of this Convention.
5. Each State Party undertakes not to use riot control agents as a method of warfare.

Source: Organisation for the Prohibition of Chemical Weapons. Opened for signature January 13, 1993. Entered into force April 29, 1997. Available online at https://www.opcw.org/chemical-weapons-convention. Used by permission of OPCW. Accessed April 30, 2018.

Australia Group

The Australia Group is an informal arrangement which aims to allow exporting or transshipping countries to minimize the risk of assisting chemical and biological weapon (CBW) proliferation. The Group meets annually to discuss ways of increasing the effectiveness of participating countries' national export licensing measures to prevent would-be proliferators from obtaining materials for CBW programs.

Participants in the Australia Group do not undertake any legally binding obligations: the effectiveness of their cooperation depends solely on a shared commitment to CBW non-proliferation goals and the strength of their respective national measures. Key considerations in the formulation of participants' export licensing measures are:

- *they should be effective in impeding the production of chemical and biological weapons;*
- *they should be practical, and reasonably easy to implement, and*
- *they should not impede the normal trade of materials and equipment used for legitimate purposes.*

All states participating in the Australia Group are parties to the Chemical Weapons Convention (CWC) and the Biological Weapons Convention (BWC), and strongly support efforts under those Conventions to rid the world of CBW.

List of Plant Pathogens for Export Control (2012)

Core List

Bacteria

1. Xanthomonas albilineans
2. Xanthomonas axonopodis pv. citri (Xanthomonas campestris pv. citri A) [Xanthomonas campestris pv. citri]
3. Xanthomonas oryzae pv. oryzae (Pseudomonas campestris pv. oryzae)
4. Clavibacter michiganensis subsp. sepedonicus (Corynebacterium michiganensis subsp. sepedonicum or Corynebacterium sepedonicum)
5. Ralstonia solanacearum, race 3, biovar 2

Fungi

1. Colletotrichum kahawae (Colletotrichum coffeanum var. virulans)
2. Cochliobolus miyabeanus (Helminthosporium oryzae)
3. Microcyclus ulei (syn. Dothidella ulei)
4. Puccinia graminis ssp. graminis var. graminis / Puccinia graminis ssp. graminis var. stakmanii (Puccinia graminis [syn. Puccinia graminis f. sp. tritici])
5. Puccinia striiformis (syn. Puccinia glumarum)
6. Magnaporthe oryzae (Pyricularia oryzae)
7. Peronosclerospora philippinensis (Peronosclerospora sacchari)
8. Sclerophthora rayssiae var. zeae
9. Synchytrium endobioticum
10. Tilletia indica
11. Thecaphora solani

Viruses

1. Andean potato latent virus (Potato Andean latent tymovirus)
2. Potato spindle tuber viroid

Genetic Elements and Genetically-modified Organisms:

1. Genetic elements that contain nucleic acid sequences associated with the pathogenicity of any of the microorganisms in the Core List.
2. Genetically-modified organisms that contain nucleic acid sequences associated with the pathogenicity of any of the microorganisms in the Core List.

Technical note: Genetically-modified organisms includes organisms in which the genetic material (nucleic acid sequences) has been altered in a way that does not occur naturally by mating and/or natural recombination, and encompasses those produced artificially in whole or in part.

Genetic elements include inter alia chromosomes, genomes, plasmids, transposons, and vectors whether genetically modified or unmodified, or chemically synthesized in whole or in part.

Nucleic acid sequences associated with the pathogenicity of any of the microorganisms in the list means any sequence specific to the relevant listed microorganism:

- that in itself or through its transcribed or translated products represents a significant hazard to human, animal or plant health; or
- that is known to enhance the ability of a listed micro-organism, or any other organism into which it may be inserted

or otherwise integrated, to cause serious harm to human, animal or plant health.

Items for Inclusion in Awareness-raising Guidelines

Bacteria
1. Xylella fastidiosa

Fungi
1. Phoma tracheiphila (Deuterophoma tracheiphila)
2. Moniliophthora roreri (Monilia roreri)

Viruses
1. Banana bunchy top virus

Genetic Elements and Genetically-modified Organisms:
1. Genetic elements that contain nucleic acid sequences associated with the pathogenicity of any of the microorganisms in the Awareness-raising Guidelines.
2. Genetically-modified organisms that contain nucleic acid sequences associated with the pathogenicity of any of the microorganisms in the Awareness-raising Guidelines.

Technical note: Genetically-modified organisms includes organisms in which the genetic material (nucleic acid sequences) has been altered in a way that does not occur naturally by mating and/or natural recombination, and encompasses those produced artificially in whole or in part.

Genetic elements include inter alia chromosomes, genomes, plasmids, transposons, and vectors whether genetically modified or unmodified, or chemically synthesized in whole or in part.

Nucleic acid sequences associated with the pathogenicity of any of the micro-organisms in the list means any sequence specific to the relevant listed micro-organism:

- that in itself or through its transcribed or translated products represents a significant hazard to human, animal or plant health; or
- that is known to enhance the ability of a listed micro-organism, or any other organism into which it may be inserted or otherwise integrated, to cause serious harm to human, animal or plant health.

Source: The Australia Group, June 2012. Available online at http://www.australiagroup.net/en/plants.html. Accessed April 30, 2018.

Control List of Dual-Use Biological Equipment and Related Technology and Software (2017)

I. Equipment
  1. Containment facilities and related equipment as follows:
     a. Complete containment facilities that meet the criteria for P3 or P4 (BL3, BL4, L3, L4) containment as specified in the WHO Laboratory Biosafety Manual (3rd edition, Geneva, 2004)
     b. Equipment designed for fixed installation in containment facilities specified in a., as follows:
        i. Double-door pass-through decontamination autoclaves;
        ii. Breathing air suit decontamination showers;
        iii. Mechanical-seal or inflatable-seal walkthrough doors.

2. Fermenters

Fermenters capable of cultivation of micro-organisms or of live cells for the production of viruses or toxins, without the propagation of aerosols, having a total internal volume of 20 litres or greater.

Components designed for such fermenters, as follows:

a. cultivation chambers designed to be sterilized or disinfected in situ;

b. cultivation chamber holding devices; or

c. process control units capable of simultaneously monitoring and controlling two or more fermentation system parameters (e.g. temperature, pH, nutrients, agitation, dissolved oxygen, air flow, foam control).

Fermenters include bioreactors (including single-use (disposable) bioreactors), chemostats and continuous-flow systems.

3. Centrifugal Separators

Centrifugal separators capable of the continuous separation of pathogenic micro-organisms, without the propagation of aerosols, and having all the following characteristics:

a. one or more sealing joints within the steam containment area;

b. a flow rate greater than 100 litres per hour;

c. components of polished stainless steel or titanium;

d. capable of in-situ steam sterilisation in a closed state.

Technical note: Centrifugal separators include decanters.

4. Cross (tangential) Flow Filtration Equipment

Cross (tangential) flow filtration equipment capable of separation of micro-organisms, viruses, toxins or cell cultures having all the following characteristics:

a. a total filtration area equal to or greater than 1 square metre; and

b. having any of the following characteristics:

i. capable of being sterilized or disinfected in-situ; or

ii. using disposable or single-use filtration components.

(Note – This control excludes reverse osmosis and hemodialysis equipment, as specified by the manufacturer.)

5. Freeze-drying Equipment

Steam, gas or vapour sterilisable freeze-drying equipment with a condenser capacity of 10 kg of ice or greater in 24 hours and less than 1000 kg of ice in 24 hours.

6. Spray-drying Equipment

Spray drying equipment capable of drying toxins or pathogenic micro-organisms having all of the following characteristics:

i. a water evaporation capacity of ≥ 0.4 kg/h and ≤ 400 kg/h

ii. the ability to generate a typical mean product particle size of ≤ 10 micrometers with existing fittings or by minimal modification of the spray-dryer with atomization nozzles enabling generation of the required particle size; and

iii. capable of being sterilized or disinfected in situ.

7. Protective and containment equipment as follows:

    a. protective full or half suits, or hoods dependent upon a tethered external air supply and operating under positive pressure;

    Technical note: This does not control suits designed to be worn with self-contained breathing apparatus.

    b. biocontainment chambers, isolators, or biological safety cabinets having all of the following characteristics, for normal operation:

      ii. fully enclosed workspace where the operator is separated from the work by a physical barrier;

      iii. able to operate at negative pressure;

      iv. means to safely manipulate items in the workspace;

      v. supply and exhaust air to and from the workspace is HEPA filtered.

    Note 1 – this control includes class III biosafety cabinets, as described in the latest edition of the WHO Laboratory Biosafety Manual or constructed in accordance with national standards, regulations or guidance.

    Note 2 – this control does not include isolators specially designed for barrier nursing or transportation of infected patients.

8. Aerosol inhalation equipment

    Aerosol inhalation equipment designed for aerosol challenge testing with micro-organisms, viruses or toxins as follows:

    a. Whole-body exposure chambers having a capacity of 1 cubic metre or greater.

    b. Nose-only exposure apparatus utilising directed aerosol flow and having capacity for exposure of 12 or more rodents, or 2 or more animals other than rodents; and, closed animal restraint tubes designed for use with such apparatus.

9. Spraying or fogging systems and components therefor, as follows:

    a. Complete spraying or fogging systems, specially designed or modified for fitting to aircraft, lighter than air vehicles or UAVs, capable of delivering, from a liquid suspension, an initial droplet "VMD" of less than 50 microns at a flow rate of greater than two litres per minute.

    b. Spray booms or arrays of aerosol generating units, specially designed or modified for fitting to aircraft, lighter than air vehicles or UAVs, capable of delivering, from a liquid suspension, an initial droplet "VMD" of less than 50 microns at a flow rate of greater than two litres per minute.

    c. Aerosol generating units specially designed for fitting to systems that fulfil all the criteria specified in paragraphs 9.a and 9.b.

Technical Notes

Aerosol generating units are devices specially designed or modified for fitting to aircraft such as nozzles, rotary drum atomisers and similar devices.

This entry does not control spraying or fogging systems and components as specified in paragraph 8 above that are demonstrated not to be capable of delivering biological agents in the form of infectious aerosols.

Pending definition of international standards, the following guidelines should be followed:

Droplet size for spray equipment or nozzles specially designed for use on aircraft or UAVs should be measured using either of the following methods:

a. Doppler laser method
b. Forward laser diffraction method

10. Nucleic acid assemblers and synthesizers

Nucleic acid assemblers and synthesizers, which are partly or entirely automated, and designed to generate continuous nucleic acids greater than 1.5 kilobases in length with error rates less than 5% in a single run.

Items for inclusion in Awareness Raising Guidelines

Experts propose that the following items be included in awareness raising guidelines to industry:

1. Equipment and technology (not specified elsewhere in the control list of Dual-use Biological Equipment and Related Technology and Software) for the encapsulation of live pathogenic micro-organisms, viruses and toxins, with a typical mean product particle size of 10 μm or less.

2. Fermenters of less than 20 litre capacity with special emphasis on aggregate orders or designs for use in combined systems.

3. Conventional or turbulent air-flow clean-air rooms and self-contained fan-HEPA filter units that may be used for P3 or P4 (BL3, BL4, L3, L4) containment facilities.

II. Related Technology

Technology, including licenses, directly associated with:

• AG-controlled pathogens and toxins; or
• AG-controlled dual-use biological equipment items

to the extent permitted by national legislation.

This includes

a. transfer of 'technology' ('technical data') by any means, including electronic media, fax or telephone;
b. transfer of 'technology' in the form of 'technical assistance'.

Controls on 'technology' do not apply to information 'in the public domain' or to 'basic scientific research' or the minimum necessary information for patent application.

The approval for export of any AG-controlled item of dual-use equipment also authorises the export to the same end-user of the minimum 'technology' required for the installation, operation, maintenance, or repair of that item.

III. Software

Controls on 'software' transfer only apply where specifically indicated in sections I and II above, and do not apply to 'software' which is either:

1. Generally available to the public by being:
   a. Sold from stock at retail selling points without restriction, by means of:
      i. Over-the-counter transactions;
      ii. Mail order transactions;
      iii. Electronic transactions; or
      iv. Telephone call transactions; and
   b. Designed for installation by the user without further substantial support by the supplier; or
2. 'In the public domain'.

Definition of Terms

'Basic scientific research'
Experimental or theoretical work undertaken principally to acquire new knowledge of the fundamental principles of phenomena or observable facts, not primarily directed towards a specific practical aim or objective.

'Development'
'Development' is related to all stages before 'production' such as: design, design research, design analysis, design concepts, assembly of prototypes, pilot production schemes, design data, process or transforming design data into a product, configuration design, integration design, and layouts.

'Export'
An actual shipment or transmission of AG-controlled items out of the country. This includes transmission of 'technology' by electronic media, fax or telephone.

'In the public domain'
'In the public domain', as it applies herein, means 'technology' or 'software' that has been made available without restrictions upon its further dissemination. (Copyright restrictions do not remove 'technology' or 'software' from being in the public domain.)

'Lighter than air vehicles'
Balloons and airships that rely on hot air or on lighter-than-air gases such as helium or hydrogen for their lift.

'Microprogram'
A sequence of elementary instructions maintained in a special storage, the execution of which is initiated by the introduction of its reference instruction into an instruction register.

'Production'
'Production' means all production phases such as: construction, production engineering, manufacture, integration, assembly (mounting), inspection, testing, and quality assurance.

'Program'
A sequence of instructions to carry out a process in, or convertible into, a form executable by an electronic computer.

'Software'
A collection of one or more 'programs' or 'microprograms' fixed in any tangible medium of expression.

'Technical assistance'
May take forms, such as: instruction, skills, training, working knowledge, consulting services. 'Technical assistance' includes oral forms of assistance. 'Technical assistance' may involve transfer of 'technical data'.

'Technical data'
May take forms such as blueprints, plans, diagrams, models, formulae, tables,

engineering designs and specifications, manuals and instructions written or recorded on other media or devices such as disk, tape, read-only memories.

'Technology'
Specific information necessary for the 'development', 'production', or 'use' of a product. The information takes the form of 'technical data' or 'technical assistance'.

'UAVs'
Unmanned Aerial Vehicles.

'Use'
Operation, installation, (including on-site installation), maintenance, (checking), repair, overhaul or refurbishing.

'VMD'
Volume Median Diameter *(note: for water-based systems, VMD equates to MMD – the Mass Median Diameter)*.

Source: The Australia Group, May 2017. Available online at http://www.australiagroup.net/en/dual_biological.html. Accessed April 30, 2018.

Control List of Dual-Use Chemical Manufacturing Facilities and Equipment and Related Technology and Software (2017)

I. Manufacturing Facilities and Equipment
   Note 1. The objective of these controls should not be defeated by the transfer of any non-controlled item containing one or more controlled components where the controlled component or components are the principal element of the item and can feasibly be removed or used for other purposes.
   N.B. In judging whether the controlled component or components are to

be considered the principal element, governments should weigh the factors of quantity, value, and technological know-how involved and other special circumstances which might establish the controlled component or components as the principal element of the item being procured.
   Note 2. The objective of these controls should not be defeated by the transfer of a whole plant, on any scale, which has been designed to produce any CW agent or AG-controlled precursor chemical.
   Note 3. The materials used for gaskets, packing, seals, screws, washers or other materials performing a sealing function do not determine the status of control of the items listed below, provided that such components are designed to be interchangeable.

1. Reaction Vessels, Reactors or Agitators
   Reaction vessels or reactors, with or without agitators, with total internal (geometric) volume greater than 0.1 m³ (100 l) and less than 20 m³ (20000 l), where all surfaces that come in direct contact with the chemical(s) being processed or contained are made from the following materials:
   a) nickel or alloys with more than 40% nickel by weight;
   b) alloys with more than 25% nickel and 20% chromium by weight;
   c) fluoropolymers (polymeric or elastomeric materials with more than 35% fluorine by weight);
   d) glass or glass-lined (including vitrified or enamelled coating);
   e) tantalum or tantalum alloys;

f)   titanium or titanium alloys;

g)   zirconium or zirconium alloys; or

h)   niobium (columbium) or niobium alloys.

Agitators designed for use in the above-mentioned reaction vessels or reactors; and impellers, blades or shafts designed for such agitators where all surfaces of the agitator that come in direct contact with the chemical(s) being processed or contained are made from any of the following materials:

a)   nickel or alloys with more than 40% nickel by weight;

b)   alloys with more than 25% nickel and 20% chromium by weight;

c)   fluoropolymers (polymeric or elastomeric materials with more than 35% fluorine by weight);

d)   glass or glass-lined (including vitrified or enamelled coating);

e)   tantalum or tantalum alloys;

f)   titanium or titanium alloys;

g)   zirconium or zirconium alloys; or

h)   niobium (columbium) or niobium alloys.

Prefabricated repair assemblies and their specially designed components, that:

i)   are designed for mechanical attachment to glass-lined reaction vessels or reactors that meet the parameters above; and,

ii) have metallic surfaces that come in direct contact with the chemical(s) being processed which are made from tantalum or tantalum alloys.

2.   Storage Tanks, Containers or Receivers

Storage tanks, containers or receivers with a total internal (geometric) volume greater than 0.1 m³ (100 l) where all surfaces that come in direct contact with the chemical(s) being processed or contained are made from the following materials:

a)   nickel or alloys with more than 40% nickel by weight;

b)   alloys with more than 25% nickel and 20% chromium by weight;

c)   fluoropolymers (polymeric or elastomeric materials with more than 35% fluorine by weight);

d)   glass or glass-lined (including vitrified or enamelled coating);

e)   tantalum or tantalum alloys;

f)   titanium or titanium alloys;

g)   zirconium or zirconium alloys; or

h)   niobium (columbium) or niobium alloys.

Prefabricated repair assemblies and their specially designed components, that:

i)   are designed for mechanical attachment to glass-lined reaction vessels or reactors that meet the parameters above; and,

ii) have metallic surfaces that come in direct contact with the chemical(s) being processed which are made from tantalum or tantalum alloys.

3.   Heat Exchangers or Condensers

Heat exchangers or condensers with a heat transfer surface area of greater than 0.15 m², and less than

20 m²; and tubes, plates, coils or blocks (cores) designed for such heat exchangers or condensers, where all surfaces that come in direct contact with the chemical(s) being processed are made from the following materials:

a) nickel or alloys with more than 40% nickel by weight;

b) alloys with more than 25% nickel and 20% chromium by weight;

c) fluoropolymers (polymeric or elastomeric materials with more than 35% fluorine by weight);

d) glass or glass-lined (including vitrified or enamelled coating);

e) graphite or carbon-graphite;

f) tantalum or tantalum alloys;

g) titanium or titanium alloys;

h) zirconium or zirconium alloys;

i) silicon carbide;

j) titanium carbide; or

k) niobium (columbium) or niobium alloys.

4. Distillation or Absorption Columns
Distillation or absorption columns of internal diameter greater than 0.1 m; and liquid distributors, vapour distributors or liquid collectors designed for such distillation or absorption columns, where all surfaces that come in direct contact with the chemical(s) being processed are made from the following materials:

a) nickel or alloys with more than 40% nickel by weight;

b) alloys with more than 25% nickel and 20% chromium by weight;

c) fluoropolymers (polymeric or elastomeric materials with more than 35% fluorine by weight);

d) glass or glass-lined (including vitrified or enamelled coating);

e) graphite or carbon-graphite;

f) tantalum or tantalum alloys;

g) titanium or titanium alloys;

h) zirconium or zirconium alloys; or

i) niobium (columbium) or niobium alloys.

5. Filling Equipment
Remotely operated filling equipment in which all surfaces that come in direct contact with the chemical(s) being processed are made from the following materials:

a) nickel or alloys with more than 40% nickel by weight; or

b) alloys with more than 25% nickel and 20% chromium by weight.

6. Valves

a) Valves, having both of the following:

i) A nominal size greater than 1.0 cm (3/8"), and

ii) All surfaces that come in direct contact with the chemical(s) being produced, processed, or contained are made from the materials of construction in Technical Note 1 of this entry

b) Valves, not already identified in paragraph 6.a., having all of the following:

i) A nominal size equal to or greater than 2.54 cm (1") and equal to or less than 10.16 cm (4")

ii) Casings (valve bodies) or preformed casing liners,

iii) A closure element designed to be interchangeable, and

iv) All surfaces of the casing (valve body) or preformed case liner that come in direct contact with the chemical(s) being produced, processed, or contained are made from the materials of construction in Technical Note 1 of this entry

c) Components, as follows:

i) Casings (valve bodies) designed for valves in paragraphs 6.a. or 6.b., in which all surfaces that come in direct contact with the chemical(s) being produced, processed, or contained are made from the materials of construction in Technical Note 1 of this entry;

ii) Preformed casing liners designed for valves in paragraphs 6.a. or 6.b., in which all surfaces that come in direct contact with the chemical(s) being produced, processed, or contained are made from the materials of construction in Technical Note 1 of this entry.

. . .

7. Incinerators

Incinerators designed to destroy CW agents, AG-controlled precursors or chemical munitions, having specially designed waste supply systems, special handling facilities, and an average combustion chamber temperature greater than 1000°C, in which all surfaces in the waste supply system that come into direct contact with the waste products are made from or lined with the following materials:

a) nickel or alloys with more than 40% nickel by weight;

b) alloys with more than 25% nickel and 20% chromium by weight; or

c) ceramics.

Statement of Understanding

These controls do not apply to equipment which is specially designed for use in civil applications (for example food processing, pulp and paper processing, or water purification, etc.) and is, by the nature of its design, inappropriate for use in storing, processing, producing or conducting and controlling the flow of chemical warfare agents or any of the AG-controlled precursor chemicals.

II. Toxic Gas Monitors and Monitoring Systems, and their Dedicated Detecting Components

Toxic gas monitors and monitoring systems, and their dedicated detecting components as follows: detectors; sensor devices; replaceable sensor cartridges; and dedicated software for such equipment;

a) designed for continuous operation and usable for the detection of chemical warfare agents or AG-controlled precursors at concentrations of less than 0.3 mg/m³; or

b) designed for the detection of cholinesterase-inhibiting activity.

III. Related Technology

'Technology', including licenses, directly associated with -

- CW agents;

- AG-controlled precursors; or
- AG-controlled dual-use equipment items,

to the extent permitted by national legislation.

This includes:

- transfer of 'technology' ('technical data') by any means, including electronic media, fax or telephone;
- transfer of 'technology' in the form of 'technical assistance'.

Controls on 'technology' do not apply to information 'in the public domain' or to 'basic scientific research' or the minimum necessary information for patent application.

The approval for export of any AG-controlled item of dual-use equipment also authorises the export to the same end-user of the minimum 'technology' required for the installation, operation, maintenance or repair of that item.

IV. Software

Controls on 'software' transfer only apply where specifically indicated in sections I and II above, and do not apply to 'software' which is either:

1) Generally available to the public by being:
   (a) Sold from stock at retail selling points without restriction, by means of:
      ii) Over-the-counter transactions;
      iii) Mail order transactions;
      iv) Electronic transactions; or
      v) Telephone call transactions; and
   (b) Designed for installation by the user without further substantial support by the supplier; or
2) 'In the public domain'.

Definition of Terms

'Basic scientific research'

Experimental or theoretical work undertaken principally to acquire new knowledge of the fundamental principles of phenomena or observable facts, not primarily directed towards a specific practical aim or objective.

'Development'

'Development' is related to all phases before 'production' such as: Design, design research, design analysis, design concepts, assembly of prototypes, pilot production schemes, design data, process or transforming design data into a product, configuration design, integration design, and layouts.

'Export'

An actual shipment or transmission of AG-controlled items out of the country. This includes transmission of 'technology' by electronic media, fax or telephone.

'in the public domain'

'In the public domain', as it applies herein, means 'technology' or 'software' that has been made available without restrictions upon its further dissemination. (Copyright restrictions do not remove 'technology' or 'software' from being in the 'public domain').

'Microprogramme'

A sequence of elementary instructions maintained in a special storage, the execution of which is initiated by the introduction of its reference instruction register.

'Production'

'Production' means all production phases such as:

Construction, production engineering, manufacture, integration, assembly (mounting), inspection, testing, and quality assurance.

'Programme'

A sequence of instructions to carry out a process in, or convertible into, a form executable by an electronic computer.

'Software'

A collection of one or more 'programmes' or 'microprogrammes' fixed in any tangible medium of expression.

'Technology'

Specific information necessary for the 'development', 'production' or 'use' of a product. The information takes the form of 'technical data' or 'technical assistance'.

'Technical assistance'

May take forms, such as: instruction, skills, training, working knowledge, consulting services. 'Technical assistance' includes oral forms of assistance. 'Technical assistance' may involve transfer of 'technical data'.

'Technical data'

May take forms such as blueprints, plans, diagrams, models, formulae, tables, engineering designs and specifications, manuals and instructions written or recorded on other media or devices such as disk, tape, read-only memories.

'Use'

Operation, installation (including on-site installation), maintenance (checking), repair, overhaul or refurbishing.

Source: The Australia Group, May 2017. Available online at http://www.australiagroup.net/en/dual_chemicals.html. Accessed April 30, 2018.

Export Control List: Chemical Weapons Precursors (2017)

Precursor Chemical	CAS No.	CWC-Schedule
Thiodiglycol	(111-48-8)	2B
Phosphorus oxychloride	(10025-87-3)	3B
Dimethyl methylphosphonate	(756-79-6)	2B
Methylphosphonyl difluoride (DF)	(676-99-3)	1B
Methylphosphonyl dichloride (DC)	(676-97-1)	2B
Dimethyl phosphite (DMP)	(868-85-9)	3B
Phosphorus trichloride	(7719-12-2)	3B
Trimethyl phosphite (TMP)	(121-45-9)	3B
Thionyl chloride	(7719-09-7)	3B
3-Hydroxy-1-methylpiperidine	(3554-74-3)	Not Listed
N,N-Diisopropyl-(beta)-aminoethyl chloride	(96-79-7)	2B
N,N-Diisopropyl-(beta)-aminoethane thiol	(5842-07-9)	2B
3-Quinuclidinol	(1619-34-7)	2B
Potassium fluoride	(7789-23-3)	Not Listed
2-Chloroethanol	(107-07-3)	Not Listed
Dimethylamine	(124-40-3)	Not Listed
Diethyl ethylphosphonate	(78-38-6)	2B
Diethyl N,N-dimethylphosphoramidate	(2404-03-7)	2B
Diethyl phosphite	(762-04-9)	3B
Dimethylamine hydrochloride	(506-59-2)	Not Listed
Ethylphosphinyl dichloride	(1498-40-4)	2B
Ethylphosphonyl dichloride	(1066-50-8)	2B
Ethylphosphonyl difluoride	(753-98-0)	1B
Hydrogen fluoride	(7664-39-3)	Not Listed
Methyl benzilate	(76-89-1)	Not Listed
Methylphosphinyl dichloride	(676-83-5)	2B
N,N-Diisopropyl-(beta)-amino-ethanol	(96-80-0)	2B
Pinacolyl alcohol	(464-07-3)	2B
O-Ethyl O-2-diisopropylaminoethyl methylphosphonite (QL)	(57856-11-8)	1B
Triethyl phosphite	(122-52-1)	3B
Arsenic trichloride	(7784-34-1)	2B
Benzilic acid	(76-93-7)	2B
Diethyl methylphosphonite	(15715-41-0)	2B
Dimethyl ethylphosphonate	(6163-75-3)	2B
Ethylphosphinyl difluoride	(430-78-4)	2B
Methylphosphinyl difluoride	(753-59-3)	2B

Precursor Chemical	CAS No.	CWC-Schedule
3-Quinuclidone	(3731-38-2)	Not Listed
Phosphorus pentachloride	(10026-13-8)	3B
Pinacolone	(75-97-8)	Not Listed
Potassium cyanide	(151-50-8)	Not Listed
Potassium bifluoride	(7789-29-9)	Not Listed
Ammonium bifluoride	(1341-49-7)	Not Listed
Sodium bifluoride	(1333-83-1)	Not Listed
Sodium fluoride	(7681-49-4)	Not Listed
Sodium cyanide	(143-33-9)	Not Listed
Triethanolamine	(102-71-6)	3B
Phosphorus pentasulphide	(1314-80-3)	Not Listed
Diisopropylamine	(108-18-9)	Not Listed
Diethylaminoethanol	(100-37-8)	Not Listed
Sodium sulphide	(1313-82-2)	Not Listed
Sulphur monochloride	(10025-67-9)	3B
Sulphur dichloride	(10545-99-0)	3B
Triethanolamine hydrochloride	(637-39-8)	Not Listed
N,N-Diisopropyl-2-aminoethyl chloride hydrochloride	(4261-68-1)	2B
Methylphosphonic acid	(993-13-5)	2B
Diethyl methylphosphonate	(683-08-9)	2B
N,N-Dimethylaminophosphoryl dichloride	(677-43-0)	2B
Triisopropyl phosphite	(116-17-6)	Not Listed
Ethyldiethanolamine	(139-87-7)	3B
O,O-Diethyl phosphorothioate	(2465-65-8)	Not Listed
O,O-Diethyl phosphorodithioate	(298-06-6)	Not Listed
Sodium hexafluorosilicate	(16893-85-9)	Not Listed
Methylphosphonothioic dichloride	(676-98-2)	2B
Diethylamine	(109-89-7)	Not Listed
N,N-Diisopropylaminoethanethiol hydrochloride	(41480-75-5)	2B

Source: The Australia Group, July 2017. Available online at http://www.australiagroup.net/en/precursors.html. Accessed April 30, 2018.

List of Human and Animal Pathogens and Toxins for Export Control[1] (2017)

Viruses

1. African horse sickness virus
2. African swine fever virus
3. Andes virus
4. Avian influenza virus[2]
5. Bluetongue virus
6. Chapare virus
7. Chikungunya virus
8. Choclo virus
9. Classical swine fever virus (Hog cholera virus)
10. Crimean-Congo hemorrhagic fever virus
11. Dobrava-Belgrade virus
12. Eastern equine encephalitis virus
13. Ebolavirus: all members of the Ebolavirus genus
14. Foot-and-mouth disease virus
15. Goatpox virus
16. Guanarito virus
17. Hantaan virus
18. Hendra virus (Equine morbillivirus)
19. Japanese encephalitis virus
20. Junin virus
21. Kyasanur Forest disease virus
22. Laguna Negra virus
23. Lassa virus
24. Louping ill virus
25. Lujo virus
26. Lumpy skin disease virus
27. Lymphocytic choriomeningitis virus
28. Machupo virus
29. Marburgvirus: all members of the Marburgvirus genus
30. Monkeypox virus
31. Murray Valley encephalitis virus
32. Newcastle disease virus
33. Nipah virus
34. Omsk hemorrhagic fever virus
35. Oropouche virus
36. Peste-des-petits-ruminants virus
37. Porcine Teschovirus
38. Powassan virus
39. Rabies virus and other members of the Lyssavirus genus
40. Reconstructed 1918 influenza virus
41. Rift Valley fever virus
42. Rinderpest virus
43. Rocio virus
44. Sabia virus
45. Seoul virus
46. Severe acute respiratory syndrome-related coronavirus (SARS-related coronavirus)
47. Sheeppox virus
48. Sin Nombre virus
49. St. Louis encephalitis virus
50. Suid herpesvirus 1 (Pseudorabies virus; Aujeszky's disease)
51. Swine vesicular disease virus
52. Tick-borne encephalitis virus (Far Eastern subtype)
53. Variola virus
54. Venezuelan equine encephalitis virus
55. Vesicular stomatitis virus
56. Western equine encephalitis virus
57. Yellow fever virus

Bacteria

1. Bacillus anthracis
2. Brucella abortus
3. Brucella melitensis
4. Brucella suis
5. Burkholderia mallei (Pseudomonas mallei)
6. Burkholderia pseudomallei (Pseudomonas pseudomallei)
7. Chlamydia psittaci (Chlamydophila psittaci)
8. Clostridium argentinense (formerly known as Clostridium botulinum Type G), botulinum neurotoxin producing strains
9. Clostridium baratii, botulinum neurotoxin producing strains

10. Clostridium botulinum
11. Clostridium butyricum, botulinum neurotoxin producing strains
12. Clostridium perfringens, epsilon toxin producing types[3]
13. Coxiella burnetii
14. Francisella tularensis
15. Mycoplasma capricolum subspecies capripneumoniae ("strain F38")
16. Mycoplasma mycoides subspecies mycoides SC (small colony)
17. Rickettsia prowazekii
18. Salmonella enterica subspecies enterica serovar Typhi (Salmonella typhi)
19. Shiga toxin producing Escherichia coli (STEC) of serogroups O26, O45, O103, O104, O111, O121, O145, O157, and other shiga toxin producing serogroups[4]
20. Shigella dysenteriae
21. Vibrio cholerae
22. Yersinia pestis

Toxins as follows and subunits thereof:[5]
1. Abrin
2. Aflatoxins
3. Botulinum toxins[6]
4. Cholera toxin
5. Clostridium perfringens alpha, beta 1, beta 2, epsilon and iota toxins
6. Conotoxins [6]
7. Diacetoxyscirpenol
8. HT-2 toxin
9. Microcystins (Cyanoginosins)
10. Modeccin
11. Ricin
12. Saxitoxin
13. Shiga toxins (shiga-like toxins, verotoxins, and verocytotoxins)
14. Staphylococcus aureus enterotoxins, hemolysin alpha toxin, and toxic shock syndrome toxin (formerly known as Staphylococcus enterotoxin F)
15. T-2 toxin
16. Tetrodotoxin

17. Viscumin (Viscum album lectin 1)
18. Volkensin

Fungi
1. Coccidioides immitis
2. Coccidioides posadasii

[1] An agent/pathogen is covered by this list except when it is in the form of a vaccine. A vaccine is a medicinal product in a pharmaceutical formulation licensed by, or having marketing or clinical trial authorisation from, the regulatory authorities of either the country of manufacture or of use, which is intended to stimulate a protective immunological response in humans or animals in order to prevent disease in those to whom or to which it is administered.

Biological agents and pathogens are controlled when they are an isolated live culture of a pathogen agent, or a preparation of a toxin agent which has been isolated or extracted from any source, or material including living material which has been deliberately inoculated or contaminated with the agent. Isolated live cultures of a pathogen agent include live cultures in dormant form or in dried preparations, whether the agent is natural, enhanced or modified.

[2] This includes only those Avian influenza viruses of high pathogenicity as defined by the World Organization for Animal Health (OIE), the European Union (EU), or competent national regulatory bodies.

[3] It is understood that limiting this control to epsilon toxin-producing strains of Clostridium perfringens therefore exempts from control the transfer of other Clostridium perfringens strains to be used as positive control cultures for food testing and quality control.

[4] Shiga toxin producing *Escherichia coli* (STEC) includes *inter alia* enterohaemorrhagic *E. coli* (EHEC), verotoxin producing *E. coli* (VTEC) or verocytotoxin producing *E. coli* (VTEC).

[5] Excluding immunotoxins

[6] Excluding botulinum toxins and conotoxins in product form meeting all of the following criteria:

- are pharmaceutical formulations designed for testing and human administration in the treatment of medical conditions;
- are pre-packaged for distribution as clinical or medical products; and
- are authorised by a state authority to be marketed as clinical or medical products.

Warning List[1]

Bacteria

1. Clostridium tetani[2]
2. Legionella pneumophila
3. Yersinia pseudotuberculosis
4. Other strains of Clostridium species that produce botulinum neurotoxin[3]

Fungi

1. Fusarium langsethiae
2. Fusarium sporotrichioides

[1] Biological agents are controlled when they are an isolated live culture of a pathogen agent, or a preparation of a toxin agent which has been isolated or extracted from any source, or material including living material which has been deliberately inoculated or contaminated with the agent. Isolated live cultures of a pathogen agent include live cultures in dormant form or in dried preparations, whether the agent is natural, enhanced or modified.

An agent is covered by this list except when it is in the form of a vaccine. A vaccine is a medicinal product in a pharmaceutical formulation licensed by, or having marketing or clinical trial authorisation from, the regulatory authorities of either the country of manufacture or of use, which is intended to stimulate a protective immunological response in humans or animals in order to prevent disease in those to whom or to which it is administered.

[2] The Australia Group recognizes that this organism is ubiquitous, but, as it has been acquired in the past as part of biological warfare programs, it is worthy of special caution.

[3] It is the intent of Australia Group members to add to the control list strains of species of Clostridium identified as producing botulinum neurotoxin.

Genetic Elements and Genetically-modified Organisms:

Any genetically-modified organism[1] which contains, or genetic element[2] that codes for:

1. any gene or genes specific to any listed virus; or
2. any gene or genes specific to any listed bacterium[3] or fungus, and which
   a. in itself or through its transcribed or translated products represents a significant hazard to human, animal or plant health, or
   b. could endow or enhance pathogenicity[4]; or
3. any listed toxins or their sub-units.

Source: The Australia Group, July 2017. Available online at http://www.australiagroup.net/en/human_animal_pathogens.html. Accessed April 30, 2018.

Primary Documents: Nuclear Weapons

Atomic Energy Act (1946)

A BILL

For the development and control of atomic energy

Be it enacted by the Senate and House of Representatives of the United States of America in congress assembled,

DECLARATION OF POLICY

Section 1. (a) Findings and Declaration. Research and experimentation in the field of nuclear fission have attained the stage at which the release of atomic energy on a large scale is practical. The significance of the atomic bomb for military purposes is evident. The effect of the use of atomic energy for civilian purposes upon the social, economic, and political structures of today cannot now be determined. It is reasonable to anticipate, however, that tapping this new source of energy will cause profound changes in our present way of life. Accordingly, it is hereby declared to be the policy of the people of the United States that the development and utilization of atomic energy shall be directed toward improving the public welfare, increasing the standard of living, strengthening free competition among private enterprises so far as practicable, and cementing world peace.

(b) Purpose of Act. It is the purpose of this Act to effectuate these policies by providing, among others, for the following major programs;

(1) A program of assisting and fostering private research and development on a truly independent basis to encourage maximum scientific progress;

(2) A program for the free dissemination of basic scientific information and for maximum liberality in dissemination of related technical information;

(3) A program of federally conducted research to assure the Government of adequate scientific and technical accomplishments;

(4) A program for Government control of the production, ownership, and use of fissionable materials to protect the national security and to insure the broadest possible exploitation of the field;

(5) A program for simultaneous study of the social, political, and economic effects of the utilization of atomic energy; and

(6) A program of administration which will be consistent with international agreements made by the United States,

and which will enable the Congress to be currently informed so as to take further legislative action as may hereafter be appropriate.

Source: Pub. L. 79-585; Ch. 724, 60 Stat. 755.

North Atlantic Treaty (1949)

Washington D.C. – 4 April 1949

The Parties to this Treaty reaffirm their faith in the purposes and principles of the Charter of the United Nations and their desire to live in peace with all peoples and all governments. They are determined to safeguard the freedom, common heritage and civilisation of their peoples, founded on the principles of democracy, individual liberty and the rule of law. They seek to promote stability and well-being in the North Atlantic area. They are resolved to unite their efforts for collective defence and for the preservation of peace and security. They therefore agree to this North Atlantic Treaty:

Article 1

The Parties undertake, as set forth in the Charter of the United Nations, to settle any international dispute in which they may be involved by peaceful means in such a manner that international peace and security and justice are not endangered, and to refrain in their international relations from the threat or use of force in any manner inconsistent with the purposes of the United Nations.

Article 2

The Parties will contribute toward the further development of peaceful and friendly international relations by strengthening their free institutions, by bringing about a better understanding of the principles upon which these institutions are founded, and by promoting conditions of stability and well-being. They will seek to eliminate conflict in their international economic policies and will encourage economic collaboration between any or all of them.

Article 3

In order more effectively to achieve the objectives of this Treaty, the Parties, separately and jointly, by means of continuous and effective self-help and mutual aid, will maintain and develop their individual and collective capacity to resist armed attack.

Article 4

The Parties will consult together whenever, in the opinion of any of them, the territorial integrity, political independence or security of any of the Parties is threatened.

Article 5

The Parties agree that an armed attack against one or more of them in Europe or North America shall be considered an attack against them all and consequently they agree that, if such an armed attack occurs, each of them, in exercise of the right of individual or collective self-defence recognised by Article 51 of the Charter of the United Nations, will assist the Party or Parties so attacked by taking forthwith, individually and in concert with the other Parties, such action as it deems necessary, including the use of armed force, to restore and maintain the security of the North Atlantic area.

Any such armed attack and all measures taken as a result thereof shall immediately be reported to the Security Council. Such measures shall be terminated when the Security Council has taken the measures necessary to restore and maintain international peace and security.

Article 6 (1)

For the purpose of Article 5, an armed attack on one or more of the Parties is deemed to include an armed attack:

on the territory of any of the Parties in Europe or North America, on the Algerian Departments of France (2), on the territory of or on the Islands under the jurisdiction of any of the Parties in the North Atlantic area north of the Tropic of Cancer;

on the forces, vessels, or aircraft of any of the Parties, when in or over these territories or any other area in Europe in which occupation forces of any of the Parties were stationed on the date when the Treaty entered into force or the Mediterranean Sea or the North Atlantic area north of the Tropic of Cancer.

Article 7

This Treaty does not affect, and shall not be interpreted as affecting in any way the rights and obligations under the Charter of the Parties which are members of the United Nations, or the primary responsibility of the Security Council for the maintenance of international peace and security.

Article 8

Each Party declares that none of the international engagements now in force between it and any other of the Parties or any third State is in conflict with the provisions of this Treaty, and undertakes not to enter into any international engagement in conflict with this Treaty.

Article 9

The Parties hereby establish a Council, on which each of them shall be represented, to consider matters concerning the implementation of this Treaty. The Council shall be so organised as to be able to meet promptly at any time. The Council shall set up such subsidiary bodies as may be necessary; in particular it shall establish immediately a defence committee which shall recommend measures for the implementation of Articles 3 and 5.

Article 10

The Parties may, by unanimous agreement, invite any other European State in a position to further the principles of this Treaty and to contribute to the security of the North Atlantic area to accede to this Treaty. Any State so invited may become a Party to the Treaty by depositing its instrument of accession with the Government of the United States of America. The Government of the United States of America will inform each of the Parties of the deposit of each such instrument of accession.

Article 13

After the Treaty has been in force for twenty years, any Party may cease to be a Party one year after its notice of denunciation has been given to the Government of the United States of America, which will inform the Governments of the other Parties of the deposit of each notice of denunciation.

Footnotes :

(1) The definition of the territories to which Article 5 applies was revised by Article 2 of the Protocol to the North Atlantic Treaty on the accession of Greece and Turkey signed on 22 October 1951.

(2) On January 16, 1963, the North Atlantic Council noted that insofar as the former Algerian Departments of France were concerned, the relevant clauses of this Treaty had become inapplicable as from July 3, 1962.

(3) The Treaty came into force on 24 August 1949, after the deposition of the ratifications of all signatory states.

Source: U.S. Department of State. *American Foreign Policy. 1950–1955; Basic Documents.* Washington, D.C.: GPO, 1957.

Statute of the International Atomic Energy Agency (1956)

Opened for signature at New York on 26 October 1956
Entered into force on 29 July 1957
Depositary: US government

Article II. *Objectives*

The Agency shall seek to accelerate and enlarge the contribution of atomic energy to peace, health and prosperity throughout the world. It shall ensure, so far as it is able, that assistance provided by it or at its request or under its supervision or control is not used in such a way as to further any military purpose.

Article III. *Functions*

A. The Agency is authorized:

5. To establish and administer safeguards designed to ensure that special fissionable and other materials, services, equipment, facilities, and information made available by the Agency or at its request or under its supervision or control are not used in such a way as to further any military purpose; and to apply safeguards, at the request of the parties, to any bilateral or multilateral arrangement, or at the request of a State, to any of that State's activities in the field of atomic energy;

Article XII. *Agency Safeguards*

A. With respect to any Agency project, or other arrangement where the Agency is requested by the parties concerned to apply safeguards, the Agency shall have the following rights and responsibilities to the extent relevant to the project or arrangement:

1. To examine the design of specialized equipment and facilities, including nuclear reactors, and to approve it only from the view-point of assuring that it will not further any military purpose, that it complies with applicable health and safety standards, and that it will permit effective application of the safeguards provided for in this article;

2. To require the observance of any health and safety measures prescribed by the Agency;

3. To require the maintenance and production of operating records to assist in ensuring accountability for source and special fissionable materials used or produced in the project or arrangement;

4. To call for and receive progress reports;

5. To approve the means to be used for the chemical processing of irradiated materials solely to ensure that this chemical processing will not lend itself to diversion of materials for military purposes and will comply with applicable health and safety standards; to require that special fissionable materials recovered or produced as a by-product be used for peaceful purposes under continuing Agency safeguards for research or in reactors, existing or under construction, specified by the member or members concerned; and to require deposit with the Agency of any excess of any special fissionable materials recovered or produced as a by-product over what is needed for the above-stated uses in order to prevent stockpiling of these materials,

provided that thereafter at the request of the member or members concerned special fissionable materials so deposited with the Agency shall be returned promptly to the member or members concerned for use under the same provisions as stated above;

6. To send into the territory of the recipient State or States inspectors, designated by the Agency after consultation with the State or States concerned, who shall have access at all times to all places and data and to any person who by reason of his occupation deals with materials, equipment, or facilities which are required by this Statute to be safeguarded, as necessary to account for source and special fissionable materials supplied and fissionable products and to determine whether there is compliance with the undertaking against use in furtherance of any military purpose referred to in sub-paragraph F-4 of article XI, with the health and safety measures referred to in sub-paragraph A-2 of this article, and with any other conditions prescribed in the agreement between the Agency and the State or States concerned. Inspectors designated by the Agency shall be accompanied by representatives of the authorities of the State concerned, if that State so requests, provided that the inspectors shall not thereby be delayed or otherwise impeded in the exercise of their functions;

7. In the event of non-compliance and failure by the recipient State or States to take requested corrective steps within a reasonable time, to suspend or terminate assistance and withdraw any materials and equipment made available by the Agency or a member in furtherance of the project.

B. The Agency shall, as necessary, establish a staff of inspectors. The Staff of inspectors shall have the responsibility of examining all operations conducted by the Agency itself to determine whether the Agency is complying with the health and safety measures prescribed by it for application to projects subject to its approval, supervision or control, and whether the Agency is taking adequate measures to prevent the source and special fissionable materials in its custody or used or produced in its own operations from being used in furtherance of any military purpose. The Agency shall take remedial action forthwith to correct any non-compliance or failure to take adequate measures.

C. . . . The inspectors shall report any non-compliance to the Director General who shall thereupon transmit the report to the Board of Governors. The Board shall call upon the recipient State or States to remedy forthwith any non-compliance which it finds to have occurred. The Board shall report the non-compliance to all members and to the Security Council and General Assembly of the United Nations. In the event of failure of the recipient State or States to take fully corrective action within a reasonable time, the Board may take one or both of the following measures: direct curtailment or suspension of assistance being provided by the Agency or by a member, and call for the return of materials and equipment made available to the recipient member or group of members. The Agency may also, in accordance with article XIX, suspend any non-complying member from the exercise of the privileges and rights of membership.

Source: International Atomic Energy Agency. Available online at https://www.iaea.org/about/statute. Accessed February 24, 2018.

Hot Line Agreement Summary (1963)

Memorandum of Understanding Between The United States of America and The Union of Soviet Socialist Republics Regarding the Establishment of a Direct Communications Link

Signed at Geneva June 20, 1963

Entered into force June 20, 1963

For use in time of emergency the Government of the United States of America and the Government of the Union of Soviet Socialist Republics have agreed to establish as soon as technically feasible a direct communications link between the two Governments.

Each Government shall be responsible for the arrangements for the link on its own territory. Each Government shall take the necessary steps to ensure continuous functioning of the link and prompt delivery to its head of government of any communications received by means of the link from the head of government of the other party.

Arrangements for establishing and operating the link are set forth in the Annex which is attached hereto and forms an integral part hereof.

Source: U.S. Department of State. Available online at https://www.state.gov/t/isn/4785.htm. Accessed February 24, 2018.

Treaty of Tlatelolco (1967)

Treaty for the Prohibition of Nuclear Weapons in Latin America and the Caribbean

Opened for Signature: 14 February 1967. Entered into Force: 22 April 1968.

Preamble

In the name of their peoples and faithfully interpreting their desires and aspirations, the Governments of the States which sign the Treaty for the Prohibition of Nuclear Weapons in Latin America,

Desiring to contribute, so far as lies in their power, towards ending the armaments race, especially in the field of nuclear weapons, and towards strengthening a world at peace, based on the sovereign equality of States, mutual respect and good neighbourliness,

Recalling that the United Nations General Assembly, in its resolution 808 (IX), adopted unanimously as one of the three points of a coordinated programme of disarmament "the total prohibition of the use and manufacture of nuclear weapons and weapons of mass destruction of every type",

Recalling that militarily denuclearized zones are not an end in themselves but rather a means for achieving general and complete disarmament at a later stage,

Recalling United Nations General Assembly resolution 1911 (XVIII), which established that the measures that should be agreed upon for the denuclearization of Latin America should be taken "in the light of the principles of the Charter of the United Nations and of regional agreements",

Recalling United Nations General Assembly resolution 2028 (XX), which established the principle of an acceptable balance of mutual responsibilities and duties for the nuclear and non-nuclear powers, and

Recalling that the Charter of the Organization of American States proclaims that it is an essential purpose of the Organization to strengthen the peace and security of the hemisphere,

Convinced:

That the incalculable destructive power of nuclear weapons has made it imperative that the legal prohibition of war should be strictly observed in practice if the survival of civilization and of mankind itself is to be assured,

That nuclear weapons, whose terrible effects are suffered, indiscriminately and inexorably, by military forces and civilian population alike, constitute, through the persistence of the radioactivity they release, an attack on the integrity of the human species and ultimately may even render the whole earth uninhabitable,

That general and complete disarmament under effective international control is a vital matter which all the peoples of the world equally demand,

That the proliferation of nuclear weapons, which seems inevitable unless States, in the exercise of their sovereign rights, impose restrictions on themselves in order to prevent it, would make any agreement on disarmament enormously difficult and would increase the danger of the outbreak of a nuclear conflagration,

That the establishment of militarily denuclearized zones is closely linked with the maintenance of peace and security in the respective regions,

That the military denuclearization of vast geographical zones, adopted by the Sovereign decision of the States comprised therein, will exercise a beneficial influence on other regions where similar conditions exist,

That the privileged situation of the signatory States, whose territories are wholly free from nuclear weapons, imposes upon them the inescapable duty of preserving that situation both in their own interests and for the good of mankind,

That the existence of nuclear weapons in any country of Latin America would make it a target for possible nuclear attacks and would inevitably set off, throughout the region a ruinous race in nuclear weapons which would involve the unjustifiable diversion, for warlike purposes, of the limited resources required for economic and social development,

That the foregoing reasons, together with the traditional peace-loving outlook of Latin America, give rise to an inescapable necessity that nuclear energy should be used in that region exclusively for peaceful purposes, and that the Latin American countries should use their right to the greatest and most equitable possible access to this new source of energy in order to expedite the economic and social development of their peoples,

Convinced finally:

That the military denuclearization of Latin America -being understood to mean the undertaking entered into internationally in this Treaty to keep their territories forever free from nuclear weapons -will constitute a measure which will spare their peoples from the squandering of their limited resources on nuclear armaments and will protect them against possible nuclear attacks on their territories, and will also constitute a significant contribution towards preventing the proliferation of nuclear weapons and a powerful factor for general and complete disarmament, and

That Latin America, faithful to its tradition of universality, must not only endeavour to banish from its homelands the scourge of a nuclear war, but must also strive to promote the well-being and advancement of its peoples, at the same time cooperating in the fulfilment of the ideals of mankind, that is to say, in the consolidation of a permanent peace based on equal rights, economic fairness and social justice for all, in accordance with the principles and purposes set forth in the Charter of the United Nations and in the Charter of the Organization of American States,

Have agreed as follows:

Obligations

Article I

1. The Contracting Parties hereby undertake to use exclusively for peaceful purposes the nuclear material and facilities which are under their jurisdiction, and to prohibit and prevent in their respective territories:

    (a) The testing, use, manufacture, production or acquisition by any means whatsoever of any nuclear weapons, by the Parties themselves, directly or indirectly, on behalf of anyone else or in any other way, and

    (b) The receipt, storage, installation, deployment and any form of possession of any nuclear weapons, directly or indirectly, by the Parties themselves, by anyone on their behalf or in any other way.

2. The Contracting Parties also undertake to refrain from engaging in, encouraging or authorizing, directly or indirectly, or in any way participating in the testing, use, manufacture, production, possession or control of any nuclear weapon.

Source: U.S. Department of State. Available online at https://www.state.gov/p/wha/rls/70658. htm. Accessed February 24, 2018.

Treaty on the Non-Proliferation of Nuclear Weapons (1968)

Signed at Washington, London, and Moscow July 1, 1968

Ratification advised by U.S. Senate March 13, 1969

Ratified by U.S. President November 24, 1969

Entered into force March 5, 1970

The States concluding this Treaty, hereinafter referred to as the "Parties to the Treaty",

Considering the devastation that would be visited upon all mankind by a nuclear war and the consequent need to make every effort to avert the danger of such a war and to take measures to safeguard the security of peoples,

Believing that the proliferation of nuclear weapons would seriously enhance the danger of nuclear war,

In conformity with resolutions of the United Nations General Assembly calling for the conclusion of an agreement on the prevention of wider dissemination of nuclear weapons,

Undertaking to cooperate in facilitating the application of International Atomic Energy Agency safeguards on peaceful nuclear activities,

Expressing their support for research, development and other efforts to further the application, within the framework of the International Atomic Energy Agency safeguards system, of the principle of safeguarding effectively the flow of source and special fissionable materials by use of instruments and other techniques at certain strategic points,

Affirming the principle that the benefits of peaceful applications of nuclear technology, including any technological by-products which may be derived by nuclear weapon States from the development of nuclear explosive devices, should be available for peaceful purposes to all Parties of the Treaty, whether nuclear-weapon or non-nuclear weapon States,

Convinced that, in furtherance of this principle, all Parties to the Treaty are entitled to participate in the fullest possible exchange of scientific information for, and to contribute alone or in cooperation with other States to, the further development of the applications of atomic energy for peaceful purposes,

Declaring their intention to achieve at the earliest possible date the cessation of the nuclear arms race and to undertake effective measures in the direction of nuclear disarmament,

Urging the cooperation of all States in the attainment of this objective,

Recalling the determination expressed by the Parties to the 1963 Treaty banning nuclear weapon tests in the atmosphere, in outer space and under water in its Preamble to seek to achieve the discontinuance of all test explosions of nuclear weapons for all time and to continue negotiations to this end,

Desiring to further the easing of international tension and the strengthening of trust between States in order to facilitate the cessation of the manufacture of nuclear weapons, the liquidation of all their existing stockpiles, and the elimination from national arsenals of nuclear weapons and the means of their delivery pursuant to a Treaty on general and complete disarmament under strict and effective international control,

Recalling that, in accordance with the Charter of the United Nations, States must refrain in their international relations from the threat or use of force against the territorial integrity or political independence of any State, or in any other manner inconsistent with the Purposes of the United Nations, and that the establishment and maintenance of international peace and security are to be promoted with the least diversion for armaments of the worlds human and economic resources,

Have agreed as follows:

Article I

Each nuclear-weapon State Party to the Treaty undertakes not to transfer to any recipient whatsoever nuclear weapons or other nuclear explosive devices or control over such weapons or explosive devices directly, or indirectly; and not in any way to assist, encourage, or induce any non-nuclear weapon State to manufacture or otherwise acquire nuclear weapons or other nuclear explosive devices, or control over such weapons or explosive devices.

Article II

Each non-nuclear-weapon State Party to the Treaty undertakes not to receive the transfer from any transferor whatsoever of nuclear weapons or other nuclear explosive devices or of control over such weapons or explosive devices directly, or indirectly; not to manufacture or otherwise acquire nuclear weapons or other nuclear explosive devices; and not to seek or receive any assistance in the manufacture of nuclear weapons or other nuclear explosive devices.

Article III

1. Each non-nuclear-weapon State Party to the Treaty undertakes to accept safeguards, as set forth in an agreement to be negotiated and concluded with the International Atomic Energy Agency in accordance with the Statute of the International Atomic Energy Agency and the Agency's safeguards system, for the exclusive purpose of verification of the fulfillment of its obligations assumed under this Treaty with a view to preventing diversion of nuclear energy from peaceful uses to nuclear weapons or other nuclear explosive devices. Procedures for the safeguards required by this article shall be followed with respect to source or special fissionable material whether it is being produced, processed or used in any

principal nuclear facility or is outside any such facility. The safeguards required by this article shall be applied to all source or special fissionable material in all peaceful nuclear activities within the territory of such State, under its jurisdiction, or carried out under its control anywhere.

2. Each State Party to the Treaty undertakes not to provide: (a) source or special fissionable material, or (b) equipment or material especially designed or prepared for the processing, use or production of special fissionable material, to any non-nuclear-weapon State for peaceful purposes, unless the source or special fissionable material shall be subject to the safeguards required by this article.

3. The safeguards required by this article shall be implemented in a manner designed to comply with article IV of this Treaty, and to avoid hampering the economic or technological development of the Parties or international cooperation in the field of peaceful nuclear activities, including the international exchange of nuclear material and equipment for the processing, use or production of nuclear material for peaceful purposes in accordance with the provisions of this article and the principle of safeguarding set forth in the Preamble of the Treaty.

4. Non-nuclear-weapon States Party to the Treaty shall conclude agreements with the International Atomic Energy Agency to meet the requirements of this article either individually or together with other States in accordance with the Statute of the International Atomic Energy Agency. Negotiation of such agreements shall commence within 180 days from the original entry into force of this Treaty. For States depositing their instruments of ratification or accession after the 180-day period, negotiation of such agreements shall commence not later than the date of such deposit. Such agreements shall enter into force not later than eighteen months after the date of initiation of negotiations.

Article IV

1. Nothing in this Treaty shall be interpreted as affecting the inalienable right of all the Parties to the Treaty to develop research, production and use of nuclear energy for peaceful purposes without discrimination and in conformity with articles I and II of this Treaty.

2. All the Parties to the Treaty undertake to facilitate, and have the right to participate in, the fullest possible exchange of equipment, materials and scientific and technological information for the peaceful uses of nuclear energy. Parties to the Treaty in a position to do so shall also cooperate in contributing alone or together with other States or international organizations to the further development of the applications of nuclear energy for peaceful purposes, especially in the territories of non-nuclear-weapon States Party to the Treaty, with due consideration for the needs of the developing areas of the world.

Article V

Each party to the Treaty undertakes to take appropriate measures to ensure that, in accordance with this Treaty, under appropriate international observation and through appropriate international procedures, potential benefits from any peaceful applications of nuclear explosions will be made available to non-nuclear-weapon States Party to the Treaty on a nondiscriminatory basis and that the charge to such Parties for the explosive devices used will be as low as possible and exclude any charge for research and development. Non-nuclear-weapon States Party to the Treaty shall be able to obtain such benefits, pursuant to a special international agreement or agreements, through an appropriate international body with adequate representation of non-nuclear-weapon States. Negotiations on this subject shall commence as soon as possible after the Treaty enters into force. Non-nuclear-weapon States Party to the Treaty so desiring may also obtain such benefits pursuant to bilateral agreements.

Article VI

Each of the Parties to the Treaty undertakes to pursue negotiations in good faith on effective measures relating to cessation of the nuclear arms race at an early date and to nuclear disarmament, and on a Treaty on general and complete disarmament under strict and effective international control.

Article VII

Nothing in this Treaty affects the right of any group of States to conclude regional treaties in order to assure the total absence of nuclear weapons in their respective territories.

Article VIII

3. Five years after the entry into force of this Treaty, a conference of Parties to the Treaty shall be held in Geneva, Switzerland, in order to review the operation of this Treaty with a view to assuring that the purposes of the Preamble and the provisions of the Treaty are being realized. At intervals of

five years thereafter, a majority of the Parties to the Treaty may obtain, by submitting a proposal to this effect to the Depositary Governments, the convening of further conferences with the same objective of reviewing the operation of the Treaty.

Article X

1. Each Party shall in exercising its national sovereignty have the right to withdraw from the Treaty if it decides that extraordinary events, related to the subject matter of this Treaty, have jeopardized the supreme interests of its country. It shall give notice of such withdrawal to all other Parties to the Treaty and to the United Nations Security Council three months in advance. Such notice shall include a statement of the extraordinary events it regards as having jeopardized its supreme interests.

2. Twenty-five years after the entry into force of the Treaty, a conference shall be convened to decide whether the Treaty shall continue in force indefinitely, or shall be extended for an additional fixed period or periods. This decision shall be taken by a majority of the Parties to the Treaty.

Source: United Nations. Available online at https://www.un.org/disarmament/wmd/nuclear/npt/text. Accessed February 24, 2018.

Nuclear War Risk Reduction Measures Agreement (1971)

Agreement on Measures to Reduce the Risk of Outbreak of Nuclear War Between the United States of America and the Union of Soviet Socialist Republics

Signed at Washington September 30, 1971

Entered into force September 30, 19715

The United States of America and the Union of Soviet Socialist Republics, hereinafter referred to as the Parties:

Taking into account the devastating consequences that nuclear war would have for all mankind, and recognizing the need to exert every effort to avert the risk of outbreak of such a war, including measures to guard against accidental or unauthorized use of nuclear weapons,

Believing that agreement on measures for reducing the risk of outbreak of nuclear war serves the interests of strengthening international peace and security, and is in no way contrary to the interests of any other country,

Bearing in mind that continued efforts are also needed in the future to seek ways of reducing the risk of outbreak of nuclear war,

Have agreed as follows:

Article 1

Each Party undertakes to maintain and to improve, as it deems necessary, its existing organizational and technical arrangements to guard against the accidental or unauthorized use of nuclear weapons under its control.

Article 2

The Parties undertake to notify each other immediately in the event of an accidental, unauthorized or any other unexplained incident involving a possible detonation of a nuclear weapon which could create a risk of outbreak of nuclear war. In the event of such an incident, the Party whose nuclear weapon is involved will immediately make every effort to take necessary measures to render harmless or destroy such weapon without its causing damage.

Article 3

The Parties undertake to notify each other immediately in the event of detection by missile warning systems of unidentified objects, or in the event of signs of interference with these systems or with related communications facilities, if such occurrences could create a risk of outbreak of nuclear war between the two countries.

Article 4

Each Party undertakes to notify the other Party in advance of any planned missile launches if such launches will extend beyond its national territory in the direction of the other Party.

Article 5

Each Party, in other situations involving unexplained nuclear incidents, undertakes to act in such a manner as to reduce the possibility of its actions being misinterpreted by the other Party. In any such situation, each Party may inform the other Party or request information when in its view, this is warranted by the interests of averting the risk of outbreak of nuclear war.

Article 6

For transmission of urgent information, notifications and requests for information in situations requiring prompt clarification, the Parties shall make primary use of the Direct Communications Link between the Governments of the United States of America and the Union of Soviet Socialist Republics.

For transmission of other information, notification and requests for information, the Parties, at their own discretion, may use any communications facilities, including diplomatic channels, depending on the degree of urgency.

Article 7

The Parties undertake to hold consultations, as mutually agreed, to consider questions relating to implementation of the provisions of this Agreement, as well as to discuss possible amendments thereto aimed at further implementation of the purposes of this Agreement.

Article 8

This Agreement shall be of unlimited duration.

Source: U.S. State Department. Available online at https://www.state.gov/t/isn/4692.htm. Accessed February 24, 2018.

Seabed Treaty (1972)

Treaty on the Prohibition of the Emplacement of Nuclear Weapons and Other Weapons of Mass Destruction on the Seabed and the Ocean Floor and in the Subsoil Thereof

Signed at Washington, London, and Moscow February 11, 1971

Ratification advised by U.S. Senate February 15, 1972

Ratified by U.S. President April 26, 1972

Entered into force May 18, 1972

The States Parties to this Treaty,

Recognizing the common interest of mankind in the progress of the exploration and use of the seabed and the ocean floor for peaceful purposes,

Considering that the prevention of a nuclear arms race on the seabed and the ocean floor serves the interests of maintaining world peace, reduces international tensions and strengthens friendly relations among States,

Convinced that this Treaty constitutes a step towards the exclusion of the seabed, the ocean floor and the subsoil thereof from the arms race,

Convinced that this Treaty constitutes a step towards a Treaty on general and complete disarmament under strict and effective international control, and determined to continue negotiations to this end,

Convinced that this Treaty will further the purposes and principles of the Charter of the United Nations, in a manner consistent with the principles of international law and without infringing the freedoms of the high seas,

Have agreed as follows:

Article I

1. The States Parties to this Treaty undertake not to emplant or emplace on the seabed and the ocean floor and in the subsoil thereof beyond the outer limit of a seabed zone, as defined in article II, any nuclear weapons or any other types of weapons of mass destruction as well as structures, launching installations or any other facilities specifically designed for storing, testing or using such weapons.

2. The undertakings of paragraph 1 of this article shall also apply to the seabed zone referred to in the same paragraph, except that within such seabed zone, they shall not apply either to the coastal State or to the seabed beneath its territorial waters.

3. The States Parties to this Treaty undertake not to assist, encourage or induce any State to carry out activities referred to in paragraph 1 of this article and not to participate in any other way in such actions.

Article II

For the purpose of this Treaty, the outer limit of the seabed zone referred to in article I shall be coterminous with the twelve-mile outer limit of the zone referred to in part II of the Convention on the Territorial Sea and the Contiguous Zone, signed at Geneva on April 29, 1958, and shall be measured in accordance with the provisions of part I, section II, of that Convention and in accordance with international law.

Source: United Nations. Available online at http://www.un-documents.net/seabed.htm. Accessed February 24, 2018.

Anti-Ballistic Missile Treaty (1972)

Treaty Between the United States of America and the Union of Soviet Socialist Republics on the Limitation of Anti-Ballistic Missile Systems

Signed at Moscow May 26, 1972

Ratification advised by U.S. Senate August 3, 1972

Ratified by U.S. President September 30, 1972

Entered into force October 3, 1972

The United States of America and the Union of Soviet Socialist Republics, hereinafter referred to as the Parties,

Proceeding from the premise that nuclear war would have devastating consequences for all mankind,

Considering that effective measures to limit anti-ballistic missile systems would be a substantial factor in curbing the race in strategic offensive arms and would lead to a decrease in the risk of outbreak of war involving nuclear weapons,

Proceeding from the premise that the limitation of anti-ballistic missile systems, as well as certain agreed measures with respect to the limitation of strategic offensive arms, would contribute to the creation of more favorable conditions for further negotiations on limiting strategic arms,

Mindful of their obligations under Article VI of the Treaty on the Non-Proliferation of Nuclear Weapons,

Declaring their intention to achieve at the earliest possible date the cessation of the nuclear arms race and to take effective measures toward reductions in strategic arms, nuclear disarmament, and general and complete disarmament,

Desiring to contribute to the relaxation of international tension and the strengthening of trust between States,

Have agreed as follows:

Article I

1. Each Party undertakes to limit anti-ballistic missile (ABM) systems and to adopt other measures in accordance with the provisions of this Treaty.

2. Each Party undertakes not to deploy ABM systems for a defense of the territory of its country and not to provide a base for such a defense, and not to deploy ABM systems for defense of an individual region except as provided for in Article III of this Treaty.

Article III

Each Party undertakes not to deploy ABM systems or their components except that:

(a) within one ABM system deployment area having a radius of one hundred and fifty kilometers and centered on the Party's national capital, a Party may deploy: (1) no more than one hundred ABM launchers and no more than one hundred ABM interceptor missiles at launch sites, and (2) ABM radars within no more than six ABM radar complexes, the area of each complex being circular and having a diameter of no more than three kilometers; and

(b) within one ABM system deployment area having a radius of one hundred and fifty kilometers and containing ICBM silo launchers, a Party may deploy: (1) no more than one hundred ABM launchers and no more than one hundred ABM interceptor missiles at launch sites, (2) two large phased-array ABM radars comparable in potential to corresponding ABM radars operational or under construction on the date of signature of the Treaty in an ABM system deployment area containing ICBM silo launchers, and (3) no more than eighteen ABM radars each having a potential less than the potential of the smaller of the above-mentioned two large phased-array ABM radars.

DONE at Moscow on May 26, 1972, in two copies, each in the English and Russian languages, both texts being equally authentic.

Source: *United States Treaties and Other International Agreements* 23, pt. 3435. Available online at https://www.state.gov/t/isn/trty/16332.htm. Accessed February 24, 2018.

Interim Agreement on Strategic Offensive Arms (SALT I) (1972)

Signed at Moscow May 26, 1972

Approval authorized by U.S. Congress September 30, 1972

Approved by U.S. President September 30, 1972

Entered into force October 3, 1972

The United States of America and the Union of Soviet Socialist Republics, hereinafter referred to as the Parties,

Convinced that the Treaty on the Limitation of Anti-Ballistic Missile Systems and this Interim Agreement on Certain Measures with Respect to the Limitation of Strategic Offensive Arms will contribute to the creation of more favorable conditions for active negotiations on limiting strategic arms as well as to the relaxation of international tension and the strengthening of trust between States,

Taking into account the relationship between strategic-offensive and defensive arms,

Mindful of their obligations under Article VI of the Treaty on the Non-Proliferation of Nuclear Weapons,

Have agreed as follows:

Article I

The Parties undertake not to start construction of additional fixed land-based intercontinental ballistic missile (ICBM) launchers after July 1, 1972.

Article II

The Parties undertake not to convert land-based launchers for light ICBMs, or for ICBMs of older types deployed prior to 1964, into land-based launchers for heavy ICBMs of types deployed after that time.

Article III

The Parties undertake to limit submarine-launched ballistic missile (SLBM) launchers and modern ballistic missile submarines to the numbers operational and under construction on the date of signature of this Interim Agreement, and in addition to launchers and submarines constructed under procedures established by the Parties as replacements for an equal number of ICBM launchers of older types deployed prior to 1964 or for launchers on older submarines.

DONE at Moscow on May 26, 1972, in two copies, each in the English and Russian languages, both texts being equally authentic.

Protocol to the Interim Agreement

The United States of America and the Union of Soviet Socialist Republics, hereinafter referred to as the Parties,

Having agreed on certain limitations relating to submarine-launched ballistic missile launchers and modern ballistic missile submarines, and to replacement procedures, in the Interim Agreement,

Have agreed as follows:

The Parties understand that, under Article III of the Interim Agreement, for the period during which that Agreement remains in force:

The United States may have no more than 710 ballistic-missile launchers on submarines (SLBMs) and no more than 44 modern ballistic missile submarines. The Soviet Union may have no more than 950 ballistic missile launchers on submarines and no more than 62 modern ballistic missile submarines.

Additional ballistic missile launchers on submarines up to the above-mentioned levels, in the United States—over 656 ballistic missile launchers on nuclear-powered submarines, and in the USSR—over 740 ballistic missile launchers on nuclear-powered submarines, operational and under construction, may become operational as replacements for equal numbers of ballistic missile launchers of older types deployed prior to 1964 or of ballistic missile launchers on older submarines.

The deployment of modern SLBMs on any submarine, regardless of type, will be counted against the total level of SLBMs permitted for the United States and the USSR.

This Protocol shall be considered an integral part of the Interim Agreement.

Source: "Interim Agreement between the United States of America and the Union of Soviet Socialist Republics on Certain Measures with Respect to the Limitation of Strategic Offensive Arms," May 26, 1972. *United States Treaties and Other International Agreements* 23, pt. 3435.

Prevention of Nuclear War Agreement (1973)

Agreement Between The United States of America and The Union of Soviet Socialist Republics on the Prevention of Nuclear War

Signed at Washington June 22, 1973
Entered into force June 22, 1973

The United States of America and the Union of Soviet Socialist Republics, hereinafter referred to as the Parties,

Guided by the objectives of strengthening world peace and international security, Conscious that nuclear war would have devastating consequences for mankind, Proceeding from the desire to bring about conditions in which the danger of an outbreak of nuclear war anywhere in the world would be reduced and ultimately eliminated,

Proceeding from their obligations under the Charter of the United Nations regarding the maintenance of peace, refraining from the threat or use of force, and the avoidance of war, and in conformity with the agreements to which either Party has subscribed,

Proceeding from the Basic Principles of Relations between the United States of America and the Union of Soviet Socialist Republics signed in Moscow on May 29, 1972,

Reaffirming that the development of relations between the United States of America and the Union of Soviet Socialist Republics is not directed against other countries and their interests,

Have agreed as follows:

Article I

The United States and the Soviet Union agree that an objective of their policies is to remove the danger of nuclear war and of the use of nuclear weapons.

Accordingly, the Parties agree that they will act in such a manner as to prevent the development of situations capable of causing a dangerous exacerbation of their relations, as to avoid military confrontations, and as to exclude the outbreak of nuclear war between them and between either of the Parties and other countries.

Article II

The Parties agree, in accordance with Article I and to realize the objective stated in that Article, to proceed from the premise that each Party will refrain from the threat or use of force against the other Party, against the allies of the other Party and against other countries, in circumstances which may endanger international peace and security. The Parties agree that they will be guided by these considerations in the formulation of their foreign policies and in their actions in the field of international relations.

Article III

The Parties undertake to develop their relations with each other and with other countries in a way consistent with the purposes of this Agreement.

Article IV

If at any time relations between the Parties or between either Party and other countries appear to involve the risk of a nuclear conflict, or if relations between countries not parties to this Agreement appear to involve the risk of nuclear war between the United States of America and the Union of Soviet Socialist Republics or between either Party and other countries, the United States and the Soviet Union, acting in accordance with

the provisions of this Agreement, shall immediately enter into urgent consultations with each other and make every effort to avert this risk.

Article V

Each Party shall be free to inform the Security Council of the United Nations, the Secretary General of the United Nations and the Governments of allied or other countries of the progress and outcome of consultations initiated in accordance with Article IV of this Agreement.

Article VI

Nothing in this Agreement shall affect or impair:
(a) the inherent right of individual or collective self-defense as envisaged by Article 51 of the Charter of the United Nations,*
(b) the provisions of the Charter of the United Nations, including those relating to the maintenance or restoration of international peace and security, and
(c) the obligations undertaken by either Party towards its allies or other countries in treaties, agreements, and other appropriate documents.

Source: U.S. State Department. Available online at https://www.state.gov/t/isn/5186.htm. Accessed February 24, 2018.

Threshold Test Ban Treaty (1974)

Treaty Between The United States of America and The Union of Soviet Socialist Republics on the Limitation of Underground Nuclear Weapon Tests
Signed at Moscow July 3, 1974
Ratified December 8, 1990
Entered into force December 11, 1990

The United States of America and the Union of Soviet Socialist Republics, hereinafter referred to as the Parties,

Declaring their intention to achieve at the earliest possible date the cessation of the nuclear arms race and to take effective measures toward reductions in strategic arms, nuclear disarmament, and general and complete disarmament under strict and effective international control,

Recalling the determination expressed by the Parties to the 1963 Treaty Banning Nuclear Weapon Tests in the Atmosphere, in Outer Space and Under Water in its Preamble to seek to achieve the discontinuance of all test explosions of nuclear weapons for all time, and to continue negotiations to this end,

Noting that the adoption of measures for the further limitation of underground nuclear weapon tests would contribute to the achievement of these objectives and would meet the interests of strengthening peace and the further relaxation of international tension,

Reaffirming their adherence to the objectives and principles of the Treaty Banning Nuclear Weapon Tests in the Atmosphere, in Outer Space and Under Water and of the Treaty on the Non-Proliferation of Nuclear Weapons,

Have agreed as follows:

Article I

1. Each Party undertakes to prohibit, to prevent, and not to carry out any underground nuclear weapon test having a yield exceeding 150 kilotons at any place under its jurisdiction or control, beginning March 31, 1976.
2. Each Party shall limit the number of its underground nuclear weapon tests to a minimum.
3. The Parties shall continue their negotiations with a view toward achieving a solution to the problem of the cessation of all underground nuclear weapon tests.

Article II

1. For the purpose of providing assurance of compliance with the provisions of this Treaty, each Party shall use national technical means of verification at its disposal in a manner consistent with the generally recognized principles of international law.
2. Each Party undertakes not to interfere with the national technical means of verification of the other Party operating in accordance with paragraph 1 of this Article.

DONE at Moscow on July 3, 1974, in duplicate, in the English and Russian languages, both texts being equally authentic.

Source: U.S. State Department. Available online at https://www.state.gov/t/isn/5204.htm. Accessed February 24, 2018.

Peaceful Nuclear Explosions Treaty (1976)

Treaty Between the United States of America and the Union of Soviet Socialist Republics on Underground Nuclear Explosions for Peaceful Purposes

Signed at Washington and Moscow May 28, 1976

Entered into force December 11, 1990

The United States of America and the Union of Soviet Socialist Republics, hereinafter referred to as the Parties,

Proceeding from a desire to implement Article III of the Treaty Between the United States of America and the Union of Soviet Socialist Republics on the Limitation of Underground Nuclear Weapon Tests, which calls for the earliest possible conclusion of an agreement on underground nuclear explosions for peaceful purposes,

Reaffirming their adherence to the objectives and principles of the Treaty Banning Nuclear Weapon Tests in the Atmosphere, in Outer Space and Under Water, the Treaty on Non-Proliferation of Nuclear Weapons, and the Treaty on the Limitation of Underground Nuclear Weapon Tests, and their determination to observe strictly the provisions of these international agreements,

Desiring to assure that underground nuclear explosions for peaceful purposes shall not be used for purposes related to nuclear weapons,

Desiring that utilization of nuclear energy be directed only toward peaceful purposes,

Desiring to develop appropriately cooperation in the field of underground nuclear explosions for peaceful purposes,

Have agreed as follows:

Article I

1. The Parties enter into this Treaty to satisfy the obligations in Article III of the Treaty on the Limitation of Underground Nuclear Weapon Tests, and assume additional obligations in accordance with the provisions of this Treaty.
2. This Treaty shall govern all underground nuclear explosions for peaceful purposes conducted by the Parties after March 31, 1976.

Article III

1. Each Party, subject to the obligations assumed under this Treaty and other international agreements, reserves the right to:
   (a) carry out explosions at any place under its jurisdiction or control outside the geographical boundaries of test sites specified under the provisions of the Treaty on the Limitation of Underground Nuclear Weapon Tests; and
   (b) carry out, participate or assist in carrying out explosions in the territory of another State at the request of such other State.
2. Each Party undertakes to prohibit, to prevent and not to carry out at any place under its jurisdiction or control, and further undertakes not to carry out, participate or assist in carrying out anywhere:
   (a) any individual explosion having a yield exceeding 150 kilotons;
   (b) any group explosion:
      (1) having an aggregate yield exceeding 150 kilotons except in ways that will permit identification of each individual explosion and determination of the yield of each individual explosion in the group in accordance with the provisions of Article IV of and the Protocol to this Treaty;
      (2) having an aggregate yield exceeding one and one-half megatons;
   (c) any explosion which does not carry out a peaceful application;
   (d) any explosion except in compliance with the provisions of the Treaty Banning Nuclear Weapon Tests in the Atmosphere, in Outer Space and Under Water, the Treaty on the Non-Proliferation of Nuclear Weapons, and other international agreements entered into by that Party.
3. The question of carrying out any individual explosion having a yield exceeding the yield specified in paragraph 2(a) of this article will be considered by the

Parties at an appropriate time to be agreed.

Source: U.S. State Department. Available online at https://www.state.gov/t/isn/5182.htm. Accessed February 24, 2018.

Harmel Report and NATO Dual-Track Decision (1979)

At a special meeting of Foreign and Defence Ministers in Brussels on 12th December 1979:

Ministers recalled the May 1978 Summit where governments expressed the political resolve to meet the challenges to their security posed by the continuing momentum of the Warsaw Pact military build-up.

The Warsaw Pact has over the years developed a large and growing capability in nuclear systems that directly threaten Western Europe and have a strategic significance for the Alliance in Europe. This situation has been especially aggravated over the last few years by Soviet decisions to implement programmes modernizing and expanding their long-range nuclear capability substantially. In particular, they have deployed the SS-20 missile, which offers significant improvements over previous systems in providing greater accuracy, more mobility, and greater range, as well as having multiple warheads, and the Backfire bomber, which has a much better performance than other Soviet aircraft deployed hitherto in a theatre role. During this period, while the Soviet Union has been reinforcing its superiority in Long-Range Theatre Nuclear Forces (LRTNF) both quantitatively and qualitatively, Western LRTNF capabilities have remained static. Indeed these forces are increasing in age and vulnerability and do not include land-based, long-range theatre nuclear missile systems

At the same time, the Soviets have also undertaken a modernization and expansion of their shorter-range TNF and greatly improved the overall quality of their conventional forces. These developments took place against the background of increasing Soviet inter-continental capabilities and achievement of parity in intercontinental capability with the United States.

These trends have prompted serious concern within the Alliance, because, if they were to continue, Soviet superiority in theatre nuclear systems could undermine the stability achieved in inter-continental systems and cast doubt on the credibility of the Alliance's deterrent strategy by highlighting the gap in the spectrum of NATO's available nuclear response to aggression.

Ministers noted that these recent developments require concrete actions on the part of the Alliance if NATO's strategy of flexible response is to remain credible. After intensive consideration, including the merits of alternative approaches, and after taking note of the positions of certain members, Ministers concluded that the overall interest of the Alliance would best be served by pursuing two parallel and complementary approaches of TNF modernization and arms control.

Accordingly Ministers have decided to modernize NATO's LRTNF by the deployment in Europe of US ground-launched systems comprising 108 Pershing II launchers, which would replace existing US Pershing I-A, and 464 Ground Launched Cruise Missiles (GLCM), all with single warheads. All the nations currently participating in the integrated defence structure will participate in the programme: the missiles will be stationed in selected countries and certain support costs will be met through NATO's existing common funding arrangements. The programme will not increase NATO's reliance upon nuclear weapons. In this connection, Ministers agreed that as an integral part of TNF modernization, 1.000 US nuclear warheads will be withdrawn from Europe as soon as feasible. Further, Ministers decided that the 572 LRTNF warheads should be accommodated within that reduced level, which necessarily implies a numerical shift of emphasis away from warheads for delivery systems of other types and shorter ranges In addition they noted with satisfaction-that the Nuclear Planning Group is undertaking an examination of the precise nature, scope and basis of the adjustments resulting from the LRTNF deployment and their possible implications for the balance of roles and systems in NATO's nuclear armoury as a whole. This examination will form the basis of a substantive report to NPG Ministers in the Autumn of 1980.

Ministers attach great importance to the role of arms control in contributing to a more stable military relationship between East and West and in advancing the process of detente. This is reflected in a broad set of initiatives being examined within the Alliance to further the course of arms control and detente in the 1980s. Ministers regard arms control as an integral part of the Alliance's efforts to assure the undiminished security of its member States and to make the strategic situation between East and West more stable, more predictable, and more manageable at lower levels of armaments on both sides. In this regard they welcome the contribution which the SALT II Treaty makes towards achieving these objectives.

Ministers consider that, building on this accomplishment and taking account of the expansion of Soviet LRTNF capabilities of concern to NATO, arms control efforts to achieve a more stable overall nuclear balance at lower levels of nuclear weapons on both sides should therefore now include certain US and Soviet long-range theatre nuclear systems This would reflect previous Western suggestions to include such Soviet and US systems in arms control negotiations and more recent expressions by Soviet President Brezhnev of willingness to do so. Ministers fully support the decision taken by the United States following consultations within the Alliance to negotiate arms limitations on LRTNF and to propose to the USSR to begin negotiations as soon as possible along the following lines which have been elaborated in intensive consultations within the Alliance...

The Ministers have decided to pursue these two parallel and complementary approaches in order to avert an arms race in Europe caused by the Soviet TNF build-up, yet preserve the viability of NATO's strategy of deterrence and defence and thus maintain the security of its member States.

1. A modernization decision, including a commitment to deployments, is necessary to meet NATO's deterrence and defence needs, to provide a credible response to unilateral Soviet TNF deployments, and to provide the foundation for the pursuit of serious negotiations on TNF.

2. Success of arms control in constraining the Soviet build-up can enhance Alliance security, modify the scale of NATO's TNF requirements, and promote stability and detente in Europe in consonance with NATO's basic policy of deterrence, defence and detente as enunciated in the Harmel Report. NATO's TNF requirements will be examined in the light of concrete results reached through negotiations.

Convention on the Physical Protection of Nuclear Material (1980)

Signed at New York March 3, 1980

Ratification advised by U.S. Senate July 30, 1981

Ratified by U.S. President September 4, 1981

Entered into force February 8, 1987

The States Parties to This Convention,

Recognizing the right of all States to develop and apply nuclear energy for peaceful purposes and their legitimate interests in the potential benefits to be derived from the peaceful application of nuclear energy,

Convinced of the need for facilitating international cooperation in the peaceful application of nuclear energy,

Desiring to avert the potential dangers posed by the unlawful taking and use of nuclear material,

Convinced that offenses relating to nuclear material are a matter of grave concern and that there is an urgent need to adopt appropriate and effective measures to ensure the prevention, detection and punishment of such offenses,

Aware of the Need for international cooperation to establish, in conformity with the national law of each State Party and with this Convention, effective measures for the physical protection of nuclear material,

Convinced that this Convention should facilitate the safe transfer of nuclear material,

Stressing also the importance of the physical protection of nuclear material in domestic use, storage and transport,

Recognizing the importance of effective physical protection of nuclear material used for military purposes, and understanding that such material is and will continue to be accorded stringent physical protection,

Have Agreed as follows:

Article 1

For the purposes of this Convention:

(a) "nuclear material" means plutonium except that with isotopic concentration exceeding 80% in plutonium-238; uranium-233; uranium enriched in the isotopes 235 or 233; uranium containing the mixture of isotopes as occurring in nature other than in the form of ore or ore-residue; any material containing one or more of the foregoing;

(b) "uranium enriched in the isotopes 235 or 233" means uranium containing the isotopes 235 or 233 or both in an amount such that the abundance ratio of the sum of these isotopes to the isotope 238 is greater than the ratio of the isotope 235 to the isotope 238 occurring in nature;

(c) "international nuclear transport" means the carriage of a consignment of nuclear material by any means of transportation intended to go beyond the territory of the State where the shipment originates beginning with the departure from a facility of the shipper in that State and ending with the arrival at a facility of the receiver within the State of ultimate destination.

Article 3

Each State Party shall take appropriate steps within the framework of its national law and consistent with international law to ensure as far as practicable that, during international nuclear transport, nuclear material within its territory, or on board a ship or aircraft under its jurisdiction insofar as such ship or aircraft is engaged in the transport to or from that State, is protected at the levels described in Annex I.

Article 4

1. Each State Party shall not export or authorize the export of nuclear material unless the State Party has received assurances that such material will be protected during the international nuclear transport at the levels described in Annex I.
2. Each State Party shall not import or authorize the import of nuclear material from a State not party to this Convention unless the State Party has received assurances that such material will during the international nuclear transport be protected at the levels described in Annex I.
3. A State Party shall not allow the transit of its territory by land or internal waterways or through its airports or seaports of nuclear material between States that are not parties to this Convention unless the State Party has received assurances as far as practicable that this nuclear material will be protected during international nuclear transport at the levels described in Annex I.
4. Each State Party shall apply within the framework of its national law the levels of physical protection described in Annex I to nuclear material being transported from a part of that State to another part of the same State through international waters or airspace.
5. The State Party responsible for receiving assurances that the nuclear material

will be protected at the levels described in Annex I according to paragraphs 1 to 3 shall identify and inform in advance States which the nuclear material is expected to transit by land or internal waterways, or whose airports or seaports it is expected to enter.
6. The responsibility for obtaining assurances referred to in paragraph 1 may be transferred, by mutual agreement, to the State Party involved in the transport as the importing State.
7. Nothing in this article shall be interpreted as in any way affecting the territorial sovereignty and jurisdiction of a State, including that over its airspace and territorial sea.

Source: "No. 24631. Multilateral," in Treaty Series 2511: Treaties and International Agreements Registered or Filed and Recorded with the Secretariat of the United Nations, UN, New York. Available online at http://dx.doi.org/10.18356/a1f3f630-en-fr. Accessed February 24, 2018.

Nuclear Risk Reduction Centers Agreement (1987)

Agreement Between the United States of American and the Union of Soviet Socialist Republics on the Establishment of Nuclear Risk Reduction Centers

Signed at Washington September 15, 1987

Entered into force September 15, 1987

The United States of America and the Union of Soviet Socialist Republics, hereinafter referred to as the Parties,

Affirming their desire to reduce and ultimately eliminate the risk of outbreak of nuclear war, in particular, as a result of misinterpretation, miscalculation, or accident,

Believing that a nuclear war cannot be won and must never be fought,

Believing that agreement on measures for reducing the risk of outbreak of nuclear war serves the interests of strengthening international peace and security,

Reaffirming their obligations under the Agreement on Measures to Reduce the Risk of Outbreak of Nuclear War between the United States of America and the Union of Soviet Socialist Republics of September 30, 1971, and the Agreement between the Government of the United States of America and the Government of the Union of Soviet Socialist Republics on the Prevention of Incidents on and over the High Seas of May 25, 1972,

Have agreed as follows:

Article 1

Each Party shall establish, in its capital, a national Nuclear Risk Reduction Center that shall operate on behalf of and under the control of its respective Government.

Article 2

The Parties shall use the Nuclear Risk Reduction Centers to transmit notifications identified in Protocol I which constitutes an integral part of this Agreement.

In the future, the list of notifications transmitted through the Centers may be altered by agreement between the Parties, as relevant new agreements are reached.

Article 5

The Parties shall hold regular meetings between representatives of the Nuclear Risk Reduction Centers at least once each year to consider matters related to the functioning of such Centers.

Source: U.S. State Department. Available online at https://www.state.gov/t/isn/215573.htm. Accessed February 24, 2018.

Ballistic Missile Launch Notification Agreement (1988)

Agreement Between The United States of America and The Union of Soviet Socialist Republics on Notifications of Launches of Intercontinental Ballistic Missiles and Submarine-Launched Ballistic Missiles

Signed at Moscow May 31, 1988

Entered into Force May 31, 1988

The United States of America and the Union of Soviet Socialist Republics, hereinafter referred to as the Parties,

Affirming their desire to reduce and ultimately eliminate the risk of outbreak of nuclear war, in particular, as a result of misinterpretation, miscalculation, or accident,

Believing that a nuclear war cannot be won and must never be fought,

Believing that agreement on measures for reducing the risk of outbreak of nuclear war serves the interests of strengthening international peace and security,

Reaffirming their obligations under the Agreement on Measures to Reduce the Risk of Outbreak of Nuclear War between the United States of America and the Union of Soviet Socialist Republics of September 30, 1971, the Agreement between the Government of the United States of America and the Government of the Union of Soviet Socialist Republics on the Prevention of Incidents on and over the High Seas of May 25, 1972, and the Agreement between the United States of America and the Union of Soviet Socialist Republics on the Establishment of Nuclear Risk Reduction Centers of September 15, 1987,

Have agreed as follows:

Article I

Each Party shall provide the other Party notification, through the Nuclear Risk

Reduction Centers of the United States of America and the Union of Soviet Socialist Republics, no less than twenty-four hours in advance, of the planned date, launch area, and area of impact for any launch of a strategic ballistic missile: an intercontinental ballistic missile (hereinafter "ICBM") or a submarine-launched ballistic missile (hereinafter "SLBM").

DONE at Moscow on May 31, 1988, in two copies, each in the English and Russian languages, both texts being equally authentic.

Source: U.S. Department of State. Available online at https://www.state.gov/t/isn/4714.htm. Accessed February 24, 2018.

Strategic Arms Reduction Treaty (START I) (1991)

Treaty Between the United States of America and the Union of Soviet Socialist Republics on the Reduction and Limitation of Strategic Offensive Arms

Signed in Moscow, 31 July 1991

The United States of America and the Union of Soviet Socialist Republics, hereinafter referred to as the Parties,

Conscious that nuclear war would have devastating consequences for all humanity, that it cannot be won and must never be fought,

Convinced that the measures for the reduction and limitation of strategic offensive arms and the other obligations set forth in this Treaty will help to reduce the risk of outbreak of nuclear war and strengthen international peace and security,

Recognizing that the interests of the Parties and the interests of international security require the strengthening of strategic stability,

Mindful of their undertakings with regard to strategic offensive arms in Article VI of the Treaty on the Non-Proliferation of Nuclear Weapons of July 1, 1968; Article XI of the Treaty on the Limitation of Anti-Ballistic Missile Systems of May 26, 1972; and the Washington Summit Joint Statement of June 1, 1990, [ABA]

Have agreed as follows:

Article I

Each Party shall reduce and limit its strategic offensive arms in accordance with the provisions of this Treaty, and shall carry out the other obligations set forth in this Treaty and its Annexes, Protocols, and Memorandum of Understanding.

Article II

1. Each Party shall reduce and limit its ICBMs and ICBM launchers, SLBMs and SLBM launchers, heavy bombers, ICBM warheads, SLBM warheads, and heavy bomber armaments, so that seven years after entry into force of this Treaty and thereafter, the aggregate numbers, as counted in accordance with Article III of this Treaty, do not exceed:
   (a) 1600, for deployed ICBMs and their associated launchers, deployed SLBMs and their associated launchers, and deployed heavy bombers, including 154 for deployed heavy ICBMs and their associated launchers; [RF MOU, Section II] [US MOU, Section II] [Agreed State 33]
   (b) 6000, for warheads attributed to deployed ICBMs, deployed SLBMs, and deployed heavy bombers, [RF MOU, Section II] [US MOU, Section II] including: [Agreed State 33] [START II, Art. I,3]
      (i) 4900, for warheads attributed to deployed ICBMs and deployed SLBMs; [RF MOU,

Section II] [US MOU, Section II] [START II, Art. I,4] [Agreed State 33]

(ii) 1100, for warheads attributed to deployed ICBMs on mobile launchers of ICBMs; [RF MOU, Section II]

(iii) 1540, for warheads attributed to deployed heavy ICBMs. [phased heavy reductions [RF MOU, Section II] ABA

2. Each Party shall implement the reductions pursuant to paragraph 1 of this Article in three phases, so that its strategic offensive arms do not exceed:

(a) by the end of the first phase, that is, no later than 36 months after entry into force of this Treaty, and thereafter, the following aggregate numbers:

(i) 2100, for deployed ICBMs and their associated launchers, deployed SLBMs and their associated launchers, and deployed heavy bombers;

(ii) 9150, for warheads attributed to deployed ICBMs, deployed SLBMs, and deployed heavy bombers;

(iii) b 8050, warheads attributed to deployed ICBMs and deployed SLBMs;

(b) by the end of the second phase, that is, no later than 60 months after entry into force of this Treaty, and thereafter, the following aggregate numbers:

(i) 1900, for deployed ICBMs and their associated launchers, deployed SLBMs and their associated launchers, and deployed heavy bombers;

(ii) 7950, for warheads attributed to deployed ICBMs, deployed

SLBMs, and deployed heavy bombers;

(iii) 6750, warheads attributed to deployed ICBMs and deployed SLBMs;

(c) by the end of the third phase, that is, no later than 84 months after entry into force of this Treaty: the aggregate numbers provided for in paragraph 1 of this Article .ABA

3. Each Party shall limit the aggregate throw-weight [RF MOU, Section II] [US MOU Section II] of its deployed ICBMs [RF MOU, Section I] [US MOU Section I] and deployed SLBMs [RF MOU, Section I] [US MOU Section I] so that seven years after entry into force of this Treaty and thereafter such aggregate throw-weight does not exceed 3600 metric tons. ABA [Throw-weight Limits/Provisions for Types of ICBMs and SLBMs]

Article III

1. For the purposes of counting toward the maximum aggregate limits provided for in subparagraphs 1(a), 2(a)(i), and 2(b)(i) of Article II of this Treaty:

(a) Each deployed ICBM and its associated launcher shall be counted as one unit; each deployed SLBM and its associated launcher; shall be counted as one unit.

(b) Each deployed heavy bombers shall be counted as one unit. ABA

2. For the purposes of counting deployed ICBMs and their associated launchers and deployed SLBMs and their associated launchers

(a) Each deployed launcher of ICBMs and each deployed launcher of SLBMs shall be considered to contain one deployed ICBM or one deployed SLBM, respectively. ABA

(b) If a deployed ICBM has been removed from its launcher and another missile has not been installed in that launcher, such an ICBM removed from its launcher and located at that ICBM base shall continue to be considered to be contained in that launcher. ABA

(c) If a deployed SLBM has been removed from its launcher and another missile has not been installed in that launcher, such an SLBM removed from its launcher shall be considered to be contained in that launcher. Such an SLBM removed from its launcher shall be located only at a facility at which non-deployed SLBMs may be located pursuant to subparagraph 9(a) of Article IV of this Treaty or be in movement to such a facility. ABA

Article VI

1. Deployed road-mobile launchers of ICBMs and their associated missiles shall be based only in restricted areas. A restricted area shall not exceed five square kilometers in size and shall not overlap another restricted area. No more than ten deployed road-mobile launchers of ICBMs and their associated missiles may be based or located in a restricted area. A restricted area shall not contain deployed ICBMs for road-mobile launchers of ICBMs of more than one type of ICBM. [RF MOU Annex A] [Agreed State 19]

Article IX

1. For the purpose of ensuring verification of compliance with the provisions of this Treaty, each Party shall use national technical means of verification at its

disposal in a manner consistent with generally recognized principles of international law.

2. Each Party undertakes not to interfere with the national technical means of verification of the other Party operating in accordance with paragraph 1 of this Article.

3. Each Party undertakes not to use concealment measures that impede verification, by national technical means of verification, of compliance with the provisions of this Treaty. In this connection, the obligation not to use concealment measures includes the obligation not to use them at test ranges, including measures that result in the concealment of ICBMs, SLBMs, mobile launchers of ICBMs, or the association between ICBMs or SLBMs and their launchers during testing. The obligation not to use concealment measures shall not apply to cover or concealment practices at ICBM bases and deployment areas, or to the use of environmental shelters for strategic offensive arms.

4. To aid verification, each ICBM for mobile launchers of ICBMs shall have a unique identifier as provided for in the Inspection Protocol.

Article XII

1. To enhance the effectiveness of national technical means of verification, each Party shall, if the other Party makes a request in accordance with paragraph 1 of Section V of the Notification Protocol, carry out the following cooperative measures:

(a) a display in the open of the road-mobile launchers of ICBMs located within restricted areas specified by the requesting Party. The number of road-mobile launchers of ICBMs based at the restricted areas specified in each such request shall not exceed ten percent of the total number of deployed road-mobile launchers of ICBMs of the requested Party, and such launchers shall be contained within one ICBM base for road-mobile launchers of ICBMs. For each specified restricted area, the roofs of fixed structures for road-mobile launchers of ICBMs shall be open for the duration of a display. The road-mobile launchers of ICBMs located within the restricted area shall be displayed either located next to or moved halfway out of such fixed structures; [RF MOU Annex A]

Done at Moscow on July 31, 1991, in two copies, each in the English and Russian languages, both texts being equally authentic.

Source: U.S. Congress. Senate. *Treaty on the Reduction and Limitation of Strategic Offensive Arms.* July 31, 1991. S. Treaty Doc. No. 102-20.

Joint Declaration on the Denuclearization of the Korean Peninsula (1992)

Entry into force on February 19, 1992

South and North Korea,

In order to eliminate the danger of nuclear war through the denuclearization of the Korean peninsula, to create conditions and an environment favourable to peace and the peaceful unification of Korea, and thus to contribute to the peace and security of Asia and the world,

Declare as follows:

1. South and North Korea shall not test, manufacture, produce, receive, possess, store, deploy or use nuclear weapons.

2. South and North Korea shall use nuclear energy solely for peaceful purposes.

3. South and North Korea shall not possess nuclear reprocessing and uranium enrichment facilities.

4. In order to verify the denuclearization of the Korean peninsula, South and North Korea shall conduct inspections of particular subjects chosen by the other side and agreed upon between the two sides, in accordance with the procedures and methods to be determined by the South-North Joint Nuclear Control Commission.

5. In order to implement this joint declaration, South and North Korea shall establish and operate a South-North Joint Nuclear Control Commission within one month of the entry into force of this joint declaration;

6. This joint declaration shall enter into force from the date the South and the North exchange the appropriate instruments following the completion of their respective procedures for bringing it into effect.

Source: Joint Declaration of the Denuclearization of the Korean Peninsula. Available online at http://peacemaker.un.org/korea-denuclearization92. Accessed February 24, 2018.

Treaty on Open Skies (1992)

The States concluding this Treaty, hereinafter referred to collectively as the States Parties or individually as a State Party,

Recalling the commitments they have made in the Conference on Security and Co-operation in Europe to promoting greater openness and transparency in their military activities and to enhancing security by means of confidence-and security-building measures,

Welcoming the historic events in Europe which have transformed the security situation from Vancouver to Vladivostok,

Wishing to contribute to the further development and strengthening of peace, stability and co-operative security in that area by the creation of an Open Skies regime for aerial observation,

Recognizing the potential contribution which an aerial-observation regime of this type could make to security and stability in other regions as well,

Noting the possibility of employing such a regime to improve openness and transparency, to facilitate the monitoring of compliance with existing or future arms control agreements and to strengthen the capacity for conflict prevention and crisis management in the framework of the Conference on Security and Co-operation in Europe and in other relevant international institutions,

Envisaging the possible extension of the Open Skies regime into additional fields, such as the protection of the environment,

Seeking to establish agreed procedures to provide for aerial observation of all the territories of States Parties, with the intent of observing a single State Party or groups of States Parties, on the basis of equity and effectiveness while maintaining flight safety,

Noting that the operation of such an Open Skies regime will be without prejudice to States not participating in it,

Have agreed as follows:

Article I: General Provisions

1. This Treaty establishes the regime, to be known as the Open Skies regime, for the conduct of observation flights by States Parties over the territories of other States Parties, and sets forth the rights and obligations of the States Parties relating thereto.

2. Each of the Annexes and their related Appendices constitutes an integral part of this Treaty.

Article III: Quotas
Section I. General Provisions

1. Each State Party shall have the right to conduct observation flights in accordance with the provisions of this Treaty.

2. Each State Party shall be obliged to accept observation flights over its territory in accordance with the provisions of this Treaty.

3. Each State Party shall have the right to conduct a number of observation flights over the territory of any other State Party equal to the number of observation flights which that other State Party has the right to conduct over it.

4. The total number of observation flights that each State Party is obliged to accept over its territory is the total passive quota for that State Party. The allocation of the total passive quota to the States Parties is set forth in Annex A, Section I to this Treaty.

5. The number of observation flights that a State Party shall have the right to conduct each year over the territory of each of the other States Parties is the individual active quota of that State Party with respect to that other State Party. The sum of the individual active quotas is the total active quota of that State Party. The total active quota of a State Party shall not exceed its total passive quota.

6. The first distribution of active quotas is set forth in Annex A, Section II to this Treaty.

7. After entry into force of this Treaty, the distribution of active quotas shall be subject to an annual review for the following calendar year within the

framework of the Open Skies Consultative Commission. In the event that it is not possible during the annual review to arrive within three weeks at agreement on the distribution of active quotas with respect to a particular State Party, the previous year's distribution of active quotas with respect to that State Party shall remain unchanged.

8. Except as provided for by the provisions of Article VIII, each observation flight conducted by a State Party shall be counted against the individual and total active quotas of that State Party.

9. Notwithstanding the provisions of paragraphs 3 and 5 of this Section, a State Party to which an active quota has been distributed may, by agreement with the State Party to be overflown, transfer a part or all of its total active quota to other States Parties and shall promptly notify all other States Parties and the Open Skies Consultative Commission thereof. Paragraph 10 of this Section shall apply.

10. No State Party shall conduct more observation flights over the territory of another State Party than a number equal to 50 per cent, rounded up to the nearest whole number, of its own total active quota, or of the total passive quota of that other State Party, whichever is less.

11. The maximum flight distances of observation flights over the territories of the States Parties are set forth in Annex A, Section III to this Treaty.

ANNEX A

QUOTAS AND MAXIMUM FLIGHT DISTANCES SECTION
I. ALLOCATION OF PASSIVE QUOTAS

1. The allocation of individual passive quotas is set forth as follows and shall be effective only for those States Parties having ratified the Treaty:

For the Federal Republic of Germany	12
For the United States of America	42
For the Republic of Belarus and the Russian Federation group of States Parties	42
For Benelux	6
For the Republic of Bulgaria	4
For Canada	12
For the Kingdom of Denmark	6
For the Kingdom of Spain	4
For the French Republic	12
For the United Kingdom of Great Britain and Northern Ireland	12
For the Hellenic Republic	4
For the Republic of Hungary	4
For the Republic of Iceland	4
For the Italian Republic	12
For the Kingdom of Norway	7
For the Republic of Poland	6
For the Portuguese Republic	2
For Romania	6
For the Czech and Slovak Federal Republic	4
For the Republic of Turkey	12
For Ukraine	12

Source: U.S. Department of State. Available online at https://www.state.gov/t/avc/trty/102337.htm. Accessed February 24, 2018.

Strategic Arms Reduction Treaty (START II) (1993)

Treaty Between the United States of America and the Russian Federation on Further Reduction and Limitation of Strategic Offensive Arms

Signed in Moscow, January 3, 1993
Never entered into force

The United States of America and the Russian Federation, hereinafter referred to as the Parties,

REAFFIRMING their obligations under the Treaty Between the United States of America and the Union of Soviet Socialist Republics on the Reduction and Limitation of Strategic Offensive Arms of July 31, 1991, hereinafter referred to as the START Treaty,

STRESSING their firm commitment to the Treaty on the Non-Proliferation of Nuclear Weapons of July 1, 1968, and their desire to contribute to its strengthening,

TAKING into account the commitment by the Republic of Belarus, the Republic of Kazakhstan, and Ukraine to accede to the Treaty on the Non-Proliferation of Nuclear Weapons of July 1, 1968, as non-nuclear-weapon States Parties,

MINDFUL of their undertakings with respect to strategic offensive arms under Article VI of the Treaty on the Non-Proliferation of Nuclear Weapons of July 1, 1968, and under the Treaty Between the United States of America and the Union of Soviet Socialist Republics on the Limitation of Anti-Ballistic Missile Systems of May 26, 1972, as well as the provisions of the Joint Understanding signed by the Presidents of the United States of America and the Russian Federation on June 17, 1992, and of the Joint Statement on a Global Protection System signed by the Presidents of the United States of America and the Russian Federation on June 17, 1992,

DESIRING to enhance strategic stability and predictability, and, in doing so, to reduce further strategic offensive arms, in addition to the reductions and limitations provided for in the START Treaty,

CONSIDERING that further progress toward that end will help lay a solid foundation for a world order built on democratic values that would preclude the risk of outbreak of war,

RECOGNIZING their special responsibility as permanent members of the United Nations Security Council for maintaining international peace and security,

TAKING note of United Nations General Assembly Resolution 47/52K of December 9, 1992.

CONSCIOUS of the new realities that have transformed the political and strategic relations between the Parties, and the relations of partnership that have been established between them,

Have agreed as follows:

Article I

1. Each Party shall reduce and limit its intercontinental ballistic missiles (ICBMs) and ICBM launchers, submarine-launched ballistic missiles (SLBMs) and SLBM launchers, heavy bombers, ICBM warheads, SLBM warheads, and heavy bomber armaments, so that seven years after entry into force of the START Treaty and thereafter, the aggregate number for each Party, as counted in accordance with Articles III and IV of this Treaty, does not exceed, for warheads attributed to deployed ICBMs, deployed SLBMs, and deployed heavy bombers, a number between 3800 and 4250 or such lower number as each Party shall decide for itself, but in no case shall such number exceed 4250.

2. Within the limitations provided for in paragraph 1 of this Article, the aggregate numbers for each Party shall not exceed:

    (a) 2160, for warheads attributed to deployed SLBMs;

    (b) 1200, for warheads attributed to deployed ICBMs of types to which more than one warhead is attributed; and

(c) 650, for warheads attributed to deployed heavy ICBMs.

3. Upon fulfillment of the obligations provided for in paragraph 1 of this Article, each Party shall further reduce and limit its ICBMs and ICBM launchers, SLBMs and SLBM launchers, heavy bombers, ICBM warheads, SLBM warheads, and heavy bomber armaments, so that no later than January 1, 2003, and thereafter, the aggregate number for each Party, as counted in accordance with Articles III and IV of this Treaty, does not exceed, for warheads attributed to deployed ICBMs, deployed SLBMs, and deployed heavy bombers, a number between 3000 and 3500 or such lower number as each Party shall decide for itself, but in no case shall such number exceed 3500.

4. Within the limitations provided for in paragraph 3 of this Article, the aggregate numbers for each Party shall not exceed:

(a) a number between 1700 and 1750, for warheads attributed to deployed SLBMs or such lower number as each Party shall decide for itself, but in no case shall such number exceed 1750;

(b) zero, for warheads attributed to deployed ICBMs of types to which more than one warhead is attributed; and

(c) zero, for warheads attributed to deployed heavy ICBMs.

Article II

1. No later than January 1, 2003, each Party undertakes to have eliminated or to have converted to launchers of ICBMs to which one warhead is attributed all its deployed and non-deployed launchers of ICBMs to which more than one warhead is attributed under Article III of this Treaty (including test launchers and training launchers), with the exception of those launchers of ICBMs other than heavy ICBMs at space launch facilities allowed under the START Treaty, and not to have thereafter launchers of ICBMs to which more than one warhead is attributed. ICBM launchers that have been converted to launch an ICBM of a different type shall not be capable of launching an ICBM of the former type. Each Party shall carry out such elimination or conversion using the procedures provided for in the START Treaty, except as otherwise provided for in paragraph 3 of this Article.

Article IV

1. For the purposes of this Treaty, the number of warheads attributed to each deployed heavy bomber shall be equal to the number of nuclear weapons for which any heavy bomber of the same type or variant of a type is actually equipped, with the exception of heavy bombers reoriented to a conventional role as provided for in paragraph 7 of this Article. Each nuclear weapon for which a heavy bomber is actually equipped shall count as one warhead toward the limitations provided for in Article I of this Treaty. For the purpose of such counting, nuclear weapons include long-range nuclear air-launched cruise missiles (ALCMs), nuclear air-to-surface missiles with a range of less than 600 kilometers, and nuclear bombs.

Source: U.S. Senate. *Treaty between the United States of America and the Russian Federation on Further Reduction and Limitation of Strategic Offensive Arms.* 103rd Cong., 1st sess., 1993. S. Treaty Doc. 103-1.

Missile Technology Control Regime, U.S. Guidelines (1993)

The United States Government has, after careful consideration and subject to its international treaty obligations, decided that, when considering the transfer of equipment and technology related to missiles, it will act in accordance with the attached Guidelines beginning on January 7, 1993. These Guidelines replace those adopted on April 16, 1987.

Guidelines For Sensitive Missile-Relevant Transfers

1. The purpose of these Guidelines is to limit the risks of proliferation of weapons of mass destruction (i.e. nuclear, chemical and biological weapons), by controlling transfers that could make a contribution to delivery systems (other than manned aircraft) for such weapons. The Guidelines are not designed to impede national space programs or international cooperation in such programs as long as such programs could not contribute to delivery systems for weapons of mass destruction. These Guidelines, including the attached Annex, form the basis for controlling transfers to any destination beyond the Government's jurisdiction or control of all delivery systems (other than manned aircraft) capable of delivering weapons of mass destruction, and of equipment and technology relevant to missiles whose performance in terms of payload and range exceeds stated parameters. Restraint will be exercised in the consideration of all transfers of items contained within the Annex and all such transfers will be considered on a case-by-case basis. The Government will implement the Guidelines in accordance with national legislation.

2. The Annex consists of two categories of items, which term includes equipment and technology. Category I items, all of which are in Annex Items 1 and 2, are those items of greatest sensitivity. If a Category I item is included in a system, that system will also be considered as Category I, except when the incorporated item cannot be separated, removed or duplicated. Particular restraint will be exercised in the consideration of Category I transfers regardless of their purpose, and there will be a strong presumption to deny such transfers. Particular restraint will also be exercised in the consideration of transfers of any items in the Annex, or of any missiles (whether or not in the Annex), if the Government judges, on the basis of all available, persuasive information, evaluated according to factors including those in paragraph 3, that they are intended to be used for the delivery of weapons of mass destruction, and there will be a strong presumption to deny such transfers. Until further notice, the transfer of Category I production facilities will not be authorized. The transfer of other Category I items will be authorized only on rare occasions and where the Government (A) obtains binding government-to-government undertakings embodying the assurances from the recipient government called for in paragraph 5 of these Guidelines and (B) assumes responsibility for taking all steps necessary to ensure that the item is put only to its stated end-use. It is understood that the decision to transfer remains the sole and sovereign judgment of the United States Government.

Source: U.S. Department of State. Available online at https://www.state.gov/t/avc/trty/187155.htm. Accessed February 24, 2018.

The Wassenaar Arrangement on Export Controls for Conventional Arms and Dual-Use Goods and Technologies (1995)

Final Declaration

1. Representatives of Australia, Austria, Belgium, Canada, the Czech Republic, Denmark, Finland, France, Germany, Greece, Hungary, Ireland, Italy, Japan, Luxembourg, the Netherlands, New Zealand, Norway, Poland, Portugal, the Russian Federation, the Slovak Republic, Spain, Sweden, Switzerland, Turkey, the United Kingdom and the United States met in Wassenaar, the Netherlands, on 18 and 19 December 1995.

2. The representatives agreed to establish The Wassenaar Arrangement on Export Controls for Conventional Arms and Dual-Use Goods and Technologies.

3. The representatives established initial elements of the new arrangement, to be submitted to their respective Governments for approval.

4. They also established a Preparatory Committee of the Whole to start work in January 1996.

5. The representatives agreed to locate the Secretariat of The Wassenaar Arrangement in Vienna, Austria. The first plenary meeting will take place in Vienna on 2 and 3 April 1996.

Purposes, Guidelines & Procedures, including the Initial Elements
(as amended and updated by the Plenary of December 2003)

Initial Elements

I. Purposes

1. The Wassenaar Arrangement has been established in order to contribute to regional and international security and stability, by promoting transparency and greater responsibility in transfers of conventional arms and dual-use goods and technologies, thus preventing destabilising accumulations. Participating States will seek, through their national policies, to ensure that transfers of these items do not contribute to the development or enhancement of military capabilities which undermine these goals, and are not diverted to support such capabilities.

2. It will complement and reinforce, without duplication, the existing control regimes for weapons of mass destruction and their delivery systems, as well as other internationally recognised measures designed to promote transparency and greater responsibility, by focusing on the threats to international and regional peace and security which may arise from transfers of armaments and sensitive dual-use goods and technologies where the risks are judged greatest.

Source: Wassenaar Arrangement. Available online at http://www.wassenaar.org. Accessed February 24, 2018.

Strategic Offensive Reductions Treaty (2002)

Signed in Moscow, May 24, 2002

The United States of America and the Russian Federation, hereinafter referred to as the Parties,

Embarking upon the path of new relations for a new century and committed to the goal of strengthening their relationship through cooperation and friendship,

Believing that new global challenges and threats require the building of a qualitatively new foundation for strategic relations between the Parties,

Desiring to establish a genuine partnership based on the principles of mutual security, cooperation, trust, openness, and predictability,

Committed to implementing significant reductions in strategic offensive arms,

Proceeding from the Joint Statements by the President of the United States of America and the President of the Russian Federation on Strategic Issues of July 22, 2001 in Genoa and on a New Relationship between the United States and Russia of November 13, 2001 in Washington,

Mindful of their obligations under the Treaty Between the United States of America and the Union of Soviet Socialist Republics on the Reduction and Limitation of Strategic Offensive Arms of July 31, 1991, hereinafter referred to as the START Treaty,

Mindful of their obligations under Article VI of the Treaty on the Non-Proliferation of Nuclear Weapons of July 1, 1968, and

Convinced that this Treaty will help to establish more favorable conditions for actively promoting security and cooperation, and enhancing international stability,

Have agreed as follows:

Article I

Each Party shall reduce and limit strategic nuclear warheads, as stated by the President of the United States of America on November 13, 2001 and as stated by the President of the Russian Federation on November 13, 2001 and December 13, 2001 respectively, so that by December 31, 2012 the aggregate number of such warheads does not exceed 1700-2200 for each Party. Each Party shall determine for itself the composition and structure of its strategic offensive arms, based on the established aggregate limit for the number of such warheads.

Article II

The Parties agree that the START Treaty remains in force in accordance with its terms.

Article III

For purposes of implementing this Treaty, the Parties shall hold meetings at least twice a year of a Bilateral Implementation Commission.

Article IV

1. This Treaty shall be subject to ratification in accordance with the constitutional procedures of each Party. This Treaty shall enter into force on the date of the exchange of instruments of ratification.
2. This Treaty shall remain in force until December 31, 2012 and may be extended by agreement of the Parties or superseded earlier by a subsequent agreement.
3. Each Party, in exercising its national sovereignty, may withdraw from this Treaty upon three months written notice to the other Party.

Source: U.S. State Department. Available online at https://www.state.gov/t/isn/10527.htm. Accessed February 24, 2018.

G8 Global Partnership Against the Spread of Weapons and Materials of Mass Destruction (2002)

Statement by the Group of Eight Leaders
  Kananaskis, Canada, June 27, 2002

The attacks of September 11 demonstrated that terrorists are prepared to use any means to cause terror and inflict appalling casualties on innocent people. We commit ourselves to prevent terrorists, or those that harbour them, from acquiring or developing nuclear, chemical, radiological and biological weapons; missiles; and related materials, equipment and technology. We call on all countries to join us in adopting the set of nonproliferation principles we have announced today.

In a major initiative to implement those principles, we have also decided today to launch a new G8 Global Partnership against the Spread of Weapons and Materials of Mass Destruction. Under this initiative, we will support specific cooperation projects, initially in Russia, to address non-proliferation, disarmament, counter-terrorism and nuclear safety issues. Among our priority concerns are the destruction of chemical weapons, the dismantlement of decommissioned nuclear submarines, the disposition of fissile materials and the employment of former weapons scientists. We will commit to raise up to $20 billion to support such projects over the next ten years. A range of financing options, including the option of bilateral debt for program exchanges, will be available to countries that contribute to this Global Partnership. We have adopted a set of guidelines that will form the basis for the negotiation of specific agreements for new projects, that will apply with immediate effect, to ensure effective and efficient project development, coordination and implementation. We will review over the next year the applicability of the guidelines to existing projects.

Recognizing that this Global Partnership will enhance international security and safety, we invite other countries that are prepared to adopt its common principles and guidelines to enter into discussions with us on participating in and contributing to this initiative. We will review progress on this Global Partnership at our next Summit in 2003.

Source: U.S. Department of State Archive. Available online at https://2001-2009.state.gov/e/eeb/rls/othr/11514.htm. Accessed February 24, 2018.

National Strategy to Combat Weapons of Mass Destruction (2002)

December 2002

Introduction

Weapons of mass destruction (WMD)—nuclear, biological, and chemical—in the possession of hostile states and terrorists represent one of the greatest security challenges facing the United States. We must pursue a comprehensive strategy to counter this threat in all of its dimensions. An effective strategy for countering WMD, including their use and further proliferation, is an integral component of the National Security Strategy of the United States of America. As with the war on terrorism, our strategy for homeland security, and our new concept of deterrence, the U.S. approach to combat WMD represents a fundamental change from the past. To succeed, we must take full advantage of today's opportunities, including the application of new technologies, increased emphasis on intelligence collection and analysis, the strengthening of alliance relationships, and the establishment of new partnerships with former adversaries. Weapons of mass destruction could enable adversaries to inflict massive harm on the United States, our military forces at home and abroad, and our friends and allies. Some states, including several that have supported and continue to support terrorism, already possess WMD and are seeking even greater capabilities, as tools of coercion and intimidation. For them, these are not weapons of last resort, but militarily useful weapons of choice intended to overcome our nation's advantages in conventional forces and to deter us from responding to aggression against our friends and allies in regions of vital interest. In addition, terrorist groups are seeking to acquire WMD with the stated purpose of killing large numbers of our people and those of friends and allies—without compunction and without warning.

We will not permit the world's most dangerous regimes and terrorists to threaten us with the world's most destructive weapons. We must accord the highest priority to the protection of the United States, our forces, and our friends and allies from the existing and growing WMD threat.

> "The gravest danger our Nation faces lies at the crossroads of radicalism and technology. Our enemies have openly declared that they are seeking weapons of mass destruction, and evidence indicates that they are doing so with determination The United States will not allow these efforts to succeed.... History will judge harshly those who saw this coming danger but failed to act. In the new world we have entered, the only path to peace and security is the path of action."

Pillars Of Our National Security

Our National Strategy to Combat Weapons of Mass Destruction has three principal pillars:

Counterproliferation to Combat WMD Use

Strengthened Nonproliferation to Combat WMD Proliferation

Consequence Management to Respond to WMD Use

Source: Available online at https://fas.org/irp/off-docs/nspd/nspd-wmd.pdf. Accessed February 24, 2018.

New START Treaty (2010)

Treaty between the United States of America and the Russian Federation on Measures for the Further Reduction and Limitation of Strategic Offensive Arms

The United States of America and the Russian Federation, hereinafter referred to as the Parties,

Believing that global challenges and threats require new approaches to interaction across the whole range of their strategic relations,

Working therefore to forge a new strategic relationship based on mutual trust, openness, predictability, and cooperation,

Desiring to bring their respective nuclear postures into alignment with this new relationship, and endeavoring to reduce further the role and importance of nuclear weapons,

Committed to the fulfillment of their obligations under Article VI of the Treaty on the Non-Proliferation of Nuclear Weapons of July 1, 1968, and to the achievement of the historic goal of freeing humanity from the nuclear threat,

Expressing strong support for on-going global efforts in non-proliferation,

Seeking to preserve continuity in, and provide new impetus to, the step-by-step process of reducing and limiting nuclear arms while maintaining the safety and security of their nuclear arsenals, and with a view to expanding this process in the future, including to a multilateral approach,

Guided by the principle of indivisible security and convinced that measures for the reduction and limitation of strategic offensive arms and the other obligations set forth in this Treaty will enhance predictability and stability, and thus the security of both Parties,

Recognizing the existence of the interrelationship between strategic offensive arms and strategic defensive arms, that this interrelationship will become more important as strategic nuclear arms are reduced, and that current strategic defensive arms do not undermine the viability and effectiveness of the strategic offensive arms of the Parties,

Mindful of the impact of conventionally armed ICBMs and SLBMs on strategic stability,

Taking into account the positive effect on the world situation of the significant, verifiable reduction in nuclear arsenals at the turn of the 21st century,

Desiring to create a mechanism for verifying compliance with the obligations under this Treaty, adapted, simplified, and made less costly in comparison to the Treaty Between the United States of America and the Union of Soviet Socialist Republics on the Reduction and Limitation of Strategic Offensive Arms of July 31, 1991, hereinafter referred to as the START Treaty,

Recognizing that the START Treaty has been implemented by the Republic of Belarus, the Republic of Kazakhstan, the Russian Federation, Ukraine, and the United States of America, and that the reduction levels envisaged by the START Treaty were achieved,

Deeply appreciating the contribution of the Republic of Belarus, the Republic of Kazakhstan, and Ukraine to nuclear disarmament and to strengthening international peace and security as non-nuclear-weapon states under the Treaty on the Non-Proliferation of Nuclear Weapons of July 1, 1968,

Welcoming the implementation of the Treaty Between the United States of America and the Russian Federation on Strategic Offensive Reductions of May 24, 2002,

Have agreed as follows:

Article I

1. Each Party shall reduce and limit its strategic offensive arms in accordance with the provisions of this Treaty and shall carry out the other obligations set forth in this Treaty and its Protocol.
2. Definitions of terms used in this Treaty and its Protocol are provided in Part One of the Protocol.

Article II

1. Each Party shall reduce and limit its ICBMs and ICBM launchers, SLBMs and SLBM launchers, heavy bombers, ICBM warheads, SLBM warheads, and heavy bomber nuclear armaments, so that seven years after entry into force of this Treaty and thereafter, the aggregate numbers, as counted in accordance with Article I11 of this Treaty, do not exceed:
   (a) 700, for deployed ICBMs, deployed SLBMs, and deployed heavy bombers;
   (b) 1550, for warheads on deployed ICBMs, warheads on deployed SLBMs, and nuclear warheads counted for deployed heavy bombers;
   (c) 800, for deployed and non-deployed ICBM launchers, deployed and non-deployed SLBM launchers, and deployed and non-deployed heavy bombers.
2. Each Party shall have the right to determine for itself the composition and structure of its strategic offensive arms.

Article III

1. For the purposes of counting toward the aggregate limit provided for in subparagraph 1(a) of Article II of this Treaty:

(a) Each deployed ICBM shall be counted as one.

(b) Each deployed SLBM shall be counted as one.

(c) Each deployed heavy bomber shall be counted as one.

2. For the purposes of counting toward the aggregate limit provided for in sub-paragraph 1(b) of Article II of this Treaty:

(a) For ICBMs and SLBMs, the number of warheads shall be the number of reentry vehicles emplaced on deployed ICBMs and on deployed SLBMs.

(b) One nuclear warhead shall be counted for each deployed heavy bomber.

3. For the purposes of counting toward the aggregate limit provided for in subpara-graph 1(c) of Article I1 of this Treaty:

(a) Each deployed launcher of ICBMs shall be counted as one.

(b) Each non-deployed launcher of ICBMs shall be counted as one.

(c) Each deployed launcher of SLBMs shall be counted as one.

(d) Each non-deployed launcher of SLBMs shall be counted as one.

(e) Each deployed heavy bomber shall be counted as one.

(f) Each non-deployed heavy bomber shall be counted as one.

Source: U.S. State Department. Available online at https://www.state.gov/t/avc/newstart/c44126.htm. Accessed February 24, 2018.

NATO Deterrence and Defence Posture Review (2012)

Agreed at the Chicago Summit, 12 May 2012

I. Introduction / Context

1. At the Lisbon Summit, the Heads of State and Government mandated *a review of NATO's overall posture* in deterring and defending against the full range of threats to the Alliance, taking into account the changes in the evolving international security environment. Over the past year, NATO has undertaken a rigorous analysis of its deterrence and defence posture. The results of this review are set out below.

2. The greatest responsibility of the Alliance is to protect and defend our territory and our populations against attack, as set out in Article 5 of the Washington Treaty. The Alliance does not consider any country to be its adversary. However, no one should doubt NATO's resolve if the security of any of its members were to be threatened. NATO will ensure that it maintains the full range of capabilities necessary to deter and defend against any threat to the safety and security of our populations, wherever it should arise. Allies' goal is to bolster deterrence as a core element of our collective defence and contribute to the indivisible security of the Alliance.

3. The review has reinforced Alliance cohesion and the continuing credibility of its posture. The review has also demonstrated anew the value of the Alliance's efforts to influence the international security environment in positive ways through cooperative security and the contribution that arms control, disarmament and non-proliferation can play in achieving its security

objectives, objectives that are fully in accord with the purposes and principles of the UN Charter and the North Atlantic Treaty. NATO will continue to seek security at the lowest possible level of forces.

4. NATO's Strategic Concept describes a *security environment* that contains a broad and evolving set of opportunities and challenges to the security of NATO territory and populations. While the threat of conventional attack against NATO is low, the conventional threat cannot be ignored. The persistence of regional conflicts continues to be a matter of great concern for the Alliance as are increasing defence spending in other parts of the world and the acquisition of increasingly advanced capabilities by some emerging powers. Globalisation, emerging security challenges, such as cyber threats, key environmental and resource constraints, including the risk of disruption to energy supplies, and the emergence of new technologies will continue shaping the future security environment in areas of interest to NATO. A number of vulnerable, weak and failed or failing states, together with the growing capabilities of non-state actors, will continue to be a source of instability and potential conflict. These factors, alongside existing threats and challenges such as the proliferation of ballistic missiles and weapons of mass destruction, piracy, and terrorism, will continue to contribute to an unpredictable security environment.

5. Developments in the strategic environment since the Lisbon Summit and the review itself have confirmed the validity of the three essential core tasks identified in the Strategic Concept. We reaffirm our commitment to *collective defence*, which remains the cornerstone of our Alliance, to *crisis management*, and to *cooperative security*.

7. A robust deterrence and defence posture strengthens Alliance cohesion, including the transatlantic link, through an equitable and sustainable distribution of roles, responsibilities, and burdens.

II. The Contribution of Nuclear Forces

8. Nuclear weapons are a core component of NATO's overall capabilities for deterrence and defence alongside conventional and missile defence forces. The review has shown that the Alliance's nuclear force posture currently meets the criteria for an effective deterrence and defence posture.

9. The circumstances in which any use of nuclear weapons might have to be contemplated are extremely remote. As long as nuclear weapons exist, NATO will remain a nuclear alliance. The supreme guarantee of the security of the Allies is provided by the strategic nuclear forces of the Alliance, particularly those of the United States; the independent strategic nuclear forces of the United Kingdom and France, which have a deterrent role of their own, contribute to the overall deterrence and security of the Allies.

10. Allies acknowledge the importance of the independent and unilateral

negative security assurances offered by the United States, the United Kingdom and France. Those assurances guarantee, without prejudice to the separate conditions each State has attached to those assurances, including the inherent right to self-defence as recognised under Article 51 of the United Nations Charter, that nuclear weapons will not be used or threatened to be used against Non-Nuclear Weapon States that are party to the Non-Proliferation Treaty and in compliance with their nuclear non-proliferation obligations. Allies further recognise the value that these statements can have in seeking to discourage nuclear proliferation. Allies note that the states that have assigned nuclear weapons to NATO apply to these weapons the assurances they have each offered on a national basis, including the separate conditions each state has attached to these assurances.

11. While seeking to create the conditions and considering options for further reductions of non-strategic nuclear weapons assigned to NATO, Allies concerned[1] will ensure that all components of NATO's nuclear deterrent remain safe, secure, and effective for as long as NATO remains a nuclear alliance. That requires sustained leadership focus and institutional excellence for the nuclear deterrence mission and planning guidance aligned with 21st century requirements.

12. Consistent with our commitment to remain a nuclear alliance for as long as nuclear weapons exist, Allies agree that the NAC will task the appropriate committees to develop concepts for how to ensure the broadest possible participation of Allies concerned[1] in their nuclear sharing arrangements, including in case NATO were to decide to reduce its reliance on non-strategic nuclear weapons based in Europe.

III. The Contribution of Conventional Forces

13. The Allies' conventional forces, their effectiveness amplified by the Alliance structures and procedures that unite them, make indispensable contributions to deterrence of a broad range of threats and to defence. By their nature, they can be employed in a flexible fashion and can provide the Alliance with a range of options with which to respond to unforeseen contingencies. They also contribute to providing visible assurance of NATO's cohesion as well as the Alliance's ability and commitment to respond to the security concerns of each and every Ally.

IV. The Contribution of Missile Defence

18. The proliferation of ballistic missiles is a growing concern for the Alliance and constitutes an increasing threat to Alliance security. NATO's ballistic missile defence capacity will be an important addition to the Alliance's capabilities for deterrence and defence. It will strengthen our collective defence commitment against 21st century threats. In Lisbon, Allies agreed on a missile defence capability that provides full coverage and protection for all NATO European

populations, territory and forces, against the threat posed by the proliferation of ballistic missiles, based on the principles of the indivisibility of Allied security and NATO solidarity, equitable sharing of risks and burdens, as well as reasonable challenge, taking into account the level of threat, affordability, and technical feasibility, and in accordance with the latest common threat assessments agreed by the Alliance. Missile defence will become an integral part of the Alliance's overall defence posture, further strengthen the transatlantic link, and contribute to the indivisible security of the Alliance.

V. The Contribution of Arms Control, Disarmament and Non-proliferation

22. Arms control, disarmament and non-proliferation play *an important role* in the achievement of the Alliance's security objectives. Both the success and failure of these efforts can have a direct impact on the threat environment of NATO and therefore affect NATO's deterrence and defence posture. When successful, they have contributed to more secure, stable and predictable international relations at lower levels of military forces and armaments, through effective and verifiable arms control agreements, and in the case of disarmament, through the elimination or prohibition of whole categories of armaments. Existing agreements cut across almost all aspects of the Alliance's work. However, they have not yet fully achieved their objectives and the world continues to face proliferation crises, force concentration problems, and lack of transparency.

VI. Conclusions – Maintaining the "Appropriate Mix" of Capabilities

31. The review of NATO's deterrence and defence posture has confirmed that NATO must have the full range of capabilities necessary to deter and defend against threats to the safety of its populations and the security of its territory, which is the Alliance's greatest responsibility. As outlined above, NATO has determined that, in the current circumstances, the existing mix of capabilities and the plans for their development are sound.

32. NATO is committed to maintaining an appropriate mix of nuclear, conventional, and missile defence capabilities for deterrence and defence to fulfil its commitments as set out in the Strategic Concept. These capabilities, underpinned by NATO's integrated Command Structure, offer the strongest guarantee of the Alliance's security and will ensure that it is able to respond to a variety of challenges and unpredictable contingencies in a highly complex and evolving international security environment. Allies are resolved to developing ways to make their forces more effective by working creatively and adaptively together and with partners as appropriate to maximise value and strengthen interoperability, so that their forces are better able to respond to the full range of 21st century security threats, achieving greater security than any one Ally could attain acting alone.

33. Allies are committed to providing the resources needed to ensure that NATO's overall deterrence and defence posture remains credible, flexible, resilient, and adaptable, and to implementing the forward-looking package of defence capabilities, which will also be agreed in Chicago. In the course of normal Alliance processes, we will revise relevant Alliance policies and strategies to take into account the principles and judgements in this posture review.

34. NATO will continue to adjust its strategy, including with respect to the capabilities and other measures required for deterrence and defence, in line with trends in the security environment. In this context, Allies will keep under review the consequences for international stability and Euro-Atlantic security of the acquisition of modern military capabilities in the regions and countries beyond NATO's borders. This posture review confirms that the Alliance is committed to maintaining the deterrence and defence capabilities necessary to ensure its security in an unpredictable world.

Source: Available online at https://www.nato.int/cps/en/natohq/official_texts_87597.htm. Accessed February 24, 2018.

Joint Comprehensive Plan of Action (2015)

Vienna, 14 July 2015

Preface

The E3/EU+3 (China, France, Germany, the Russian Federation, the United Kingdom and the United States, with the High Representative of the European Union for Foreign Affairs and Security Policy) and the Islamic Republic of Iran welcome this historic Joint Comprehensive Plan of Action (JCPOA), which will ensure that Iran's nuclear programme will be exclusively peaceful, and mark a fundamental shift in their approach to this issue. They anticipate that full implementation of this JCPOA will positively contribute to regional and international peace and security. Iran reaffirms that under no circumstances will Iran ever seek, develop or acquire any nuclear weapons.

Iran envisions that this JCPOA will allow it to move forward with an exclusively peaceful, indigenous nuclear programme, in line with scientific and economic considerations, in accordance with the JCPOA, and with a view to building confidence and encouraging international cooperation. In this context, the initial mutually determined limitations described in this JCPOA will be followed by a gradual evolution, at a reasonable pace, of Iran's peaceful nuclear programme, including its enrichment activities, to a commercial programme for exclusively peaceful purposes, consistent with international nonproliferation norms.

The E3/EU+3 envision that the implementation of this JCPOA will progressively allow them to gain confidence in the exclusively peaceful nature of Iran's programme. The JCPOA reflects mutually determined parameters, consistent with practical needs, with agreed limits on the scope of Iran's nuclear programme, including enrichment activities and R&D. The JCPOA addresses the E3/EU+3's concerns, including through comprehensive measures providing for transparency and verification.

The JCPOA will produce the comprehensive lifting of all UN Security Council sanctions as well as multilateral and national sanctions related to Iran's nuclear programme, including steps on access in areas of trade, technology, finance, and energy.

Preamble and general provisions

i.   The Islamic Republic of Iran and the E3/EU+3 (China, France, Germany, the Russian Federation, the United Kingdom and the United States, with the High Representative of the European Union for Foreign Affairs and Security Policy) have decided upon this long-term Joint Comprehensive Plan of Action (JCPOA). This JCPOA, reflecting a step-by-step approach, includes the reciprocal commitments as laid down in this document and the annexes hereto and is to be endorsed by the United Nations (UN) Security Council.

ii.   The full implementation of this JCPOA will ensure the exclusively peaceful nature of Iran's nuclear programme.

iii.   Iran reaffirms that under no circumstances will Iran ever seek, develop or acquire any nuclear weapons.

iv.   Successful implementation of this JCPOA will enable Iran to fully enjoy its right to nuclear energy for peaceful purposes under the relevant articles of the nuclear Non-Proliferation Treaty (NPT) in line with its obligations therein, and the Iranian nuclear programme will be treated in the same manner as that of any other non-nuclear-weapon state party to the NPT.

v.   This JCPOA will produce the comprehensive lifting of all UN Security Council sanctions as well as multilateral and national sanctions related to Iran's nuclear programme, including steps on access in areas of trade, technology, finance and energy.

vi.   The E3/EU+3 and Iran reaffirm their commitment to the purposes and principles of the United Nations as set out in the UN Charter.

vii.   The E3/EU+3 and Iran acknowledge that the NPT remains the cornerstone of the nuclear non-proliferation regime and the essential foundation for the pursuit of nuclear disarmament and for the peaceful uses of nuclear energy.

viii.   The E3/EU+3 and Iran commit to implement this JCPOA in good faith and in a constructive atmosphere, based on mutual respect, and to refrain from any action inconsistent with the letter, spirit and intent of this JCPOA that would undermine its successful implementation. The E3/EU+3 will refrain from imposing discriminatory regulatory and procedural requirements in lieu of the sanctions and restrictive measures covered by this JCPOA. This JCPOA builds on the implementation of the Joint Plan of Action (JPOA) agreed in Geneva on 24 November 2013.

ix.   A Joint Commission consisting of the E3/EU+3 and Iran will be established to monitor the implementation of this JCPOA and will carry out the functions provided for in this JCPOA. This Joint Commission will address issues arising from the implementation of this JCPOA and will operate in accordance with the provisions as detailed in the relevant annex.

x.   The International Atomic Energy Agency (IAEA) will be requested to monitor and verify the voluntary nuclear-related measures as detailed in this JCPOA. The IAEA will be requested to provide regular updates to the Board of Governors, and as provided for in this JCPOA, to the UN

Security Council. All relevant rules and regulations of the IAEA with regard to the protection of information will be fully observed by all parties involved.

xii. Technical details of the implementation of this JCPOA are dealt with in the annexes to this document.

xiii. The EU and E3+3 countries and Iran, in the framework of the JCPOA, will cooperate, as appropriate, in the field of peaceful uses of nuclear energy and engage in mutually determined civil nuclear cooperation projects as detailed in Annex III, including through IAEA involvement.

xiv. The E3+3 will submit a draft resolution to the UN Security Council endorsing this JCPOA affirming that conclusion of this JCPOA marks a fundamental shift in its consideration of this issue and expressing its desire to build a new relationship with Iran. This UN Security Council resolution will also provide for the termination on Implementation Day of provisions imposed under previous resolutions; establishment of specific restrictions; and conclusion of consideration of the Iran nuclear issue by the UN Security Council 10 years after the Adoption Day.

xv. The provisions stipulated in this JCPOA will be implemented for their respective durations as set forth below and detailed in the annexes.

xvi. The E3/EU+3 and Iran will meet at the ministerial level every 2 years, or earlier if needed, in order to review and assess progress and to adopt appropriate decisions by consensus.

Source: Joint Comprehensive Plan of Action (JCPOA), July 14, 2015. United Nations, S/2015/544.

Treaty on the Prohibition of Nuclear Weapons (2017)

Signed in New York, 7 July 2017.

The States Parties to this Treaty,

Determined to contribute to the realization of the purposes and principles of the Charter of the United Nations,

Deeply concerned about the catastrophic humanitarian consequences that would result from any use of nuclear weapons, and recognizing the consequent need to completely eliminate such weapons, which remains the only way to guarantee that nuclear weapons are never used again under any circumstances,

Mindful of the risks posed by the continued existence of nuclear weapons, including from any nuclear-weapon detonation by accident, miscalculation or design, and emphasizing that these risks concern the security of all humanity, and that all States share the responsibility to prevent any use of nuclear weapons,

Cognizant that the catastrophic consequences of nuclear weapons cannot be adequately addressed, transcend national borders, pose grave implications for human survival, the environment, socioeconomic development, the global economy, food security and the health of current and future generations, and have a disproportionate impact on women and girls, including as a result of ionizing radiation,

Acknowledging the ethical imperatives for nuclear disarmament and the urgency of achieving and maintaining a nuclear-weapon-free world, which is a global public good of the highest order, serving both national and collective security interests,

Mindful of the unacceptable suffering of and harm caused to the victims of the use of nuclear weapons (hibakusha), as well as of those affected by the testing of nuclear weapons,

Recognizing the disproportionate impact of nuclear-weapon activities on indigenous peoples,

Reaffirming the need for all States at all times to comply with applicable international law, including international humanitarian law and international human rights law,

Basing themselves on the principles and rules of international humanitarian law, in particular the principle that the right of parties to an armed conflict to choose methods or means of warfare is not unlimited, the rule of distinction, the prohibition against indiscriminate attacks, the rules on proportionality and precautions in attack, the prohibition on the use of weapons of a nature to cause superfluous injury or unnecessary suffering, and the rules for the protection of the natural environment,

Considering that any use of nuclear weapons would be contrary to the rules of international law applicable in armed conflict, in particular the principles and rules of international humanitarian law,

Reaffirming that any use of nuclear weapons would also be abhorrent to the principles of humanity and the dictates of public conscience,

Recalling that, in accordance with the Charter of the United Nations, States must refrain in their international relations from the threat or use of force against the territorial integrity or political independence of any State, or in any other manner inconsistent with the Purposes of the United Nations, and that the establishment and maintenance of international peace and security are to be promoted with the least diversion for armaments of the world's human and economic resources,

Recalling also the first resolution of the General Assembly of the United Nations, adopted on 24 January 1946, and subsequent resolutions which call for the elimination of nuclear weapons,

Concerned by the slow pace of nuclear disarmament, the continued reliance on nuclear weapons in military and security concepts, doctrines and policies, and the waste of economic and human resources on programmes for the production, maintenance and modernization of nuclear weapons,

Recognizing that a legally binding prohibition of nuclear weapons constitutes an important contribution towards the achievement and maintenance of a world free of nuclear weapons, including the irreversible, verifiable and transparent elimination of nuclear weapons, and determined to act towards that end,

Determined to act with a view to achieving effective progress towards general and complete disarmament under strict and effective international control,

Reaffirming that there exists an obligation to pursue in good faith and bring to a conclusion negotiations leading to nuclear disarmament in all its aspects under strict and effective international control,

Reaffirming also that the full and effective implementation of the Treaty on the Non-Proliferation of Nuclear Weapons, which serves as the cornerstone of the nuclear disarmament and non-proliferation regime, has a vital role to play in promoting international peace and security,

Recognizing the vital importance of the Comprehensive Nuclear-Test-Ban Treaty and its verification regime as a core element of the nuclear disarmament and non-proliferation regime,

Reaffirming the conviction that the establishment of the internationally recognized nuclear-weapon-free zones on the basis of arrangements freely arrived at among the States of the region concerned enhances global and regional peace and security, strengthens the nuclear non-proliferation regime and contributes towards realizing the objective of nuclear disarmament,

Emphasizing that nothing in this Treaty shall be interpreted as affecting the inalienable right of its States Parties to develop research, production and use of nuclear energy for peaceful purposes without discrimination,

Recognizing that the equal, full and effective participation of both women and men is an essential factor for the promotion and attainment of sustainable peace and security, and committed to supporting and strengthening the effective participation of women in nuclear disarmament,

Recognizing also the importance of peace and disarmament education in all its aspects and of raising awareness of the risks and consequences of nuclear weapons for current and future generations, and committed to the dissemination of the principles and norms of this Treaty,

Stressing the role of public conscience in the furthering of the principles of humanity as evidenced by the call for the total elimination of nuclear weapons, and recognizing the efforts to that end undertaken by the United Nations, the International Red Cross and Red Crescent Movement, other international and regional organizations, non-governmental organizations, religious leaders, parliamentarians, academics and the hibakusha,

Have agreed as follows:

Article 1
Prohibitions

1. Each State Party undertakes never under any circumstances to:
    (a) Develop, test, produce, manufacture, otherwise acquire, possess or stockpile nuclear weapons or other nuclear explosive devices;
    (b) Transfer to any recipient whatsoever nuclear weapons or other nuclear explosive devices or control over such weapons or explosive devices directly or indirectly;
    (c) Receive the transfer of or control over nuclear weapons or other nuclear explosive devices directly or indirectly;
    (d) Use or threaten to use nuclear weapons or other nuclear explosive devices;
    (e) Assist, encourage or induce, in any way, anyone to engage in any activity prohibited to a State Party under this Treaty;
    (f) Seek or receive any assistance, in any way, from anyone to engage in any activity prohibited to a State Party under this Treaty;
    (g) Allow any stationing, installation or deployment of any nuclear weapons or other nuclear explosive devices in its territory or at any place under its jurisdiction or control.

Source: United Nations. A/CONF.229/2017/8. Available online at http://undocs.org/A/CONF.229 /2017/8. Accessed February 24, 2018.

Chronology of Chemical and Biological Weapons

6th Century BCE

The Assyrians use ergot fungus (*Claviceps purpurea*) to poison their enemy's water wells.

595 BCE

During the siege of Kirra, the Athenian Cleisthenes cuts off water to the town and waits for thirst to take over its inhabitants. He then acquires Hellebore root and inserts it into the main pipes that supply water to the city, resulting in widespread diarrhea among its population.

429 BCE

Spartan troops burn tar and sulfur to issue noxious smoke in its siege of Platea.[1]

200 BCE

Hannibal's army adulterates wine with mandrake (a plant that contains a number of toxic belladonna-like alkaloids) to cause delirium among African rebels.

189 BCE

During its siege of Ambracia, Rome deploys sappers to dig beneath the city. The Ambracians countertunnel and fit a large pot with burning feathers that create a noxious smoke, forcing the Romans to cease their mining operations.

1040 CE

Scottish armies poison wine with belladonna nightshade and give it to Norwegian troops. The Scots then slaughter the incapacitated Norwegians.

1346

Mongolian troops suffering from plague decide to hurl their dead over the city walls of Kaffa in an attempt to spread the disease among the citizens inside.

July 21, 1456

Christian defenders in Belgrade throw burning brush with sulfur down to the besieging Turks. Thousands of Turks reportedly die from the fire and smoke.

1649

Venetian intelligence operatives plot to use plague-ridden bodies by harvesting their fluids and disseminating them among enemy Turkic military forces. It was never carried out.

1672

The bishop of Münster attempts the use of an atropine-like drug in grenades in the siege against the city of Gröningen. Unfavorable winds cause the belladonna to blow back against the attacking forces.

1767

The British plot to supply cloths from a smallpox hospital ward to American Indian tribes in hopes of spreading disease.

1855

Sir Lyon Playfair suggests using cyanide-containing chemicals against Russian troops during the Crimean War, but this tactic never found approval by the British High Command

1885

During the Crimean War, Lord Dundonald suggests the use of burning sulfur against Sebastopol, but his plan is rejected on the grounds that it "would contravene the laws of civilized warfare."[2]

1914

French troops use tear gas grenades against German positions in World War I.

January 31, 1915

German forces fire a barrage of artillery shells filled with xylyl bromide against Russian troops at Bolimow, Poland, but to no effect due to the extreme cold.

April 22, 1915

The German military uses a barrage of chlorine gas against Allied trenches in Ypres, Belgium.

July 12, 1917

Germany uses mustard agent against Allied troops at Ypres, Belgium.

1917–1918

German agents infect beasts of burden—including horses bound for use by Allied forces in Europe—using glanders and anthrax.

1919

In the first known instance of air-delivered chemical weapons, British aircraft drop Adamsite and diphenylchloroarsine munitions against Bolshevik forces during the civil war in Russia.[3]

June 17, 1925

The Geneva Protocol for the Prohibition of the Use in War of Asphyxiating, Poisonous or Other Gases, and of Bacteriological Methods of Warfare is signed by nearly 30 countries.

1935

Italian troops under Benito Mussolini begin using chemical weapons (mustard agent) against Ethiopians.

1937

During the Sino-Japanese War, Japan begins chemical and biological warfare against Chinese troops and civilians.

Summer 1939

Japanese bioweaponeers plot to contaminate river water with typhoid and cholera bacteria to infect Soviet troops, but they are unsuccessful in carrying out the operation.[4]

December 2, 1943

The German Luftwaffe attacks Allied ships carrying sulfur mustard in Bari, Italy, leading to more than 600 chemical warfare agent casualties; 89 of these die.

February 1956

Soviet Marshal and Defense Minister Georgy Zhukov predicts future warfare will include "various means of mass destruction, such as atomic, thermonuclear, chemical and bacteriological weapons."

April 10, 1972
The United States, Great Britain, and the Soviet Union sign the Biological and Toxin Weapons Convention.

April 1979
Anthrax spores are accidentally released from a biological weapons facility in Sverdlovsk, Russia; 68 people die from inhalation anthrax.

1983
Iraq begins using chemical warfare agents, including mustard, in the Iran-Iraq War (1980–1988).

March 16, 1988
The Iraqi government (under the leadership of Saddam Hussein) launches a three-day chemical weapons attack against the Kurdish town of Halabja in northern Iraq. Approximately 5,000 die, and another 20,000 are injured.

March 1991
After a U.S. coalition invades Iraq, the United Nations Special Commission on Iraq (UNSCOM) searches for WMD and oversees the destruction of known chemical and biological weapons arsenals and production facilities.

January 13, 1993
The Chemical Weapons Convention opens for signature.

March 20, 1995
Aum Shinrikyo releases sarin nerve agent in the Tokyo subway, killing 12 people and injuring about 1,000.

April 19, 1995
Timothy McVeigh detonates a 4,000-pound explosive device, destroying the Alfred P. Murrah Federal Building in Oklahoma City, Oklahoma, killing 168 people.

October 2001
U.S. biodefense research scientist Bruce Ivins mails four letters containing anthrax spores. Twenty-two people become infected, and five of them die from inhalation anthrax.

March–April 2003
Coalition forces undertake Operation Iraqi Freedom, with the stated goal of ridding Iraq of its weapons of mass destruction (WMD) programs.

August 21, 2013
Syrian military forces use sarin nerve agent against 12 areas in and around the Ghouta area, killing at least 1,400 people.

April 4, 2017
Syria again employs sarin nerve agent against rebel-contested areas, killing at least 70 people.

Notes
1. Elvira K. Fradkin, *The Air Menace and the Answer* (New York: Macmillan Company, 1934), 7.

2. Fradkin, *Air Menace*, 8.

3. D. Hank Ellison, *Handbook of Chemical and Biological Warfare Agents*, 2nd ed. (Boca Raton, FL: CRC Press, 2008), 427.

4. Jeffrey A. Lockwood, *Six-Legged Soldiers: Using Insects as Weapons of War* (New York: Oxford University Press, 2009), 98.

Chronology of Nuclear Weapons

1933
Hungarian physicist Leo Szilard theorizes atomic structure.

1938
Otto Hahan and Fritz Strassmann's discovery of fission steers Germany toward developing an atomic weapon.

July 1939
Szilard and Edward Teller meet with Albert Einstein in New York to describe Germany's efforts. Einstein writes a letter to President Franklin Roosevelt, warning him of the possibility of building an atomic weapon.

Fall 1939
The United States grants small funding for research into nuclear fission. Key scientists involved include Szilard, Teller, and Enrico Fermi. Early work is primarily carried out at Columbia University and the Universities of California and Chicago.

1941
By 1941, Germany leads the race for the atomic bomb. They have a heavy-water plant (in Norway), high-grade uranium compounds, a nearly complete cyclotron, capable scientists and engineers, and the greatest chemical engineering industry in the world.

June 1942
The United States begins a major research program to develop and build a usable atomic weapon. The effort is called the Manhattan Project and is directed by Major General Leslie Groves and Dr. Robert Oppenheimer.

1942–1943
Three entirely new towns are created for the sole purpose of developing the components of an atomic bomb: Los Alamos, New Mexico (center of scientific and engineering efforts); Oak Ridge, Tennessee (where uranium enrichment is centered); and Hanford, Washington (where plutonium is reprocessed from spent reactor fuel). This is the beginning of what will become a massive American atomic infrastructure.

December 2, 1942
At the University of Chicago, Fermi oversees the first controlled energy release from the nucleus of the atom using a uranium graphite reactor.

July 16, 1945
The United States tests the world's first atomic bomb at the Trinity Site in central New Mexico.

August 6, 1945
A U.S. B-29 bomber drops an atomic bomb on Hiroshima, Japan. (Another bomber drops a second bomb on Nagasaki, Japan, three days later.)

April 4, 1946
The United States passes the Atomic Energy Act (also known as the McMahon Act), creating the U.S. Atomic Energy Commission (which was abolished and absorbed into other US government agencies in 1974).

June 14, 1946
The Baruch Plan is presented by the United States to the United Nations. The plan is an early disarmament effort to place all nuclear material and weapons under UN control. (The proposal is rejected by the USSR in December 1946.)

August 29, 1949
The Soviet Union tests its first atomic bomb.

November 1, 1951
The United States tests the world's first hydrogen bomb.

October 3, 1952
Great Britain tests its first atomic bomb.

August 1953
The Soviet Union tests its first hydrogen bomb.

December 8, 1953
The United States makes an "Atoms for Peace" proposal to the UN General Assembly.

January 1954
The United States launches its first nuclear-powered submarine.

September 1954
The North Atlantic Treaty Organization (NATO) accepts US atomic weapons deployed to Europe.

October 23, 1954
In a protocol to the Brussels Treaty (which created the West European Union), and in return for permission to rearm itself with conventional weapons, West Germany pledges not to produce, procure, or possess weapons of mass destruction.

October 26, 1956
The International Atomic Energy Agency (IAEA) is created.

October 4, 1957
The USSR launches Sputnik, the world's first orbiting satellite.

October 15, 1957
The USSR and China sign a defense agreement whereby the Soviets agree to provide China with technical help in developing their own atomic bomb.

January 10, 1958
The United States tests the world's first intercontinental ballistic missile (ICBM).

October 31, 1958
The United States, the United Kingdom, and the USSR begin negotiations on a comprehensive test ban treaty (CTBT).

June 1959
The United States launches the first nuclear-powered submarine equipped with submarine-launched ballistic missiles (SLBM).

December 1, 1959
Twelve nations sign the Antarctic Treaty, demilitarizing the continent and leading the

way to future geographic nuclear-weapon-free zones.

February 13, 1960
France tests its first atomic bomb.

October 15–28, 1962
The United States and Soviet Union come close to nuclear war during the Cuban Missile Crisis.

June 20, 1963
The United States and Soviet Union establish a crisis communications link by signing the Hot Line Agreement.

August 5, 1963
The United States, United Kingdom, and USSR sign the Limited Test Ban Treaty, banning nuclear weapon tests in the atmosphere, outer space, and underwater.

1964
The United States ceases production of highly enriched uranium.

October 16, 1964
China tests its first atomic bomb.

January 27, 1967
The Outer Space Treaty is signed by 67 nations, demilitarizing space, the moon, and other celestial bodies.

February 14, 1967
The Treaty of Tlatelcolco is signed, creating the Latin American Nuclear-Weapon-Free Zone.

December 13, 1967
The United States announces that it has successfully tested ICBM warheads with multiple independently targetable reentry vehicles (MIRVs).

July 1, 1968
The Nuclear Non-Proliferation Treaty (NPT) is signed by 73 countries. (There are currently 187 states parties to the treaty.)

September 3, 1971
The Zangger Committee is created by 33 nations to voluntarily restrict nuclear-related exports.

September 30, 1971
The Nuclear War Risk Reduction Agreement is signed by the United States and Soviet Union (also called the Accidents Measures Agreement).

May 26, 1972
The Strategic Arms Limitation Treaty (SALT I) is signed in Moscow by the United States and Soviet Union. It is the first major strategic arms control treaty and consists of an Interim Agreement on Strategic Offensive Arms (freezing the number of missile launch sites) and an Anti-Ballistic Missile Treaty (ABM) (which restricts the development of missile defenses).

May 18, 1974
India tests its first atomic "device."

July 3, 1974
The United States and Soviet Union sign the Threshold Test Ban Treaty, limiting the size of allowable underground nuclear weapons test explosions.

April 23, 1975
The Nuclear Suppliers Group is created to restrict the export of sensitive technology.

August 1, 1975
The Helsinki Accords are signed by 35 states, creating the Conference on Security and Cooperation in Europe and emphasizing

the value of confidence- and security building measures.

May 28, 1976
The Peaceful Nuclear Explosions Treaty is signed by the United States and USSR.

March 28, 1979
The Three Mile Island nuclear power reactor accident occurs in Pennsylvania.

June 18, 1979
The SALT II Treaty is signed by the United States and Soviet Union, limiting the number and types of strategic delivery vehicles allowed. The treaty is never ratified.

June 7, 1981
Israeli jets strike an Iraqi nuclear reactor in a preemptive attack.

March 23, 1983
The United States announces its Strategic Defense Initiative (SDI).

August 6, 1985
The Treaty of Rarotonga is signed, creating the South Pacific Nuclear-Weapon-Free Zone.

April 26, 1986
Soviet nuclear reactors explode and melt down at Chernobyl, Ukraine.

April 7, 1987
The Missile Technology Control Regime is established to reduce proliferation risks through controls on technology transfers.

December 8, 1987
The Intermediate-Range Nuclear Forces Treaty (INF) is signed by the United States and Soviet Union, eliminating an entire category of missiles with a range of 500–5,500 kilometers.

1988
The United States closes its plutonium production facilities.

November 9, 1989
The Berlin Wall falls in peaceful revolution; within two years, NATO has declared the Cold War over (July 1990), and the Soviet Union has dissolved (December 1991).

April 3, 1991
Following the victory by the U.S.-led international military coalition that defeated Iraq in the First Gulf War, the United Nations creates a Special Commission on Iraq (UNSCOM) to find and destroy Iraqi capabilities to make weapons of mass destruction.

July 9, 1991
The Strategic Arms Reduction Treaty (START I) is signed by the United States and Soviet Union, limiting the number of strategic nuclear weapons (6000) and delivery vehicles (1600) on each side.

September 27, 1991
Under President George H. W. Bush, the United States initiates a series of reciprocated Presidential Nuclear Initiatives that eliminate or remove most tactical nuclear weapons systems from deployment and lead to the de-alerting or detargeting of strategic systems. Russia follows suit in announcements by Soviet general secretary Mikhail Gorbachev on October 5, 1991, and by Russian president Boris Yeltsin on January 29, 1992.

November 27, 1991
The U.S. Congress passes the Nuclear Threat Reduction Act (also called the Nunn-Lugar Program) to help the Soviet Union transport, store, safeguard, and destroy its

residual nuclear arsenal. This leads to the creation of the Cooperative Threat Reduction Program.

January 20, 1992
North and South Korea sign the Joint Declaration on the Denuclearization of the Korean Peninsula.

March 24, 1992
The Treaty on Open Skies is signed by 25 nations to allow intrusive aerial reconnaissance for arms control monitoring and compliance verification.

September 23, 1992
The United States conducts its last underground nuclear test.

January 3, 1993
The START II Treaty is signed by the United States and Russia. It further limits the number of strategic delivery systems and eliminates warheads with multiple independently targetable reentry vehicles and heavy ICBMs.

January 14, 1994
The United States, Russia, and Ukraine sign the Trilateral Agreement, whereby Ukraine agrees to return to Russia nuclear weapons left on its territory upon the demise of the Soviet Union.

March 24, 1994
South Africa admits it had a secret nuclear weapons program that since 1974 had produced six weapons, now destroyed.

May 30, 1994
The United States and Russia agree to detarget their ICBMs and SLBMs from each other's territory. Russia concludes similar agreements with Great Britain and China.

June 23, 1994
The United States and Russia sign an agreement on shutting down Russia's plutonium production facilities (also called the Gore-Chernomyrdin Agreement).

September 22, 1994
The United States releases its Nuclear Posture Review, calling for a smaller version of the Cold War nuclear triad.

October 23, 1994
The United States and North Korea sign the Agreed Framework to stop North Korea's attempts to develop nuclear weapons in return for food and energy assistance.

March 23, 1995
The Fissile Material Cut-Off talks begin in the UN Conference on Disarmament.

May 12, 1995
States parties to the NPT Extension Review conference agree to extend the treaty indefinitely

December 15, 1995
The Treaty of Bangkok is signed, creating the Southeast Asian Nuclear-Weapons-Free Zone.

April 11, 1996
The Pelindaba Treaty is signed, creating the African Nuclear-Weapons-Free Zone.

September 10, 1996
The United Nations adopts the Comprehensive Test Ban Treaty. (The United States is the first country to sign it, but the U.S. Congress refuses to ratify it on October 13, 1999.)

March 21, 1997
The United States and Russia agree on parameters for START III negotiations (which never occur).

May 11, 1998
India tests atomic weapons.

May 28, 1998
Pakistan tests its first atomic weapon.

September 22, 1998
The United States and Russia begin the Nuclear Cities Initiative to provide nonmilitary work for Russian scientists and engineers formerly involved in the nuclear weapons complex.

December 31, 2001
The United States releases the Nuclear Posture Review, calling for a new triad consisting of strategic strike forces, missile defenses, and an enhanced infrastructure.

May 24, 2002
The United States and Russia sign the Strategic Offensive Reductions Treaty (SORT, also known as the Moscow Treaty), calling for reductions in deployed strategic warheads to approximately 2,000 by 2012.

June 13, 2002
The United States withdraws from the ABM Treaty, citing a need to develop and deploy a working antiballistic missile system.

June 27, 2002
The G-8 countries agree to a Global Partnership against the Spread of Weapons and Materials of Mass Destruction.

October 5, 2002
North Korea admits it has an ongoing nuclear weapons program in defiance of its responsibilities under the NPT.

January 10, 2003
North Korea withdraws from the Nuclear Nonproliferation Treaty.

March 18, 2003
A U.S.-led coalition of the willing invades Iraq to effect regime change and to find and eliminate Iraqi WMD.

May 31, 2003
The Proliferation Security Initiative is signed by 11 countries in an effort to reduce the global trafficking of WMD, delivery vehicles, and related materiel to and from states of proliferation concern.

December 19, 2003
Muammar Qaddafi of Libya renounces WMD, including the Libyan nuclear weapons program, and invites international inspectors into the country.

October 9, 2006
North Korea conducts its first nuclear weapons test.

April 5, 2009
President Barack Obama calls for a world free of nuclear weapons in a speech in Prague, Czech Republic.

April 8, 2010
The United States and Russia sign the New START Treaty in Prague, reducing allowable limits on strategic weapons to 1,550 warheads and 700 deployed delivery vehicles. It entered into force on February 5, 2011, and expires 10 years later.

April 12, 2010
The United States hosts the first Nuclear Security Summit in Washington, D.C., to draw attention to the need to secure fissile materials. Subsequent summits are held in Seoul, The Hague, and Washington, D.C.

April 2010
The United States releases a Nuclear Posture Review that supports President Obama's

Prague Agenda goals for moving toward a world free of nuclear weapons, and removes chemical-weapons attack as rationale for nuclear response.

March 11, 2011
The Fukushima Daiichi Nuclear Power Plant accident occurs after a severe earthquake off the coast of Japan and resulting tsunami.

March 19, 2011
A NATO-led coalition begins military intervention in Libya, leading to regime change and loss of control over remaining Libyan WMD capabilities.

May 20, 2012
At the Chicago Summit, NATO releases its Deterrence and Defense Posture Review, as called for in the 2010 NATO Strategic Concept. This document recommends the continued status quo regarding NATO's nuclear posture.

February 27, 2014
Russia begins its conquest of Crimea, annexing it one month later. In April, it foments civil war in the Donbas region of Eastern Ukraine.

January 2015
Russia informs the United States that it will no longer accept U.S. assistance to secure weapons-grade nuclear material (through the Cooperative Threat Reduction Program).

March 10, 2015
Russia formally withdraws from the Conventional Forces in Europe Treaty after years of noncompliance.

July 14, 2015
The P5+1 nations sign the Joint Comprehensive Plan of Action (JCPOA) with Iran, limiting Iran's nuclear development capability for 10 years.

December 31, 2015
A new Russian national security strategy emphasizes the role of nuclear weapons.

October 19, 2016
The United States formally accuses Russia of violating the INF Treaty with tests of a new cruise missile.

July 7, 2017
The United Nations passes the Treaty on the Prohibition of Nuclear Weapons, with 122 states supporting. All nuclear weapons states and all but one NATO member state abstain from voting.

February 2, 2018
The United States releases the new Nuclear Posture Review under the Trump administration, calling for the return of sea-based tactical nuclear weapons.

April 27, 2018
At a summit meeting between the leaders of North and South Korea, both sides pledge to pursue a denuclearized Korean Peninsula.

Bibliography

Chemical and Biological Weapons

Alibek, Ken, with Stephen Handelman. *Biohazard: The Chilling True Story of the Largest Covert Biological Weapons Program in the World—Told from the Inside by the Man Who Ran It.* New York: Random House, 1999.

Bower, William A., Katherine Hendricks, Satish Pillai, Julie Guarnizo, and Dana Meaney-Delman. "Clinical Framework and Medical Countermeasure Use during an Anthrax Mass-Casualty Incident CDC Recommendations," *MMWR Recommendations & Reports* 64, no. 4 (December 4, 2015): 1–21.

Bozheyeva, Gulbarshyn, Yerlan Kunakbayev, and Dastan Yeleukenov. *Former Soviet Biological Weapons Facilities in Kazakhstan: Past, Present, and Future,* Occasional Paper No. 1. Monterey, CA: Center for Nonproliferation Studies, June 1999.

Brackett, D. W. *Holy Terror: Armageddon in Tokyo.* New York: Weatherhill, 1996.

Burger, Marlène, and Chandré Gould. *Secrets and Lies: Wouter Basson and South Africa's Chemical and Biological Warfare Programme.* Cape Town: Zebra, 2002.

Carefoot, G. L., and E. R. Sprott. *Famine on the Wind: Plant Diseases and Human History.* New York: Rand McNally & Company, 1967.

Compton, James A. F. *Military Chemical and Biological Agents.* Caldwell, NJ: Telford, 1987.

Cox, Christopher S., and Christopher M. Wathes, eds. *Bioaerosols Handbook.* Boca Raton, FL: CRC Press, 1995.

Croddy, Eric. *Chemical and Biological Warfare: A Comprehensive Survey for the Concerned Citizen.* New York: Copernicus, 2001.

Croddy, Eric, James J. Wirtz, and Jeffrey A. Larsen, eds. *Weapons of Mass Destruction: An Encyclopedia of Worldwide Policy, Technology, and History,* vol. 1, *Chemical and Biological Weapons.* Santa Barbara, CA: ABC-CLIO, 2005.

Drogin, Bob. *Curveball: Spies, Lies, and the Con Man Who Caused a War.* New York: Random House, 2007.

Federov, Lev. *Chemical Weapons in Russia: History, Ecology, Politics.* Moscow: Center of Ecological Policy of Russia, 1994.

Fenn, Elizabeth. *Pox Americana: The Great Smallpox Epidemic of 1775–1782.* New York: Hill & Wang, 2001.

Fradkin, Elvira K. *The Air Menace and the Answer.* New York: Macmillan, 1934.

Franke, Siegfried. *Manual of Military Chemistry,* vol. 1, *Chemistry of Chemical Warfare* [*Lehrbuch der Militärchemie der Kampfstoffe*]. East Berlin: Deutscher Militärverlag, 1967.

Franz, David R. *Defense against Toxin Weapons.* Fort Detrick, MD: U.S. Army Medical Research and Material Command, 1997.

Fries, Amos A., and Clarence J. West. *Chemical Warfare.* New York: McGraw-Hill, 1921.

Gardner, John H. *Covert Use of Psychochemicals and Other Agents to Influence National Policy.* Chevy Chase, MD: Johns Hopkins University, 1956.

Geissler, Erhard, and John Ellis von Courtland Moon, eds. *Biological and Toxin Weapons: Research, Development, and Use from the Middle Ages to 1945.* Oxford: Oxford University Press, 1999.

Gould, Chandré, and Peter Folb. *Project Coast: Apartheid's Chemical and Biological Warfare Programme.* Geneva, Switzerland: United Nations Institute for Disarmament Research, 2002.

Guillemin, Jeanne. *Anthrax: Investigation of a Deadly Outbreak.* Berkeley: University of California Press, 1999.

Hirsch, Walter. *Soviet BW and CW Preparations and Capabilities.* Washington, D.C.: Office of the Chief, Chemical Corps, 1947.

Hoenig, Steven L. *Compendium of Chemical Warfare Agents.* New York: Springer-Verlag, 2007.

Hoffman, David E. *The Cold Hand: The Untold Story of the Cold War Arms Race and Its Dangerous Legacy.* New York: Doubleday, 2009.

Ketchum, James S. *Chemical Warfare Secrets Almost Forgotten: A Personal Story of Medical Testing of Army Volunteers.* Santa Rosa, CA: ChemBooks, Inc., 2007.

Kleber, B. E., and D. Birdell. *The Chemical Warfare Service: Chemicals in Combat, United States Army in World War II: The Technical Services.* Washington, D.C.: U.S. Government Printing Office, 1966.

Langmuir, Alexander D. "Epidemiology of Airborne Infection," *Bacteriological Reviews* 25, no. 3 (September 1961): 173–187.

Leitenberg, Milton, and Raymond A. Zilinskas, with Jens Kuhn. *The Soviet Biological Weapons Program.* Cambridge, MA: Harvard University Press, 2012.

Lohs, Karlheinz. *Synthetic Poisons.* 2nd ed. East Berlin: German Military Publishing House, 1963.

Marrs, Timothy C., Robert L. Maynard, and Frederick R. Sidell. *Chemical Warfare Agents: Toxicology and Treatment.* New York: John Wiley & Sons, 1996.

Marty, Aileen M., ed. *Clinics in Laboratory Medicine: Laboratory Aspects of Biowarfare.* Vol. 21, no. 1. Philadelphia: W. B. Saunders Company, September 2001.

Mauroni, Al. *Chemical and Biological Warfare.* Santa Barbara, CA: ABC-CLIO, 2003.

Mayor, Adrienne. *Greek Fire, Poison Arrows, and Scorpion Bombs: Biological and Chemical Warfare in the Ancient World.* New York: Overlook Duckworth, 2003.

Miller, Judith, Stephen Engelberg, and William J. Broad. *Germs: Biological Weapons and America's Secret War.* New York: Simon & Schuster, 2001.

Neer, Robert M. *Napalm: An American Biography.* Cambridge, MA: Belknap Press of Harvard University Press, 2013.

O'Brien, Richard D. *Toxic Phosphorus Esters.* New York: Academic Press, 1960.

Prentiss, Augustin M. *Chemicals in War—A Treatise on Chemical Warfare.* New York: McGraw-Hill, 1937.

Price, Richard M. *The Chemical Weapons Taboo.* Ithaca, NY: Cornell University Press, 1997.

Purkitt, Helen E., and Stephen F. Burgess. *South Africa's Weapons of Mass Destruction.* Bloomington: Indiana University Press, 2005.

Regis, Ed. *The Biology of Doom.* New York: Henry Holt, 1999.

Richter, Donald. *Chemical Soldiers: British Gas Warfare in World War I.* Lawrence: University Press of Kansas, 1992.

Saunders, Bernard Charles. *Some Aspects of the Chemistry and Toxic Action of Organic Compounds Containing Phosphorus and Fluorine.* Cambridge: Oxford University Press, 1957.

Spiers, Edward. *Chemical Warfare.* Hong Kong: Macmillan, 1986.

Stockholm International Peace Research Institute (SIPRI). *The Problem of Chemical and Biological Warfare.* Vols. 1–6. Stockholm: SIPRI, 2000.

Tucker, Jonathan B. *War of Nerves: Chemical Warfare from World War I to Al-Qaeda.* New York: Pantheon Books, 2006.

U.S. Congress, Office of Technology Assessment. *Technologies Underlying Weapons* of Mass Destruction, OTA-BP-ISC-115. Washington, D.C.: U.S. Government Printing Office, December 1993.

Utgoff, Victor A. *The Challenge of Chemical Weapons: An American Perspective.* New York: St. Martin's Press, 1991.

Vedder, Edward B. *The Medical Aspects of Chemical Warfare.* Baltimore: Williams & Wilkins, 1925.

Veenema, Tener Goodwin, ed. *Disaster Nursing and Emergency Preparedness for Chemical, Biological, and Radiological Terrorism and Other Hazards.* 3rd ed. New York: Springer, 2012.

Vilensky, Joel A. *Dew of Death: The Story of Lewisite, America's World War I Weapon of Mass Destruction.* Indianapolis: Indiana University Press, 2005.

Wachtel, Curt. *Chemical Warfare.* Brooklyn, NY: Chemical, 1941.

Williams, Peter, and David Wallace. *The Japanese Army's Secret of Secrets.* London: Hodder & Stoughton, 1989.

Williams, Peter, and David Wallace. *Unit 731: Japan's Secret Biological Warfare in World War II.* New York: Free Press, 1989.

Wise, David. *Cassidy's Run: The Secret Spy War over Nerve Gas.* New York: Random House, 2000.

Nuclear Weapons

Ackland, Len. *Making a Real Killing: Rocky Flats and the Nuclear West.* Albuquerque: University of New Mexico Press, 1999.

Ahmed, Samina, and David Cortright. *South Asia at the Nuclear Crossroads.* Washington, D.C.: Fourth Freedom Forum, April 2001.

Albright, David, and Kevin O'Neill, eds. *Solving the North Korea Nuclear Puzzle.* Washington, D.C.: Institute for Science and International Security, 2000.

Alexander, Brian, and Alistair Millar, eds. *Tactical Nuclear Weapons: Emergent Threats in an Evolving Security Environment.* Dulles, VA: Brassey's, 2003.

Allison, Graham T., Albert Carnesale, and Joseph S. Nye Jr., eds. *Hawks, Doves, & Owls: An Agenda for Avoiding Nuclear War.* New York: W. W. Norton & Company, 1985.

Allison, Graham, Ashton B. Carter, Steven E. Miller, and Philip Zelikow. *Cooperative Denuclearization: From Pledges to Deeds.* Cambridge, MA: Harvard University, Center for Science and International Affairs, January 1993.

Allison, Graham, Owen R. Cote Jr., Richard A. Falkenrath, and Steven E. Miller. *Avoiding Nuclear Anarchy: Containing the Threat of Loose Russian Nuclear Weapons and Fissile Material.* Cambridge, MA: MIT Press, 1996.

Alperovitz, Gar. *The Decision to Use the Atomic Bomb.* New York: Vintage Books, 1995.

Anderson, Justin V., and Jeffrey A. Larsen. *Extended Deterrence and Allied Assurance: Key Concepts and Current Challenges for U.S. Policy.* INSS Occasional Paper 69. USAF Academy, CO: Institute for National Security Studies, September 2013.

Arkin, William M., Thomas B. Cochran, and Milton M. Hoenig. *Nuclear Weapons Databook,* vol. 1, *U.S. Nuclear Forces and Capabilities.* Cambridge, MA: Ballinger Publishing Company, 1984.

Arkin, William M., and Robert S. Norris. *Nuclear Weapons Databook,* vol. 2, *U.S. Nuclear Warhead Production.* Cambridge, MA: Ballinger Publishing Company, 1987.

Arkin, William M., and Robert S. Norris. *Nuclear Weapons Databook,* vol. 3, *U.S. Nuclear Warhead Facility Profiles.* Cambridge, MA: Ballinger Publishing Company, 1987.

Arkin, William M., Thomas B. Cochran, Robert S. Norris, and Jeffrey I. Sands. *Nuclear Weapons Databook,* vol. 4, *Soviet Nuclear Weapons.* New York: Harper and Row, 1989.

Arkin, William M., and Richard W. Fieldhouse. *Nuclear Battlefields: Global Links in the Arms Race.* Cambridge, MA: Ballinger Publishing Company, 1985.

Arnold, Lorna. *Britain and the H-Bomb.* New York: Palgrave, 2001.

Axelrod, Robert. *The Evolution of Cooperation.* New York: Basic Books, 1984.

Axelrod, Robert, and Jeffrey Richelson. *Strategic Nuclear Targeting.* Ithaca, NY: Cornell University Press, 1986.

Azizian, Rouben. *Nuclear Developments in South Asia and the Future of Global Arms Control.* Wellington, New Zealand: Centre for Strategic Studies, Victoria University of Wellington, 2001.

Ball, Desmond. *Targeting for Strategic Deterrence.* London: International Institute for Strategic Studies, 1983.

Bartimus, Tad, and Scott McCartney. *Trinity's Children: America's Nuclear Highway.* Albuquerque: New Mexico University Press, 1991.

Beckman, Peter R., Larry Campbell, Paul W. Crumlish, Michael N. Dobkowski, and Steven P. Lee. *The Nuclear Predicament: Nuclear Weapons in the Cold War and Beyond.* Englewood Cliffs, NJ: Prentice-Hall, 1992.

Bergeron, Kenneth D. *Tritium on Ice: The Dangerous New Alliance of Nuclear Weapons and Nuclear Power.* Cambridge, MA: MIT Press, 2002.

Bernstein, Jeremy. *Plutonium: A History of the World's Most Dangerous Element.* Washington, D.C.: Joseph Henry Press, 2007.

Betts, Richard, ed. *Cruise Missiles: Strategy, Technology, Politics.* Washington, D.C.: Brookings Institution, 1981.

Binnendijk, Hans, and James Goodby, eds. *Transforming Nuclear Deterrence.* Washington, D.C.: National Defense University Press, 1997.

Blackwill, Robert D., and Albert Carnesale. *New Nuclear Nations: Consequences for US Policy.* New York: Council on Foreign Relations Press, 1993.

Blair, Bruce G. *The Logic of Accidental Nuclear War.* Washington, D.C.: Brookings Institution Press, 1991.

Blechman, Peter R., Larry Campbell, Paul W. Crumlish, Michael N. Dobkowski, and Steven P. Lee. *The Nuclear Predicament: Nuclear Weapons in the Cold War and Beyond.* Englewood Cliffs, NJ: Prentice-Hall, 1992.

Bowen, Wyn Q. *The Politics of Ballistic Missile Nonproliferation.* Southampton, UK: Southampton Studies in International Policy, 2000.

Bracken, Paul. *The Command and Control of Nuclear Forces.* New Haven, CT: Yale University Press, 1983.

Brodie, Bernard. *Strategy in the Missile Age.* Santa Monica, CA: RAND Corporation, 1959.

Bundy, McGeorge. *Danger and Survival: Choices about the Bomb in the First Fifty Years.* New York: Vintage Books, 1988.

Bundy, McGeorge, William J. Crowe, and Sidney D. Drell. *Reducing Nuclear Danger: The Road Away from the Brink.* New York: Council on Foreign Relations Press, 1993.

Bunn, George, and Christopher F. Chyba, eds. *US Nuclear Weapons Policy: Confronting Today's Threats.* Washington, D.C.: Brookings Institute Press, 2006.

Buteux, Paul. *The Politics of Nuclear Consultation in NATO, 1965–1980.* Cambridge: Cambridge University Press, 1983.

Campbell, Craig, and Sergey Radchenko. *The Atomic Bomb and the Origins of the Cold War.* New Haven, CT: Yale University Press, 2008.

Campbell, Kurt M., Ashton B. Carter, Steven E. Miller, and Charles A. Zraket. *Soviet Nuclear Fission: Control of the Nuclear Arsenal in a Disintegrating Soviet Union.* Cambridge, MA: Harvard University Center for Science and International Affairs, 1991.

Campbell, Kurt M., Robert J. Einhorn, and Mitchell B. Reiss, eds. *The Nuclear Tipping Point: Why States Reconsider Their Nuclear Choices.* Washington, D.C.: Brookings Institution, 2004.

Carter, Ashton B., John D. Steinbruner, and Charles A. Zraket. *Managing Nuclear Operations.* Washington, D.C.: Brookings Institution, 1987.

Center for Counterproliferation Research and Center for Global Security Research. *U.S. Nuclear Policy in the 21st Century: A Fresh Look at National Strategy and Requirements.* Washington, D.C.: National Defense University and Lawrence Livermore National Laboratory, 1998.

Chandler, Robert W. *The New Face of War: Weapons of Mass Destruction and the Revitalization of America's Transoceanic Military Strategy.* McLean, VA: AMCODA Press, 1998.

Cimbala, Stephen J., ed. *Deterrence and Nuclear Proliferation in the Twenty-First Century.* New York: Praeger Publishers, 2001.

Cimbala, Stephen J. *Extended Deterrence: The United States and NATO Europe.* Lexington, MA: Lexington Books, 1987.

Cimbala, Stephen J. *NATO Strategy and Nuclear Weapons.* New York: St. Martin's Press, 1989.

Cirincione, Joseph. *Bomb Scare: The History and Future of Nuclear Weapons.* New York: Columbia University Press, 2008.

Cirincione, Joseph, ed. *Repairing the Regime: Preventing the Spread of Weapons of Mass Destruction.* Washington, D.C.: Carnegie Endowment for International Peace, 2000.

Cirincione, Joseph, Jon Wolfsthal, and Miriam Rajkumar. *Deadly Arsenals: Nuclear, Chemical, and Biological Threats.* 2nd ed. Washington, D.C.: Carnegie Endowment for International Peace, 2007.

Clarke, Duncan L. *American Defense and Foreign Policy Institutions.* New York: Ballinger Publishers, 1989.

Commission to Assess United States National Security Space Management and Organization. *Report of the Commission to Assess United States National Security Space Management and Organization.* Washington, D.C.: United States Commission on National Security/21st Century, January 2001.

Committee on International Security and Arms Control, National Academy of Sciences. *Nuclear Arms Control.* Washington, D.C.: National Academy Press, 1985.

Cordesman, Anthony H. *The Global Nuclear Balance: A Quantitative and Arms Control Analysis.* Washington, D.C.: Center for Strategic and International Studies, January 2001.

Daalder, Ivo H. *The Nature and Practice of Flexible Response: NATO Strategy and Theater Nuclear Forces since 1967.* New York: Columbia University Press, 1991.

Daalder, Ivo H., and Terry Terriff, eds. *Rethinking the Unthinkable: New Directions for Nuclear Arms Control.* London: Frank Cass, 1993.

Davis, Jacqueline K., Charles M. Perry, and Robert L. Pfaltzgraff Jr. *The INF Controversy: Lessons for NATO Modernization and Transatlantic Relations.* Washington, D.C.: Pergamon-Brassey's, 1989.

DeGroot, Gerard J. *The Bomb: A Life.* Cambridge, MA: Harvard University Press, 2006.

Deibel, Terry L., and John Lewis Gaddis. *Containment: Concept and Policy.* 2 vols. Washington, D.C.: National Defense University Press, 1986.

Dunn, Lewis. *Global Proliferation: Dynamics, Acquisition Strategies, and Responses.* Newington, VA: Center for Verification Research, December 9, 1992.

Eden, Lynn, and Steven E. Miller. *Nuclear Arguments: Understanding the Nuclear Arms and Arms Control Debates.* Ithaca, NY: Cornell University Press, 1989.

Ferguson, Charles, Brent Scowcroft, and William Perry. *U.S. Nuclear Weapons Policy.* Task Force Report. New York: Council on Foreign Relations, April 2009.

FitzGerald, Frances. *Way Out There in the Blue: Reagan and Star Wars and the End of the Cold War.* New York: Simon & Schuster, 2000.

Foradori, Paolo, ed. *Tactical Nuclear Weapons and Euro-Atlantic Security: The Future of NATO.* London: Routledge, 2013.

Ford, James L., and C. Richard Schuller. *Controlling Threats to Nuclear Security.* Washington, D.C.: Center of Counterproliferation Research, National Defense University Press, June 1997.

Freedman, Lawrence. *The Evolution of Nuclear Strategy.* New York: St. Martin's Press, 1989.

Gaddis, John Lewis. *The Cold War: A New History.* New York: Penguin Books, 2005.

Gaddis, John Lewis. *The Long Peace: Inquiries into the History of the Cold War.* Oxford: Oxford University Press, 1987.

Gaddis, John Lewis. *Strategies of Containment: A Critical Appraisal of Postwar American National Security Policy.* Oxford: Oxford University Press, 1982.

Gardner, Gary T. *Nuclear Nonproliferation: A Primer.* Boulder, CO: Lynne Rienner Publishers, 1994.

Gardner, Gary T., and Steven A. Maaranen, eds. *Nuclear Weapons in the Changing World: Perspectives from Europe, Asia, and North America.* New York: Plenum Press, 1992.

Gibson, James N. *Nuclear Weapons of the United States: An Illustrated History.* Atglen, PA: Schiffer Publishing Ltd., 1996.

Glaser, Charles L. *Analyzing Strategic Nuclear Policy.* Princeton, NJ: Princeton University Press, 1990.

Graham, Bradley. *Hit to Kill: The New Battle over Shielding America from Missile Attack.* Washington, D.C.: Public Affairs Press, 2001.

Gray, Colin S. *Nuclear Strategy and National Style.* Lanham, MD: Hamilton Press, 1986.

Gregory, Shaun R. *Nuclear Command and Control in NATO: Nuclear Weapons Operations and the Strategy of Flexible Response.* Basingstoke, UK: Macmillan Press, 1996.

Hamza, Khidhir. *Saddam's Bombmaker: The Terrifying Inside Story of the Iraqi Nuclear and Biological Weapons Agenda.* New York: Charles Scribner's Sons, 2000.

Harvard Nuclear Study Group. *Living with Nuclear Weapons.* Toronto: Bantam Books, 1983.

Hays, Peter L., Vincent J. Jodoin, and Alan R. Van Tassel, eds. *Countering the Proliferation and Use of Weapons of Mass Destruction.* New York: McGraw Hill, 1998.

Herf, Jeffrey. *War by Other Means: Soviet Power, West German Resistance, and the Battle of the Euromissiles.* New York: Free Press, 1991.

Hersey, John. *Hiroshima.* New York: Alfred A. Knopf, 1946.

Holloway, David. *Stalin and the Bomb.* New Haven, CT: Yale University Press, 1996.

Hopkins, John C., and Weixing Hu. *Strategic Views from the Second Tier: The Nuclear-Weapons Policies of France, Britain, and China.* San Diego: University of California Institute on Global Conflict and Cooperation, 1994.

Jervis, Robert. *The Meaning of the Nuclear Revolution: Statecraft and the Prospect of Armageddon.* Ithaca, NY: Cornell University Press, 1989.

Johnson, Craig M. *The Russian Federation's Ministry of Atomic Energy: Programs and Developments.* Richland, WA: Pacific Northwest National Laboratory, February 2000.

Johnson, Jeannie, Kerry M. Kartchner, and Jeffrey A. Larsen, eds. *Strategic Culture and Weapons of Mass Destruction: Culturally Based Insights into Comparative National Security Policymaking.* New York: Palgrave, 2009.

Kahn, Herman. *On Escalation: Metaphors and Scenarios.* New York: Taylor and Frances, 1965.

Kahn, Herman. *On Thermonuclear War.* Princeton, NJ: Princeton University Press, 1960.

Kahn, Herman. *Thinking about the Unthinkable.* New York: Horizon Press, 1962.

Kartchner, Kerry M. *Negotiating START: Strategic Arms Reduction Talks and the*

Quest for Strategic Stability. New Brunswick, NJ: Transaction Press, 1992.

Katz, Arthur M. *Life after Nuclear War: The Economic and Social Impacts of Nuclear Attacks on the United States.* Cambridge, MA: Ballinger Publishing Company, 1982.

Kegley, Charles W., Jr., and Eugene R. Wittkopf, eds. *The Nuclear Reader: Strategy, Weapons, War.* New York: St. Martin's Press, 1989.

Kennan, George F. *The Nuclear Delusion: Soviet-American Relations in the Atomic Age.* New York: Pantheon Books, 1983.

Kennedy, Thomas J., Jr. *NATO Politico-Military Consultation: Shaping Alliance Decisions.* Washington, D.C.: National Defense University Press, 1984.

Kissinger, Henry. *Nuclear Weapons and Foreign Policy.* New York: Harper and Row, 1957.

Knorr, Klaus. *On the Uses of Military Power in the Nuclear Age.* Princeton, NJ: Princeton University Press, 1966.

Krepon, Michael. *Cooperative Threat Reduction, Missile Defense, and the Nuclear Future.* New York: Palgrave, 2003.

Kroenig, Matthew. *Exporting the Bomb: Technology Transfer and the Spread of Nuclear Weapons.* Ithaca, NY: Cornell University Press, 2010.

Kroenig, Matthew. *The Logic of American Nuclear Strategy: Why Strategic Superiority Matters.* Oxford, UK: Oxford University Press, 2018.

Larkin, Bruce D. *Nuclear Designs: Great Britain, France, and China in the Global Governance of Nuclear Arms.* New Brunswick, NJ: Transaction Publishers, 1996.

Larsen, Jeffrey A., Justin V. Anderson, Darci Bloyer, Thomas Devine IV, Rebecca Davis Gibbons, and Christina Vaughan. *Qualitative Considerations of Nuclear Forces at Lower Numbers and Implications for Future Arms Control Negotiation.* INSS Occasional Paper 68. USAF Academy, CO: Institute for National Security Studies, July 2012.

Larsen, Jeffrey A., and Kerry M. Kartchner. *On Limited Nuclear War in the 21st Century.* Palo Alto, CA: Stanford University Press, 2014.

Larsen, Jeffrey A., and Kurt J. Klingenberger, eds. *Controlling Non-Strategic Nuclear Weapons: Obstacles and Opportunities.* Colorado Springs, CO: USAF Institute for National Security Studies, 2001.

Larsen, Jeffrey A., and James M. Smith. *Historical Dictionary of Arms Control and Disarmament.* Lanham, MD: Scarecrow Press, 2005.

Larsen, Jeffrey A., and James J. Wirtz, eds. *Arms Control and Cooperative Security.* Boulder, CO: Lynne Rienner Publications, 2009.

Larson, Deborah Welch. *Origins of Containment: A Psychological Explanation.* Princeton, NJ: Princeton University Press, 1985.

League of Women Voters. *The Nuclear Waste Primer: A Handbook for Citizens.* Rev. ed. New York: Lyons & Burford Publishers, 1993.

Lewis, William H., and Stuart E. Johnson. *Weapons of Mass Destruction: New Perspectives on Counterproliferation.* Washington, D.C.: Institute for National Strategic Studies, NDU Press, 1995.

Lifton, Robert Jay, and Richard Falk. *Indefensible Weapons: The Political and Psychological Case against Nuclearism.* New York: Basic Books, 1982.

Lindsay, James M., and Michael E. O'Hanlon. *Defending America: The Case for a Limited National Missile Defense.* Washington, D.C.: Brookings Institution, 2001.

Lodal, Jan. *The Price of Dominance: The New Weapons of Mass Destruction and Their Challenge to American Leadership.* New York: Council on Foreign Relations Press, 2001.

Mandelbaum, Michael. *The Nuclear Question: The United States and Nuclear Weapons 1946–1976.* Cambridge: Cambridge University Press, 1979.

Mandelbaum, Michael. *The Nuclear Revolution: International Politics before and after Hiroshima*. Cambridge: Cambridge University Press, 1981.

Maroncelli, James M., and Timothy L. Karpin. *The Traveler's Guide to Nuclear Weapons: A Journey through America's Cold War Battlefields*. Silverdale, WA: Historical Odysseys Publishers, 2002.

Matlock, Jack F., Jr. *Reagan and Gorbachev: How the Cold War Ended*. New York: Random House, 2004.

May, John. *The Greenpeace Book of the Nuclear Age*. London: Victor Gollancz, Ltd., 1989.

May, Michael, and Roger Speed. "Should Nuclear Weapons Be Used?" In *The Proliferation of Advanced Weaponry: Technology, Motivations, and Responses*, edited by W. Thomas Wander and Eric H. Arnett. Washington, D.C.: American Association for the Advancement of Science, 1992, 235–253.

McLean, Scilla, ed. *How Nuclear Weapons Decisions Are Made*. Basingstoke, UK: MacMillan Press, 1987.

Mendelbaum, Michael. *The Nuclear Revolution*. Cambridge: Cambridge University Press, 1981.

Millar, Alistair, and Brian Alexander, eds. *Tactical Nuclear Weapons: Emergent Threats in an Evolving Security Environment*. New York: Brassey's, May 2003.

Miller, Steven E., ed. *Strategy and Nuclear Deterrence: An* International Security *Reader*. Princeton, NJ: Princeton University Press, 1984.

Mueller, John. *Atomic Obsession: Nuclear Alarmism from Hiroshima to Al-Qaeda*. Oxford, UK: Oxford University Press, 2009.

National Institute for Public Policy. *Rationale and Requirements for U.S. Nuclear Forces and Arms Control*. Washington, D.C.: National Institute for Public Policy, January 2001.

Newhouse, John. *War and Peace in the Nuclear Age*. New York: Vintage Books, 1990.

Nolan, Janne E. *An Elusive Consensus: Nuclear Weapons and American Security*

after the Cold War. Washington, D.C.: Brookings Institution Press, 1999.

Nye, Joseph S., Jr. *Nuclear Ethics*. New York: Free Press, 1984.

Office of Technology Assessment. *The Effects of Nuclear War*. Washington, D.C.: U.S. Government Printing Office, 1979.

Paul, Septimus H. *Nuclear Rivals: Anglo-American Atomic Relations, 1941–52*. Columbus: Ohio State University Press, 2000.

Paul, T. V., Richard J. Harknett, and James J. Wirtz, eds. *The Absolute Weapon Revisited: Nuclear Arms and the Emerging International Order*. Ann Arbor: University of Michigan Press, 1998.

Paulsen, Richard A. *The Role of U.S. Nuclear Weapons in the Post–Cold War Era*. Montgomery, AL: Air University Press, September 1994.

Payne, Keith B. *The Fallacies of Cold War Deterrence and a New Direction*. Lexington, KY: University Press of Kentucky, 2001.

Perry, William. *My Journey at the Nuclear Brink*. Palo Alto, CA: Stanford University Press, 2015.

Pikayev, Alexander A. *The Rise and Fall of START II: The Russian View*. Washington, D.C.: Carnegie Endowment for International Peace, September 1999.

Podvig, Pavel. *Russian Strategic Nuclear Forces*. Cambridge, MA: MIT Press, 2001.

Potter, William C., Nikolai Sokov, Harald Müller, and Annette Schaper. *Tactical Nuclear Weapons: Options for Control*. New York: United Nations Institute for Disarmament Research, 2001.

Pringle, Peter, and James Spigelman. *The Nuclear Barons*. New York: Holt, Rinehart, and Winston, 1981.

Ramsbotham, Oliver, ed. *Choices: Nuclear and Nonnuclear Defense Options*. London: Brassey's Defense Publishers, 1987.

Raven-Hansen, Peter, ed. *First Use of Nuclear Weapons: Under the Constitution, Who Decides?* New York: Greenwood Press, 1987.

Record, Jeffrey. *NATO's Theater Nuclear Force Modernization Program: The Real*

Issues. Cambridge, MA: Institute for Foreign Policy Analysis, Inc., 1981.

Reiss, Mitchell, and Robert S. Litwak. *Nuclear Proliferation after the Cold War.* Baltimore: Johns Hopkins University Press, 1994.

Reynolds, Wayne. *Australia's Bid for the Atomic Bomb.* Melbourne, Australia: Melbourne University Press, 2001.

Rhodes, Edward. *Power and MADness: The Logic of Nuclear Coercion.* New York: Columbia University Press, 1989.

Rhodes, Richard. *Arsenals of Folly: The Making of the Nuclear Arms Race.* New York: Alfred A. Knopf, 2007.

Rhodes, Richard. *Dark Sun: The Making of the Hydrogen Bomb.* New York: Simon & Schuster, 1995.

Rhodes, Richard. *The Making of the Atomic Bomb.* New York: Simon & Schuster, 1986.

Risse-Kappen, Thomas. *The Zero Option: INF, West Germany, and Arms Control.* Boulder, CO: Westview Press, 1988.

Roberts, Brad. *The Case for U.S. Nuclear Weapons in the 21st Century.* Palo Alto, CA: Stanford University Press, 2015.

Rose, Kenneth D. *One Nation Underground: The Fallout Shelter in American Culture.* New York: New York University Press, 2001.

Rosenthal, Debra. *At the Heart of the Bomb: The Dangerous Allure of Weapons Work.* Reading, MA: Addison-Wesley Publishing Company, Inc., 1990.

Royal United Services Institute. *Nuclear Attack: Civil Defence. Aspects of Civil Defence in the Nuclear Age.* London: Brassey's Publishers, 1981.

Sagan, Scott D. *The Limits of Safety: Organizations, Accidents, and Nuclear Weapons.* Princeton, NJ: Princeton University Press, 1993.

Sagan, Scott D. *Moving Targets: Nuclear Strategy and National Security.* Princeton, NJ: Princeton University Press, 1989.

Sagan, Scott D., and Kenneth N. Waltz. *The Spread of Nuclear Weapons: A Debate.* New York: W. W. Norton, 1995.

Schaeffer, Henry W. *Nuclear Arms Control.* Washington, D.C.: National Defense University Press, April 1986.

Schaerf, Carlo, and David Carlton, eds. *Reducing Nuclear Arsenals.* New York: St. Martin's Press, 1991.

Schelling, Thomas C. *Arms and Influence.* New Haven, CT: Yale University Press, 1966.

Schelling, Thomas C., and Morton H. Halperin. *Strategy and Arms Control.* Washington, D.C.: Pergamon-Brassey's, 1985.

Schlesinger, James. *Report of the Secretary of Defense Task Force on Nuclear Weapons Management. Phase One: The Air Force's Nuclear Mission.* Washington, D.C.: The Pentagon, September 2008.

Schlesinger, James. *Report of the Secretary of Defense Task Force on Nuclear Weapons Management. Phase Two: Review of the DOD Nuclear Mission.* Washington, D.C.: The Pentagon, December 2008.

Schlosser, Eric. *Command and Control: Nuclear Weapons, the Damascus Incident, and the Illusion of Safety.* New York: Penguin Books, 2013.

Schulz, George, Sidney Drell, Henry Kissinger, and Sam Nunn. *Nuclear Security: The Problems and the Road Ahead.* Palo Alto, CA: Hoover Institute Press, 2013.

Schwartz, David N. *NATO's Nuclear Dilemmas.* Washington, D.C.: Brookings Institution, 1983.

Schwartz, Stephen I. *Atomic Audit: The Costs and Consequences of U.S. Nuclear Weapons since 1940.* Washington, D.C.: Brookings Institution Press, 1998.

Shambroom, Paul. *Face to Face with the Bomb: Nuclear Reality after the Cold War.* Baltimore: Johns Hopkins University Press, 2003.

Sherwin, Martin J. *A World Destroyed: Hiroshima and Its Legacies.* 3rd ed. Palo Alto, CA: Stanford University Press, 2003.

Shields, John M., and William C. Potter. *Dismantling the Cold War: U.S. and NIS Perspectives on the Nunn-Lugar*

Cooperative Threat Reduction Program. Cambridge, MA: MIT Press, 1997.

Sigal, Leon V., and John D. Steinbruner, eds. *Alliance Security: NATO and the No-First-Use Question.* Washington, D.C.: Brookings Institution, 1983.

Smith, James M., ed. *Nuclear Deterrence and Defense: Strategic Considerations.* Colorado Springs, CO: USAF Institute for National Security Studies, February 2001.

Smith, Joseph, and Simon Davis. *Historical Dictionary of the Cold War.* Lanham, MD: Scarecrow Press, 2000.

Smith, P. D. *Doomsday Men: The Real Dr. Strangelove and the Dream of the Superweapon.* New York: St. Martin's Press, 2007.

Smoke, Richard. *National Security and the Nuclear Dilemma.* New York: McGraw-Hill, 1993.

Snyder, Glenn. *Deterrence and Defense.* Princeton, NJ: Princeton University Press, 1961.

Sokolski, Henry D. *Best of Intentions: America's Campaign against Strategic Weapons Proliferation.* New York: Praeger Publishers, 2001.

Sokolski, Henry D., and Patrick Clawson, eds. *Checking Iran's Nuclear Ambitions.* Carlisle, PA: Army War College Strategic Studies Institute, January 2004.

Sokolski, Henry D., and James M. Ludes, eds. *Twenty-First Century Weapons Proliferation: Are We Ready?* London: Frank Cass Publishers, 2001.

Spector, Leonard S. *Nuclear Ambitions: The Spread of Nuclear Weapons 1989–1990.* Boulder, CO: Westview Press, 1990.

Spector, Leonard S., Mark G. McDonough, and Evan S. Medeiros. *Tracking Nuclear Proliferation.* Washington, D.C.: Carnegie Endowment for International Peace, 1995.

Talbott, Strobe. *Deadly Gambits: The Reagan Administration and the Stalemate in Nuclear Arms Control.* New York: Alfred A. Knopf, 1984.

Talbott, Strobe. *The Master of the Game: Paul Nitze and the Nuclear Peace.* New York: Vintage Books, 1988.

Tannenwald, Nina. *The Nuclear Taboo: The United States and the Non-Use of Nuclear Weapons since 1945.* Cambridge, UK: Cambridge University Press, 2008.

Teller, Edward, with Judith Shoolery. *Memoirs: A Twentieth-Century Journey in Science and Politics.* New York: Perseus Books, 2001.

Tellis, Ashley J. *India's Emerging Nuclear Posture: Between Recessed Deterrent and Ready Arsenal.* Santa Monica, CA: RAND Corporation, 2001.

Treverton, Gregory. *Nuclear Weapons in Europe.* Adelphi Paper. London: International Institute for Strategic Studies, 1981.

Turner, Stansfield. *Caging the Nuclear Genie: An American Challenge for Global Security.* Boulder, CO: Westview Press, 1997.

Twigge, Stephen, and Len Scott. *Planning Armageddon: Britain, the United States and the Command of Western Nuclear Forces 1945–1964.* Newark, NJ: Harwood Academic Publishers, 2000.

Van Oudenaren, John. *West German Policymaking and NATO Nuclear Strategy.* Santa Monica, CA: RAND Corporation, September 1985.

Vanderbilt, Tom. *Survival City: Adventures among the Ruins of Atomic America.* Princeton, NJ: Princeton Architectural Press, 2002.

Wirtz, James J., Eliot Cohen, Colin Gray, and John Bayliss, eds. *Strategy in the Contemporary World.* Oxford, UK: Oxford University Press, 2002.

Wirtz, James J., and Jeffrey A. Larsen, eds. *Nuclear Transformation: The New U.S. Nuclear Doctrine.* New York: Palgrave Press, 2005.

Wirtz, James J., and Jeffrey A. Larsen, eds. *Rockets' Red Glare: Missile Defenses and the Future of World Politics.* Boulder, CO: Westview Press, 2001.

Wittner, Lawrence S. *Toward Nuclear Abolition: A History of the World Nuclear Disarmament Movement*, vol. 3, *1971 to the Present*. Palo Alto, CA: Stanford University Press, 2003.

Wolfstahl, Jon Brook, Christina-Astrid Chuen, and Emily Ewell Daughtry, eds. *Nuclear Status Report: Nuclear Weapons, Fissile Material, and Export Controls in the Former Soviet Union*. Washington, D.C.: Carnegie Endowment for International Peace, 2001.

Woolsey, R. James, ed. *Nuclear Arms: Ethics, Strategy, Politics*. San Francisco: ICS Press, 1984.

Yost, David S. *The US and Nuclear Deterrence in Europe*. Adelphi Paper 326. London: IISS, 1999.

Younger, Stephen M. *The Bomb: A New History*. New York: Harper Collins, 2009.

Contributors

Jeffrey A. Adams

Senior Analyst, Analytic Services, Inc. (ANSER), Arlington, VA

Jeffrey M. Bale

Professor, Middlebury Institute of International Studies, Monterey, CA

Zachariah Becker

President, High Street Consulting LLC, Fairfax, VA

Jennifer Brower

Budget Analyst, U.S. Government, Washington, D.C.

Kalpana Chittaranjan

Research Fellow, Observer Research Foundation, Chennai Chapter, Chennai, India

Abe Denmark

Director, Asia Program, Woodrow Wilson International Center for Scholars, Washington, D.C.

John W. Dietrich

Professor and Chair, Department of Political Science, Bryant University, Smithfield, RI

Andrew M. Dorman

Professor of International Security, King's College London, London, U.K.

Frannie Edwards

Professor, San Jose State University, San Jose, CA

Stephanie Fitzpatrick

Arms Control/Policy Analyst, Independent Consultant, Arlington, VA

Schuyler Foerster

Principal, CGST Solutions, Colorado Springs, CO

Laura Fontaine

Consultant, Quad City Health Initiative, Davenport, IA

J. Russ Forney

Walter Reed Army Medical Center, Washington, D.C.

Don Gillich

Research Development and Systems Engineer, Sandia National Laboratories, Albuquerque, NM

Dan Goodrich

Research Associate, Mineta Transportation Institute, San Jose State University, San Jose, CA

John Hart

Head of Biological and Chemical Security Project, Stockholm International Peace Research Institute, Solna, Sweden

Peter Hays

Senior Space Policy Analyst, Falcon Research, Washington, D.C.

James Joyner

Associate Professor of Security Studies, Marine Corps University, Quantico, VA

Kerry Kartchner

Visiting Professor, Brigham Young University, Provo, UT

Kimberly L. Kosteff

Policy Analyst, Science Applications International Corporation, Arlington, VA

Amy E. Krafft

Program Officer, National Institutes of Health, Bethesda, MD

Jennifer Lasecki

Analyst, Alexandria, VA

Peter R. Lavoy

Senior Advisor, Asia Pacific, ExxonMobil, Washington, D.C.

Sean Lawson

Associate Professor, University of Utah, Salt Lake City, UT

Brian L'Italien

Director of Visioneering, Decipher Technology Studios, Arlington, VA

Morten Bremer Maerli

Senior Research Fellow, Norwegian Institute of International Affairs, Oslo, Norway

Tom Mahnken

President, Center for Strategic and Budgetary Assessments, Washington, D.C.

Robert Mathews

Associate Professor at the University of Melbourne Law School, Victoria, Australia

Claudine McCarthy

Policy and Communications Advisor, Wisconsin Department of Health Services, Madison, WI

Brian Moretti

Professor, Department of Physics, U.S. Military Academy, West Point, NY

Jennifer Hunt Morstein

Senior Analyst, Science Applications International Corporation, McLean, VA

T. V. Paul

James McGill Professor of International Relations, McGill University, Montreal, Canada

Roy Pettis

Chief, Systems Analysis, Government Accountability Office, Washington, D.C.

Rich Pilch

Director, Biosciences, Raytheon Intelligence, Information, and Services, Washington, D.C.

Elizabeth Prescott

Georgetown University, Washington, D.C.

Beverley Rider

Rider Health Group, San Jose, CA

Guy Roberts

Assistant Secretary of Defense for Nuclear, Chemical and Biological Defense, Office of the Secretary of Defense, Washington, D.C.

Ken Rogers

Independent Scholar

Steven Rosenkrantz

Foreign Affairs Officer, U.S. State Department, Washington, D.C.

C. Ross Schmidtlein

Assistant Attending Physicist, Department of Medical Physics, Memorial Sloan-Kettering Cancer Center, New York, NY

Jacqueline Simon

Independent Consultant, Ottawa, Canada

Stanley R. Sloan

Visiting Scholar in Political Science at Middlebury College, VT, and Non-resident Senior Fellow, Scowcroft Center, Atlantic Council of the United States

James M. Smith

Director, USAF Institute for National Security Studies, U.S. Air Force Academy, Colorado Springs, CO

John Spykerman

Independent Scholar

Charles L. Thornton

Research Fellow, Center for International and Security Studies, School of Public

Policy, University of Maryland, College Park, MD

Rod Thornton

Senior Lecturer, Defence Studies Department, King's College London, London, U.K.

Anthony Tu

Professor Emeritus, Department of Biochemistry and Molecular Biology, Colorado State University, Fort Collins, CO

Peter Vale

Professor of Humanities, University of Johannesburg, Johannesburg, South Africa

Gilles Van Nederveen

Senior Systems Engineer, SOSACORP, Fairfax, VA

Michael Wheeler

Institute for Defense Analyses, Arlington, VA

Jolie Wood

Metropolitan State University, Saint Paul, MN

Index

Page numbers in **bold** indicate the location of main entries and primary sources. Page numbers in *italics* indicate tables and figures.

About the Editors

Eric A. Croddy specializes in weapons of mass destruction with a focus on chemical and biological warfare. Until 2017 he was a missile analyst with the Defense Intelligence Agency. He currently resides in Oregon. He authored *Chemical and Biological Warfare: An Annotated Bibliography*; *World Markets for Chemical and Biological Warfare Agent Detection*; and *Chemical and Biological Warfare: A Comprehensive Survey for the Concerned Citizen*. He is also coeditor, with James J. Wirtz and Jeffrey A. Larsen, of ABC-CLIO's *Encyclopedia of Weapons of Mass Destruction*.

Jeffrey A. Larsen, PhD, is president of Larsen Consulting Group. He has worked on U.S. nuclear policy for the U.S. Air Force, U.S. Strategic Command, the Defense Threat Reduction Agency, and the North Atlantic Treaty Organization. Until 2018 he was head of the Research Division at the NATO Defense College. His publications include *On Limited Nuclear War in the 21st Century; NATO's Response to Hybrid Threats; Strategic Culture and Weapons of Mass Destruction; Dealing with Disaster: Consequence Management; Encyclopedia of Weapons of Mass Destruction; Historical Dictionary of Arms Control and Disarmament; Arms Control: Cooperative Security in a Changing Environment; Nuclear Transformation: The New US Nuclear Doctrine;* and *Rockets' Red Glare: Missile Defenses and the Future of World Politics.*

James J. Wirtz, PhD, is professor and Dean of the School of International Graduate Studies, Naval Postgraduate School, Monterey, California. He has worked nuclear policy issues for the Department of Defense, Defense Threat Reduction Agency, the U.S. Air Force, and the U.S. Navy. He is coeditor of *Planning the Unthinkable: How New Powers Will Use Nuclear, Biological, and Chemical Weapons; Encyclopedia of Weapons of Mass Destruction; Arms Control and Cooperative Security; Nuclear Transformation: The New US Nuclear Doctrine; The Absolute Weapon Revisited;* and *Rockets' Red Glare: Missile Defenses and the Future of World Politics.*